*Women on Power*

# Women on Power

*Leadership Redefined*

EDITED BY

Sue J. M. Freeman

Susan C. Bourque

Christine M. Shelton

*With a Foreword by* Jill Ker Conway

Northeastern University Press

*Boston*

Northeastern University Press 2001

*Library of Congress Cataloging-in-Publication Data*

Women on power : leadership redefined / edited by Sue J. M. Freeman, Susan C. Bourque, Christine M. Shelton; with a foreword by Jill Ker Conway.
    p.  cm.
   Includes bibliographical references and index.
    ISBN 1–55553–478–3 (pbk. : alk. paper) — ISBN 1-55553-479-1 (cloth : alk. paper)
    1. Leadership in women.   2. Leadership.   I. Freeman, Sue Joan Mendelson, 1944–
II. Bourque, Susan Carolyn, 1943–   III. Shelton, Christine.

   HO1233 .W597   2001
   303.3'4'082—dc21           00-066216

Designed by Gary Gore

Composed in Electra by Coghill Composition in Richmond, Virginia. Printed and bound by Edwards Brothers, Inc., in Lillington, North Carolina. The paper is EB Natural, an acid-free sheet.

Manufactured in the United States of America
05  04  03  02  01     5  4  3  2  1

*To the strong and powerful women and men in our lives,
especially our mothers and fathers, who led and nurtured
in unexpected ways.*

# Acknowledgments

The Smith College Project on Women and Social Change has nurtured and sustained the editors of this volume for more than two decades. We are, as always, grateful to Jill K. Conway, who became the first woman president of Smith College one hundred years after its founding. Jill envisioned the Project as a means to foster new knowledge about women's lives and to ensure that research on women would continue at Smith whatever the scholarly fashion of the day. The contributors to this volume came together initially under the auspices of the Project and have enjoyed a wonderful scholarly collaboration and friendship since. Because of the support of presidents Jill Ker Conway, Mary Maples Dunn, and Ruth J. Simmons and the generosity of Smith alumnae, the Project is an endowed institution at Smith. Working closely with and learning from these extraordinary women leaders has inspired us.

The idea for this book began with a series of conferences on Gender, Authority, and Leadership in Business, Politics, and Sport, affectionately called the GAL project. We are grateful to all the participants in those conferences, many of whom are represented by their essays in this volume. We are indebted in particular to Kathleen Ridder, who has sponsored Project conferences and contributed to them intellectually through her attendance whenever possible.

Our colleagues in the Five College Consortium of Amherst College, Hampshire College, Mt. Holyoke College, Smith College, and the University of Massachusetts at Amherst, have joined us at conferences, work-in-progress seminars, and lectures, and as contributors to this volume. They are far too numerous to list here, but their participation and contributions always enrich our scholarly exchanges.

Although this book had been the subject of many discussions over the years, it was not until we met Elizabeth Swayze, women's studies editor at Northeastern University Press, that the volume finally took shape. Her insights into the importance of the topic, as well as her constant encouragement and penetrating suggestions, have assisted us immeasurably. We are grateful to the reviewers, who provided critical readings and urged us to make important changes that ultimately improved the manuscript.

Our thanks to the contributors to this volume, who attended meetings, received and responded to countless e-mail messages and letters, and shaped their essays to make a coherent volume. We are also grateful to several Smith students who contributed to the production of the book: Katie M. Byers did a wonderful job compiling the majority of the "Want to Learn More?" sections, and Katie Winger, president of the Smith class of 2001, contributed "down to the wire" help with those sections.

Finally, Kathleen Gauger, the Project administrative assistant for the past seventeen years, is the person who actually made it all happen. We have come to depend upon Kathy's exceptional competence, enduring patience, and infallible grace to make our work feasible. It really is the case that this book could not have been completed without her.

We three consider ourselves fortunate to have worked together compiling the essays, learning from each other, and celebrating the future of women's prospects for leadership.

# Contents

*Foreword*

# Amazons and Warriors:
# The Image of the Powerful Woman

**Jill Ker Conway**

WHY have modern feminists been so ambivalent about women's leadership? It's curious but true that the feminist leaders who sparked the battle for women's suffrage had great difficulty in thinking about how women would take political power. The early suffrage leaders had no difficulty whatsoever describing how they would shape society through volunteerism or how they would influence the delivery of welfare and the development of public policy. But they had a lot of difficulty in thinking about how women would actually take political power. What is most paradoxical is that this same difficulty persists in contemporary popular culture. Media treatment of women leaders is notoriously negative. Feminist psychologists have made an industry out of women's "relational self," presenting women as a nexus of relationships rather than an ego with boundaries and thus a potential to stand out from the group. We can't talk about women's leadership without exploring how we got to this highly gendered view and understanding its consequences.

I first thought about this subject while studying the generation of progressive women about whom I wrote my Ph.D. dissertation at Harvard. The five women I studied—Jane Addams, Julia Lathrop, Florence Kelly, Ellen Gates Starr, and Ida M. Cannon—were extremely effective political lobbyists, wonderful pressure group leaders. They were highly skillful in getting any piece of legislation on the docket, but they themselves never deemed it appropriate to think of running for political office if the suffrage were won. Aware of her enormous personal power, Jane Addams wanted to exercise it for the good of society. She idealized Abraham Lincoln and her father, who had been an associate of Lincoln's. Nevertheless, she agonized for three months before she

agreed to place Theodore Roosevelt's name in nomination at the 1912 Bull
Moose political convention, in which Roosevelt led a breakaway group from
the Republican Party. What she worried about was whether it would be seemly
for someone with her position as feminist and social critic to take part in presidential politics. She wrote private letters urging people to vote for Roosevelt,
but such public partisan involvement was inconsistent with her idea of women
as moral leaders, exempt from the wish for power.

When the feminist movement ignited in the late 1960s and early 1970s as
a popular movement, its leaders chose a strategy of using the courts to bring
about greater equality for women. The courts could grant and enforce a notion
of equality between women and men that existed in political documents and
in legislation but was not implemented. Generally, using the courts is a very
good strategy for a minority group and may be the only way to bring about
immediate change. But it is also the strategy of people who expect justice to
be granted, rather than won through building their own political movement.
Reflecting back to Jane Addams and the effectiveness of those early women
politicians who had no vote but considerable agility in Washington, it remains
puzzling why they weren't able to translate that experience into action that
would be understood and used more effectively for taking political power in
subsequent years. Today feminists are raising money to elect women to political office, to the House and Senate and to governorships. Sometime soon, it
may be hoped, there will be enough women who have had a long career in
the Senate and enough women who have been outstanding state governors
that they will be unmistakably presidential timber. But we have come to it
rather late, and there are still many feminists who disagree with this strategy.
Why have we taken such a long time to come to this particular program of
action? The answers can be found in the historical context within which modern feminism developed. Because our ideas of leadership are derived from
Greek rather than Christian models, we need to understand why those models
so influenced men in modern democratic culture and don't seem to have
touched women.

## Historical Insights: The Amazon Ideal

To understand why contemporary women don't use classical models we
need to go back to the fifteenth century. In that era, literate people, whether
female or male, knew Latin and studied classical literature. When the tiny
group of literate women thought about the gap between Christian teaching on
the equality of souls and the actual experience of female inequality in daily

life, they looked to the political ideals of Greece and Rome and their embodiment in classical literature. In the myth of the Amazons they found a valuable source for thinking about women and power. Even though classical writers made the Amazons ugly and brutal, early modern women could transpose the image of women fighters into positive imagery. They could refer to the Amazon defenders of Troy, who as an army of women were able to stand off an attacking force for a lengthy battle in which they displayed great heroism and physical courage and inflicted severe wounds on their opponents. In the imagery of those Amazon women warriors, early modern women saw a picture of women taking power, being physically courageous and ready to do violence if necessary for a cause in which they believed.[1]

*strong women*

Before the rise of democratic society, rule was something that one took for granted, and women could inherit rulership. It was not unreasonable for a female thinker to speculate about the nature of rule by women. With the arrival of the romantic movement, with its cult of childhood and the sexual innocence of women, the classics were closed as a field of study for nineteenth-century French, German, Italian, and English women. The classics were viewed as too bawdy; they dealt with "unnatural vices" and were not thought proper reading for women. Although women are educated more broadly as a group after early modern times, they are educated in a culture that has allowed them access only to the models of a world inherited from Christianity.

Because classical models were lost to women, feminist thinkers could think of women only in nonheroic terms, or possibly in terms of heroic Christian sanctity, which usually meant martyrdom. Mary Wollstonecraft goes through every source that she can possibly find to think about the political rights of women, and it never occurs to her that she could make use of imagery drawn from Greek and Roman literature. Instead she had access only to a romantic notion of the female who was nonviolent, had no political motivations, and had to see herself as exercising power in relation to her sexual and generative functions and not her political status as a potential ruler.

It is also significant that just at the point that romantic ideals and bourgeois society stopped women from studying the classics, the technology of warfare changed. As it became more complicated and distant, women could not think about military life nearly so easily. Women wrote many fantasies about living as soldiers before the seventeenth century, when the required technology was still simple. Women in crowds deployed various kinds of projectiles (lances, stones) whenever they rioted in cities. The participation of women in street violence and political riots of one kind or another is a common theme through medieval and early modern times. It was the market women of Paris who, in 1789, went out to Versailles and brought the king and queen of France back to imprisonment in Paris. What the textbooks omit is that it took half a regiment of French soldiers to prevent this crowd of women from killing the queen. They came armed with pipes and stones and other kinds of blunt instruments. Medieval women didn't have any trouble thinking about women fighting and using physical strength for a political cause; it was spontaneous and natural to them. Our notion of women as innately peaceful is one derived from study limited to the nineteenth and twentieth centuries.

With the invention of every technology of warfare from the rifle on, weapons could be mystified. Unless women were of elite classes that hunted, they didn't know how to use those weapons. Thus fantasies about warfare disappear from women's writing around the end of the eighteenth century. It is important to have fantasies about warfare in order to think about exercising political power. Politics is a stylized and ritualized version of war, and sometimes it is not so stylized.

For early modern and medieval women female leadership was defined in aristocratic terms. One had to have the skills of a knight; one had to be able to ride a horse. One had to understand the codes of chivalry and all the forms of allegiance that were part of the fusion of the political, economic, and military systems of the day. One of the most powerful writers on women as warriors in the fourteenth and fifteenth centuries, Christine de Pisan, author of the much-quoted *The Book of the City of Ladies* (1405), wrote about the nature of kingship and about chivalry and its practice. At the end of her life, she saw Joan of Arc as the absolute apotheosis of feminine virtue, as a good Amazon, and she wrote poetry about Joan of Arc as the archetypal Amazon princess and ruler. Whenever she referred to the battle of Troy, Pisan transposed the qualities assigned the Amazons. Whereas a strong misogynist tradition in classical literature described the Amazons as ferocious, bloodthirsty, and violent, an ancient example of raging hormones, Christine de Pisan wrote about her Amazon princess as the embodiment of chivalric virtue in classical dress. She describes the death of Queen Penthesilea, who led the Amazon army, as a moment of high tragedy in which the queen is defeated not because she lacks strength or military prowess but because of the deceitful military practices of the Athenian attackers. Queen Penthesilea is not defeated as a physical warrior. In Pisan's powerful and moving description, Penthesilea is a strong, beautiful, moral, ideal type of woman.

In writing about Joan of Arc, Christine de Pisan was particularly interested in the possibility that there could be a kind of military virgin, because the Maid of Orleans was thought of as a virgin. We know today that she was seriously anorexic and probably not capable of conceiving. She ate very little, weighed very little. Her boyish figure was probably due to self-starvation. Writing a poem in praise of Joan of Arc's victory leading the French army against the attackers of the French nation, Christine de Pisan calls Joan of Arc a modern Amazon. Her success at the head of her troops revived a nation demoralized by a series of defeats in the Thirty Years War. Pisan sees Joan's triumph first in raising the siege of Orleans and then defeating the British at the Battle of Patay in 1429 as an act of leadership that will restore the French nation. Joan of Arc was dressed as a male and was absolutely fearless in battle; Christine de Pisan considers her to be a holy warrior chosen by God to rescue the French nation and the French monarchy. Wherever she went on the battlefield she required that she be treated with the full honors of knighthood and chivalry. This is a contemporary description of her: "The maid, arrayed in white armor, rode on horseback before the King with her standard unfurled. When not in armor she kept state as a knight and dressed as one. Her shoes were tied with laces to her feet. Her hose and doublet were shapely. A hat was on her head. She wore very handsome attire of cloth of gold and silk, noticeably trimmed with fur."[2]

For Christine de Pisan, this is a kind of counterimage of the virgin. She is not submissive, but is a powerful woman who acts decisively to correct wrongs. She can, by her own physical courage and the power of her faith, inspire an army to bravery and successful defiance of an enemy that outnumbers them.

This powerful image was referred to frequently by subsequent French writers. Many of them in later years of French nationalism quoted Pisan's poem about Joan of Arc:

> What honor this for womankind!
> Well loved of God it would appear,
> When the sad crowd [by which she means the French nobility] at last
>     resigned,
> Fled from the kingdom in great fear.
> Now we by a woman rescued here.
> Which five thousand men could not do.
> She made the traitor disappear!
> One could scarcely believe it true.[3]

That image, powerful up to the eighteenth century, disappears thereafter to be replaced by domestic imagery or romantic sexual imagery about women.

## Periods of Transition: Subordinating the Amazon and Romanticizing the Female

In the British tradition, the Amazons surface again in comfortable Renaissance English dress. In Thomas More's *Utopia* (1516), the Utopians fight in battle, each wife beside her husband to maximize efficiency. Although More is writing satirically and mocking medieval notions of warfare, nonetheless his women are described as though they have equal physical vigor and courage with men.[4]

In England, it was during the reign of Elizabeth I that the country needed the image of the warlike woman most profoundly. Elizabeth I came to the throne of England at the time that it was most threatened as an emerging nation-state by the might of the Spanish Empire. From the day that Elizabeth I was crowned, the country daily expected the arrival of a Spanish invasion that might overrun the country. Elizabeth I used the imagery of an Amazon princess to rally the troops. When the news came that the Spanish Armada had sailed and was expected to attack, she traveled to the Port of Tilbury to join the assembled troops. Here is a contemporary description of her: "She came habited like an Amazonian queen, buskinned and plumed, having a golden truncheon, gantlet and gorget."[5]

Elizabeth exploited the imagery of herself as a warlike Amazon many times in rallying the British forces to resist the Armada. However, the fabled virgin Queen Elizabeth could not be represented in any literary tradition as actually subverting male power and authority. In 1589, when Edmund Spenser wrote his great poem about Elizabeth I, *The Faerie Queene*, he solved the problem. In place of a powerful, strong, and brave woman who subverts male authority, he has the female warrior, Britomart, standing for Elizabeth I, chosen by fate to join her male lover in leading the battle to free England from foreign invaders. But the foreign invaders in Spenser's poem are Amazons. The virtuous queen rids the country of these subversive women and then submits herself again to male authority. Spenser's poem ends with Britomart

> Changing all that form of common weal, The liberty of women did
>     repeal,
> Which they had long usurped;
> And, them restoring to men's subjection, did true justice deal.[6]

In this transitional period people still used the image of the mighty woman but were comfortable doing so only when, after a period of freedom or crisis, the female then submits to male authority. But in drama the Amazon theme persists in many forms. The French poet Marie-Anne Fiquet du Boccage wrote a 1750 drama, *Amazones*, using Amazon society as a setting for extended speculation on the nature of gender in eighteenth-century France. Just as Montesquieu used Persia as the foil for everything he thought was wrong about French society, Madame Boccage used the Amazon kingdom. The Amazon rulers tell her that "for women in the Amazon kingdom age brings dignity and wisdom. Far from being dreaded here, time brings us a prize. Here a wrinkled brow signifies authority."[7] The author parodies many of the obsessions about the attractiveness of adolescent and late adolescent females in her depiction of the Amazon rulers, who are strong, powerful, elderly, and wise. *Amazones* was well received on the French stage, only to be replaced in popularity, in a wonderful irony, by one of the early plays of Jean-Jacques Rousseau.

Rousseau's writings embodied a totally new mentality about the meaning of gender and sexuality. The earlier writers discussed so far thought of nature as a background on which political society exists as the creation of divine authority or some secularized version of it; women, as part of society, are therefore not seen as part of nature. In contrast, Rousseau's romantic idealization of nature, and of women as a sexual surrogate for nature and its infinite capacity for fruitfulness and renewal, changed the way a female is defined.

In depicting nature as opposed to the artifice of human society, observers read onto that natural order the particular political meanings that they sought. Even though the females of many species are larger than males, nineteenth-century biologists concluded that nature's fixed and unchanging categories were the key to understanding a society in which the female must be submissive to the male. Females must be smaller and less powerful—indeed, must not be seen as sexually aggressive and therefore not aggressive in any way at all. Nineteenth-century ideologists observed male competition for female mates as the only form of sexual combat. Once that natural imagery replaced a reference back to a classical world and classical models, it was impossible for nineteenth-century women to imagine themselves as military leaders or as exercising rule. This is a significant problem for the feminist movement, which became a worldwide movement in the nineteenth century.

One of the great forces at work in the idealization of nature and natural man in the period leading up to the French Revolution was the hatred by philosophes such as Rousseau of the aristocratic learned women who mocked him as a simpleton from the provinces. The political power and influence of aristocratic women was one thing that all revolutionary, democratic reformers wanted to purge from the whole social system, and they proceeded to do so in what we call the Age of the Democratic Revolution. The fighting in Paris during the French Revolution saw a great deal of female participation. When war was declared on Revolutionary France, many women wanted to join the national army. A serious petition was prepared by several claiming that they wanted full citizenship and wanted to fight beside their menfolk to defend the country. During the Reign of Terror most women who were associated with that petition somehow or other found their way to the guillotine. Indeed, the French women who tried to organize political clubs for women that could be sources of agitation for those rights also met their end at the guillotine. So too did the philosophe Marie-Jean de Caritat, Marquis de Condorcet, who argued for the political rights of women. He committed suicide en route to what he knew was certain execution.

Thus we have to go much further back than the nineteenth century and the romantic view of the female if we want to think about the political roles of women. Modern industrial society produced cities where women were moved to dwellings far away from work, and middle-class women lived in suburban settings, where they no longer had any access to technology except domestic technology. Under those conditions it was difficult to entertain fantasies of rule or military life or power outside the emotional power of influence and control in the family. In trying to think about how one could claim political rights for women to vote and to bear arms, Mary Wollstonecraft was unable to imagine it. She wrote in *The Vindication of the Rights of Women*, "Women ought to have representatives instead of being arbitrarily governed without having any direct share allowed them in the deliberations of government. It should be an equal right of representation for the female population." But she thought it difficult to imagine that women could fight alongside men, except "if it were a defensive war, the only justifiable war, if it were alone to be adopted as just and glorious"; only then, she believed, might "the true heroism of antiquity . . . again animate a female bosom." Wollstonecraft puts it all very condition-ally and is confused about what she thinks might be a just war. Instead, she says her ideal society would be one in which man must necessarily fulfill the duties of a citizen, that is, fight in times of national crisis, or be despised. While he was employed in any of the departments of civil life, his wife, also an active citizen, should be equally intent to manage her family, educate her children, and assist her neighbors. Wollstonecraft thus makes one little bow in the direc-tion of military and civic responsibility for women. But she quickly corrects it, to put it in line with the emerging notion of separation between the political roles of males and females. She ends up arguing that women's political rights rest not on their equal citizenship with men in the defense of their state but on their maternal functions.[8]

## Contemporary Opportunities: Postmodern Amazons

Where are we today in the important arenas of power and leadership in American life? Where has the feminist movement succeeded and in what realms is the struggle yet to begin? Wollstonecraft's assessment of the basis of women's political rights seems to have prevailed. Few feminist leaders have battled for women's access to military academies and for their right of participation in all ranks of the military. On the whole, we have argued about a notion of female rule that is derived from emotional control and the effort to influence rather than to take power. Today we no longer have a citizen army in the old sense of citizens sharing the responsibility for the defense of the society, but rather an army of recruited volunteers who enlist for a variety of reasons having to do with the attractions of military service. We do have an elite core of women in the U.S. armed services, women who have excelled in combat. For example, in the Gulf War the women who were flying missions over Kuwait were the best flyers, and nobody wanted to jeopardize a particular set of exercises by not using the women pilots.

While we are now used to the image of women in general's uniforms, they have arrived at that rank just when the military virtues are less resonant in popular culture, and when military women appear in the media more as victims of sexual exploitation than as figures of valor. So we need to work steadily and deliberately to forge the images of female power that can inform notions of leadership. This is difficult to do in the face of the current "relational" emphasis of feminist thought, but it is a task worthy of serious effort.

Much of my daily life in recent decades has been taken up with the governance of institutions, for-profit companies, foundations, hospitals, universities, and schools, and in that role I observe women leaders in every type of institution. They are super-efficient, visionary about the institution or the business, and able to state their views and defend them strongly against contending opinions. Some are mothers, some are not. What they all have is the personal ability to call out the best performance from others and mobilize it around a common goal. They are no more lodged in a network of relationships than their male colleagues. Somehow feminist psychologists can't see the "old boy network" for what it is—a network of sustaining and collaborative relationships. Men don't talk about those relationships because their discourse is supposed to focus on the business at hand. Women are taught to report on the

significance of relationships in their lives, and so they do it. But I see no difference in business discourse when women executives are talking, Deborah Tan-
nen to the contrary notwithstanding.

If positive models for female rule were screened out of women's education
in the eighteenth century, the same may be said for women's access to technological thinking in the nineteenth. As a result, a strong strand in modern feminism views modern technology as a male creation, and a negative one at that.
It is said to have displaced women from their great craft tradition in textiles
and as silversmiths, and worst of all, from health care. Of course, what happened was the monopolization of science-based technical skills in educational
institutions for men, and the definition of the female temperament in a manner that excluded technical thinking. We have only to look at the household
guides written by women in the eighteenth and early nineteenth centuries to
see that women wrote in technical terms about household design, the circula-
tion of air, and the construction of chimneys and plumbing systems, and that
they suggested such labor-saving devices as the first primitive washing machine. But because they were excluded from scientific training and the emerging schools of engineering of the later nineteenth century, this genre of writing
died out, and household management became the management of consumption rather than the design and management of the built environment.

Shifting the focus to the mid-twentieth century, we see women leading
in opposition to nuclear weapons and in campaigns against environmental
pollution. By that time technology has become a male field, and the orientation of science toward the conquest and manipulation of nature has been designated a male characteristic. Of course, this view ignores all the male
scientists who became opponents of nuclear weapons after seeing the destruc-
tive force of atomic weapons, and it is forgetful of an older tradition of women's
involvement with shaping material culture. Once again it is hard for contemporary women to think about controlling technology because they have no
memory of a past in which women were technological innovators.

But unless we are able to think systematically about the uses of a system
of technological control that exists, it will always control us. Historians of science and technology point out that the direction of scientific work and the
applications of scientific discovery as technology are shaped by cultural and
particularly by political factors. It is the relations of modern science to the state
and to warfare that have given it its current character.

Young women have been voting with their feet by studying science and
engineering in increasing numbers, especially fields such as electrical and
chemical engineering and genetics. Smith College, recognizing the centrality

of the electronically networked organization for the twenty-first century, has launched a school of engineering to deliver the scientific and technological training often left out of the average woman's education. We need to understand that it is left out not because technical knowledge is male but because we live in a culture that has defined the female as lacking scientific and technical motivations. Fortunately, there are women CEOs in the Internet world to serve as models, and there is growing recognition that bias has made women's pursuit of scientific and technical training doubly taxing. Witness MIT's recent announcement of plans to rectify its unequal treatment of women faculty. In theory, the arrival of the Internet should go far to rectify the isolation of women engaged in child rearing, and the capacity it provides for people to work from the home ought to be beneficial to mothers. However, this technical change alone will not provide the setting for women to exercise decisive business leadership, unless new systems of child care and redesigned home services become available.

## Concluding Thoughts

Fortunately, there is one area of great importance in popular culture in which the image of the female leader has been dramatically transformed in recent years. In the field of athletics women continue to improve the levels of their performance in ways that move the best well beyond most males in their sport. We have only to watch the times of women competitors in marathons to see that the leaders outclass all but one or two males in the field.

Recent reports in the press predict that should women's athletic performance continue to improve at the pace that it has been over the last twenty years, it is entirely conceivable that women will establish records beyond the achievement of males. Certainly there is now a great array of media images of physically vigorous and strong women; witness Olympic women athletes throwing the discus. Photographs of any marathon today reflect the change from twenty years ago, when women were excluded from the race because it was thought to be too taxing for their physiques. Images of female power are highly energizing for young women today.

In team sports, women hockey, lacrosse, and basketball players have become the idols of young girls and the objects of popular enthusiasm. In tennis the crowd is as large and involved for the women's competition as for the men's. It is clear that, with training, a female body can take in oxygen and put out energy in ways that were unthinkable a mere decade ago. And the great array of media images of powerful women triumphing conveys a powerful message. Of course, whenever I make such remarks in a public address there will always be some women in the audience who rightly point out that the world needs people who nurture and care for those around them and don't always have to win. My response is to say that all modern organizations need leaders who can nurture the young talent below them. I watch successful male leaders do that every day, and if they don't do it spontaneously, coaches have to be retained to help teach them. Society fears that if women become strong and competitive they will cease to be nurturing, but that fear is the product of a gender system created a few hundred years ago and should not be taken as a universal.

The interest of young women in athletics comes, in part, because of this extraordinary progress and the absence, at the moment, of a glass ceiling in this area of achievement. Every time in the past that women have shown a really strong likelihood of outperforming men, a way has been found to reorganize the competition. Certainly that is what happened during the admission of women to formerly all-male institutions in the nineteenth century. Whenever it looked as though women were going to outperform males academically, they were quickly streamed into other kinds of activities. Will such history repeat itself in the athletic world? It will be interesting to follow the course of women athletes as they increasingly reach highly competitive levels of performance.

The modern feminist movement, then, has restored the image of physically vigorous and powerful women. We see them all around us. We even aspire to be that ourselves. It has given us back women in the military running the same risks as their male colleagues. The question remains regarding when women will be ready to take on the responsibilities of rule. Those responsibilities go with acknowledged strength and military participation. With some wonderful and notable exceptions, women have seemed a bit shy about power and leadership. The feminist movement in the 1970s, which was shaped by the New Left ideology about the destructiveness of leadership and hierarchy, was marked by its inability to vest real power and authority in its leaders; it tried to rule itself by committee. How will the next generation think about and resolve this peculiar problem of feminism? We no longer have a memory of those early military and aristocratic models; they have been almost completely expunged from our thoughts and consciousness. We think about feminism only as a nineteenth-century bourgeois phenomenon even though it isn't. An important, albeit small, group of women has tried hard to sort out the questions of citizenship, rule, and physical and political power. We've come quite a long way in thinking about and claiming physical power, and we are now poised to take further steps in assessing the authority of leadership and power.

## Notes

1. If you are interested in looking at the use to which this imagery was put in the fourteenth and fifteenth centuries and subsequently, see Abby W. Kleinbaum, *The War against the Amazons* (New York: New Press, McGraw Hill, 1983). Kleinbaum has traced the appearance of the imagery of the Amazons in women's writing in medieval and early modern times, the uses to which those women put it, and the impact that that imagery had on their sense of themselves as people capable of rule.

2. Christine de Pisan, *La Dittie de Jeanne d'Arc*, ed. A. J. Kennedy and K. Vartz (Oxford: Oxford University Press, 1977), 19.

3. Ibid., 34.

4. *The Utopia of Thomas More, including Ropa's Life of More, and His Letters to His Daughter Margaret*, with notes and introduction by Mildred Campbell (New York: Classics Club, 1947).

5. Thomas Heywood, *The Exemplary Lives and Memorable Acts of Nine of the Most Worthy Women of the World* (London, 1640). A gorget is a shoulder decoration. A gantlet is worn on the wrist for battle.

6. Edmund Spenser, *The Faerie Queene*, V, vii, 42.

7. Marie-Anne Fiquet du Boccage, *Amazones: Tragédie en trois actes* (Paris, 1749), 21–23.

8. Mary Wollstonecraft, *A Vindication of the Rights of Women* (1792; New York: Norton, 1975), 145.

*Women on Power*

*Introduction*

# Leadership and Power: New Conceptions

**Sue J. M. Freeman and Susan C. Bourque**

*The best way for a woman to get to the top is to start there. My being a woman is just not an issue. I'm the boss. They'd better be comfortable with me or else.*

— SANDRA KURTZIG, *founder of ASK Group Computer Systems*

MANY women like Sandra Kurtzig have assumed leadership roles in America's most lucrative and predominately male occupations: business, politics, sport, and the professions. Over the past two decades, women's leadership in these fields has been embraced and resisted, accepted and denied by both institutions and individuals. The path to leadership in boardrooms, in public office, and on the playing fields has not been smooth. As recently as the 1980s, conservative political and religious figures called for women's return to the home to heal the wounds of national life, suffered, presumably, because of women's exodus from the domestic sphere. Even now, at the beginning of a new millennium, with women constituting at least half the work force and 49 percent of management, the media still reflect ambivalence about women's place.[1]

Leadership has been problematic for women. Historically it was deemed appropriate only in fields specifically defined as female or in arenas related to the home. Public leaders have been overwhelmingly male, as are public representations of leaders. The female leaders of movements for women's rights and expanded public roles have been belittled and, at times, vilified. The notion of a woman at the helm of any powerful enterprise has, until

3

recently, been jarring. For the most part (despite the recent exception of high-level Clinton administration appointments of Secretary of State Madeleine Albright and Attorney General Janet Reno), women have not set the direction of the nation's business or public policy. Nor have they been celebrated as heroes akin to men in the serious pastime and big industry of American sport. Given the long-standing male monopoly at the higher ranks of business, politics, professional life, and sport, combined with the problematic nature of female leadership in our culture, it is not surprising that women have encountered glass ceilings in their quest for positions at the top of their fields. Even today, despite the enormous changes of the past twenty-five years, men still occupy 95 percent of the top corporate positions and 85 percent of elected offices. The leadership situation for minority women is even bleaker. Despite over thirty-five years of equal pay legislation, "full-time female employees earn less than 75 cents for every dollar earned by men. Hispanic female college graduates average lower salaries than white male high school dropouts."[2] Most compelling of all, women constitute two-thirds of those living in poverty in the United States. With twenty-five years of legislation outlawing sex discrimination, how are we to understand women's continuing inequality and limited leadership?

The exercise of leadership involves power, a concept where research has suggested gender variation. Power becomes an essential link in our study of women's changing leadership roles, for it is precisely in debates about the appropriateness of women's exercise of power, particularly over men, that gender is linked to leadership in society's most prestigious and highly compensated institutions. As women's roles widen in business, politics, sports, and the professions, they will necessarily lead in areas where enormous resources are concentrated. Will our fundamental notions of leadership and gender be reshaped and the traditional limits on women's exercise of power be left behind? To what extent will race, class, and culture intersect with gender to shape the experience of different groups of women and men?

We have collected essays that examine women's experience in areas of the greatest resistance to change. In doing so, we engage the pivotal theoretical debates within the feminist community about women's leadership. We argue that theories of leadership need to be reformulated to account for women's expanded roles in the contemporary world. The evidence in these essays makes it clear that leadership qualities and requirements vary significantly from one context to another, among racial and ethnic groups and cross-nationally. Moreover, men and women are perceived differently as leaders; they are evaluated on a different scale and according to different criteria. In the pages that follow, we identify this paradox and a number of others that confront the woman leader. We argue that these paradoxes confound and restrain women's leadership. New research suggests that women's exercise of authority is judged more harshly than men's, by both men and women. Our concern is not only how to increase the number of women in leadership positions but also how best to understand our assessments of leadership. We have chosen essays that address both the content of leadership and the vision of leadership that women bring to positions of power and authority.

One of the most provocative hypotheses to emerge from these essays is that for many women leadership begins with an intensely experienced wrong. The need to protect their children and families is frequently cited as the initial catalyst for public action. Leadership becomes an imperative for many women engaged in personal struggles and it is justified—at least initially—by women's sense that they are defending their families and homes. The personally experienced wrong is eventually broadened to embrace a community and the need for an organization emerges.

At the same time, most of the material presented in this volume poses a challenge to essentialist descriptions of women, that is, the idea that there is an identifiable component found in every woman that marks her as female across cultures and over time. Although for many women the first catalyst to leadership may stem from their traditional domestic roles, women are no longer exclusively characterized by those roles. Similarly, few descriptions of women's leadership will hold across all cultures or throughout history or within American society across class, race, and ethnic lines. To maximize women's participation and leadership throughout the world, it is clear that cultural mores and proscriptions must be part of our calculations.

The international arena provides us with a number of interesting insights. The United Nations meetings held over the course of the past twenty-five years have demonstrated the desire to achieve consensus on a definition of women's rights and a plan of action to improve women's status worldwide. Among the areas of long-standing and continuing concern have been the calls for reproductive rights, educational access, improved employment opportunities, and an end to violence against women. But there are important areas where agreement has not been reached. Culture and religion contribute to severe breaches on the questions of abortion, gay and lesbian rights, and new definitions of the family. Similarly, there is ongoing debate in the international community about the impact of globalization, privatization, and structural adjustment programs on women's economic well-being.

While the category "woman" encompasses vast differences, our task will be to discern the commonalities that prevail in patterns of leadership. We learn a great deal about the dynamics of gender by sensitivity to "difference" in the experience of women. The essays in this collection look at leadership in grass-roots organizations, national-level politics, the corporate world, and international organizations. For each we ask how the experience of women fits the prevailing theoretical models of leadership. First, let us review the current theories of leadership.

## Theoretical Approaches to Leadership

Most theories of leadership have not specifically addressed gender, though they have been proposed within a cultural milieu of male leaders. Only in recent decades as women have made claims to leadership has gender been part of the analysis. Historically, female leaders were often portrayed as so unconventional in their ideas and agendas that they were ignored or ostracized. The only option for the nineteenth-century American middle-class white woman was to carve out a separate sphere of action that could be defined as appropriately female and where she could exercise her own vision and build institutions. Initially, this was an extension of the domestic sphere, capitalizing on the supposedly distinct nurturing and compassionate temperament of women. That temperament ideally suited them to lead social reform efforts to assist those left helpless in the face of aggressive and rapid industrial development. For example, in the nineteenth century Dorothea Dix led a national movement for the humane care of the mentally ill, and Frances Willard organized the temperance movement. Both insisted that their activism was an appropriate extension of women's private sphere. In the early twentieth century, Jane Addams organized the settlement movement to aid the immigrant population in the slums of Chicago, and Julia Lathrop organized the Child Protection Bureau. Both explained their public activism as an appropriate reflection of women's special concerns for the needs of children and the poor. The cost of this strategy—one that endorsed beliefs in gender-specific psychological traits and capabilities as a basis for citizenship—was high. It resulted in women's tangential relationship to the political system and an ill-defined strategy for political power.[3] Moreover, despite working-class and African American women's very different work experiences, the dominant white middle-class ideal of womanhood devalued African American women's labor and added to the complexity of gender power relations in their communities.[4]

The current women's movement has built on a fuller understanding of the limits of previous strategies. Being both broader and more specific in its demands for equal rights, the women's movement of the late twentieth century prompted unprecedented female participation at all levels of public life. The call for equality has included specific agendas for judicial and legislative action. Women have combined new levels of participation with the responsibilities of leadership even in fields marked as exclusively masculine as recently as fifty years ago.

Nevertheless, although many women are now prepared to lead, their potential constituents have not been acculturated to the notion of a female leader. The puzzle remains for the female leader: What role will she adopt toward her constituents? Images and attributes commonly associated with females or "the feminine" do not overlap with those associated with leadership. Our prevailing stereotypes of women still include gentleness, emotionality rather than rational powers, the priority of interpersonal relationships over independent achievement. In sum, our stereotypes still insist on an intuitive, subjective perspective and a domestic focus. A leader, on the other hand, is assumed to be rational, decisive, objective, and strongly motivated to achieve, with a worldview that projects concern well beyond the confines of the domestic sphere. The latter characterization still closely corresponds to our stereotyped images of men and the masculine.[5]

When we examine early leadership theories, the overlap between notions of male and leader is unmistakable. Max Weber's categories of patrimonial, legal, and charismatic authority all presumed a male leader. An obvious example comes from the eighteenth- and nineteenth-century philosophers' "great man" theory: personal traits of particular individuals predicted leadership; moreover, those traits were inherent rather than acquired through learning or experience. This theory fell by the wayside when research failed to uncover a constellation of universal traits distinguishing leaders from others.[6] In its place contextual explanations became popular: the needs and spirit of the times determined who would emerge as a leader. Because these two approaches each emphasized one part of the equation (person or situation) to the exclusion of the other, they could not account for the diversity of leaders and complexity of leadership roles. Since the 1930s a more interactive conception has held sway: individual, situational, and temporal factors are all considered operative.[7]

Today we argue that leadership depends on a combination of individual characteristics and situational requirements. What is most noteworthy about this current understanding of leadership is that it brings followers into the equation. Theorists now view leadership as heavily dependent on the acceptance of the leader by those who are led and leader-follower interactions as most important to the leader's success or failure. Moreover, in some recent formulations "leadership is seen as a means to the empowerment of follow-ers."[8] This notion is not entirely new. Ralph Stogdill concluded in 1948: "The pattern of personal characteristics of the leader must bear some relevant rela-tionship to the characteristics, activities, and goals of the followers. . . . It be-comes clear that an adequate analysis of leadership involves not only a study of leaders, but also of situations."[9]

Perhaps the most general understanding of leadership had been one that emphasized a leader's vision and the ability to translate that vision into reality.[10] Today, in contrast, the visionary leaders have been replaced by a view of leader-ship as a reciprocal relationship with followers to achieve a shared purpose.[11] It is the transaction between leader and followers that creates a unified focus.[12] The term _reciprocal leadership_ refers to the dynamic set of relationships among followers, leaders, and their mutual mission. Leaders are no longer seen as unilaterally exercising authority and power or engaged in "headship."[13] Viewed as a process, reciprocal leadership is no longer identified by a person or personal attributes. All aspects of leadership, from election or appointment to effectiveness, are now linked to followers and their context.[14] This new vi-sion appears to be more compatible with traditional stereotypes of women's strengths of interpersonal connection and care. Nevertheless, as our essays make clear, the new understanding of leadership has not necessarily translated into wider opportunities for women—why that should be the case is one of the central paradoxes addressed in this volume. We have addressed this paradox from a variety of perspectives, and the essays reach a range of conclusions.

## Women and Power

Long-standing beliefs about gender roles—what is deemed appropriate be-havior for males and females—militate against women wielding the type of power associated with male leadership. Gender-role congruency would sanc-tion, if anything, a different kind of power for women, and indeed, female power has been described as indirect, personal, and derivative as opposed to direct, authoritative, and status-derived. Indeed, women who adopt stereotypi-cally male leadership styles (autocratic and nonparticipatory) or occupy male-dominated leadership positions are apt to be evaluated negatively in light of the gender role incongruency.[15] Since it has been an unquestioned male pre-rogative to lead, men may adopt a variety of leadership styles without sanction; their success is not compromised by a so-called feminine style (democratic, collaborative, and interpersonally oriented). Women are in the untenable posi-tion of being criticized for adopting a male model of authority and devalued by the stereotyped female model. The essays in this collection explore the alternatives that exist for female leaders as they exercise power.

Women's desire for public leadership has been denied despite substantial evidence to the contrary. Even when their volunteerism dominated local political organizations, their numbers populated the ranks of middle management, and their pressure resulted in the implementation of equity legislation such as Title IX, women were still seen as lacking ambition and aspiration to leadership in large, powerful enterprises. Indeed, some women did eschew "headship," perhaps because the very top of career ladders conformed to a military model where single-minded devotion to the exclusion of all other aspects of life is the norm.[16] When queried about success and ambition, women would cite the intrinsic rewards of work satisfaction in business, worthwhile contribution in politics, and achieving according to their own internal standards of excellence rather than competition and direct power over others.[17]

This seeming reluctance to vie for leadership in their fields fueled speculation about a conflicted female relation to power. Might women's comparatively greater concerns about both the possession and use of power inhibit them from seeking high-level powerful positions?[18] A female desire for power runs contrary to the established cultural "truth" that "normal" women are not interested in power. Women are criticized for personal ambition, and the label "a powerful woman" does not carry the same unalloyed positive connotation, as does "a powerful man." Given the prevailing cultural assessments, women might reasonably conclude that a desire for power needs to be masked or disguised.[19]

Are women conflicted about power? Or is power undergoing a redefinition, as has leadership? The concept of power is no longer solely a male construction or province. The challenge of an unprecedented female influx into the strongholds of our society, coupled with a revised feminist consciousness and fortified by legislative mandates, has significantly complicated our conceptions of power.[20] But paradoxically, it has not resolved the problem of women's leadership.

## Power Redefined or Persistent Stereotypes?

Early studies of the motive to gain, hold, and use power were conducted with male subjects.[21] This custom in male-constructed psychological research reflected the belief that public power was considered a male prerogative.[22] Indeed, the very definitions of power in the social sciences reflected a decidedly male disposition: power was experienced through wealth, resources, influence, control, and physical strength. "Thus, resistance, conflict, force, domination, and control are recurrent themes in patriarchal constructions of the meaning of power, which always include a 'win-lose' and 'power-over' conceptual basis."[23]

Feminist discussions of power have focused on "power to," "empowerment" to achieve one's goals, or "shared power" to enhance another's feelings of competence.[24] In addition to this interpersonal form of power, feminist theorists have described a form of personal authority that is "the power to be self-determining, to act rather than react, to choose the terms on which to live one's own life."[25] This power to change, to move something, particularly oneself, could be considered a vital starting point for people who have been without power and status, an underclass dominated by others.[26]

The power of autonomy, personal control over oneself and the direction of one's life, may be a common aspect of the sense of new freedom that follows oppression and a necessary antecedent to more public action and visibly recognized power. That is, the primacy of personal authority may be an initial stage of an individual's claim to power; it seems likely, however, that power derived from control over resources or physical strength compounds an individual's sense of autonomy.

Do women in leadership positions think about and exercise power differently than their male counterparts? Do such women view power as reciprocal, as opposed to dominating and controlling? How do they exercise power in their relations with subordinates? Do they empower them in the process of a concerted team effort or shared vision? Do they more fully subscribe to the notion that "leadership is not so much the exercise of power itself as the empowerment of others?"[27] A descriptive study of influential political women emphasized leadership through empowerment, where power is "an expandable resource that is produced and shared through interaction by leader and followers."[28] In interviews with twenty-five prominent women politicians, Dorothy Cantor and Toni Bernay report their definition of power as "the ability to get things done." These women viewed political power as a vehicle for making a difference in society for the greater good, by setting and accomplishing an agenda. "Power in itself means nothing," claimed one respondent.[29] Is it likely that for men as well, power is to be used in the service of a shared goal?

In our estimation, the association of "power over" with men and "power to" with women borders again on another stereotype. While men generally have had higher status and more access to power than women in our society, sex differences in the power motive and in the exercise of power have been discounted by research studies.[30] A commonly held belief that men have stronger power motivation has also been refuted by research reviews.[31] The most cursory perusal of magazines and newspapers attests to a strong female power motive as women seek leadership in heretofore male preserves of business, politics, the professions, and sports. These women ordinarily do not present themselves as revolutionaries aiming to "change the system" but rather as capable, confident hard workers with a mission related to the business at hand. In fact, women have not been found to differ from men in styles of leadership or power.[32] A review of studies revealed that "power motivation predicted many of the same actions in women and men: becoming 'visible' to others, getting positions of formal social power and pursuing power-related careers, and acquiring possessions that reflect prestige."[33]

A tradition of power as a male preserve has obscured our understanding of women and power. That is, we have mistakenly attributed behavioral variation between men and women to sex rather than to power differences that were invisible by virtue of their institutionalization or because they appeared to be natural.[34] When psychological studies have attempted to disentangle the effects of gender and power, gender differences disappear. Researchers have concluded that it is the amount of power an individual has in a particular situation, as opposed to gender, that is key.[35]

If it is the case that the equalization of power eliminates sex differences, then one might predict that such differences will fade as women gain status and access to power.[36] As Lynda M. Sagrestano has noted, "unequal distribution of power results in the illusion of gender differences, which are really the result of women's and men's social statuses. As such, apparent gender differences in behavior must be understood within a context of status and power."[37] Moreover, gender differences are firmly based in stereotypic cultural conceptions of gender-appropriate social roles. Unfortunately, as the authors in this collection make clear, our gender stereotypes are remarkably resistant to change. In addition, the salience of stereotypes mutates in ways that are not entirely predictable. As we shall see in several of the essays that follow, women's attempts to use these stereotypes to their advantage have often had less than optimal outcomes.

If gender obscures the effects of power and social status, we can expect race and class to do likewise. Just as it has taken a long time to look beyond a male prototype of leadership and power, similarly it has been a slow process to revise our paradigms in relation to race, class, and culture. The influx of women in leadership positions in business, politics, sport, and the professions began in a serious way in the 1970s. In most of these enterprises, the story has been the same: women's numbers have swelled at the middle ranks and been stalled at the top. Focused consideration of the reasons for this glass-ceiling phenomenon began in the following decade. It was not until the 1990s that serious discourse appeared about the limited number of minority women to gain places of power and leadership.[38] There are few women and people of color on the tracks leading to top leadership. In business we can expect the picture to shift rapidly because of the revolutionary changes brought by technology and because rapid globalization has brought business leaders of different cultures into more immediate interaction. In politics, the professions, and sport, changes have been less radical, though there is evidence of limited change. Among the professions there has been an influx of people of color, although the top ranks of the professions are still dominated by white males. In most of these arenas, neither rapidly changing technology nor an increasingly interdependent world economy has substantially shaken white male dominance.

In the midst of the recent plethora of research on gender and leadership, there is little on the interaction of race and ethnicity with leadership. "Unlike the research on women and men, where the findings have been quite consistent, there is still much to be learned in studies of race and ethnic differences in leadership style and effectiveness."[39] Studies of race, class, and culture in relation to leadership of our most influential enterprises are just gaining momentum since the early work in the 1980s.[40]

In the United States, studies of race commonly begin with African American experience, and the leadership literature is no exception. For African Americans to assume leadership positions, they must overcome several appreciable obstacles. The presence of a substantial African American middle class has not eliminated race and gender barriers for a sizable number of African Americans. Stereotypes associated with being female and African American are not easily overcome. Further, economic disadvantage has been deep and enduring for male and female African Americans. Within-race comparisons find females better off than their male counterparts in terms of completion of education, employment opportunities, and family stability. African American females traditionally have been family caretakers as well as the family's primary financial support. Thus, the expectation for young African American women has been that they will have the dual responsibilities of work and family; in fact, marriage is seen as secondary to occupation as essential for success in life. Family and racial communities become important as motivators and beneficiaries. As African American women become members of the professional-managerial class, they identify their own success as not only an individual achievement but also a mark of pride for their community and race. In contrast to a white male model of solitary, individual mobility achieved through traditional routes, black professional women's mobility "is motivated by a desire for personal, but also collective gain and shaped by interpersonal commitments to family, partners and children, community, and the race."[41] African American women go beyond immediate family commitments to contribute to "an entire racial uplift process."[42] This kind of consciousness is reminiscent of that spawned by large-scale movements undertaken by and on behalf of an entire "class," for example, the women's and civil rights movements.

This glimpse of African American women exemplifies the incipient complexity in studying leadership. Just as we should avoid generalizing about white men and women, we cannot generalize across race or gender for African Americans. Not only can we expect leadership styles and opportunities to vary by race, but we should also expect organizational or institutional context to play a pivotal role. African American leadership of a predominantly African American organization might be quite different from such leadership of a predominantly white or a mixed group. Only limited research is available on this latter configuration.[43] There is also scant research on the leadership styles of African American women. Speculation must ultimately be put to the test of firsthand evidence gathered directly from the perspective of African American women.[44]

## Global Perspectives

Gender relations cut across all cultures, but how they are manifest in relation to the exercise of leadership and power cannot be ascertained in the absence of the social, historical, and cultural context. In recognition of this limitation, more comprehensive and finely grained research has been undertaken to further our understanding of the effects of cultural variables on leadership.[45]

Important commonalities have been reported in recent cross-cultural research. As evidenced in a number of such studies and found throughout the essays in this collection, men and women experience the conflict between work and family differently. For women it serves as a brake on their options. Even when this is not the case for an individual woman, the expectation of this dual responsibility shapes perceptions of a woman's leadership potential and often serves as a structural limit on her opportunities. There is also cross-cultural evidence that many women have come to see the difficulty of combining career and family as a structural problem rather than a matter of individual responsibility. Where women have been successful in combining the two, much has depended on the comfort of the women's male partners with women's professional visibility and success, the cultural traditions regarding male-female relations, and the value of family in the lives of men and women.[46]

When we look beyond the borders of the United States, we find our customary notions of gender differences and effective leadership overturned. For example, what has been characterized as a primarily female managerial style in America, with an emphasis on relational values, is more commonly assumed and practiced by executives in strong Asian economies. "It is not that the distinction between women and men identified in the American managerial literature is either incorrect or inconsequential, but only that it is incomplete. Without appreciating American male managers as outliers, it is impossible to begin to appreciate what men's and women's approaches can bring to global leadership in the twenty-first century."[47] American ethnocentrism may foster projection of our models of leadership and understandings of power as universal, but increasing diversity and a worldwide scope place the American view in a much larger and more complex global perspective.[48] Nonetheless, women leaders are still a rarity across the face of the globe; as such they may represent a rise to power apart from traditional structures and symbolize change, hope, and fresh possibilities.[49]

## Leadership and Power: The Recurring Paradoxes

It is clear that women are exercising leadership today in new and significant ways. In this collection, we have gathered essays from a wide array of disciplines to demonstrate the new theoretical insights that have emerged as well as the continuing puzzles and paradoxes. For more than two decades, contemporary American women have been making claims to leadership roles in business, the professions, politics, and sports. Nevertheless, much of the literature documenting women's exercise of power and leadership begins with the male prototype of the leader. This starting point invariably sets in play a dichotomy and structures the focus on how women *differ from* or *compare to* men in their attitudes toward power and the exercise of leadership. Men and male patterns are assumed to be the norm and the standard against which women's behavior will be measured. This portrayal often leads to representations of women as "less able" leaders. It also submerges other potentially interesting comparisons within gender categories such as race, ethnicity, sexual orientation, and nationality.

The assumed polarity between men and women has led some feminists to argue that women are better suited than men for contemporary leadership.[50]

They argue that we need to assign new value to women's purported emotional and empathetic qualities, and that a new and better form of leadership would emerge with an "ethic of care" based on maternal values.

We have sought to avoid dichotomous thinking and attempted to depict women in their own right, coming to positions of leadership in disparate ways and in a variety of contexts. We assume that men and women share the same capacity for intelligence, rational action, strength, and decisiveness. Thus, leadership capabilities ought to be distributed among both the male and female population. Why that is not perceived to be the case is at the core of our inquiries.

Because of women's previous exclusion from public power, we find female leadership exercised in unusual ways and in unexpected places. Moreover, because social class, race, and ethnicity have an important effect on women's opportunities, these factors also influence the strategies and tactics available to different groups of women. Thus, some women experience power in ostensibly "powerless" ways. For example, Maureen Mahoney points out in her essay that silence can represent a subjective sense of power as resistance and an active choice to "not do." Silence can be an act of protest rather than passive submission. Internal resistance, expressed as silence, can be a vital first step in the development of a private and personal sense of power that later becomes manifest in more public ways.

Another insight from these essays is the centrality of the human body as a source of the most private and personal sense of power. In the past, "science" justified restrictions on women as a result of their physiology. Reformulating such received wisdom about the female body has historically been an essential first step toward wider power for women. New and more accurate knowledge about women's physiology and their physical and mental capacity, widely accessible to women of all classes and social backgrounds, has been an important starting point in women's quest for broader leadership.[51] Expanding and extending information about the female body and female health is a fundamental aspect of widening women's potential for leadership, and the essay by Barbara Brehm explores this process in a women's collective. The members of the Boston Women's Health Book Collective saw their position as "powerless as women: powerless as patients," and they set out to change that situation. The Collective's efforts challenged the medical establishment's treatment of the female body and began a revolution in female medical care and research. The Collective members saw their efforts as a struggle for power—power that could be shared, and power that would redress a previous imbalance in the powerlessness of women. Thus, we find women's leadership in an unexpected place—far outside the formal institutions of power—but with a profound capacity to reshape those institutions.

Women's physiology—the body—is also linked to our generative capacity and to the notion of motherhood. In contemporary society, there is simply no male counterpart to the impact of motherhood—actual or potential—on women's lives and opportunities. Motherhood and how to address it remain puzzles at the heart of much feminist discourse. Disagreements and misunderstandings about it have been stumbling blocks in women's efforts to organize as women and develop a common agenda for equality.

The essays in this volume demonstrate again the role motherhood plays in structuring women's opportunities for leadership. While women's leadership has expanded, their traditional roles and responsibilities have not diminished. Thus, women throughout the world still bear the primary responsibility for home and child care. But the impact of motherhood is felt in a variety of contradictory ways and consequently is one of the central paradoxes surrounding women's leadership.

For example, Susan Bourque, in her essay on politics, points out that even as women have freed themselves from restrictive interpretations of their bodies and mental capacities, there remains an ongoing debate about the effect of motherhood on women's political activity. At the theoretical core of this debate is the degree to which motherhood prompts political action or serves as a credential for leadership.

Two essays in this collection confront this question directly. Myron and Penina Glazer and Velma García-Gorena describe mothers who begin protest movements but do not perceive themselves initially as political activists. In the case of the Madres Veracruzanas described by García-Gorena, the women eschewed association with the "corrupt" world of Mexican male politics. In both case studies, women who began as protectors of children developed strength and self-confidence through confrontations with public officials and interaction with the media. The paradox here is that motherhood and its restriction to the private domestic sphere have been the antithesis of public power and leadership—in fact, motherhood is often used as the rationale for excluding women from politics. Nonetheless, women in these mothers' movements have gained clout in ways that might not have been possible otherwise: that is, mobilization as mothers can be more effective within certain cultural contexts. Moreover, women in such movements gain a new sense of efficacy that infuses them with a more powerful sense of self and extends beyond the domain in which it originally developed.

The use of motherhood as a vehicle and justification for mobilization imposes certain limits, however. Motherhood as a claim for political participation is usually linked to a presumedly heightened sense of female morality. As such, it sets women's claims for a political voice apart from the claims of an ordinary male citizen for the right to make political demands and express political opinions. It seems to suggest that women require a justification for political action in a way that is unnecessary for men. The paradox here is that the strategy of elevating women at the same time restricts them and undermines their claims for a political voice on the basis of equality.

Our essays also suggest that what begins as private or personal power exercised in a domestic sphere frequently extends to more public arenas and transfers across domains. This may partially account for why those holding power attempt to restrict even the smallest female incursions. The first women to enter male enclaves were reluctant to distinguish themselves from their male colleagues. In business they adopted a female version of the gray flannel suit, in politics they sought to be hardworking policy wonks, in the professions they emphasized their merit and skills as exemplars of the profession, and in sports they emphasized their femininity. Seldom did they venture a feminist agenda or seek to rock the organizational or professional boat.

As we recall in this volume, major change occurred when the feminist movement of the late 1960s and 1970s developed women and men's consciousness of gender inequity. What had been viewed as individual challenges were now seen as collective and structural issues. Public policy changes created a conception of "sexual discrimination" and the legal tools to correct it. This inevitably led to more women in fields where they had been excluded.

With time and experience women become "players." Paradoxically, once numbers increase so too does an appreciation of the deeply embedded nature and broad scope of inequity. Similarly, as more women gain entry to these domains, their critiques of the domains increase. For example, sexual harassment becomes a public issue only in the late 1980s. As women gain some measure of power and prestige, they discover the ways in which institutions are structured to limit female power and leadership. The essays from the world of business, politics, the professions, and sport all underscore the commonality of this experience. This realization of the entrenched nature of sexual inequality coupled with encounters with the "glass ceiling" has led more than one female leader to abandon the field to pursue a career in a less hostile environment. Thus, the paradox develops that just as more women gain access to new opportunities for leadership, a significant number decide to abandon the high-power institutions and forge independent paths to power. The dilemma that emerges is that while women now have more choices about how and where to lead and exercise power, if substantial numbers decide to abandon traditional institutions, the pressure for structural change will diminish and successive generations of women will have to start anew.

Equally perplexing is our realization that while the content of gender stereotypes can remain unchanged, their salience may vary from one historical context to another. In the contemporary setting, Sue J. M. Freeman demonstrates that business has embraced a so-called female leadership style to the extent that it is no longer viewed as exclusively female but rather generally desirable. Thus, men have adopted more collaborative management techniques while maintaining their positions in the senior executive suites.

In the world of politics discussed by Susan Bourque, the first post–Cold War elections in 1992 reflected reduced concern with national defense and security. The election doubled the number of women in the U.S. Congress. Women's stereotypical concerns with domestic issues such as education and their reputation as less corruptible enhanced their appeal to voters. Yet their dramatic gains were not replicated in subsequent elections.

Even when gender stereotypes work for women, the gains may be short-lived. Moreover, they are still stereotypes, and in all of these seats of power they ultimately limit women. Because power and leadership based on the female stereotype currently in fashion is ephemeral, women's gains have often been temporary and reversible. Sustained cumulative improvement in women's access to leadership still eludes the modern women's movement.

Perhaps no other area of social life has been as obvious a site of change and partial triumph as that of sport. With the passage of Title IX, and the persistent activism that followed it, girls' and women's participation in organized sports has gone through a major transformation. This is a direct example of how changed conceptions of women's bodies are a critical component of wider access. It would be hard to deny the significance of the physical prowess demonstrated by women soccer players in the 1999 World Cup competition, watched by unprecedented numbers of viewers and fans. Nevertheless, as Mary Jo Kane points out, the number of women coaches and athletic directors—in other words, women's participation in the leadership structure of sports—has declined even as the number of girls and women participating in sport has increased. As Kane argues, the preference for male coaches, even for women's teams, cannot be explained by experience or skill. Moreover, among those women who achieved leadership positions, reports of an unfriendly, even hostile environment were common, and a lack of support frequent.

Kane notes, tellingly for many of the fields we consider, "It would be a mistake to assume that simply occupying a leadership position gives women equal status and power." This was certainly the case for many of the women elected to Congress who found themselves on the bottom rung of the internal hierarchy, with lower-status committee assignments and a chilly working environment. Once in leadership positions, women often discover new forms of marginalization—relegation to the less prestigious parts of the profession, lesser-status committee assignments, and limited access to the power brokers within the organizations and institutions.

The issue of sexuality has been just below the surface in many issues surrounding women's leadership. The strong female, whether physically or intellectually, finds herself open to a charge of abnormality and deviance. From there it is a short step for Americans to infer sexual deviance. Homophobia affects both men and women, and men who attempt new leadership styles often have their sexuality questioned. So too for women, and especially women in sport, lesbian baiting is an ideal mechanism for limiting women's access to leadership and for pitting women against one another.

Beyond American sport, how did the women's sports community come to adopt an international perspective and press for gender equity, linking sport to women's empowerment? New efforts to improve women's status in health, literacy, employment, and legal rights in the developing world may also be linked to wider access to sport and sport leadership for women. Christine Shelton discusses the development of an international grassroots movement to improve women's access to athletics, while Carole Oglesby raises critical questions about women's access to leadership in the profession of physical education.

As with sport, women have made substantial inroads in the professions. This success story, as related by Miriam Slater's account of veterinary medicine, is tempered by the limited change at the top of most fields. The structure and demands of leadership have not been altered to accommodate women's (and some men's) desires to combine family with work. Apparently, an increased number of women professionals is not a sufficient buttress against the persistent differences in the lives and experiences of men and women. What is true at the top level of leadership in the professions is equally true in business, politics, and sport. It is still the case that the recruitment of leaders taps into underlying differences in the way men and women structure their lives.

In light of these structural obstacles, there is mounting evidence that many women today eschew the conventional paths to leadership in corporate America, the professions, sport, and politics. Instead, they are forging independent and innovative institutions and organizations in which they can employ different leadership styles and pursue a more explicitly feminist agenda. To return to Kurtzig's comment at the beginning of this essay, women are not waiting for recognition but rather creating situations where they can start at the top. Over time, with accumulated experience and the growth of independent women's organizations, it is possible that the necessary link to more far-reaching changes in attitudes and structures will come to reshape existing institutions.[52]

But it is also true that women have not given up on institutional change. Many women are attempting change—through electoral politics, the United Nations, and the International Olympic Committee, and in corporate boardrooms and professional associations—so that each new generation of women is not forced to begin the struggle over again. It is this dual nature of women's approach to leadership that is most hopeful: it occurs both inside institutions and from organized outside pressure.

In the meantime, women's presence in the most powerful realms of American life continues to challenge the expectations and assumptions that associate men, and not women, with power and leadership. In business, sport, politics, and the professions, women are also developing alternative models of leadership and power that grow outside the entrenched structures. When they have worked within those structures, gains have often been fleeting unless they have explicitly plotted a viable course of institutional change and found cohorts of men and women willing to support the effort and sustain it past a single generation. As women assert leadership in new and unexpected ways, perhaps the cumulative effect will be greater and the gains more enduring than has been the case to date. We look forward to a future in which women leaders of all races will exercise leadership with the same ease and the same degree of respect that their male counterparts enjoy.

# Notes

1. Sandra Kurtzig, founder of the ASK Group Computer Systems, a manufacturing software system that was once the country's second largest woman-led firm, is quoted in J. Castro, "More and More, She's the Boss," *Time*, 2 December 1985, 64–66. For a full discussion of the limits on women's gains, see Deborah Rhode, *Speaking of Sex* (Cambridge, Mass.: Harvard University Press, 1997), especially 4–20. Rhode's emphasis on the denial of gender inequality is equally appropriate as an explanation for women's continuing struggle for leadership.

2. Ibid., 9.

3. Mary Katzenstein provides an insightful account of this process, emphasizing how women's "difference" became enshrined in the law in the aftermath of the successful suffrage campaign. She contrasts this pattern with the women's movement in the late twentieth century and its choice of an "equal rights" strategy to end sex discrimination. Katzenstein explores women's efforts at institutional change within the military and Catholic Church. She argues that the legal changes that begin with the 1964 Civil Rights Act have been critical to the success of feminists' transformations in American institutions. See Mary Fainsod Katzenstein, *Faithful and Fearless: Moving Feminist Protest inside the Church and Military* (Princeton, N.J.: Princeton University Press, 1998).

4. See the discussion of the historical impact of this pattern in Elsa Barkley Brown, "Negotiating and Transforming the Political Sphere: African American Political Life in the Transition from Slavery to Freedom," in *Women Transforming Politics: An Alternative Reader,* ed. Cathy Cohen, Kathleen Jones, and Joan Tronto (New York: New York University Press, 1997), 343–76.

5. Some leading feminist theorists observing this pattern conclude that adding more women to the current political system is a mistaken strategy, for women will be forced to accept the prevailing norms and values of highly masculine political institutions. Kathleen B. Jones argues instead for a new conception of authority—compassionate authority—in *Compassionate Authority: Democracy and the Representation of Women* (New York: Routledge, 1993).

6. J. B. Spotts, "The Problem of Leadership: A Look at Some Recent Findings of Behavioral Science Research," in *Leadership and Social Change,* ed. W. R. Lassey and R. R. Fernandez, 2d ed. (La Jolla, Calif.: University Associates, 1976), 44–63.

7. F. L. Denmark, "Women, Leadership, and Empowerment," *Psychology of Women Quarterly* 17, no. 3 (1993): 343–57.

8. William E. Rosenbach and Robert L. Taylor, *Contemporary Issues in Leadership,* 3d ed. (Boulder, Colo.: Westview Press, 1993), xi.

9. Quoted in V. H. Vroom and P. W. Yetton, *Leadership and Decision-Making* (Pittsburgh, Pa.: University of Pittsburgh Press, 1973).

10. W. G. Bennis and B. Nanus, *Leaders: The Strategies for Taking Charge* (New York: Harper and Row, 1985).

11. Rosenbach and Taylor, *Contemporary Issues in Leadership.*

12. This theoretical position surpasses the more circumscribed meaning of a transactional leader who exchanges desired rewards for designated follower behavior; see J. M. Burns, *Leadership* (New York: Harper and Row, 1978), and Bennis and Nanus, *Leaders.*

13. W. H. Cowley, "Three Distinctions in the Study of Leaders," *Journal of Abnormal and Social Psychology* 23 (1928): 144–57.

14. E. P. Hollander, "Leadership, Followership, Self, and Others," *Leadership Quarterly* 3 (1992): 43–54.

15. A. H. Eagly, M. G. Makhijani, and B. G. Klonsky, "Gender and the Evaluation of Leaders: A Meta-Analysis," *Psychological Bulletin* 111, no. 1 (1992): 3–22.

16. Cowley, "Three Distinctions in the Study of Leaders."

17. Sue J. M. Freeman, *Managing Lives: Corporate Women and Social Change* (Amherst: University of Massachusetts Press, 1990); D. W. Canter and T. Bernay, *Women in Power: The Secrets of Leadership* (New York: Houghton Mifflin, 1992); and L. R. Offermann and C. Beil, "Achievement Styles of Women Leaders and Their Peers: Toward an Understanding of Women and Leadership," *Psychology of Women Quarterly* 16, no. 1 (1992): 37–57.

18. L. R. Offermann and P. E. Schrier, "Social Influence Strategies: The Impact of Sex, Role, and Attitudes toward Power," *Personality and Social Psychology Bulletin* 11 (1985): 286–300.

19. D. G. Winter, "The Power Motive in Women—and Men," *Journal of Personality and Social Psychology* 54 (1988): 510–19.

20. A number of feminist political theorists have asked to what extent the presence of women challenges our conception of power and authority. They posit that leadership and authority are irrevocably gendered in Western political thought and tradition. Rather than simply adding more women to present political institutions, what is required is a thorough rethinking and restructuring of the political system as well as new conceptualizations of authority and leadership. See on this point Jones, *Compassionate Authority*, and Cohen, Jones, and Tronto, eds., *Women Transforming Politics*.

21. Winter, "The Power Motive in Women," 510–19.

22. Carol Gilligan, *In a Different Voice* (Cambridge, Mass.: Harvard University Press, 1982), 6, 69.

23. C. Miller and A. G. Cummins, "An Examination of Women's Perspectives on Power," *Psychology of Women Quarterly* 16, no. 4 (1992): 416.

24. H. M. Lips, *Women, Men, and Power* (Mountain View, Calif.: Mayfield, 1991), and Miller and Cummins, "An Examination of Women's Perspectives on Power," 415–29.

25. C. Rampage, "Personal Authority and Women's Self Stories," in *Women and Power: Perspectives for Family Therapy*, ed. T. J. Goodrich (New York: Norton, 1991), 110.

26. J. B. Miller, "Women and Power: Reflections Ten Years Later," in *Women and Power: Perspectives for Family Therapy*, ed. T. J. Goodrich (New York: Norton, 1991), 36–47.

27. Bennis and Nanus, *Leaders*, 225.

28. H. S. Astin and C. Leland, *Women of Influence, Women of Vision: A Cross-Generational Study of Leaders and Social Change* (San Francisco: Jossey-Bass, 1991), 1.

29. D. W. Canter and T. Bernay, *Women in Power: The Secrets of Leadership* (New York: Houghton Mifflin, 1992), 58.

30. D. C. McClelland, *Power: The Inner Experience* (New York: Irvington, 1975); D. C. McClelland, *Human Motivation* (New York: Cambridge University Press, 1985);

Miller and Cummins, "An Examination of Women's Perspectives on Power"; and Winter, "The Power Motive in Women."

31. A. J. Stewart and D. G. Winter, "Arousal of the Power Motive in Women," *Journal of Consulting and Clinical Psychology* 44 (1976): 495–96, and Winter, "The Power Motive in Women."

32. Eagly, Makhijani, and Klonsky, "Gender and the Evaluation of Leaders"; D. G. Winter and N. B. Barenbaum, "Responsibility and the Power Motive in Women and Men," *Journal of Personality* 53 (1985): 335–55.

33. Winter and Barenbaum, "Responsibility and the Power Motive," 337.

34. Lips, *Women, Men, and Power.*

35. L. M. Sagrestano, "Power Strategies in Interpersonal Relationships: The Effects of Expertise and Gender," *Psychology of Women Quarterly* 16, no. 4 (1992): 491.

36. Eagly, Makhijani, and Klonsky, "Gender and the Evaluation of Leaders."

37. Sagrestano, "Power Strategies," 493.

38. A. M. Morrison and M. A. Von Glinow, "Women and Minorities in Management," *American Psychologist* 45 (1990): 200–208.

39. Robert Hooijberg and Nancy DiTomaso, "Leadership in and of Demographically Diverse Organizations," *Leadership Quarterly* 7, no. 1 (1996): 7.

40. G. Hofstede, *Culture's Consequences: International Differences in Work Related Values* (Beverly Hills, Calif.: Sage, 1980).

41. E. Higginbotham and L. Weber, "Moving Up with Kin and Community: Upward Social Mobility for Black and White Women," in *Race, Class and Gender: Common Bonds, Different Voices*, ed. Esther Ngan-Ling Chow, Doris Wilkinson, and Maxine Baca Zinn (Thousand Oaks, Calif.: Sage, 1996), 147.

42. Ibid., 146.

43. A recent study of race relations in the U.S. military, where it is not unusual for African Americans to exercise leadership in mixed race groups, revealed racial tensions surrounding leadership. The *New York Times*, special series on Race in America, 4 June, 2, 10, 16 July 2000.

44. P. S. Parker and dt ogilvie, "Gender, Culture, and Leadership: Toward a Culturally Distinct Model of African-American Women Executives' Leadership Strategies," *Leadership Quarterly* 7, no. 2 (1996): 189–214.

45. M. J. Gessner and V. Arnold, eds., *Advances in Global Leadership*, vol. 1 (Stamford, Conn.: JAI Press, 1999).

46. E. Apfelbaum, "Norwegian and French Women in High Leadership Positions: The Importance of Cultural Contexts upon Gendered Relations," *Psychology of Women Quarterly* 17 (1993): 419.

47. Nancy Adler, "Global Leaders: Women Leaders," in *Advances in Global Leadership*, ed. M. Jocelyne Gessner and Val Arnold (Stamford, Conn.: JAI Press, 1999), 64.

48. Hooijberg and DiTomaso, "Leadership in and of Demographically Diverse Organizations," 7.

49. Adler, "Global Leaders," 64.

50. Amanda Sinclair, writing about the Australian corporate world, stresses that stereotypically "female" traits are better suited to the contemporary business context. Such arguments can fall into the trap of arguing for female "difference." Sinclair is eager to avoid this reductionism and stresses the availability of this style of leadership to both men and women. See Amanda Sinclair, *Doing Leadership Differently: Gender Power and Sexuality in a Changing Business Culture* (Melbourne, Australia: Melbourne University Press, 1998).

51. Thomas Laquer, "Orgasm, Generation, and the Politics of Reproductive Biology," in *The Making of the Modern Body*, ed. Catherine Gallagher and Thomas Laquer (Berkeley and Los Angeles: University of California Press, 1987), 1–41.

52. For a fascinating account of how this has occurred in the U.S. armed forces and the Catholic Church, see Katzenstein, *Faithful and Fearless*.

*Part* I

THEORETICAL ISSUES

# 1

## Women at the Top: "You've Come a Long Way, Baby"

**Sue J. M. Freeman**

■ BACKGROUND

I have been interested in the psychology of women for more than twenty-five years now. My early studies focused on how women define the moral dilemmas that they faced in their own lives. I continued this work at Smith in the early 1980s with corporate women who were pioneering managers in their companies. To my surprise I drew a blank when I questioned these women managers about moral dilemmas they had faced, but I did learn a lot about how they thought about themselves and the direction that their lives had taken. These data resulted in a book, *Managing Lives: Corporate Women and Social Change*, and a shift in my perspective. Now I was interested particularly in how women were incorporating the new possibilities for work in their self-concepts and life plans. In many ways I could identify with both the first group of women interviewed specifically about their lived moral dilemmas and with this generation of women managers. We had grown up with traditional sex-typed norms and expectations, which then changed with the most recent women's movement of the 1960s and 1970s. I, like the women interviewed for my studies, had radically revised my own conceptions of self and life path during this time of social change.

As the 1980s moved into the 1990s, it became apparent that women's choices were not as open-ended as we had hoped. They had encountered a "glass ceiling," such that their advancement up the corporate ladder was halted well below the top executive levels. Now I wanted to study how women might overcome this latest obstacle, how they might assume the top leadership positions in business. In my view, some of the same old stereotypes were keeping women at bay, and I wished to study the para-

doxes and possibilities for women now. Women were ready and wanting
to take the helm at the same time that they were reclaiming home and
hearth. The essay represents some of my thinking and findings about these
seemingly contradictory trends.

T HE title of this essay stands as a metaphor for women's current status as
leaders in the world of business. For what does it conjure but the savvy,
sophisticated young woman who has achieved freedom and independence up to a point? The sentence "You've come a long way, baby" is incomplete without the implied "but you still have a long way to go." The
advertisement from which it comes hails the triumphs of the most recent wom-
en's liberation movement, asserting that women have come so much into their
own that they are now entitled to a cigarette designed just for them. The myriad messages include explicit victory and implicit threat; women are issued a
special invitation to join the world of men and smokes (and these days cigars
included), a health-endangering world, while remaining an infantilized icon
called "baby." Moreover, the female pictured is sexy and slim like her newly
fashioned cigarette, so the old rules for female image and role remain clearly
in place.

So it is with women and business. Women have come a long way toward
assumption of leadership in the business world, but the messages about their
achievements and continued progress are many and mixed. On the one hand,
women now account for more than 40 percent of corporate middle managers
and are expected, in conjunction with minorities, to constitute the majority of
the work force in the twenty-first century. On the other hand, women account
for little more than 5 percent of top executive positions.[1] Considerable commentary on the "glass ceiling" notwithstanding, the media have reflected an
ambivalence about women's extradomestic place. Simultaneous to the publicity about successful female inroads in male business bastions are stories about
threatened stress and disease effects for women akin to those suffered by men
engaged in the public sphere of commerce. In addition, accounts of women's
exodus from the demands of corporate management and retreats to domesticity
can subtly reinforce long-standing notions that women's place is indeed in the
home. Portraits of women relinquishing high-power careers and resuming full
responsibility for husband, home, and children flourish alongside stories be-
moaning the disintegration of the American family and its dire consequences.

For women aspiring to success in business, forecasts are frequent of untold obstacles in the form of discrimination, harassment, and glass ceilings. Although they are no longer to be called "baby," successful women continue to encounter cultural confusion and resistance to their achievements and to their desire for more.

It is testament to women's determination and ability that they have made as much progress as they have in the past two decades. A pioneering 1977 study of women in corporations, Rosabeth Kanter's *Men and Women of the Corporation* detailed through participant observation the particular strains a first or only woman encounters in the male work environment.[2] A "token" female's heightened visibility fosters a skewed attribution system whereby luck is credited with her successes and women as a class are faulted for her missteps.[3] Kanter predicted that increased numbers alone could correct biased perceptions and educate for appropriate behavior. Her apt counsel included a focus on the context of gendered business transactions, indicating that a changed corporate context can foster revised behavior, expectations, and perceptions. Until recently a plausible explanation for women's absence from top executive posts has been their sparse numbers at lower management ranks. This "pipeline" or critical mass theory, however, has lost credibility, as women represent a substantial proportion of management in American companies today; their numbers and longevity are there, with women now in place for better than two and a half decades.[4]

## Women's Future as Business Leaders

What does the future hold for women in American businesses? Predictions cannot be made without considering the shape of the businesses themselves. In the wake of the 1980s boom, American corporations have had to adjust both their size and shape. Corporate change has been characterized by downsizing, whereby departments and employees have been eliminated or consolidated, and by flattening of the pyramid of managerial hierarchy. As a consequence, there are fewer layers of management and fewer managers. In this climate of reduction in labor force and shaken job security at every level, it would be reasonable to conclude that women's newcomer status would make them the most vulnerable. But to the contrary, women have been touted as possessing the very skills critical to American corporate survival as a top competitor in the world marketplace. The reality of a global economy has heightened corporate America's competition; the threat to its position is so palpable that this entrenched system has approached an uncharacteristic overhaul in philosophy and practice. In their search for enhanced effectiveness, American corporations have looked to the models of other countries and have embraced, at least in theory, a decentralized, participatory operation that is more responsive to consumer needs and preferences. Women's management style has been described as naturally suited to these new directions.

These trends raise several questions. First, how much change is feasible for large, complex organizations whose practices have become entrenched over decades? While the business literature is replete with exhortation toward new ideas and practices, what is the reality on the shop floor and in executive offices? It seems likely that women's experiences in corporations are not unlike those elsewhere, for example, academe, politics, sport. In academe, women are clustered in the part-time and lower ranks; in politics, they are most visible at the local level, considerably less at the national level. In sport, the explosion of female participation has not infused the leadership level. In business, the glass ceiling and women's exodus to independent enterprise have highlighted their stalled positions at the middle ranks. Like our essay metaphor, the message is mixed. Business needs and celebrates women, but limits remain on how far they have been allowed to go.

A second question revolves around the notion that women, by their nature, possess managerial skills particularly suited to the proposed new corporate philosophy. Sex differences in managerial style, as in many other dimensions, have been widely researched and generally found to be insignificant. Yet these findings and commensurate field experiences are for the most part ignored; the managerial styles alleged of women and men are emphasized according to the needs and purposes of the particular time and place. For women in business, this represents a conundrum. The customary struggle has been to achieve equality in access to opportunity; that is, women desire consideration in hiring and promotion that men have enjoyed. Now women are said to be more suited than their male counterparts for the new management requirements. This potential shift to better-than-equal status could be seductive for women, who had previously been stereotyped as unsuitable to management. It is stereotype that labeled female traits as unsuitable to management, however, and it is stereotype that makes those traits currently desirable. It could be said that the traits have not changed, but their perception and interpretation have. If this is the case, then women (and men) continue to be stereotyped, and acceptance of the current assessment would likely result only in short-lived progress for women.

If women are especially suited to the new corporate management, why have they not been promoted to highest executive positions? One response could be that corporate change is slow in coming, and women are more ready than their organizations to move forward. Therefore, in the absence of recognition and promotion, women change jobs or open their own businesses. Another might be that while corporations have changed size and shape, established practices and perceptions with regard to women remain resistant to revision. In that case, women are retained as managers but kept from advancing to top executive levels. The solid number of women managers and sparse number of women executives attest to this practice, but the reasons still elude us. One possible explanation could lie in the distinction between management and leadership found in the literature and in practice.

## Manager versus Leader

It is clear that women have access to management positions almost on a par with men in American corporations but very little representation at the top executive levels. Women are seen as managers but not leaders. Men are seen as both, and curiously, men can rise to executive levels from a management track, whereas women who do reach top positions often do not follow the customary male path. Distinctions between management and leadership drawn in the literature seem to render the two as distinct continua rather than simply different points on the same continuum. If management and leadership are distinct constellations of skills and tasks, then managers of either sex should experience a glass ceiling between their current positions and the executive suite. As it is, only women do. This is not to say that all male managers advance to leadership positions, but 95 percent of those who do are men.

Are women more suited to manage and men more suited to lead? The early discussions of leadership types do not include gender; most established leadership theory seemed to assume a male paradigm without reference to the sex of the leader. This is not surprising if leadership is understood as a form of social authority, traditionally a male monopoly.[5] Because of its importance in so many aspects of social and political life, leadership itself has been a subject of long-standing fascination across disciplines. That study cannot be totally without personal referent, however implicit, since theory is often derived from empirical example, and in the case of leadership that example has been male. Hence the "great man" theory of the eighteenth and nineteenth centuries imbues certain people (men) with a destiny by birth to lead. Max Weber's charismatic leader is held "apart from ordinary men [sic]," and predominantly male CEOs elucidate the idea of transformational leadership.[6] These notions paint a broad picture of an inspirational leader who arouses intense commitment to values and goals; the focus is on personal traits rather than behaviors that are more frequently associated with managing. A brief review of what constitutes leadership and how it is distinguished from management may be instructive for our understanding of women's current status in business and their future leadership prospects.

The differentiation of managers and leaders in behavior, personality, needs, and attitudes was first discussed in the business context in 1977 by Abraham Zaleznik in an award-winning *Harvard Business Review* paper.[7] Whereas managers enjoyed working with people and maintaining order, leaders were seen as loners, risk takers, and visionaries. In his Pulitzer Prize–winning book, the political scientist James McGregor Burns distinguished between transformational and transactional leaders.[8] Transactional leaders, who correspond to Zaleznik's manager, are engaged in an exchange relationship with subordinates where the focus is on teamwork, task accomplishment, and problem solving. Transformational leaders tap into followers' motives and seek to engage the full person of the follower; here the process of intellectual and emotional stimulation can convert followers into leaders and leaders into moral agents. Bernard Bass operationalized Burns's concept of transformational leadership for organizational settings as the ability to arouse followers emotionally and inspire them to greater effort and accomplishment.[9]

The characteristics of a transformational leader resemble those earlier attributed to the charismatic leader. The latter derives his authority not from position, rules, or traditions but from followers' faith in his gift of "exceptional powers and qualities."[10] This highly confident leader is wholly involved in his vision of change and inspires others to pursue his articulated goals. Followers are transformed by a leader who engages them intellectually and emotionally, acts on their belief system, and stirs their values. Through attachment to and trust in the leader, followers become strongly committed and motivated toward the mission; self-esteem and aspiration are elevated, as they are empowered by the leader's faith in their abilities and by group cohesion based on shared beliefs.[11] The relationship "binds leader and follower together in mutual and continuing pursuit of a higher purpose."[12]

Mutual involvement in a higher purpose or vision frequently is a response to a felt need for change. The origins of charismatic leadership were said to be a revolution against the tyranny of tradition.[13] Stagnation or discontent with the established order provides a ripe context for the ascendance of a charismatic or transformational leader, a context that has evoked uncertainty and feelings of helplessness and powerlessness.[14] The leader perceives opportunity in a crisis situation and mobilizes human minds and emotions toward his vision of change. The leader instills faith in followers, and their consequent empowerment reduces helplessness and instability. Thus, Weber envisioned charismatic leadership as transitory, creating and institutionalizing new orders. If power is vested solely in the leader, however, visionary leadership could create a system that fails to function in the leader's absence.[15] Bernard Bass points out that the most significant component of transformational leadership may be charisma, but that charisma alone may not be transforming enough to sustain and institutionalize change in business organizations.[16] The charismatic leader may encourage followers to adopt only his worldview, but the transformational leader seeks to instill in followers the propensity to continue to question views established by the leader. One solution is to lead others to lead themselves.[17]

Although classic leadership theory and our enduring cultural images seem to perpetuate the association of male with charismatic or transformational leadership, recent studies have found no difference between men and women as transformational or transactional leaders.[18] That is, subordinates rate the actual leadership behaviors of their male and female supervisors quite similarly. Through emotional arousal of values and motives, leaders inspire followers to work in the interest of the company as opposed to the self. The strength of charismatic/transformational leadership has been endorsed as an ideal type and found universally superior to transactional leadership.[19] Transformational leadership is characterized cross-culturally by integrity, honesty, trustworthiness, team orientation, decisiveness, intelligence, and win-win problem solving.[20] These descriptors are not gender specific.

There is considerable evidence, however, that stereotypes for male and female leaders remain robust, and these are almost invariably to the detriment of women.[21] To further complicate matters, the nature of the stereotyping differs by gender, wherein males and females may hold differing expectations of male and female leadership, and those expectations may in turn affect perceptions of a leader and ultimately his or her effectiveness. For males, perceptions of effective leadership are associated with men and not with women. Females express more mixed reactions; depending on the circumstance, though, they frequently express a preference for a male leader. In the absence of information or experience to the contrary, people act in accordance with their stereotyped perceptions, and women are less likely to be chosen by men for leadership positions.[22]

Although it is the case that men dominate the upper echelons of leadership and are in the position of selecting their successors, these extant leaders are certainly not invariably transformational or charismatic. Studies of charismatic leadership have taken men as their subject, but male leadership is not ipso facto charismatic or transformational.[23] One cannot assume that a given leader is charismatic or transformational by virtue of his sex or assumed sex-related inherent characteristics. Men may dominate top leadership but not necessarily because they are "great men."

Since the "great man" theory, wherein leaders are born rather than made, failed to fully explain leadership, the "big bang" notion promoted the idea that great events can make leaders out of otherwise ordinary people.[24] That is, situations and followers can combine to promote a leader where there had been none. Within a complex context of apathy, increasing change, and uncertainty, this leader would be required to instill vision, meaning, and trust in followers. Although women were unlikely to fit the "great man" paradigm, they might better qualify for the "big bang" theory's emergent leader. The only real difference between these two theories, however, is the origin or source of leadership; "great men" are born leaders, "big bang" creates leaders. The actual leadership characteristics associated with each of these theories are indistinguishable, so that even though the "big bang" seemingly opens the door to women, in practice it continues to be men who emerge as leaders in organizations needing change.

While leaders are primarily concerned with macrocosmic purposes and directions of the organization, managers are more intimately involved with daily work functions. Paradoxically, followers are more personally engaged with leaders while directly supervised by managers. Leaders may be physically distant, but they have a hold on followers psychologically, as their message centers on needs, values, aspirations. Leaders articulate ideals and overall direction; managers involve employees in short-range decision making and provide feedback for continued learning.[25] Managers are highly skilled problem solvers and staff experts who aim for teamwork and consistently stable working relations. Responsible for the more immediate task accomplishment, managers remove obstacles and support the development of specific competencies required for effective performance. Ideally, an effective manager promotes employees' development through challenging tasks and increasingly autonomous working conditions.[26]

Thus, managing involves know-how and problem solving, whereas leading calls for knowing why and problem finding.[27] Leaders empower through direction and inspiration, managers through action and participation.[28] The distinction between top- and lower-level management is strong even cross-culturally, whereby innovation, vision, persuasion, long-term orientation, diplomacy, and courage are associated with top levels, while lower-level managers are team builders, participative, and attentive to subordinates.[29] Leaders need managers for implementation. A leadership typology attributed to Abraham Zaleznik and Manfred Kets de Vries describes the "maximum man," who leads by charisma and builds the institution, leaving the dailies to the "minimum man," or consensus builder.[30] The "maximum man" is an innovator with high self-confidence, conviction, and independence; people are drawn to his strength and vision. The "minimum man" or modern manager is concerned with peers' opinions and prefers egalitarian relations to distant, exalted ones. The latter resemble the qualities frequently associated with female managers.

If we examine the qualities and behaviors associated with managers and leaders, respectively, we see once again that many of those stereotypically touted as women's talents line up in the manager column rather than the leader column. For example, Zaleznik's manager, as opposed to the solitary leader, prefers to work with people and enables others through a process of coordinating and balancing.[31] While a leader's sense of self is separate from the environment and his identity is derived from personal mastery of events, a manager's sense of self is strongly connected to the environment and his identity depends on roles and memberships. This is reminiscent of the developmental tasks psychologists have traditionally attributed to males and females, such that males are more concerned with separation and individuation, females with connection and care.[32] In the Burns schema, a manager (transactional leader) is involved with the task, its people, and its accomplishment; a short-range focus on problem solution seeks conformity from and smooth, steady relations with subordinates. On the other hand, a (transformational) leader is involved with the ideals and vision of the institution; a long-range focus may create problems and intense and turbulent feelings in subordinates.[33] In times of turmoil and rapid change for American business through globalization, there is a call for a leadership that breaks with tradition and envisions unforeseen opportunity and unconventional strategies. There is evidence that in the cases of successfully managed companies transformational leaders have arisen, instilled purpose, shaped values, and engendered excitement.[34] In fact, the potency and effectiveness of transformational leadership have now been documented across a variety of enterprises and even cross-culturally.[35] Are these emergent leaders inevitably male?

Historically, leadership theory and studies have been unconcerned with gender. Both the form and content of leadership literature, however, reflected the assumption of a male leader. Even if we eschew the "great man" notion and the idea that leadership resides in personal attributes, we are still left with a view that depends on the relation between leaders' attributes and followers' needs, beliefs, and perceptions.[36] If leaders and followers must share basic beliefs and values to validate the leaders' power to lead, then those values and beliefs are likely to be gender related. In the case of transformational leadership, a powerful and charismatic leader prompts followers to transcend self-interest to embrace the values, mission, and future trajectory of the organization. This process is facilitated by followers' high level of personal identification with their leaders, and such identification more readily occurs with gender similarity.[37] If leadership is less one-sided and more of a transaction between leaders and followers such that a unity of focus is established, it is likely that the majority of male executives will perceive leadership in their male, rather than female, colleagues. Female leaders have been the recipients of more negative social interpretations and responses.[38] Indeed, males' familiarity and comfort with other males are repeatedly cited as the primary obstacles to women seeking top corporate executive positions.[39] If nothing else, men have the weight of time and tradition shaping perceptions and long-standing practice.

## Gender and Leadership

We have seen that several theories of leadership have been developed since Weber's original treatise. We have seen also that gender considerations have not ordinarily been part of these discussions, but a shift precipitated by the women's movement has brought formerly held assumptions under scholarly scrutiny here as elsewhere. Hence, several studies of gender and leadership have emerged during the last decade. These studies might reveal if and how gender intersects with leadership and what the implications might be for women in business.

Current understandings of leadership could be termed contextual, that is, personal requirements for leadership are examined with reference to the particular circumstances calling for its emergence.[40] Thus, a leader's effectiveness depends on situational elements, including those of the constituent followers. In business, situational requirements can vary enormously from one industry to another and among companies within industries where components such as size, culture, and philosophy must be taken into account. Moreover, in today's global business environment, cultural variables such as individualism versus collectivism and culturally endorsed implicit leadership theories may interact to change significantly the leadership-follower equation.[41] Similarly, companies' constituencies, including their leaders, contribute to their diverse climates; variation among companies in working conditions conducive to female opportunity is generally acknowledged and openly discussed in articles and books.[42] However, the expansion of our understanding of leadership to include race and gender diversity is in a fledgling stage.[43]

How does a contextual concept of leadership affect women? Surely it would seem to afford more opportunity than the formerly held "great man" theory, whose title accurately reflected the idea that it was men, not women, who were born leaders. Opportunity could be equalized by the notion that leadership consists of a set of behaviors, learned and learnable, that are largely defined by contextual needs. That is, unless one sex is deemed more capable of particular kinds of learning or more commonly associated with certain contexts. Unfortunately for women, these two conditions are extant in business.

First, the question of context. Variation among industries and companies notwithstanding, for most of its history American business has been a male preserve. Men have populated the blue- and white-collar ranks of worker, manager, executive, while women have been consigned to the pink-collar clerical world of considerable responsibility with little authority.[44] Over the past two decades, women's unprecedented inroads into management have changed the complexion of American business; in addition, today's global economy demands fresh ideas and practices. Although women are said to possess a management style suited to today's business demands, perceptions of leaders and followers alike linger behind research and experiential evidence of female suitability for top leadership positions. That is, people's long-standing perceptions of male leadership in general, and in business particularly, could be a major obstacle to women's entry to the executive suite. Moreover, stereotypic notions that attribute emotional reactivity and relationship priority to women may render them lacking the aptitude supposedly required for the rational, objective decisiveness required for business leadership. Thus, people may not readily perceive women as leaders, and they may continue to associate female traits as incompatible with the kinds of learning leadership requires.

The relevance of perception and attribution to interpersonal relations has long been recognized in psychology. An early and startling study discovered in 1970 that mental health professionals characterized, through adjective attribution, the "healthy female" and the mental patient in similar terms that were significantly different from the "healthy male" and "healthy person."[45] The next two decades in psychology saw a burgeoning study of so-called sex differences, their validity and import. While we continue to struggle with what constitute real and imagined sex differences, we have established a clear distinction between sex and gender. Sex is understood as biologically based, while gender is defined as the sociocultural understanding of the sexes.[46] In business, therefore, even though we repeatedly find little or no sex differences in leadership style, gender-based expectations and perceptions seem to persist.[47]

A brief examination of the components of effective business leadership and their connection to gender perceptions will reveal some psychological obstacles to female leadership. Regarding leadership effectiveness, two major categories of behavior are generally used by subordinates in judging their leaders. One, called consideration, is concerned with employee-oriented interpersonal relations, while the other, initiating structure, centers on task accomplishment.[48] Both stereotypic expectation and research findings corroborate the respective feminine and masculine associations with each of these independent dimensions.[49] In field studies, however, male and female business leaders have not been found to differ significantly in their behavior, nor are their subordinates differentially satisfied with them; the sex of the leader does not significantly influence either leader behavior or subordinate satisfaction.[50] When sex differences are found, they are in laboratory experiments with non-employees making judgments about imaginary leaders. Thus, under conditions of ambiguous or insufficient information and experience, people fill in the gaps with stereotypic gender expectations and their implicit leadership theories.[51]

In their emphasis on lay conceptions of leadership, implicit leadership theories reflect widely shared beliefs about leader behaviors and traits.[52] While a vast array of traits have been associated with leadership, Robert Lord et al. found that intelligence emerges as the trait that should predict leadership in almost all situations.[53] These authors further report significant correlations between leadership perception and masculinity-femininity and dominance. That is, leaders are generally perceived as outgoing, verbally skilled, aggressive, decisive, unemotional, caring, and understanding. All but the last two of these traits have customarily been associated with maleness.

The point here is that there are critical differences between reality and perception, but to date perception has held sway at the leadership gate. This should not be surprising if we acknowledge, as Carl Rogers asserted, that reality pales in the face of perception.[54] While studies consistently have shown that effective male and female leaders demonstrate similar characteristics and behaviors, including those commonly termed both masculine and feminine, people still associate leadership with a male trait constellation. Thus, leadership selection and success are not a unilateral matter of the traits and behaviors of the leader, but rather strongly a function of the social cognitions and perceptions of followers.[55] Followers will accept and endorse a leader who matches their perceptions and understandings of what constitutes leadership.[56] "While

leadership perceptions may not be reality, they are used by perceivers to evaluate and subsequently distinguish leaders from non-leaders or effective from
ineffective leaders. This type of attribution process provides a basis for social
power and influence."[57] Moreover, followers can not only influence a leader's
effectiveness but also determine his or her selection. Who is seen as a leader
can be shaped by how closely an individual matches the leadership prototype
held.[58] "Thus, successful leadership is dependent upon others' perceptions. . . .
Leaders derive their status from their followers, who may choose to grant it or
take it away."[59]

Where the culture and both the perception and practice of leadership
have been predominantly male, as they have in business, it is not surprising
that females are not normally considered for top executive positions. "Cultural
images govern promotion at least as much as actual performance."[60] Once a
woman is functioning as a leader, she is as likely as her male counterpart to be
favorably judged. It is at the point of entry that entrenched perceptions and
cognitions associating leadership with maleness block her. Like subjects in
experimental studies of leadership, leaders and followers who have not been
exposed to female leadership will fall back on their implicit leadership theories
to guide their selection. Those theories are susceptible to bias and stereotype
when they function in the absence of sufficient information, uncorrected by
actual experience.

At first glance, a contextual model of leadership, where leader qualifications are considered in light of situational demands, could hold the promise of
equalizing opportunity. That there is no one ideal leader personality or set of
behaviors, and that different situations require different leader behaviors are
now considered "well-established conclusions about leadership."[61] Research
and reality attest to similarity, rather than difference, between male and female
leaders in behavior and effectiveness. The dearth of women in leadership positions can no longer be attributed to female traits, disposition, or qualifications.
It seems likely, however, that some of the most recalcitrant resistance remains
on the level of perception and social cognition. That is, there has yet to be a
perceptual shift in people's notions of gender and leadership; in both experience and expectation, people are unaccustomed to female leadership. It would
be a mistake to underestimate the importance and endurance of perception.
The paradox is that once in a leadership position women are seen as effective
in their own right; however, being perceived as a leader may be prerequisite to
becoming one.[62] While blatant sex discrimination has been greatly diminished
through long and arduous effort, discrimination that is subtle and rooted in
such intangibles as perception and cognition has proved more recalcitrant.[63]

## Change and Opportunity

So it seems that much of what happens to women and men in organizations is a function of the perceptions and judgments made by others. Current
study of information processing is aimed to expand our understanding of the
power of social cognition and gender-based perception.[64] Psychology's long
study of perception and cognition is beyond the scope of this essay, but suffice
it to say that the complex interconnections among perception, thought, and
behavior have relevance to our analyses of leadership opportunities for women
in business. If we assume that gender-based perceptions are likely to work
against women's leadership opportunities, a critical question becomes how to
change perception and social cognition.

When American human rights movements could not sufficiently change
entrenched perceptions and social belief systems, legal means were brought to
bear. If we could not change people's minds, we would compel them to
change their behavior, on the principle that behavior change can be the impetus to revised thought, feeling, perception.[65] This has been the strategy applied
in America's institutions, including corporate organizations. Affirmative action
has mandated that women and minorities be given full consideration in hiring,
and now, having hired women in goodly numbers, companies are being urged
to follow affirmative action guidelines more consistently in promotion.[66] The
reasons are both equity and bottom-line productivity; both work force and consumers promise to become increasingly diverse in the twenty-first century.[67]
Not only will profitability increasingly depend on companies' inclusiveness in
employment and marketing, but the global economy also adds a complexity to
the mix of gender, culture, and race that undoubtedly affects leadership in
theory and practice.

It seems clear that women are not about to be promoted into leadership
positions without considerable prompting of those currently in power. We can
no longer rely on pipeline or critical mass explanations for women's absence
from top executive positions. Women now account for more than 40 percent
of corporate managers but hold less than 5 percent of senior management
positions, up from 3 percent in 1979.[68] A 1992 study conducted by *Fortune*
found that 16 percent of 201 CEOs believed it "very" or "somewhat" likely that
a woman could become CEO of their large companies within that decade,
and only 18 percent believed it likely in twenty years. These CEOs cited discrimination as the biggest obstacle. Specifically, CEOs "want to pass their jobs
along to someone who is the image and likeness of themselves," and that image
is first and foremost male.[69]

Thus, presence alone is not going to remove the barriers to women's ascent. Moreover, outstanding performance and bottom-line productivity may not hold as much promise for women as they do for men. In fact, women have reported feeling that they are evaluated by more stringent performance measures than men; that they have to work twice as hard and longer for promotion in companies that are "less willing to take risks on women."[70] "Men seem to be promoted on their potential. Women get promoted on their performance, and it takes longer."[71] A *Business Week* survey revealed that 70 percent (up from 60 percent two years prior) of four hundred female managers polled believe that the male-dominated corporate culture was an obstacle to their success.[72] Further, one-third of the respondents predicted that the number of female senior executives at their companies will have either remained the same or dropped in five years. Thus, the current reality and widely held prediction of women's limited opportunity for leadership in America's corporations is commonly reported by both men and women at various levels of the work force.

It is now established that "artificial barriers" and not qualifications, performance, or experience are inhibiting female advancement.[73] The U.S. Department of Labor has defined the glass ceiling as "those artificial barriers based on attitudinal or organizational bias that prevent qualified individuals from advancing upward in their organization into management level positions."[74] Women have recognized these obstacles for some time and have garnered strategies for overcoming them. While revising perception is not their sole or primary purpose, these strategies may ultimately validate women's leadership ability.

Women who want increasing autonomy and responsibility at work are not staying at their jobs in an endless wait for promotion. Many have done all within their power to climb a corporate ladder where the top steps were missing. When the limits became clear to them and they still felt the need for further advancement, they took initiative and sought other prospects.[75] Sometimes this meant switching companies; contrary to expectation, the *Wall Street Journal* has reported that women are less company loyal than men and leave not for personal or family reasons but for expanded opportunity. Whereas in the past women were characterized as not wanting top positions, their desire for leadership can no longer be denied. What is most crucial is that women are discovering that rather than waiting to be chosen by a male culture, they can manufacture and provide opportunity for themselves.

Increasingly, women have been leaving large corporations and starting their own businesses in unprecedented numbers. Women business owners now

employ more people, 11 million, than all of the Fortune 500 companies combined. "During the past decade, women have been starting their own companies at nearly twice the national average and now own 38 percent of all U.S.
firms."[76] This substantial exodus has been carefully documented by the media;
a negative spin on it could imply that it reflects female failure to advance in
big business.[77] Here an alternative explanation offers the view that these moves
by women are normal and typical phases of a business career. Gaining experience in an established company, women (and men) can clarify and articulate
their own visions and become better able to implement their independent
creations. Moreover, for women, whose rights to independence are still young,
this is an extraordinarily positive and powerful move to make.

Through their entrepreneurial behavior, women are asserting their right
and ability to lead, even in the absence of opportunity in more conventionally
established settings. Contrary to old stereotypes of passivity, dependence, and
a need only for vicarious success through family achievement, women have
seized opportunity in a most active, assertive, and self-promoting way. Their
purpose may be the more immediate one of freedom to do the kind of work
they choose, make the decisions, be their own boss. But the long-term effects
could be a critical shift in cultural perception. That is, women are reshaping
perception of their leadership potential by being leaders. Women were not
perceived as having what it takes to be managers until their employment in
those positions became commonplace. Through revised behavior and practice,
perceptions and cognitions of what is suitable for a woman have changed significantly. Now women are readily seen as managers, but not necessarily as
leaders. Feeling ready and able to lead, and unwilling to wait for permission,
women have seized the reins of leadership in independent enterprise. Here as
elsewhere, behavior change can precede and precipitate a perceptual shift. It
does seem likely that people will more readily perceive women as leaders if
they are occupying those roles. "When you see more women running big companies, it seems more doable. . . . And it's changed other people's perceptions
of whether women can do the job."[78]

The boom in women's business ownership and its predicted expansion
into this new century further attest to female desire and ability to lead. Entrepreneurs resemble leaders more than they do managers.[79] Guided by a vision
of what they want their business to be, they are able to harness their strong
achievement needs in the service of building a business while maintaining a
hands-on relation to the work itself. Whereas effective managers, in becoming
leaders, must delegate the work that had heretofore been the basis of their

satisfaction and success, business owners can maintain a close relation to all aspects of the work-in-progress.

Our current notions of leadership do not uphold many of the distinctions from management drawn earlier. An interactive and reciprocal relation between leaders and followers also includes situational factors and requirements of the task at hand, just as it did for managers. No longer a unilateral and static position, leadership now emerges as "a process, and not just a person."[80] This process includes mutual expectations, perceptions, and a need for responsiveness. In leading their own businesses, women can combine their strengths as managers with their vision as leaders. If it can be assumed that people are passionately motivated in relation to a business they begin and lead, then women entrepreneurs have the opportunity of combining the closeness to staff that comes with managing them with the emotional arousal and commitment that comes with leading them. In this circumstance, employees might achieve a more holistic identification with the enterprise instead of the bifurcation of feeling closer to the more physically distant leaders than to their proximal, daily managers in large corporate organizations.

Qualities currently emphasized as germane to successful leadership are well within a female repertoire; in fact, they might even be recognized as stereotypically gender linked. The interpersonal or relational realm plays a significant role, as followers characterize good leadership as providing sensitivity, support, praise, increased participation, and a sense of being valued.[81] While a need for power and achievement may be instrumental in seeking a leadership position, qualities of empathy, creativity, and flexibility become more salient in sustaining effectiveness in ongoing leadership.[82] Moreover, the emotional arousal associated with transformational leadership could be linked to conventional notions of femaleness. While further stereotyping is not desirable, a model of "relational competence" developed in response to the needs of a global business community resonates with what have been traditional female domains.[83] "Relational Competence is a way of looking at the world in which one's personal life and business life is viewed as a series of highly interconnected relationships with others. . . . This model supports a shift in what is valued in human and organizational relationships. . . . We support a cultural shift from competition to cooperation; a shift from impersonal to personal communication; a shift from disconnection to connection; a shift from using people to valuing people; a shift in the way we view relationships."[84] Indeed, the shifts represented by this model are viewed as essential to meeting the challenge of the global responsibility of business, "the dominant institution on our planet."[85]

As in management, women who assume leadership positions are equal to the task. The most recurring obstacle for women has been attaining legitimacy, first to gain entry and then to be promoted. This is not to gainsay the more stringent criteria applied to women once in a managerial position. These hurdles notwithstanding, women managers have provided widespread evidence of their competence. Similarly, given the opportunity to lead, there is every reason to believe that women will again be successful.

Thus, women have put their desire to lead to work for them and, in so doing, have begun to reshape our expectations and perceptions about women and leadership in business. As we have seen in the past, large-scale movement by women into domains previously deemed unsuitable initially arouses suspicion and draws critical skepticism. Undaunted in business, as elsewhere, women have not turned back, but on the contrary have pressed forward even further. When they are not granted opportunity to vie for what they want, they have found ways around, through, and above obstacles. In the end, they often have had to manufacture their own opportunities and, in so doing, have precipitated undeniable social change. In the case of women and business leadership, the significant expansion of female-owned businesses will ultimately redound to our perceptions and beliefs about a woman's place.

## Successful Female Leadership

Increasingly, women's successes have been chronicled. We read about women who have become successful entrepreneurs, CEOs, educational leaders. What would these women say about some of the "truths" found in scholarly literature? What are their views regarding what constitutes leadership and women's styles of leadership in particular?

We know that there can be a significant gulf between published work and lived reality. Thus, it is of utmost importance to discover women's views, experiences, and thoughts about their leadership of large organizations. This review would offer only part of the story without the contributions of two prominent women leaders today.

Having read so much about the difficulties faced by women aspiring to lead and the presumed reasons for them, I was eager to glean information about these issues from women who are recognized as successful leaders in their fields. I interviewed two women about various aspects of leadership and their relation to women's opportunities and found some confirmation and difference from the oft-cited literature. Shelly Lazarus is the CEO of Ogilvy and Mather Worldwide, a multibillion-dollar company and the sixth largest advertising firm in the world. Ruth J. Simmons, youngest of twelve children of a Texas sharecropper, is the first black president of Smith College, having previously served as vice-provost of Princeton University.

Regarding what constitutes leadership, Ruth Simmons clearly subscribed to the current view of contextual fit between the person and the needs of an organization at a particular time:

> Leadership can come to someone for lots of different reasons. It can come to people who are reluctant to assume that role. It can come to people who want the role desperately and who worked hard to get it. It can come to people who have not done anything basically to deserve it but who happen to be good at it for one reason or another. . . . As far as we know, there is no one path to leadership. A leader is a leader in a particular time and place . . . a leader is a person for their time. . . . That's the great thing about leadership: it's not who you are, it's what the institution that you're serving needs. That's what makes leadership, really.

Leadership cannot be solely defined in the abstract; there is no formula for leadership. Nor can one be guaranteed a leadership position even with special preparation for it. Thus, Simmons points up the limits of career planning. Lazarus also sheds doubt on its value for advancement when she states, "I still don't think about it. I just love what I'm doing every day, and I think that's why I do it well." Simmons elucidates the somewhat fortuitous nature of opportunity, as opposed to the alleged security of career planning:

> A lot of people think that you can . . . simply follow those guidelines and become a leader . . . but when you finish following all those guidelines . . . it is not at all clear that there will be a place for you. . . . And so it's not exactly fortuitous, but it is a small set of circumstances that fit together like a puzzle. So, having said that, that is the reason a lot of people who seem to offer good leadership skills don't happen into those circumstances—because it is hard to plan for them. And there is no guarantee. . . . It doesn't make what you have done in preparing yourself less valuable. It just means that it might not end up the same way that you think. So one myth that is very disturbing to me about the discussion about leadership, is the assumption that all leaders will find a place to use their leadership skills. That's not necessarily the case.

While Simmons looks at the confluence of situational and personal factors that conspire to make a leader, Lazarus addresses the idea that leaders possess a certain something. People can be what she calls "instinctive leaders" who are optimistic, self-confident, and able to delegate to and connect with people. While this may seem to be an endorsement of a kind of "great (wo)man" or charismatic leader theory, Lazarus's own rise to CEO corresponded more to the "big bang" or emergence of a leader at a time of crisis and much-needed change in the organization's life. Reminiscent of the distinction between managing and leading, Lazarus's emphasis was on a leader's articulation of the values of an organization. She speaks of "the importance of the philosophy of the person at the top . . . eventually someone sets the values, standards, beliefs. . . . One of my jobs as a CEO is to make it explicit, to articulate the beliefs, values." Lazarus wants employees to know what the organization's values are so that those who don't agree can leave rather than stay, "behaving in ways that are not productive for the organization." She and Simmons agree that the leader's primary responsibility is to preserve and strengthen the organization for which she is responsible.

What makes for a successful leader? Again, the ingredients for success are a combination of personal qualities and interactions with an organizational context. Simmons says, "A leader can never be good enough. Ever. A good leader always feels that way, it seems to me. . . . Leaders . . . want to know what can be done better and how to do it better, they listen to advice, and they improve on what they're doing. It's a very hard thing to do." Lazarus stresses the importance of trusting employees with the responsibility of doing the job. Aware of her own penchant for autonomy, Lazarus warns against micromanaging. "I learned so much about how to get the most out of people, to make them feel that they have the maximum power, to make them feel engaged: you should set the objectives but don't tell them how to go about it. . . . If you are too directive about what to do, the good people are not going to be willing to work for you. . . . So I afford people enormous freedom on the how to do it as long as they get there and as long as they live up to the principles and values of the organization." Once again, the difference between managing and leading is articulated.

A key difference between Simmons and Lazarus is the type of organizations they lead. Simmons does not address the issue of autonomy probably because that is a sine qua non of an academic environment. While Lazarus articulates the need for a leader to surround herself with talented people who can do the job, Simmons's professorial environment presumably comes that way. The challenge for academe, perhaps more so than a corporate organization, is change; academic institutions are notoriously slow to change. Thus, Simmons emphasizes a leader's courage to take the steps necessary for change, to be unafraid to do so for fear of making a mistake. "Because whenever you take the next step you have to acknowledge it could be a mistake, and that's what keeps most people from doing it." A leader must know how to keep a steady step even during a period of significant change. "Because that's how change occurs: when people are willing to let go enough and feel comfortable enough that their world is not going to collapse. They trust enough to think that it will be okay in the end. That's how they allow the best kind of change."

Lazarus is aware of people's frailties in times of upheaval. Having successfully turned around her organization, Lazarus recognized that when employees feel overwhelmed by failure, they lose hope. When hope and faith are lost, people give up; "they leave when it's too dark." Assuming leadership did not mean taking over and telling people what to do, but rather giving them a small piece to turn around, creating the opportunity for them to succeed again and applauding them when they did. A leader, then, has the courage to move forward, guiding but not dictating, providing just the right balance of support and leeway. The trust must be mutual: a leader trusts her constituency's capabilities, and those she leads trust her to preserve the center even during significant change. Lazarus's pride was that her company's turnaround occurred with all the same employees in place.

How does gender enter the leadership picture? While the literature may have touted a collaborative style as a female contribution to leadership, it is now universal rather than gendered. Simmons declares "that collaborative style is beginning to affect the whole culture of leadership in this country because now people talk quite openly about participatory leadership as a virtue. And corporations now, when they are looking for leaders, are no longer looking for that autocratic individual." Lazarus also dismisses the notion of a female style of leadership and asserted that no one who is really effective today is of the "power over" style. Cross-cultural findings relegate an autocratic, dictatorial style to the negative side of the leadership ledger.[86] Interestingly, the "lonely leader" icon is also viewed as undesirable cross-culturally, thus contradicting the myth of the distant and solitary male leader.

If women are not at a disadvantage, then, why are so few of them in leadership positions? Lazarus points out in response to this that, gender aside, there are very few leadership positions, and these few leaders must come from a sizable pool of managers. Moreover, now that the pool of female candidates is becoming large enough from which leaders may be drawn or emerge, women are going home. Lazarus has observed women's discouragement when they look up the line and fail to see others like themselves in the highest positions. The literature has attested to the tendency for extant leadership to choose others like themselves, and those successors are predominantly male. When their prospects for advancement look slim and other possibilities arise, women take advantage of those possibilities. For example, women focused on career often have delayed motherhood, and if her income is not essential to the family's well-being and the work is no longer gratifying, a woman may choose the baby over the corporation. Later these women often start their own businesses, where they have more control over their work lives.

Explaining why women are stalled in positions below the top, Simmons echoed some of the conventional wisdom. Women and minorities face the same problem: being in the wrong lines of business, spending "their lifetimes in areas that do not lead to leadership roles in that particular field. . . . Most of the people who come to see me to ask about assuming a leadership role believe that they can achieve excellence in one area and transform that into leadership of the whole. And it's almost impossible to do that." Simmons observes that "many minorities and women are advised into positions or choose positions in organizations which do not lead to greater and greater levels of responsibility within the organization." Those who aspire to leadership must be willing to alter their paths, even when it means going into aspects of the enterprise that are less palatable to them. Simmons goes on to describe what might be considered another version of career planning, one that is intimately tied to the idea of mentoring. Simmons characterizes her model as

> fairly didactic . . . and very old-fashioned. . . . Frankly, someone who starts off on a path to leadership doesn't know what they're going to need. They have to trust in other people to tell them several very important things. You have to trust other people to tell you where your abilities lie because those people are going to be closer to the perspective of the people you will one day lead. So trust them and not yourself. Particularly if, over time, people are saying the same thing about you. . . . But one of the most serious mistakes that people make, in my view, is that they don't listen to that . . . because so imbued are we at a certain age with the idea that we know how to configure things that we very rarely take advice when we're given it. And so I think that's probably the greatest problem—people don't know how to find their way to the right mentor and . . . once they have that mentor, they don't follow that advice.

Women and minorities may have more difficulty in a mentoring relationship, not only because there are fewer people willing to mentor them, as the literature suggests, but also because of their complicated history with advice. Simmons explains:

> There are so many instances in your life in which people have told you negative things about yourself that it's very hard for you to sort out whether this is one of those instances or whether this is someone trying to help you. We become so accustomed to blocking out negative criticism because we know that when we're young that adversely affects us. . . . What's the difference? That's why the quality of discernment is a skill that every leader must have. And when you find that mentor, that person is not a mentor to you unless you have complete trust in them, because you will not listen to them if you don't. So finding the right mentor means finding someone who can hold your hand and look you in the eye and say, "If you continue on this course you will never be successful," and you will believe them. . . . That's the way most CEOs are made. If you talk to the average CEO and the average leader, somebody held their hand and said to them, "I think you can do this, but you know what? In order to do it, here are some things that you really need to change. Now let's go."

But even in a mentor relationship one exercises discernment and selectively follows advice. Simmons continues, "On the side of truth I have to say to you that there were many cases, times in which I simply did not follow the advice. You can never lose yourself in these mentor relationships because that's what makes you unique. And so I did fight when there were things that I thought were important to me. And I fought to retain myself because I didn't want to become a leader and lose myself."

Ultimately, the individual must be true to herself, particularly if she is going to serve others as a leader. It is her authenticity as a person that generates trust, and we have seen how important it is for the trust to be reciprocal, for leaders and their constituencies to trust each other. Both Simmons and Lazarus stress that even in the leadership role, they must be themselves. Lazarus plainly says, "I've always felt that I am who I am, and if it doesn't work then I'll leave, and if you don't like it I'll go, but I'm not going to pretend to be somebody else because life's too short." Simmons addresses her own strength: "I think my greatest asset as a leader is the truth about me. And whatever faults there are, they are true. They are not fabricated for a time, they are what they are. And that allows me to enter into relationships on a management basis so that people, I hope, can trust what I say and believe what I say. That's the most important thing to me."

Both women interviewed present a complex picture of leadership that combines the subtleties of knowing oneself and others with the ability to make the most difficult decisions. We learn that leadership is not simply the stereotype of objective, rational decisiveness and vision. Certainly those are required, but they are only part of the story. Leadership is also an affective relationship, between employees and their leader, that engages the hearts and minds of both. We have seen this most clearly and strikingly in findings that attest to the universal applicability of transformational leadership.[87] Lazarus declares, "I think all any company really has is the people, and if, as the senior person, you don't worry about them every day, you're not doing your job." Simmons agrees that "leadership is also, most of the time, about people and managing people." She points out, however, that "that's getting harder and harder to do." As our institutions become increasingly diverse, their leadership will be much more challenging. Homogeneous institutions made for common assumptions that no longer hold within or across national boundaries. It is not surprising that Simmons, an educational leader, espouses the importance of both formal and informal education as preparation for leadership.

> In today's organization every step you take involves sorting through the heterogeneity of the enterprise and determining whether or not you have the right mix of symbols, language, and so on to include your entire group. It's a completely different phenomenon, completely different. And that's why I think education has such an important task in the coming era in educating students both internationally and from the standpoint of more local diversity, because leaders who do not have those experiences simply will not be able to function. . . . To the extent that this concerns women and ways in which they can keep themselves open to leadership opportunities, I always feel that the fundamental advice that I would give anyone is that a leader has to be extraordinarily curious. Curious enough to learn about everything that they can learn about. And so it begins with education and a disposition to learn about everything that passes your way. . . . That's such a simple thing, but very few people do it . . . when it's essential to do if you want to win the confidence of a broad constituency.

## Conclusion

As these extraordinary women attest, the face of leadership is changing, as is the nature of the enterprise to be led. As we move swiftly toward a global consciousness and economy, the interdependence of our countries and citizens becomes inescapable. We may feel as though we are experiencing "future shock," unable to keep pace with change nor predict and prepare for the immediate or more distant future. The nature and pace of change in our environments at home and at work are undeniably radical. New skill and flexibility are surely required in both additive and transformative ways. That is, the shape of our work and our approaches to it will take new forms that are not just extensions of the old. Nevertheless, the knowledge base will in many ways retain its recognizability but be significantly expanded. Thus, we extend what we already know and do, as well as venture into new knowledge forms and functions. We add to and transform what we do and how we do it.

Technology is a good example of change that can be both additive and transformative. That is, technology can be used to enhance and facilitate business practice, making communication and transaction easier, faster, and more efficient; evidence the ubiquitous cellular phone, e-mail, fax machine, and so on. More astounding, however, is the revolution in incipient Internet businesses that have converted young entrepreneurs to multimillionaires in record time. Twenty-something men and women, even adolescents, have reaped stunning financial rewards from this new way of doing business. People without requisite degrees or work experience have had meteoric rises in fortune. Sudden riches in conjunction with the rather long-running stock market advances have a potentially enormous impact on our business conceptions and practices.

What do these seismic shifts mean for our traditional notions about what it takes to prepare for a career in business and for top executive positions? If one can manufacture and captain his or her own ship through an Internet start-up and be far more successful than decades in rank would bring, what will become of our customary ways of doing business? Certainly no one knows fully the answers to these and countless other questions. We might speculate, however, that there has been a leveling of the playing field such that one's gender, race, ethnicity, and status can become less salient features. These individual and group dimensions do not have to become intervening variables between one's aspirations and achievements. Others' perceptions are necessarily less operative in environments where the players are not seen and do not interact in person. Negative social perception and stereotyping are less likely to occur when interactions are electronic rather than personal. With conditions of increased anonymity, there is more safety and potential for creativity.[88] With increased use of technology, there is the prospect and expectation of more immediate learning rather than extensive preparatory expertise.[89] This is not to say that knowledge and experience will no longer be instrumental, but rather there may be opportunities for women and others who might not have gotten across a leadership threshold heretofore. Gender, race, and status will be diminished as considerations when the work environment becomes more technologically and less personally based. This is not to say that people and their abilities to work cooperatively with others will become less critical. It is to say that there may be the opportunity to be judged first by what you can do, as opposed to who you are.

Indeed, there has been a significant influx of women starting their own Internet businesses. The top positions at existing companies are not as attractive as they once were. Women's numbers are scant; only three women head a Fortune 500 corporation, and occupancy of the upper ranks of corporations is no longer so appealing. Many young women who have the technical and business preparation that their pioneer sisters lacked coming into the company are not spending much time on the traditional track to advancement. New MBAs look up the line, as Lazarus suggested above, and what they see is not inviting. Instead of being models to emulate, "women . . . in upper management . . . just seemed miserable."[90] Now corporations are facing a shortage of female talent and are revising promotion and instituting family-friendly policies in an effort to slow the escalating exodus of "good women."[91]

Thus, current prospects for women differ from the past in several ways. First, longtime women employees who have been stalled at the middle ranks have left their corporate employers to become their own boss, as noted above. Second, women who are just entering the business environment need less on-the-job training because they are far more likely to have the credentials at the gate; women earned 39 percent of all business and management degrees in 1997.[92] Third, women, at least, no longer hold the perception of business and technology as male preserves. They have confidence in their own expertise and abilities to forge a successful business career and are not waiting for permission to do so. Finally, a significantly different business landscape primarily due to technology has made choices available that were heretofore unknown. "With their young workforces and fast-paced environment, technology companies as a group appear more likely to ignore gender in the quest to find the best people. . . . In addition, high tech firms tend to attract a younger group that is more likely to go up the ladder gender-blind. 'Fifty percent of the people three to five years out of school have already worked for a woman. It's nothing unusual to them.' "[93]

In the face of all this promise and its fruition, there remain obstacles for women. Parenthood still disproportionately affects the careers of women. Men still dominate the directorships of Internet companies.[94] Moreover, when women entrepreneurs seek funding for their enterprises, they often encounter the male bastion of venture capitalism. This obstacle is not insurmountable, but women must be educated and prompted to win access and funding through these sources. This is a good example of the depth and breadth of male monopoly in business. Even as women seem to be moving ahead by leaps and bounds in attaining credentials and expertise and in heading their own enterprises, they encounter a financial gatekeeper that remains in the hands of men. Women are now preparing for those encounters, however, and forming networks to help each other in doing so. Moreover, as women gain momentum, they too will become venture capitalists and yet another playing field will be equalized by gender. Perhaps the crux of change lies in women's expectations. "Younger women just expect their names to be on the list [for CEO]. That's the way it should be."[95] And now there are mounting indicators that the way it should be will become the way it is.

# Notes

I am indebted to many friends and colleagues and especially my co-editors who have supported me during this work. I am particularly grateful to Ruth J. Simmons and Shelly Braff Lazarus for being so generous with their time and thoughts in our interviews. Their experiences and teachings not only complemented the scholarly literature but most crucially added the invaluable element of firsthand accounts. I was fortunate, also, to have the help of several Smith students: Katie M. Byers, my Smith STRIDE student and research assistant; my seminar students, Dunreith Kelly, Charity Ritscher, and Stacy Betts, who read and offered a student's perspective on the essays. Finally, my family, Emily, Owen, and Evan, have given me all that I need to work freely and productively. My mother, Sally E. Freeman, passed away while this work was in progress, but her strength, fortitude, and love made my life possible. I dedicate this and all my accomplishments to her.

1. Catalyst, *The 1999 Catalyst Census of Women Corporate Officers*, 1999. See www.catalystwomen.org.

2. Rosabeth M. Kanter, *Men and Women of the Corporation* (New York: Basic Books, 1977).

3. A paradox of visibility exists for women in that they need visibility to be promoted, but increased visibility also brings more scrutiny. Because of women's minority status, this paradox is more pronounced for women than for men. Edward Klein, Faith Gabelnick, and Peter Herr, eds., *The Dynamics of Leadership* (Madison, Conn.: Psychosocial Press, 1998).

4. Because a female presence as chief financial officer is a relatively recent (within the past ten years) phenomenon, some women in senior financial positions continue to believe in the viability of the pipeline theory. Julie C. Dalton, "More Room at the Top," *CFO: The Magazine for Senior Financial Executives* 14, no. 8 (August 1998): 30.

5. M. Weber, *The Theory of Social and Economic Organization* (1924), trans. A. M. Henderson and T. Parsons, ed. T. Parsons (New York: Free Press, 1947).

6. Ibid., 358; C. C. Manz and H. P. Sims, *Superleadership: Leading People to Lead Themselves* (Englewood Cliffs, N.J.: Prentice-Hall, 1989); J. A. Conger and R. N. Kanungo, *Charismatic Leadership: The Elusive Factor in Organizational Effectiveness* (San Francisco: Jossey-Bass, 1988); S. Srivastva, *Executive Power* (San Francisco: Jossey-Bass, 1986); W. G. Bennis and B. Nanus, *Leaders: The Strategies for Taking Charge* (New York: Harper and Row, 1985); and V. H. Vroom and P. W. Yetton, *Leadership and Decision-Making* (Pittsburgh, Pa.: University of Pittsburgh Press, 1973).

7. A. Zaleznik, "Managers and Leaders: Are They Different?" *Harvard Business Review* 55, no. 3 (May–June 1977): 67–78.

8. James McGregor Burns, *Leadership* (New York: Harper and Row, 1978).

9. Conger and Kanungo, *Charismatic Leadership*.

10. Weber, *Theory of Social and Economic Organization*, 358.

11. Conger and Kanungo, *Charismatic Leadership*.

12. Ibid., 20.

13. Weber, *Theory of Social and Economic Organization*.

14. Conger and Kanungo, *Charismatic Leadership*.

15. Manz and Sims, *Superleadership*.

16. Conger and Kanungo, *Charismatic Leadership*.

17. Manz and Sims, *Superleadership*.

18. K. Maher, "Gender-Related Stereotypes of Transformational and Transactional Leadership," *Sex Roles* 37 (1997): 209–25.

19. Deanne N. Den Hartog et al., "Culture Specific and Cross-Culturally Generalizable Implicit Leadership Theories: Are Attributes of Charismatic/Transformational Leadership Universally Endorsed?" *Leadership Quarterly* 10, no. 2 (1999): 219–56; B. M. Bass, "Does the Transactional-Transformational Leadership Paradigm Transcend Organizational and National Boundaries?" *American Psychologist* 52, no. 2 (1977): 130–39; B. M. Bass and B. J. Avolio, "Potential Biases in Leadership Measures: How Prototypes, Leniency, and General Satisfaction Relate to Ratings and Rankings of Transformational and Transactional Leadership Constructs," *Educational and Psychological Measurement* 49 (1989): 509–27.

20. Den Hartog et al., "Culture Specific."

21. Maher, "Gender-Related Stereotypes."

22. G. Dobbins and S. Platz, "Sex Differences in Leadership: How Real Are They?" *Academy of Management Review* 11, no. 1 (1986): 118–27.

23. R. Hooijberg and N. DiTomaso, "Leadership in and of Demographically Diverse Organizations," *Leadership Quarterly* 7, no. 1 (1996): 1–19.

24. F. Denmark, "Women, Leadership, and Empowerment," *Psychology of Women Quarterly* 17 (1993): 343–56; Bennis and Nanus, *Leaders.*

25. Srivastva, *Executive Power.*

26. R. House, J. Woycke, and E. Fodor, "Charismatic and Non-Charismatic Leaders: Differences in Behavior and Effectiveness," in *Charismatic Leadership*, ed J. A. Conger and R. N. Kanungo (San Francisco: Jossey-Bass, 1988).

27. Bennis and Nanus, *Leaders.*

28. Srivastva, *Executive Power.*

29. Den Hartog et al., "Culture Specific."

30. A. Zaleznik and M. F. R. Kets de Vries, *Power and the Corporate Mind* (Boston: Houghton Mifflin, 1975); Conger and Kanungo, *Charismatic Leadership.*

31. Zaleznik, "Managers and Leaders."

32. Carol Gilligan, *In a Different Voice* (Cambridge, Mass.: Harvard University Press, 1982); Nancy Chodorow, *The Reproduction of Mothering* (Berkeley and Los Angeles: University of California Press, 1978); and Dorothy Dinnerstein, *The Mermaid and the Minotaur: Sexual Arrangements and Human Malaise* (New York: Harper and Row, 1976).

33. Burns, *Leadership.*

34. T. J. Peters and R. H. Waterman, *In Search of Excellence* (New York: Harper and Row, 1982).

35. D. Jung and B. Avolio, "Examination of Transformational Leadership and Group Process among Caucasian- and Asian-Americans: Are They Different?" in *Research in International Business and International Relations*, vol. 7, ed. T. Scandura and M. Serapio, 29–66 (Stamford, Conn.: JAI Press, 1998); K. Klein and R. House, "On Fire: Charismatic Leadership and Levels of Analysis," *Leadership Quarterly* 6 (1995): 183–98.

36. Conger and Kanungo, *Charismatic Leadership.*

37. B. M. Bass and R. M. Stogdill, *Handbook of Leadership* (New York: Free Press, 1990).

38. H. M. Rosen and K. Korabik, "Workplace Variables, Affective Responses, and Intention to Leave among Women Managers," *Journal of Occupational Psychology* 64, no. 4 (1991): 317–30; D. Butler and F. Geis, "Nonverbal Affect Responses to Male and Female Leaders: Implications for Leadership Evaluations," *Journal of Personality and Social Psychology* 58, no. 1 (1990): 48–59.

39. M. Jensen, *Women Who Want to Be Boss: Business Revelations and Success Strategies* (New York: Doubleday, 1987); J. A. Sonnenfeld, P. G. Washington, M. S.

Barry, and R. A. Bradley, "Gender Comparison of CEO Leadership Styles," working paper (Atlanta: Center for Leadership and Career Studies, Emory Business School, Emory University, 1993).

40. Denmark, "Women, Leadership, and Empowerment."

41. Jung and Avolio, "Examination of Transformational Leadership"; Den Hartog et al., "Culture Specific."

42. P. L. Ryan, "Ten Best Lesbian Places to Work," *Girlfriends*, June 2000, 27–29; R. B. Will and S. D. Lydenberg, "Twenty Corporations That Listen to Women," *Ms.*, 1987, 45–52; and Rosabeth M. Kanter, *The Change Masters: Innovations for Productivity in the American Corporation* (New York: Simon and Schuster, 1983).

43. Hooijberg and DiTomaso, "Leadership in and of Demographically Diverse Organizations"; P. S. Parker and dt ogilvie, "Gender, Culture, and Leadership: Toward a Culturally Distinct Model of African-American Women Executives' Leadership Strategies," *Leadership Quarterly* 7, no. 2 (1996): 189–214.

44. G. Baruch, R. Barnett, and C. Rivers, *Lifeprints: New Patterns of Love and Work for Today's Women* (New York: McGraw-Hill, 1983).

45. I. Broverman, D. Broverman, F. Clarkson, P. Rosenkrantz, and S. Vogel, "Sex-role Stereotypes and Clinical Judgments of Mental Health," *Journal of Consulting Psychology* 34 (1970): 1–7.

46. Susan C. Bourque and Kay B. Warren, *Women of the Andes: Patriarchy and Social Change in Two Peruvian Towns* (Ann Arbor: University of Michigan Press, 1981), 42–56, 211–18.

47. L. K. Brown, "Women and Business Management," *Signs: Journal of Women in Culture and Society* 5 (1979): 266–88; Dobbins and Platz, "Sex Differences"; G. N. Powell, *Women and Men in Management* (Newbury Park, Calif.: Sage, 1988); A. H. Eagly and B. T. Johnson, "Gender and Leadership Style: A Meta-Analysis," *Psychological Bulletin* 108, no. 2 (1990): 233–56; and A. H. Eagly, M. G. Makhijani, and B. G. Klonsky, "Gender and the Evaluation of Leaders: A Meta-Analysis," *Psychological Bulletin* 111, no. 1 (1992): 3–22.

48. F. E. Fiedler and R. J. House, "Leadership Theory and Research: A Report of Progress," in *International Review of Industrial and Organizational Psychology*, ed. C. L. Cooper and I. Robertson, 73–92 (London: Wiley, 1988).

49. A. Cann and W. Siegfried, "Gender Stereotypes and Dimensions of Effective Leader Behavior," *Sex Roles* 23 (1990): 413–19.

50. Eagly et al., "Gender and the Evaluation of Leaders"; Dobbins and Platz, "Sex Differences."

51. R. G. Lord, C. L. DeVader, and G. M. Alliger, "A Meta-Analysis of the Relation between Personality Traits and Leadership Perceptions: An Application of Validity Generalization Procedures," *Journal of Applied Psychology* 71 (1986): 402–9.

52. Lord et al., "A Meta-Analysis of the Relation between Personality Traits and Leadership Perceptions."

53. R. G. Lord, R. J. Foti, and C. L. DeVader, "A Test of Leadership Categoriza-

tion Theory: Internal Structure, Information Processing, and Leadership Perceptions," *Organizational Behavior and Human Performance* 34 (1984): 343–78.

54. G. Corey, *Theory and Practice of Counseling and Psychotherapy*, 5th ed. (Pacific Grove, Calif.: Brooks/Cole, 1996).

55. E. Hollander, "Leadership, Followership, Self, and Others," *Leadership Quarterly* 3, no. 1 (1992): 43–54; Fiedler and House, "Leadership Theory and Research"; Lord et al., "A Meta-Analysis of the Relation between Personality Traits and Leadership Perceptions."

56. Lord et al., "A Meta-Analysis of the Relation between Personality Traits and Leadership Perceptions."

57. R. G. Lord and K. J. Maher, *Leadership and Information Processing* (London: Routledge, 1991), 98.

58. Den Hartog et al., "Culture Specific"; L. R. Offermann, J. K. Kennedy, and P. W. Wirtz, "Implicit Leadership Theories: Content, Structure, and Generalizability," *Leadership Quarterly* 5, no. 1 (1994): 43–55; and R. J. Foti and C. H. Luch, "The Influence of Individual Differences on the Perception and Categorization of Leaders," *Leadership Quarterly* 3 (1992): 55–66.

59. Denmark, "Women, Leadership, and Empowerment," 350.

60. Mary Ellen Guy, "Workplace Productivity and Gender Issues," *Public Administration Review* 53, no. 3 (1993): 281.

61. Fiedler and House, "Leadership Theory and Research," 87.

62. Lord and Maher, *Leadership and Information Processing*.

63. S. M. Freedman and J. S. Phillips, "The Changing Nature of Research on Women at Work," *Journal of Management* 14, no. 2 (1988): 231–51.

64. Ibid.

65. Corey, *Theory and Practice of Counseling* (1996).

66. U.S. Department of Labor, *Pipelines of Progress: A Status Report on the Glass Ceiling* (Washington, D.C.: Government Printing Office, 1992).

67. T. Cox and S. Blake, "Managing Cultural Diversity: Implications for Organizational Competitiveness," *Academy of Management Executives* 5 (1991): 45–56.

68. Sonnenfeld et al., "Gender Comparison of CEO Leadership Styles."

69. Ibid., 4.

70. U.S. Department of Labor, *Pipelines of Progress*, 35.

71. Ibid., 36.

72. Ibid.

73. U.S. Department of Labor, *A Report on the Glass Ceiling Initiative* (Washington, D.C.: Government Printing Office, 1991).

74. Ibid., 1.

75. Rosen and Korabik, "Workplace Variables."

76. M. McDonald, "A Start-up of Her Own," *U.S. News and World Report*, 15 May 2000, 36.

77. Ibid.

78. Ibid., 37.

79. Srivastva, *Executive Power*.

80. Hollander, "Leadership, Followership, Self, and Others," 46.

81. Ibid.

82. Ibid.

83. B. Clark and M. Matze, "A Core of Global Leadership: Relational Competence," in *Advances in Global Leadership*, vol. 1, ed. W. Mobley, M. J. Gessner, and V. Arnold, 127–61 (Stamford, Conn.: JAI Press, 1999).

84. Ibid., 131–32, 147.

85. Ibid., 127.

86. Den Hartog et al., "Culture Specific."

87. Ibid.

88. Jung and Avolio, "Examination of Transformational Leadership."

89. J. Baum and L. Russell, "Technology in Executive Learning," in *Advances in Global Leadership*, vol. 1, ed. W. Mobley, M. J. Gessner, and V. Arnold, 355–69 (Stamford, Conn.: JAI Press, 1999).

90. McDonald, "A Start-up of Her Own," 40.

91. Ibid., 40.

92. Ibid.

93. Dalton, "More Room at the Top," 30–38. Quote within is by Marian O'Leary, Senior Vice President and CFO at Security Dynamics Technologies, Inc., in Bedford, Massachusetts.

94. Ibid.

95. Ibid., 30.

## Want to Learn More?

### Online Women's Business Center

The Online Women's Business Center is an interactive business skills training website dedicated to helping entrepreneurial women realize their goals and aspirations for their personal and professional development. The center's goal is to provide women with the information and expertise necessary for planning their economic independence through owning their own businesses.

www.onlinewbc.org

### National Association of Women Business Owners

NAWBO is a resource/information organization that connects women business owners to each other and provides resources such as news, conferences, and research. It allows members to exchange ideas and information with other members across the country who have encountered similar business challenges and experiences.

National Association of Women Business Owners
1100 Wayne Avenue, Suite 830
Silver Spring, MD 20910
Telephone (301) 608-2590
Fax (301) 608-2596
www.nawbo.org

**American Woman's Economic Development Corporation**
AWED is a national nonprofit organization helping women achieve economic equity through business ownership and entrepreneurship. AWED serves women from all social and economic backgrounds with training and counseling in all phases of business development, from beginners to CEOs.

American Woman's Economic Development Corporation
71 Vanderbilt Avenue, Suite 320
New York, NY 10169
Telephone (212) 692-9100
Fax (212) 692-9296
www.onlinewbc.org/docs/wbcs/NYNYAWED.html

**An Income of Her Own/Independent Means**
AIOHO has one mission: economic empowerment for girls. Were you clueless about money and economic power when you were a teenager? Do you have an interest in giving the next generation the economic tools we never had? Brought to you by Independent Means, Inc., AIOHO On-Line offers teenage girls resources, programs, articles, and information that will help them on their path toward independence.

An Income of Her Own/Independent Means
P.O. Box 987
Santa Barbara, CA 93102
Telephone (800) 350-1816
Fax (805) 965-3148
www.independentmeans.com

**Euro-American Women's Council**
EAWC has the mission to strengthen the status of women in the business community worldwide. It attempts to aid women business owners and executives by building alliances between the private sector and government while providing groundbreaking research to document the economic and social contributions of women-owned firms.

Euro-American Women's Council
163-15 Oak Avenue, Suite 2A
Flushing, NY 11355
Telephone (313) 203-3352
Fax (718) 321-3362
www.eawc.org

**National Women's Business Center**

WBC provides women with the resources, training, support, and network to start or expand their own business successfully. The WBC is a public-private partnership that is partially funded by the U.S. Small Business Administration's Office of Women's Business Ownership, which is the only office in the federal government established to help women become full partners in economic development through small business ownership.

National Women's Business Center
1250 24th Street, NW, Suite 350
Washington, DC 20037
Telephone (202) 466-0544
Fax (202) 466-0581
www.womensbusinesscenter.org

**National Women's Business Council**

NWBC is a federal advisory panel created to serve as an independent source of advice and counsel to the president, the Congress, and the Interagency Committee on Women's Business Enterprise on economic issues of importance to women business owners and the effectiveness of federal programs and policies designed to foster women's entrepreneurship.

National Women's Business Council
409 Third Street, SW, Suite 210
Washington, DC 20024
Telephone (202) 205-3850
Fax (202) 205-6825
www.nwbc.gov

**National Association for Female Executives**

NAFE provides the resources and services—through education, networking, and public advocacy—to empower its members to achieve career success and financial security. Since its founding in 1972, NAFE has served as a leading authority on issues and trends affecting women in business.

Telephone (800) 634-6233
www.nafe.com

# 2

# The Problem of Silence
# in Feminist Psychology

**Maureen A. Mahoney**

■ BACKGROUND

This essay represents the coming together of my professional work as a developmental psychologist and my long-standing interest in women's studies and the psychology of women. Moreover, it joins my professional understandings with reflections about my own experiences as a child and developing young female. By looking at my own life in light of what the scholarly literature was saying about voice and silence, I came to realize the inadequacies of academic formulations in accounting for actual experience, in this case most notably my own. In considering the interaction of the personal and the scholarly, I came to a more complex understanding of voice than that depicted by currently popular academic literature.

These more complex understandings, stemming from my own psychological interpretations of personal experiences, have contributed enormously to my current work with college students. In individual work with and advising of students, I was always intrigued by so-called shy female students who have difficulty articulating what they want. I realize that this reticence is not necessarily a function of low self-esteem as so often assumed, but rather that it is far more complex, that there is much going on beneath the surface of silence, and that silence is not necessarily a sign of weakness but can be a reflection of strength and resolve. In the classroom and in the professor's or dean's office, the student who speaks the most is not necessarily the one feeling the most power or the highest level of self-esteem. These personal discoveries gave conviction to my challenge to popular assumptions about the meaning of female students' silence and have significantly facilitated my work with students.

THIS article reassesses the meaning of silence and voice in feminist psychologies of women. Just as "voice" has been seen by some feminist writers—most notably Carol Gilligan—as central to women's experience and exercise of power, I suggest that silence can also be understood as an avenue to power. The simple equation of voice with authority, and silence with victimization, needs to be reexamined in the spirit of recent challenges to the notion of women's unitary "voice." Just as women's voices are as multiple and diverse as our cultural and personal histories, so the meaning of silence—being unwilling or unable to speak—can be seen as complex and multidimensional. Such a reassessment is timely because it allows for a new perspective on the psychological sources of women's—indeed, anyone's—subjective experience of power.

Current discussions about the psychological meanings of voice and silence exist within two competing stories about the psychological source of women's power. These stories have developed in different sectors of the academy: on the one hand, among American feminist psychologists who have constructed a theory and practice of "relational" women's psychology, and on the other, among feminist theorists who work in the domains of literary criticism and philosophy and are influenced by postmodernism's declaration of the "death of the subject."[1]

The view within U.S. feminist psychology, most clearly represented by Carol Gilligan and her colleagues, sees women's strength emerging from the recovery of an authentic "voice" and the capacity to express it, and a woman's subordination as rooted in the silencing of voice.[2] The anthropologist Susan Gal points out that women's historians, similarly, have justified their work on the basis of recapturing the "silent" past: "In these writings, silence is generally deplored" as "a symbol of passivity and powerlessness: those who are denied speech cannot make their experience known and thus cannot influence the course of their lives or history."[3] The conflation here of individual and collective experience is not coincidental: individual women's voices become easily confused in this view with Woman's voice.[4] Equally important, women's silence is equated with Woman's silence, divesting silence itself from the possibility of multiple meanings anchored in different social roles and shifting subject positions. For example, Gal points out that in certain contexts, such as a job interview, confession, or psychotherapy, the silent party is the one with power.[5] Carla Kaplan adds yet another dimension to the meaning of silence, as when silence represents a heroic act of defiance among slaves and, more subtly, when gaps in a slave narrative represent a subversive plot.[6] More generally, feminist literary critics have recognized that textual silences reveal not only cultural suppression but also, alternatively, "women's deployment of silence as a form of resistance to the dominant discourse."[7]

These insights about the shifting literary and social meaning of silence are crucial in understanding that silence is not a one-dimensional concept. My emphasis is not on silence as part of an identified social role or as a gap in a text. Rather, it is on the less-than-conscious experience of feeling unable or unwilling to speak and feeling bad about it, due in part to feminist writing that conveys the expectation that silence is a sign of inauthenticity, of failure to be a "real" feminist. Academic discourse outside of feminist psychology, however, has been strongly influenced by a postmodern perspective that disputes the notion of "authentic" individual voice.[8] Indeed, postmodern feminists reject the possibility of a whole identity that gives rise to a single, true voice and see liberatory potential in playing at numerous, contradictory identities. These feminists attack the idea that any fixed identity is healthy, especially a stable gender identity, which they see as a sentimental and dangerously limiting construction. However, in the United States feminist psychologists have not shared the enthusiasm of feminist writers in other disciplines for a theory of contradictory identities.[9]

This essay suggests that the particular contradiction between U.S. psychological and postmodernist discourse illuminates a painful and productive psychological experience: an intellectual rejection of the notion of "authentic selves" juxtaposed with a continuing intrapsychic resonance of that very concept. It is the psychological embeddedness of the ideas of integrity and authenticity that motivates, in part, concern about voicing contradictory thoughts and feelings. Creative disruption of given identities suggested by the postmodern agenda requires the transformation of contradiction from a shameful experience to an empowering one. This process, in turn, requires silence as an important psychological space of resistance and negotiation.

I became acutely aware of a contradiction in my own thinking about issues of voice when I participated in a writing seminar to which I had brought a work-in-progress about split subjectivity and shifting identities as a path to change.[10] At the end of the seminar, the instructor asked us to write a statement about our writing process during the week-long workshop. With great enthusiasm and a surprising lack of self-awareness, I wrote a piece about "writing from the self," testifying to the exhilaration I had experienced of locating my own voice and feeling free to express it. The subjective experience was of finding *my* voice, as if there was one, a unified whole, a source of clarity and power waiting to be uncovered and unleashed. Only later did I realize, with a feeling of hot shame, that I had contradicted my own arguments in the scholarly paper I was writing.

I have come to recognize the feeling of hot shame as an alarm signal warning me of the need to be careful about exposing what I "really" feel or think and to take into account the expectations of others who are listening and judging. This subjective experience linking shame and silence is echoed in the clinical literature: "Shame teaches us the value of privacy: the privacy that protects us from shame, and the private place to which we must repair when humiliated. Just as shame follows the exposure of whatever we wished to keep private, the wish to withdraw provides a reasonable compensatory stratagem."[11] From childhood I have been a close observer, standing on the edge of the playground, trying to figure out how to become part of the group that was playing in the center. To this child the center was populated by one group of happy, secure, enviable participants. (I now know that those "happy" children were no doubt struggling with their own insecurities and contradictions, but nothing would have convinced me of that then.) The intense activity in observing and anticipating, and occasionally making a foray toward the social center, was not a playful exercise in taking on various roles but an enterprise of deadly seriousness. Standing on the margin, by myself, did not seem to be a position of power but of possible annihilation. The quest to belong was far from a passive exercise in conformity, although someone observing from the outside might assume this was so. I was determined and single-minded, using the only tools I had available, my intelligence and insight, to figure out how to get what I wanted. Apparent passivity and silence obscured an intensely focused enterprise.

My position at the margin of the playground was reproduced several times in my life because my father held a government job in which he was transferred three times before I entered fifth grade. The child of a ranger, born in Yosemite National Park, I became the envy of anyone who heard about it. From the child's perspective, however, the spectacular beauty of the setting was a matter of mundane, everyday life. Before the first job transfer, I enjoyed the security of a small-town community where everyone knew me, where everyone was "Park Service." This relatively seamless social existence was challenged within days of the first move from the huge national park isolated in the Sierra Nevada to Muir Woods, a small national monument near San Francisco. There I attended for the first time an upper-middle-class elementary school in Mill Valley, even then an exclusive, progressive suburb of the city. In my first life I had been a member of a community where all the families lived on minimal government salaries subsidized by assigned housing and reduced prices at the concessionaire's grocery store. Clothing was purchased from the Sears catalog; television signals could not penetrate the granite of the Sierra Nevada. Now I was on my own in a school where the principal, Miss Grimm, wore tailored suits and three-inch-high heels and where my classmates took lessons in English riding or interpretive dance.

What became clear to me was that I was now an outsider. I did not understand how to be like the other kids, and I made humiliating mistakes. One morning I went to school in corduroy pedal pushers, as I had done nearly every day in the mountains for warmth and ease of movement, only to realize that all the girls wore skirts. Indeed, there was a school rule that forbade girls to wear pants. I berated myself in my shame. I should have seen beforehand; I should have been able to protect myself from this; why didn't my mother warn me? Difference meant isolation, so the trick was to cover over difference and make oneself seem to be part of the group. I wore skirts every day after that. I looked the same (more or less—the colored scarves I wore around my neck every day in an attempt, along with my ponytail, to achieve the 1950s poodle skirt look may have marked me as a bit unusual). But I was convinced now that I lived in a world where inadvertent mistakes could exclude and isolate and the solution was to be "advertent"—so that I could recover a sense of control. The fact of difference, carried with me as surely as my new wardrobe, was the secret that must not be told. Behaving *as if* I were wholly like the others, I felt that I was split into different selves, one outer, one inner; one public, one domestic; one shared, one private. The particular "error" was small—one of the stories parents laugh about when, after years have gone by, children sometimes reveal them. And indeed, compared with the trauma of many children's lives, my stories are relatively inconsequential. However, the shame experienced over small mistakes can create a sense of the splitting off of an "inner," or private, self that propels conformity out of fear of exclusion. Silence about difference emerges from the threat of public humiliation. But the very awareness of difference equally depends on social experiences of comparison and judgment.

Not only was I having a difficult time "adjusting" to a recent move, but in taking action to protect myself and to gain acceptance I felt doubly disgraced. I had learned the moral stricture to be honest from my mother, a woman whose own experience of being raised in the poverty of a rural Northern California lumber town by German immigrant parents positioned her far outside middle-class comfort. Like other immigrant parents, hers (no doubt unconsciously but nevertheless very effectively) attempted to insulate her from social humiliation by instilling a quiet but stubborn pride that viewed all the others as more or less lacking in intelligence, responsibility, morality.

A family belief in personal integrity may have allowed a moral superiority that was a salve for the humiliation of being German in the United States during the world wars as well as for the disgrace of being poor in a culture that values money. But for me, the stricture to be consistent and honest meant that my shame grew. Being like the others required a degradation and suppression of the "truth" about my background. I experienced this move as dishonest and felt it as a betrayal of my mother. I now had to pretend to be confident and normal when the ground of normality had shifted wildly. This is a story about pain and conflict and struggle over authenticity beginning (for me) in second grade, long before the female adolescent crisis on which Carol Gilligan insists.[12]

Of course, the same experience can be seen as early training in conscious awareness of split subjectivity, an experience of the controlled expression of public behavior, as opposed to concealed private thoughts and vulnerabilities that can be protected. For me, however, the language of a "true self" covered over by falseness described my subjective situation. Shame merged into guilt over lack of integrity, locating the experience within the moral domain. Obviously, as a girl I was not taking pleasure in the playful possibilities of being different selves, of being complicated, of being smart, or even of being a child. The playfulness that such a perspective prescribes as a project for personal and political change requires an amused detachment—a psychological maturity and sophistication unavailable to me as a child. But even in adulthood it is problematic, because it idealizes the notion of fun and invention and ignores the pain that moments of contradiction also evoke.[13]

My story about a young girl's first realization that clothing makes a statement about inclusion and exclusion—that is, my discomfort and the meaning I made of it—initiated a lifetime of active (but mostly silent) attention to the public message that apparel conveys. Such chance, highly charged encounters of childhood located me in the social world, operating in multiple and contradictory psychological directions, both to silence through humiliation and to energize the psychological work required to gain control and avoid being taken unawares in the future.[14] Writing about her experiences growing up as the working-class child of a single mother in 1950s England, Carolyn Steedman,

in *Landscape for a Good Woman: A Story of Two Lives*, argues that the puzzlement and shock of such experiences "can provide a sharp critical faculty in a
child." Steedman suggests that the processing of such experiences and the
relocation of oneself in the newly altered world is a paradigmatic developmental moment (thus, she emphasizes meaning and narrative in her account
rather than emotional loss and defense against it). Accordingly, she understands power as the capacity to understand and reinterpret one's past, incorporating multiple layers and retellings, as the child moves through geographical
and social space. "The only point," she writes, "lies in interpretation." But this
interpretation is far from passive, a postmodern description of subjects who
"are spoken" rather than who "speak" might imply: "worked upon and reinter-
preted, the landscape becomes a historical landscape; but only through continual and active reworking." Steedman suggests the possibility of continual play
between unconscious and conscious experience, awareness of contradictions
provoked by social circumstances, and the act of making meaning about them.
While meaning shifts and contradicts itself, Steedman places a reflective subject at the center of the process: "It's not the outcome [of confrontation] that
signifies. It's the children watching the confrontation . . . that we should look
at, watch their watching this disjuncture."[15] Here we see the possibility of a
subject who speaks within language and culture but who occupies changing
positions at the convergence of continually conflicting histories and interpretations. Her subjectivity, anchored to her particular position in the social and
cultural grid, consists in interpreting these contradictions, moved and motivated by the emotional impact they have on her.

But what is the relationship between reinterpreting one's history and acting in the world? And what is the psychological source of women's capacity to
act and to resist, in other words, of women's personal power? Although many
feminist theorists have justifiably criticized any psychological analysis as drawing attention away from the economic, social, and political realities that reproduce women's subordination, the nagging question of personal change
reappears again and again and needs to be confronted as both a psychological
and a social issue.[16] Yet an adequate theory of psychological empowerment
must incorporate social and historical circumstances and, in particular, class
and concepts of femininity.

## Carol Gilligan and the Politics of Voice

From her first major work to her most recent one, Carol Gilligan has
single-mindedly developed the notion of "voice" as the linchpin of her theory

of women's development. Arguing that voice connects psyche and body as well as psyche and culture, Gilligan presents a developmental model that depicts young girls as forthright, outspoken, and matter-of-fact about conflict and hurt feelings. The dawning of adolescence, however, "muffles" that clear voice, silencing girls and rendering them confused about what they want to communicate. Gilligan and Lyn Mikel Brown provide evidence from their interviews with girls at a private school in Cleveland, Ohio, that developmental progress in the realms of cognition and insight "goes hand in hand with evidence of a loss of voice, a struggle to authorize or take seriously their own experience . . . increased confusion, sometimes defensiveness, as well as evidence for the replacement of real with inauthentic or idealized relationships." They go on to assert: "If we consider responding to oneself, knowing one's feelings and thoughts, clarity, courage, openness, and free-flowing connections with others and the world as signs of psychological health, as we do, then these girls are in fact not developing, but are showing evidence of loss and struggle and signs of an impasse in their ability to act in the face of conflict."[17] In Gilligan's view, the power of voice, the freedom to speak one's mind and act on one's feelings, emerges from a specific relational context, a context of "real" or "authentic" relationships: "We speak about authentic or resonant relationships, that is, relationships that are as open and mutual as possible, in which partially formed thoughts and strong feelings can be spoken and heard. . . . A shift from encouraging (enforcing) consensus or agreement to engaging diversity creates the possibility for real rather than fraudulent relationships with those with whom we engage in our work." Thus, paradoxically, personal power for women emerges from relationships that are already mutual. That is, she argues that personal power is born in social circumstances devoid of unequal power struggles (and this hardly seems likely). False relationships are those "in which people cannot speak or are not heard" because the power imbalance is too great.[18]

Gilligan, along with self-in-relation theorists at Wellesley College's Stone Center, arrive at a conception of "power with" in favor of "power over"—power as "capacity" versus domination. For example, Jean Baker Miller states that "most women would be most comfortable in a world in which we feel we are not limiting, but are enhancing the power of other people while simultaneously increasing our own power."[19] Jessica Benjamin's work, as well as my own with Barbara Yngvesson, attempts to go beyond this dichotomy.[20] Following Benjamin, I use D. W. Winnicott's developmental model to help conceptualize a psychological dynamic in which "power as capacity" is born of the infant's struggle between the disparate desires to be omnipotent and to be recognized by an other over whom one does not have complete control.[21] Thus, "power with" and "power over" are linked in a psychological dialectic. Tension between the two can easily be ruptured in favor of insistence on one aspect of the dynamic or the other—a kind of splitting that produces a false dichotomy. This dynamic is discussed more fully below.

Gilligan's developmental model of relationship, authenticity, and power represents only one side of this dichotomy and carries with it several implications. First, the model suggests that relationships of mutuality, relatively free of power dynamics, are not only possible but desirable because they set the social context for girls' feelings of empowerment. Second, in idealizing girlhood as a time when conflicts are met openly and an authentic voice is readily available, the model suggests that the struggles of development begin only in adolescence. Third, it assumes that the struggles themselves limit rather than propel development. The silence that they may produce is seen as pathological, a defensive reaction born of confusion or the desire to appear in a way that one is not "really" feeling. In this view, silence should be understood as defeat rather than an active choice and an ingredient in resistance, either now or in the future.

Notions of true selves covered over by false appearances are not confined to white middle-class psychologies. They also appeal to writers trying to understand their own experiences of marginalization. In an essay on her dissonant experience as a black female law student at Harvard, Patricia Williams describes the way relations of power and the legacy of slavery render some in this culture "masters" while others are constructed as "servants." Then "the struggle of the self becomes not a true mirroring of self-in-other, but a hierarchically inspired series of distortions. . . . It is essential at some stage that the self be permitted to retreat into itself and make its own decisions with self-love and self-confidence. . . . Since the self's power resides in another, little faith is placed in the true self, in one's own experiential knowledge." Here, in a brief aside on human nature, Williams evokes a story of true selves denied by unequal power relations as a way of arguing that women, children, and blacks operate in a dual world, one in which intuitive experience challenges the socially prescribed "reality" of the dominant power structure. The paradox is that Williams herself is a master of the politics of split subjectivity. She confronts audiences with the contradictions of her own subjective experience to expose power relations and sources of subordination, as when she surprises a formal academic meeting by describing how she wrote the paper she is delivering only by overcoming a depression that left her wanting to stay in her frayed bathrobe and spend the day in bed.[22] In juxtaposing her fear and lack of confidence with her skill and power as a public speaker, Williams hints at a possibility that Gilligan does not fully explore—that silence can reflect a posture of resistance rather than defeat. Williams overcomes the isolation implied by the impulse to spend the day in bed by using it to launch her argument and to disarm and provoke her audience. The move is an intellectual version of Freud's original observation that trauma is overcome and development occurs when the subject engages in "making passive active"; in this case, a narrative of a true self denied by racism helps mobilize a resistant stance based on the playful possibilities of split subjectivity.

D. W. Winnicott, the British object relations theorist, used a similarly provocative technique to gain the attention of his audience when he was invited in 1962 to address the San Francisco Psychoanalytic Institute. He began his remarks with the comment "Starting from no fixed place I soon came, while preparing this paper for a foreign society, to staking a claim, to my surprise, to the right not to communicate."[23] Winnicott's refreshing opener provides the entrée to his psychoanalytic analysis of the meaning of not communicating. I cite his account to complicate Brown and Gilligan's assumptions about the necessary pathology of silence. Winnicott helps us see that silence contains the possibility of power as well as pathology, of action as well as passivity (although, of course, not necessarily so).

## Winnicott on Communicating and Not Communicating

Winnicott takes a stance opposed to Gilligan's, seeing silence as an active protest against intrusion rather than a passive, submissive position. Ironically, this active use of silence, or resisting communication, is illustrated in Brown and Gilligan's own study. They describe "signs of an emerging underground" as the initial reaction of the students to the researchers' presence at their school. This underground consisted of whispered hallway conversations about the questions on the researchers' interviews so that friends could be properly prepared. Brown and Gilligan write that "the girls responded to our research by aligning themselves against this strange intrusion." Brown and Gilligan view the girls' reaction as an unfortunate obscuring and muting of voice, a sign that the girls know that the "dominant culture" is "out of tune" with their voices "and for the most part uninterested in girls' experiences." They see the girls as victims of a misattuned patriarchy, not rebels against the power of adults.[24]

Winnicott suggests an alternative motivation for the response of the underground, one that is more respectful of the possibility that the girls are agents of change as well as victims of the dominant patriarchal culture. In his view, silence or secret conspiracy to prepare responses are healthy forms of resistance to unwelcome probing. Brown and Gilligan deny the power of their own position as researchers and adults vis-à-vis the girls and seek to find "a way of working that sustained other people's voices and our own—to voice the relationship that was at the heart of our psychological work."[25] By translating the young girls into simply "other people," Brown and Gilligan muffle the power dynamics between adults and children; the girls, acutely aware of such disparities, become suspicious and take action to protect themselves.

Although Gilligan does discuss adolescent girls' use of silence as "a way of maintaining integrity" when someone does not listen to them, "a way to avoid further invalidation," she nonetheless goes on to assert that "willingness to speak and to risk disagreement is central to the process of adolescent development, making it possible to reweave attachment, and informing the distinction between true and false relationships."[26] Winnicott makes the story more complicated psychologically:

> I suggest that in health there is a core to the personality that corresponds to the true self of the split personality; I suggest that this core never communicates with the world of perceived objects, and that the individual person knows that it must never be communicated with or influenced by external reality. . . . Although healthy persons communicate and enjoy communicating, the other fact is equally true, that *each individual is an isolate, permanently non-communicating, permanently unknown, in fact unfound.*[27]

Winnicott plays on the notion of opposites, on the paradox of simultaneous sociality and isolation, setting up dual motivations to communicate and to be silent. Perfect communication is as threatening as absence of communication, because it obscures the difference between subject and object and threatens to annihilate the subject's sense of agency and creativity in the world. Paradoxically, it is *im*perfect communication that Winnicott values, because these "adaptation failures" help the child understand that although adults are in control, they are not in absolute control. The anger that results from a failure of communication motivates a subjective sense of agency and resistance. This sense does not exist sui generis; it is not a natural or inborn part of the personality, nor is it the *result* of isolation. Rather, it emerges from social relations and efforts to communicate that are not fully successful and that may evoke painful emotions such as shame.

Here we can begin to see a theory of psychological power that paradoxically locates the capacity for creativity and resistance in the delicate balance between being heard and not being heard, between speaking and refusing to speak. Winnicott understands that the struggle of interpersonal power relations, far from obscuring one's own sense of agency, as Gilligan suggests, actually may set the conditions that give rise to it.

Part of the problem is Gilligan's concept of "voice." In her earlier work, Gilligan restricts her use of the term *voice* to "ways of speaking about moral problems" and "modes of describing the relationship between other and self." She sees voice as a way of representing a mode of thought and discerns different themes in the moral reasoning of women and men, one representing an ethic of care and the other an ethic of justice.[28] Ten years later, with the publication of a recent book, the term *voice* has taken on a broader meaning. More than representing a mode of thought, or a moral logic, voice now signifies for Gilligan the ability to express feelings as well as thoughts, to embody "strength, courage and a healthy resistance to losing voice and relationship." Having a voice enables one to "speak freely of feeling angry, of fighting or open conflict in relationships, . . . [to] take difference and disagreement for granted in daily life." Uncertainty about such outspokenness is construed not as "a different voice" but as a "loss of voice," the result of confusion.

In shifting her analysis from speaking about different voices to dichotomizing voice as either present or absent, Gilligan has transformed her discussion from one of moral logic to one of self-esteem and agency; girls' struggle to "voice their feelings and thoughts and experiences in relationships" affects "their feelings about themselves, their relationships with others, and *their ability to act in the world.*" Loss of voice, or silence, becomes both the cause and result of low self-esteem, poor or inauthentic relationships, and inability to take action in the world. In other words, loss of voice is equated with loss of self or at best with an inauthentic or "fraudulent" self: "Voice became key insofar as girls feel pressure to become selfless or without a voice in relationships, and the experience of self in the sense of having a voice became central to girls' experience of authentic relationships." False relationships are those "in which people cannot speak or are not heard."[29]

Gilligan's notion of not being able to speak or not being heard ignores more instrumental sources of a sense of accomplishment, such as work, and also attributes infinite power to the listener and little to the would-be speaker. In this view, not speaking is not a legitimate response but rather the result of "silencing" by cultural and political forces outside the subject's control. Further, although Brown and Gilligan do note in passing that voice is "polyphonic and complex," their way of writing about it implies that it is a unitary thing, which one either possesses or does not.[30] "Voice" becomes reified in much the same way that concepts of id, ego, and superego were reified by Freud's popularizers (much to his distress). It is this reified notion of authentic voice, and the related concept of the whole self, that the postmodern critics ridicule and reject in favor of a notion of split subjectivity, shifting identifications, and selves constructed retrospectively out of cultural myths, distorted memories, and psychological fantasies.

In rejecting the unitary account of voice and self, however, postmodernists have also given up a major insight of the object relations theorists and of Winnicott in particular. Although Winnicott introduced the concept of "true" and "false" self into the psychoanalytic lexicon, he himself was less interested in a thing possessed or achieved in development than in a quality of experience, a subjective state that he describes as "feeling real." His major question was, What "makes a baby begin to be, to feel that life is real, to find life worth living"?[31]

Winnicott argues that the sense of feeling real begins to emerge in the earliest stages of infancy, in the interaction between a responsive caregiver and a baby who cannot exist outside of the caregiver's willingness to nurture. Paradoxically, however, the caregiver must collaborate with the infant in producing the infant's subjective sense of control in the world. The caregiver must help create the illusion that the infant produces that which she or he desires.[32]

This process goes wrong when the caregiver demands too much, either by being neglectful or by being excessively intrusive. Winnicott suggested that the overzealous caregiver is particularly threatening because relentless attention forces the baby into a reactive mode. A reactive mode, in turn, is a state in which "coping" substitutes for "being." The infant cannot *not* respond to the impinging environment. When the infant's experience is more of impingement than sensitivity, the state of "feeling real" is overcome by the state of "feeling false," or living with a false self characterized by a mode of reacting and compliance.

Daniel Stern's research on mothers and infants provides some empirical evidence for Winnicott's theory. Stern finds that mothers who pursue their babies excessively, who do not recognize or respond to the baby's delicate signal to let go of eye-to-eye contact for a moment, dispose their babies to less healthy development.[33] Although neither Winnicott nor Stern offers a gender analysis of these experiences, I speculate that the dangers of compliance are more immanent for girls than for boys in many cultures, not because mothers of girls are more disturbed but because girls are expected to be more relationally oriented than boys.[34]

Living reactively produces a socially compliant subject and communication itself becomes linked to a sense of being controlled, to producing a response demanded by the other. Silence, or not communicating, can be a healthy response, then, to a sense of being controlled. Such a compliant subject can be seen in Brown and Gilligan's example of the fifteen-year-old girl Neeti, who, in the researchers' new open style of "mutual" communication, had been given a draft of the analysis of her own words. Neeti's response to the researchers reveals her discomfort in taking up the given terms of the analysis:

> Neeti then conversed with us about our interpretation of the changes in her life. She told us of her dismay when at fifteen she was asked to write an essay called "Who Am I?" and she realized she did not know. Unhappy with her "fascination" with the "perfect girl" and her "fraudulent view" of herself (phrases from our writing that resonated with her feelings about herself), Neeti spoke of a "voice inside" her that "has been muffled": "The voice that stands up for what I believe in has been buried deep inside of me."[35]

Here we see Neeti taking up the terms of a discourse of true and false selves that has been given her by the relatively powerful psychologists, who, the girl might reasonably believe, know her better than she knows herself. From this infinite regress of reaction and compliance, noncommunication may be the only possible escape.

Carla Kaplan, in a brilliant study of Harriet Jacobs's *Incidents in the Life of a Slave Girl*, shows that the girl's silences in this slave narrative are active and resistant responses to a repressive social order. Whereas white silence, in the context of the debate about emancipation, is "cowardly," slave silence can be heroic and is to be "valued, privileged, and protected." Jacobs notes at the outset that "I have not written my experiences in order to attract attention to myself; on the contrary, it would have been more pleasant to me to have been silent about my own history."[36] Seen from this perspective, Neeti's silent refusal to accept the narrative of true self offered by Gilligan might have served to protect her own sense of integrity.

Gilligan and her colleagues go wrong, I believe, in reifying the notion of "authentic voice" as a precious object buried and available to be uncovered, freed in the process of being listened to and heard. According to Gilligan, this listening requires mutuality in relationship, an absence of power relations or inequality. Gilligan and her colleagues imply that some relationships are mutual and therefore freeing, whereas others are infused with power and therefore

restraining. Winnicott sees that power and defiance within the intimate relationship constitute the essential ground for experiencing a self that feels authentic: "Shall I say that, for a child to be brought up so that he can discover
the deepest part of his nature, someone has to be defied, and even at times
hated, without there being a danger of a complete break in the relationship?"[37]

## A Developmental Story: The Convergence
## of the Social World and the Psyche

Winnicott's account provides us with insight into the developmental importance of secrets and silence, of their place in allowing a subjective sense of
authenticity or feeling real, of the necessity of resistance to powerful others on
whom the child depends. This, in itself, challenges Gilligan's notions about
the relational conditions for feeling "free." But it is a story detached from the
historical and cultural grid, told as if all that matters is the child and her
mother.[38] In her autobiographical *Landscape for a Good Woman*, Carolyn
Steedman adds another essential dimension to the story about secrets: the dimension of social class, or more generally, social marginality. She focuses on
the child watching disjunctures between "systems of authority." Children in
impoverished families are often confronted with discontinuity between the domestic authority of the parent, on the one hand, and on the other, the power
of representatives of the dominant culture, such as social workers, who may
have authority over the parents. White middle-class children, by contrast, tend
to have a more seamless experience of domestic and public authority. Their
fathers, and often their mothers, hold positions of power both within and outside the family (i.e., in the public world of work). Steedman begins her book
with an account of having moved with her mother to a house on Streathem
Hill in 1951, just after her younger sister was born. She and her mother "both
watched the dumpy retreating figure of the health visitor through the curtain-
less windows. The woman had said: 'This house isn't fit for a baby.' "[39]

The child watched the retreating figure and recalls the image decades
later. She remembers her mother weeping and then picking up the pieces with
the offhand comment: "Hard lines, eh, Kay?" Here is what the adult, who has
carried this confrontation all her life, has made of it:

> And I? I will do everything and anything until the end of my days to
> stop anyone ever talking to me like that woman talked to my mother.
> It is in this place, this bare curtainless bedroom, that lies my secret
> and shameful defiance. I read a woman's book, meet such a woman

at a party (a woman now, like me) and think quite deliberately as we
talk: we are divided: a hundred years ago I'd have been cleaning your
shoes. I know this and you don't.

Thus, Steedman argues, "all children experience a first loss of exclusion, lives
shape themselves around this sense of being cut off or denied."[40] But, as Steedman herself is at pains to demonstrate, some exclusions signify more than others because they combine psychological with social marginalization. They
become embedded in the unconscious, in Elizabeth Abel's words, through
"the complexity of feeling and class positioning."[41] My experience on the alien
playground was trivial in social or historical terms, but momentous psychologically. As an adult, I now see the moment as a metaphor, throwing into relief
not only my strangeness and exclusion but also my private uniqueness, my
separateness not only from the other children but from my mother as well. My
refusal to speak about the matter to my mother or anyone else reveals shame
but also determination to keep on the course of inventing myself as distinct
from my family.

There are myriad ways of constructing and reinterpreting such a moment.
Another seven-year-old may have turned to her mother in her distress and
learned that her family had a long tradition of opposition to bourgeois values
such as those that require girls to wear skirts to school. Mediation of a family
narrative through a mother might set the ground for an experience of inclusion
(in a family and cultural tradition) rather than exclusion (from a desirable
public world) and estrangement (from the mother). Whether the mother is
available for such a reinterpretation depends on the relationship between
mother and daughter and on the cultural meanings available to the mother.

Audre Lorde, in her biomythography *Zami: A New Spelling of My Name*,
offers several examples of the limits of a mother's efforts to reinterpret, among
which is the following. As a small girl living in Harlem during the 1930s, Lorde
often had the experience of walking with her mother in "racially mixed zones
of transition," hearing a "hoarsely sharp, guttural rasp," and having a "nasty
glob of grey spittle upon my coat or shoe an instant later." Wiping it off,
Lorde's mother

> fussed about low-class people who had no better sense nor manners
> than to spit into the wind no matter where they went, impressing
> upon me that this humiliation was totally random. . . . It was not until
> years later once in conversation I said to her: "Have you noticed peo-
> ple don't spit into the wind so much the way they used to?" And the

> look on my mother's face told me that I had blundered into one of
> those secret places of pain that must never be spoken of again.[42]

Lorde may never have spoken to her mother about it again. But this experience of her mother's protectiveness and later refusal to speak about the pain of knowing that the protection must crumble, indeed be revealed as a lie, as the daughter faced the world of racism in the United States, inspired Lorde's deep insights about the disjuncture between black women's personal power and social powerlessness. The strength and resistance of Lorde's own adult voice were no doubt fed by these paradoxes of power and powerlessness, experienced acutely and personally, in a delicately negotiated balance between words and silence.

We can see now that the simple story of voice and silence that Gilligan tells is both an attractive and coherent story and a misleading one that denies girls their own complications, their anger at the powerlessness they experience in the face of experts who want to know their secrets, and their active struggles—both spoken and silent—to resist such intrusion and authority. Gilligan's story of voice and silence denies them their own knowledge of their marginalized position; their experiences "out of the borderlands"; the sense of exclusion and uniqueness that comes of such experiences; and the motivation to respond, reinterpret, reposition, and transform themselves. In doing so, it misses the complications of silence and its potential richness as a state of developmental change.

The process of responding to marginalization, full of contradiction and discomfort, mobilizes silence as one among many possible responses and recognizes the importance of incoherence, defiance, and the constructive possibility of not being heard. Cultural prescriptions of personal integrity based on coherence and rationality may help motivate the interpretations of her life that the child makes. Whatever the story, however, it is the capacity to feel real that allows her sense of herself as its inventor. This feeling real, in turn, as Winnicott suggests, depends on the experience of feeling false. Mobilizing possibilities and enjoying contradictions depend on the capacity to shift between states of "feeling real" and "feeling false," not, crucially, between *being* real or *being* false. Indeed, "feeling real" is quite compatible with experiencing the incoherence and contradictions of a nonunitary self, just as "feeling false" is often the subjective experience of expectations for a self that is whole and seamless.[43] Winnicott helps us see that communication itself may set the condition for "feeling false," because it inevitably implies the possibility of conformity or compliance. Silence, then, should not be understood unidimensionally as the condition of disempowerment, or "being silenced," but carries the potential for strength and resistance. As Winnicott suggests, "feeling real" may be more easily experienced in moments of noncommunication. This may help to explain why women treasure the solitude of their own rooms (if we are so fortunate as to have them) as the most fertile sites for creativity.

Standing and watching at the side of the playground, creating secret alliances with girlfriends while responding silently to adults perceived as intrusive, lying in bed in an old bathrobe contemplating a public speech—these moments of withdrawal create a space of silence, where one does not have to be accountable. The capacity to speak out is nurtured in these episodes of nonspeaking that are often experienced subjectively as times of shame, confusion, and anxiety. Far from being (only) moments of defeat, they also contain the possibility of strength and action through the subjective state of noncompliance. Rather than relegating a girl or a woman to a life of acquiescence and loss of power, then, such silences may help foster the capacity to speak out with confidence and authority—indeed, with "authenticity."

I might have become a little girl who defiantly wore pedal pushers all my life. I could rewrite myself on the playground as a triumphant nonconformist. But it would not be my story. My story has to do with humiliation felt so strongly that it took forty years for me to rethink it. Those intervening years, filled with the contradictions of life lived now toward the center, now on the margins, of experience sometimes shared and sometimes secret, brought me to this interpretation.

# Notes

I would like to thank *Feminist Studies* reviewers for their comments on earlier drafts of this essay. Also thanks to colleagues at Hampshire College—Nina Payne and her faculty writing seminar, Barbara Yngvesson, Penina Glazer, Miriam Slater, and Margaret Cerullo. Finally, thanks to Betty Farrell for several careful readings and to Aurora Smaldone for reminding me of the complications of adolescence. This article was originally published in *Feminist Studies* 22, no. 3 (spring 1996): 603–26, by permission of the publisher, Feminist Studies, Inc.

1. Psychoanalytically oriented feminist theorists have been among the few who have engaged the issue of the relationship between postmodernism and relational psychology directly. See Jane Flax, *Thinking Fragments: Psychoanalysis, Feminism, and*

*Postmodernism in the Contemporary West* (Berkeley and Los Angeles: University of California Press, 1990), for a useful overview. Elizabeth Abel's "Race, Class, and Psychoanalysis? Opening Questions," in *Conflicts in Feminism*, ed. Marianne Hirsch and Evelyn Fox Keller, 184–204 (New York: Routledge, 1990), also takes up object relations theory and Lacanian psychology and charges both theoretical perspectives with paying insufficient attention to the social context of gender relations.

2. The "authentic voice" position infuses the writing not only of Carol Gilligan (*In a Different Voice: Psychological Theory and Women's Development* [Cambridge, Mass.: Harvard University Press, 1982]) but also of Jean Baker Miller and her colleagues. See Judith Jordan et al., *Women's Growth in Connection: Writings from the Stone Center* (New York: Guilford Press, 1991); Mary Field Belenky et al., *Women's Ways of Knowing: The Development of Self, Voice, and Mind* (New York: Basic Books, 1986); and Dana Crowley Jack, *Silencing the Self: Women and Depression* (Cambridge, Mass.: Harvard University Press, 1991).

3. Susan Gal, "Between Speech and Silence: The Problematics of Research on Language and Gender," in *Gender at the Crossroads of Knowledge: Feminist Anthropology in the Postmodern Era*, ed. Micaela di Leonardo (Berkeley and Los Angeles: University of California Press, 1991), 175.

4. See Teresa de Lauretis, *Alice Doesn't: Feminism, Semiotics, Cinema* (Bloomington: Indiana University Press, 1984), on the distinction between women and Woman.

5. See Gal, "Between Speech and Silence." Similarly, Japanese businessmen may mobilize silence as a sign of power—in a negotiation, the most silent participant is the one with the most control over decision making (Robert Cunningham, personal communication, February 1994).

6. Carla Kaplan, "Narrative Contract and Emancipatory Readers: *Incidents in the Life of a Slave Girl*," *Yale Journal of Criticism* 1 (1993): 93–119.

7. Elaine Hedges and Shelly Fisher Fishkin, introduction to *Listening to Silence: New Essays in Feminist Criticism*, ed. Elaine Hedges and Shelley Fisher Fishkin (New York: Oxford University Press, 1994), 5.

8. This perspective is represented clearly by Judith Butler's work, *Gender Trouble: Feminism and the Subversion of Identity* (New York: Routledge, 1990).

9. Psychologists in Britain and France have developed a postmodernist account. See, for example, Julien Henriques et al., *Changing the Subject: Psychology, Social Regulation, and Subjectivity* (New York: Methuen, 1984), and Juliet Mitchell and Jacqueline Rose, eds., *Feminine Sexuality: Jacques Lacan and the Ecole Freudienne* (New York: Norton, 1982).

10. See Maureen A. Mahoney and Barbara Yngvesson, "The Construction of Subjectivity and the Paradox of Resistance: Reintegrating Feminist Anthropology and Psychology," *Signs* 18 (autumn 1992): 44–73.

11. Donald L. Nathanson, *Shame and Pride: Affect, Sex, and the Birth of the Self* (New York: Norton, 1992), 319. Nathanson's chapter on withdrawal explicates the links between shame, humiliation, and withdrawal and the importance of therapy in providing a "safe" setting in which to voice shameful memories.

12. Lyn Mikel Brown and Carol Gilligan, *Meeting at the Crossroads: Women's Psychology and Girls' Development* (Cambridge, Mass.: Harvard University Press, 1992). See also Mary Pipher, *Reviving Ophelia: Saving the Selves of Adolescent Girls* (New York: Ballantine Books, 1994).

13. I am grateful to Jessica Benjamin for her thoughtful comments about the issue of idealization.

14. Nathanson too recognizes a positive moment in the withdrawal response to shame that allows an individual to recover self-esteem and return more fully into the world of others (*Shame and Pride*, 322).

15. Carolyn Steedman, *Landscape for a Good Woman: A Story of Two Lives* (New Brunswick, N.J.: Rutgers University Press, 1987), 72, 5, 78, 73.

16. See Mahoney and Yngvesson, "Construction of Subjectivity," for a discussion.

17. Brown and Gilligan, *Meeting at the Crossroads*, 20, 6.

18. Ibid., 40, 36.

19. Jean Baker Miller, "Women and Power" (work-in-progress, Stone Center for Developmental Services and Studies, Wellesley College, Wellesley, Mass., 1982).

20. Jessica Benjamin, *The Bonds of Love: Psychoanalysis, Feminism, and the Problem of Domination* (New York: Pantheon, 1988), and "'The Shadow of the Other (Subject): Intersubjectivity and Feminist Theory," *Constellations* 1, no. 2 (1994): 231–54. Also see Mahoney and Yngvesson, "Construction of Subjectivity."

21. This argument builds on Jessica Benjamin's analysis in *The Bonds of Love*, shifting the emphasis from the struggle between dependence and independence to the struggle between silence and voice.

22. Patricia Williams, *Alchemy of Race and Rights: Diary of a Law Professor* (Cambridge, Mass.: Harvard University Press, 1991), 56–79, esp. 63.

23. D. W. Winnicott, "On Communicating and Not Communicating Leading to a Study of Certain Opposites," in *The Maturational Processes and the Facilitating Environment: Studies in the Theory of Emotional Development* (Madison, Conn.: International Universities Press, 1965), 179–92, esp. 179.

24. Brown and Gilligan, *Meeting at the Crossroads*, 9, 10. It is significant that, in the popular culture of the United States, the silence of adolescent boys is construed as an active struggle against parents and adults in general.

25. Ibid., 11.

26. Carol Gilligan, "Remapping the Moral Domain: New Images of the Self in Relationship," in *Reconstructing Individualism: Autonomy, Individuality, and the Self in Western Thought*, ed. Thomas C. Heller, Morton Sosna, and David E. Wellbery (Stanford, Calif.: Stanford University Press, 1986), 251.

27. Winnicott, "On Communicating and Not Communicating," 187.

28. Gilligan, *In a Different Voice*, 1, 2.

29. Brown and Gilligan, *Meeting at the Crossroads*, 3, 4 (emphasis added), 20–21, 36.

30. Ibid., 23.

31. D. W. Winnicott, "The Location of Cultural Experience," in *Playing and Reality* (1967; rpt., New York: Tavistock, 1982), 98.

32. For cross-cultural examples, see Mahoney and Yngvesson, "Construction of Subjectivity."

33. Daniel Stern, *The First Relationship: Infant and Mother* (Cambridge, Mass.: Harvard University Press, 1977). See also Daniel Stern, *The Interpersonal World of the Infant: A View from Psychoanalysis and Developmental Psychology* (New York: Basic Books, 1985).

34. Much of the research on the development of sex differences has focused on the assertion that girls are more relationally oriented than boys. Gilligan (*In a Different Voice*), Nancy Chodorow (*The Reproduction of Mothering: Psychoanalysis and the Sociology of Gender* [Berkeley and Los Angeles: University of California Press, 1978]), and to some extent, Jessica Benjamin (*The Bonds of Love*), take this assertion as a description of reality and try to give a developmental account of how it came to be. Others (critics of Gilligan) argue that there is no empirical documentation of such a difference; see, for example, Ann Colby and William Damon, "Listening to a Different Voice: A Review of Gilligan's *In a Different Voice*," *Merrill-Palmer Quarterly* 29, no. 4 (1983): 473–81. That the assumption of such a difference has influenced thinking about proper roles for women and men, at least since the nineteenth century in the United States, is indisputable.

35. Brown and Gilligan, *Meeting at the Crossroads*, 40.

36. Kaplan, "Narrative Contract," 112. Jacobs quoted in ibid., 99.

37. Winnicott quoted in Adam Phillips, *Winnicott* (Cambridge, Mass.: Harvard University Press, 1988), 70.

38. Indeed, this narrative about the isolation of mother and child, as if they interacted "in a bell jar," isolated from history and culture, is one of the major weaknesses of classical object relations theory. See Henriques et al., *Changing the Subject*.

39. Steedman, *Landscape for a Good Woman*, 2.

40. Ibid., 2, 6.

41. Abel, "Race, Class, and Psychoanalysis," 191.

42. Audre Lorde, *Zami: A New Spelling of My Name* (Trumansburg, N.Y.: Crossing Press, 1982), 17–18.

43. This latter experience is related to what has been termed the "impostor syndrome." See P. R. Clance, *The Impostor Phenomenon: When Success Makes You Feel Like a Fake* (New York: Bantam Books, 1985); see also Peggy McIntosh, "Feeling Like a Fraud," Stone Center Working Papers Series, Paper no. 18 (Wellesley, Mass.: Wellesley College, 1985).

# Want to Learn More?

### Wellesley Centers for Women

Two organizations, the Center for Research on Women and the Stone Center, compose Wellesley's Centers for Women. Both are committed to facilitating research on women's issues. Their mission is not only to conduct the research but to make information and education about women available to policy makers and the general public. The Stone Center, in particular, focuses on women's psychological development, providing workshops and training for clinicians and others.

Wellesley Centers for Women
Wellesley College
106 Central Street
Wellesley, MA 02481
Telephone (781) 283-2500
www.wellesley.edu/wcw

### American Association of University Women

Among its other activities, the AAUW has recently been a leader in assessing research on the problems girls face in schools. Two reports have generated national debate on this issue: "Shortchanging Girls, Shortchanging America" and "Gender Gaps: Where Schools Still Fail Our Children." Although the core of the AAUW's mission is related to education, the organization also seeks to influence public debate and policy on sex discrimination in general, welfare reform, pay equity, and other matters of great concern to women.

American Association of University Women
1111 Sixteenth Street, NW
Washington, DC 20036
Telephone (800) 326-AAUW
www.AAUW.org

### Radcliffe Institute for Advanced Study

Founded in the fall of 1999, the Radcliffe Institute carries on the tradition of Radcliffe College in supporting interdisciplinary research on women, gender, and society. Included in the institute is the Murray Research Center, which makes available the nation's largest database on human development across the life span. Scholars come to the center to pursue projects on a variety of topics, including women's psychological development.

Radcliffe Institute for Advanced Study
10 Garden Street
Cambridge, MA 02138
Telephone (617) 495-8601
www.radcliffe.edu

### The Institute for Research on Women and Gender, Stanford University

The Institute for Research on Women and Gender supports interdisciplinary scholarship on women's economic and social roles. Recent projects have focused on adolescent pregnancy, women's autobiographies, and redefining family values. The institute seeks to make research on women and gender available to the public and to policy makers.

The Institute for Research on Women and Gender
Serra House
556 Salvatierra Walk
Stanford University
Stanford, CA 94305-8640
Telephone (650) 723-1994
www.stanford.edu/group/IRWG

# 3

# Political Leadership for Women: Redefining Power and Reassessing the Political

**Susan C. Bourque**

## ■ BACKGROUND

The day after I graduated from Cornell University in 1965 I flew to Lima to spend the next two years conducting research in coastal and Andean Peru. The focus of my research was the study of social change in peasant societies, and my particular area of concern was how the process affected women's attitudes and opportunities. That experience profoundly shaped my life and intellectual pursuits.

From the outset I have been fascinated by the study of women and politics. Initially I was puzzled by the lack of attention to women's political activity and sought to understand how women—whom I saw as active and politically engaged—could be dismissed and discounted in academic studies. My work in Latin America made it clear to me that this pattern was not limited to the United States but rather deeply embedded in international development politics. I came to see that when governments overlooked, ignored, or minimized women's interests or contributions, the results would be detrimental not only for women but ultimately for the community and nation.

Over the past thirty years, as I have been writing about women's lives in a variety of cultural settings, I have been heartened by the widespread institutional change that has occurred both in the United States and throughout the world. There is also significant reform in the way scholars today treat women's experience, and the study of politics has broadened to capture women's experience in both formal and informal political action. The United Nations conferences have done a great deal to identify areas for collaboration across national borders and have clarified the location of resistance to change.

Nevertheless, I am concerned that our pool of women leaders has not expanded more rapidly or more extensively. In this essay I have addressed some of the factors that continue to limit women's opportunities for political leadership. I am eager to see opportunities for leadership expanded and remain painfully aware that the social change necessary to make this possible is only beginning to be recognized in the political world.

POLITICAL leadership in modern democracies remains unconquered territory for women. This is as true in the United States as it is throughout much of the world.[1] Because culture and gender relations are embedded in political life, focus on this redoubt of masculine dominance clarifies the obstacles to women's leadership. In politics the stakes are high: to a remarkable extent political institutions structure public and private life as well as the distribution of resources and opportunities. Access to leadership in those institutions is critical for any group that wishes to shape the public agenda, or more particularly, wishes to reshape the distribution of resources and public goods.[2] The paradox explored in this paper is why American women—who today constitute 52 percent of the electorate—enjoy so little political leadership. During the 106th Congress (1998–2000) women held only 12.9 percent of the seats in the U.S. House of Representatives and constituted only 9 percent of the Senate. In the entire history of the republic only one woman has been nominated for the vice-presidency by a major party.[3]

When we speak of political leadership we deal with a controlling mechanism of public life, one imbued with enormous capacity to effect change, and one marked by some of the most conservative elements in American culture. Here as elsewhere, the picture that emerges of women's political leadership over the past twenty-five years is mixed: there have been some substantial gains, but there is still significant inequity.

Despite rates of political participation comparable to men, political leadership continues to elude women. Even as one barrier after the next fades away and women gain seats on the Supreme Court, leading cabinet positions, governorships, and Senate seats, their numbers remain small, and those in the pipeline for the presidency, vice-presidency, and Congress remain very limited

indeed.[4] Even as our perceptions of the appropriateness of women's political
and public life are broadened, we must ask what factors continue to restrict
women's political leadership. It is noteworthy that the United States is 49th out
of 176 countries ranked on the percentage of women in the national legislature,
well behind all the Scandinavian countries as well as Germany, Austria, South
Africa, Australia, and Great Britain.[5] In this essay I argue that four aspects of
American life continue to limit women's political leadership and that these
factors have proved remarkably resistant. Nevertheless, there are promising av-
enues of change in the way we have broadened our understanding of women's
political behavior and deepened our critique of women's absence from the
nation's political elite.

## Four Factors That Limit Women's Political Leadership

### The Sexual Division of Domestic Labor

The sexual division of labor for home and child care has not altered to
keep step with women's increased labor force participation. The passage of the
Equal Pay Act in 1963 and antidiscrimination laws that followed the passage of
the Civil Rights Act of 1964 were followed by the reentry of married white
women into the labor force (following their exit after World War II). By 1992 a
majority of all mothers worked, and over two-thirds of employed mothers with
children under six were full-time workers.[6]

Nevertheless, as a number of recent studies have demonstrated, men's
share of household labor has not increased significantly over the past twenty-
five years.[7] Moreover, younger men are just as likely as middle-aged men to
expect that their wives will be responsible for the majority of child care and
housework. The lack of affordable child care results in a demanding set of
expectations for working women, especially in homes of moderate or modest
means or for single mothers.

### The Structure of Work and the Persistence of Sex Role Expectations

The American workplace is only beginning to adapt to the reality of the
generative needs of the work force. While there have been some advances in
flextime and decentralized workplaces, the "fast track" and career ladders to
the high-paying, high-prestige positions are limited to those who can dedicate
long hours and weekends to their jobs. To a significant extent the American
workplace is still geared to the model of one worker with a support staff at
home.

Both of these first two factors reflect the persistence over time of sex role

expectations. Despite the significant changes in women's responsibilities outside the home, their responsibilities within have not lessened. As study after
study suggests, this lack of change has had enormous impact on the lives of
women who pursue political leadership.[8] "Republican motherhood" is as old
as the Republic, and its Aristotelian roots still have deep resonance in American life.[9] Public assumptions about the home and family as the bedrock of
democracy and women's roles in that family place important parameters
around women's leadership in politics.

It is still the case that a woman candidate will face much closer public
scrutiny about the care of her family than a comparably situated man. The
male candidate with young children encounters little constituent concern
about the impact of a rigorous congressional career or political campaign on
his family. And the presence of an admiring spouse and handsome children is
deemed an important assurance of the candidate's heterosexual credentials.[10]
A man without such credentials might encounter probing questions about his
private life and sexual proclivities.[11]

On the other hand, a woman with the same young children still encounters questions about the likely impact of the campaign and the demands of the
job she seeks on her children. Her admiring spouse may encounter other concerns about who is truly the head of the household. Consequently, women
with young children often delay their political careers. Only five women under
forty served in the 106th U.S. Congress, while there were twenty-seven men in
the same age group. This "late start" sets in motion a series of restrictions on
women's political careers, often limiting their opportunities for leadership.

*Ambivalence about Women Exercising Power*

A third and more subtle factor that confronts the woman leader is the
continuing ambivalence in American society about women and the exercise
of power. Freudians attribute this to the overwhelming power of mothers in
the early years of a child's life and the desire of adults to disassociate themselves
from their early memories of dependence. Non-Freudians simply note the dis-
sonance powerful women create for our conceptions of which sex is powerful.

Feminist thinkers have also expressed conflicting attitudes about women's
exercise of power, and a lively debate continues on the subject. Concern about
the abuse of power has led some women to redefine power, claiming that
women leaders have less interest in exercising power "over" others and instead
wish to "empower" others, or wish only the power "to effect social change."[12]
They argue that women desire political power not for selfish personal aggran-

dizement but rather for an "other-regarding" power to effect change for the public good. There is a certain romanticism and essentialism inherent in this position. It is reminiscent of late-nineteenth-century suffragist claims that women's moral superiority would reshape and improve the political order if they gained the vote.

Related to this concern with power is another central debate in the feminist community over political leadership. *Transformational* feminists have argued that political institutions as presently constructed will never be adequately responsive to the disadvantaged or address the needs of those in poverty or those who suffer discrimination and oppression.[13] For these analysts, an emphasis on placing more women into office is a failed strategy. For despite the evidence that women leaders address questions of concern to women to a far greater degree than men — regardless of political party — transformational feminists feel that politics as currently structured fails to address the needs of the majority of women.

They argue that for women to be successful candidates in the current system, they must moderate their positions to such a degree that they become ineffective as agents of change. As a consequence class, race, and ethnicity remain submerged issues. Transformational feminists conclude that adding more women to the current political structures will not be adequate; instead, a transformation of American political institutions is necessary.

In addition, transformational feminists suggest that a much broader focus and definition of politics are essential to capturing the full spectrum of women's political leadership. They include community activism and church leadership as important realms where women's leadership emerges. They argue that in these arenas the muting of women's voices that is essential to women's success in formal politics on the national or state level is not necessary. As a result, more effective restructuring and reordering of priorities and agendas can take place. Moreover, they remind us that race and ethnicity have an enormous impact on gender relations, and for nonwhite women, ties to racial and ethnic communities may be far more important than gender issues.

*Perceptual Issues: First Ladies and "No Problem" Problems*

Not all feminists reach the same conclusions as the transformational feminists. Many women are interested in political leadership and comfortable with the idea of exercising power within existing institutions. Nevertheless, even these women will encounter constituents who are resistant to women leaders. That resistance is exacerbated in the United States by an idealized nonpolitical role assigned to women: the first lady. Women candidates encounter the high-profile role of "first lady" and the ambiguity this role creates for women in elected office. Strong first ladies with interests in political life elicit criticism and even censure if they are deemed too involved in the nonceremonial aspects of their husband's political careers. Media attention to the high-profile first lady positions puts an emphasis on women in a subordinate, nonpolitical status. Women who pursue electoral politics, and seek to enter the fray as leaders in their own right, challenge the idealized widespread symbol of female as helpmate.[14]

The media play a major role in how we perceive women leaders. There is solid evidence that the media shape public perceptions of the strengths, weaknesses, and political viability of candidates.[15] There is also evidence that media coverage of women can be particularly harsh.[16] The media also shape our perception of women's presence or absence in leadership positions, at times clarifying women's absence and galvanizing action and at other times overemphasizing their presence and perhaps giving a false impression of their impact.[17]

The third perceptual issue for the woman leader is the denial of sexual inequality. As Deborah Rhode writes:

> "Women's growing opportunities are taken as evidence that the 'woman problem' has been solved." This perception has itself become a central problem. The "no problem" problem prevents Americans from noticing that on every major measure of wealth, power, and status, women still are significantly worse off than men. . . . While we have made considerable progress in encouraging women to pursue traditional male roles, we have been less effective in encouraging men to assume traditional female ones. Women continue to shoulder the vast majority of responsibilities in the home, a burden that limits their responsibilities outside it.[18]

Each of these factors contributes to women's limited leadership roles. But before we can fully appreciate women's roles in contemporary politics we need to examine how the context for women's leadership has changed.

## Sources of Change

Despite the challenges and obstacles noted above, women's roles in politics have undergone marked change in the past twenty-five years. First, there have been significant changes in public perceptions of women as political actors. Second, there have been marked changes in women's political behavior, including voting and officeholding. Third, there have been notable changes in how we study women in political life. In some arenas the breadth and depth of change are so notable that it begs the question of why leadership rates lag so far behind. But in a number of areas, such as the public perception of women as political actors and the recruitment patterns for women leaders, change is accompanied by persistent and limiting sex stereotypes.

### Public Acceptance of Women as Political Actors

Nancy McGlen and Karen O'Connor report that in 1969, 40 percent of those interviewed responded that they would not vote for a woman for president. From 1967 to 1975 support for a female president among women college graduates rose from 51 to 88 percent and among male college graduates from 58 to 91 percent. By 1992 a Gallop poll found 92 percent of women and 88 percent of men indicated they would vote for a qualified woman for president if their party nominated her.[19]

While there has been growing support for women's leadership, survey data indicate that the public distinguished between the arenas of public life best suited for men and women along sex-stereotyped lines. Women were perceived as better suited for domestic issues and men for international affairs. Respondents to a 1990 Virginia Slims survey indicated they felt that men in public office would be better at "directing the military and making war decisions," while women would be better at "working for world peace." Women in public life were deemed better at maintaining honesty and integrity in government, assisting the poor, improving education, and protecting the environment, among a host of other "domestic" concerns.[20]

While these are sex-stereotyped characteristics, in 1992 the characteristics associated with women became attractive to many American voters and enhanced the appeal of women candidates. Sue Thomas points out the difficulties that women leaders face when confronted with these persistent stereotypes of the appropriate political arenas for women's leadership.

> Simply put, women politicians are between a rock and a hard place. If they reject and fight against depictions that women's skills and knowledge are superior to men's on certain issues, they will lose the advantage of support from an electorate that, at least at the moment, wants people in office with those qualities. On the other hand, if

female candidates play to those expectations they risk limiting their current and future political input to those areas.[21]

What makes these gender stereotypes pernicious is the ease with which they become linked to "essentialist" conceptions of women and serve as limiting factors on women's careers. As long as women are not seen as competent in the areas of national defense, it is hard to imagine that they will gain the powerful committee chairs in the Congress or become viable candidates for the presidency. Pat Schroeder, who fought long and hard for a seat on the House Armed Services Committee, recounts the resistance of the committee chair and its members to her lack of military service. She was able to silence her challengers when she pointed out that a substantial proportion of the men on the committee also lacked military service. Men without military service had been deemed appropriate members of the committee, whereas a woman was challenged on that basis.[22]

### Women's Political Behavior

Women's political behavior has also changed. Until the 1970s political scientists dismissed women as political actors, claiming—with sparse, dated, and ambiguous evidence—that women voted as their husbands did.[23] The tendency of the discipline was to discount women. Several events occurred simultaneously in the 1970s and 1980s that altered this perception of women's political interest.

First, women's rates of political participation increased. Women today turn out to vote at higher rates than men. That was not the case as recently as the 1970s, when *The American Voter* reported a 10 percent difference in voter turnout (controlling for SES, social and economic status), with men more likely to vote than women.[24] Political scientists attributed the differences to women's lesser interest in politics and argued that the discrepancy was unlikely to change. Few had noted that the presence of preschool children accounted for almost all the variation between men's and women's turnout rates. Still fewer noted that African American women consistently had higher voter turnout rates than predicted by SES factors. The pioneering work of Sandra Baxter and Marjorie Lansing opened up the examination of race and gender differences in voter participation that continues in today's discussions of the gender gap.[25]

### The Gender Gap

Along with the increased turnout rates, a "gender gap" emerged in the 1980 presidential election and captured the imagination of the American press.

Suddenly women had a political agenda and a political voice. The "discovery" of a gender gap has contributed to the recognition of women's interest in politics. Gender gap studies are an important addition to the study of political behavior that was unthinkable even twenty-five years ago.

When Maurice Duverger wrote about women's voting preferences in the 1950s, he characterized women as much more conservative than men. Basing his data on French and German women's support for conservative Catholic and anticommunist parties, Duverger's characterization stuck until the gender gap forced political scientists to take a different view of the data.[26] The term *gender gap* was coined to describe women's higher level of support for the Democratic presidential candidate. Women were more supportive of Walter Mondale (the losing Democratic candidate) than men, and less supportive of Ronald Reagan, the Republican victor. This pattern has held in every presidential race since 1980, with women far more supportive of the Democrats' candidate. In every instance the Democrat has been viewed as the more liberal candidate. Political scientists today report the greater tendency of women to support the liberal position on most policy concerns.

The preference of women voters for the Democratic nominees led to new political aspirations for women within the party and a demand for better representation at party conventions. Women made up 40 percent of the convention delegates by the early 1970s, and in 1978 the Democratic National Committee endorsed parity for future conventions. In 1984, just four years after the emergence of the gender gap, the Democrats were the first major party to place a woman on the national ticket.[27] Geraldine Ferraro was nominated for vice-president and became Walter Mondale's running mate in their spectacularly unsuccessful campaign against Ronald Reagan in 1984. Organized Democratic women were in large part responsible for the Ferraro nomination.[28] The Republicans initially responded to the challenge by trying to dismiss the Ferraro nomination, characterizing it as "the Democrats catering to special interests." Nevertheless, over time they have sought to improve their appeal to women and to increase the number of female Republican candidates.

Because women throughout the 1990s had a higher turnout rate than men, both candidates in the 2000 presidential race made efforts to appeal to women voters. The past preference of women for Democratic presidential candidates led to considerable concerns in Al Gore's campaign when he did not appear to have the same appeal to women voters.[29] The Gore campaign made one attempt after another to attract female voters and by mid-August of the 2000 presidential campaign the gender gap was again apparent and very much in Gore's favor. The Republicans also made efforts to improve their appeal to women voters through their rhetoric of "compassionate conservatism." Nevertheless, this direct appeal to the gender stereotype of women's concerns may not be sufficient to offset the party's anti-choice platform plank.

### The Women's Movement

Along with increased and more liberal voting, women have become more politically active. First and foremost, they increased their activism through the women's movement and the other social movements of the late 1960s and 1970s (civil rights and antiwar movements in particular). But they also increased their rates of electoral participation as candidates at the state and local level. There was as well a gradual increase in women officeholders throughout the period, with the proportion rising to 5 percent in the U.S. Congress and 20 percent in the state legislatures by 1990. Women held 14 percent of mayoral offices and positions on local governing boards in 1985.

Moreover, the gender consciousness that accompanied women's increased participation made many women leaders acutely aware of how an organized women's movement could lobby for an enhanced role for women in electoral politics. The women's movement also had a substantial impact on the increased "gender consciousness" of women legislators and consequently on the policy agendas they supported.[30] Gender consciousness also enhanced the appeal of women candidates to female constituents.[31]

In addition, the passage of gender equity legislation meant that many more women had been able to pursue professional and graduate education. That meant more women with the business and law backgrounds that placed them in what scholars have referred to as the social eligibility pool.[32] That is, they had the background characteristics traditionally associated with male political leaders.

Given these important shifts in women's political behavior and the changing attitudes of the public, what has this meant for women's political leadership? One way of addressing this question is to look at the experience of women leaders over the course of the past twenty-five years.

## 1975 to 2000: Twenty-five Years of Women Leaders

### Studies of Women Leaders

When political scientists sought to understand the basis for women's exclusion from political leadership, they looked to elected women officials to assess what allowed their success. A number of studies of women state legislators were done in the 1970s, including Jeane Kirkpatrick's *Political Woman*

(1972) and Irene Diamond's *Sex Roles in the State House* (1977). Both studies were based on surveys and interviews with women in state legislatures because there were too few women in the U.S. Congress to provide an adequate sample. Susan Carroll's *Women as Candidates in American Politics* (1985) contained material on both state and national female candidates for office. In contrast to studies that emphasized sex role socialization as a barrier to women's political leadership, Carroll's analysis emphasized the obstacles built into the political structure that limited women's opportunities for leadership. Regardless of changes in sex role socialization, these are factors external to individual women that nevertheless shape their opportunities.

All of these studies concluded that it was the tremendous hold of incumbency and financial factors that explained women's limited numbers. Incumbents, the majority of whom were men, had too great an advantage over any competitors, male or female.

Political party leadership was also a restraint. When open seats occurred (the incumbent retired), party leadership would be eager to nominate a candidate they felt would win. Women, at least until the 1990s, were thought to be less likely to be successful candidates. Many in the party leadership feared women would be unable to attract financial support for their campaigns.[33] The notion that women might support other women was not seriously considered, and the belief was widespread that men would prefer the male candidate—not because of maleness per se, but rather because of the greater likelihood of a victory. In addition, Kirkpatrick reported male resistance to women's claims on political leadership:

> Some women encountered resistance from male party leaders when
> they sought nominations, others did not. Almost all were met with
> doubts and reservations when they first entered the legislature. . . .
> The women who rose into leadership roles report male efforts to
> freeze them out; and they report overcoming these obstacles. Most of
> the women legislators feel that members of their sex would be barred
> from the top offices, e.g., Speaker, Majority Leader; male legislators
> interviewed in this study agree.[34]

But Kirkpatrick concludes that there was no conscious conspiracy of males to exclude women from office. "There is some resistance to nominating women, voting for them, accepting them as legislative colleagues, [and] admitting them to leadership positions." The studies from the 1970s indicate that male legislators did not welcome women into their ranks. Women were perceived as outsiders and different, and there was clear evidence of a "male reluctance to share power."[35] Women legislators were equally aware that they were unwelcome.

The life circumstances and self-perception of women elected to state office in the 1970s are revealing. The women were older than their male colleagues, and most had married and raised children before entering the legislature. They had successfully combined traditional gender roles with political leadership. Kirkpatrick reports that all of them expected to meet their obligations to husbands and children and saw those obligations as primary, their political careers as secondary. None of the women expected equal contributions to housework or child rearing from their husbands, and none seemed to resent their dual roles.

While accepting the prevailing beliefs about sex role responsibilities in marriage and the home, these women had not accepted the cultural message that women were unsuited for politics. Socialization had not limited their aspirations for leadership. Finally, women in the state legislatures in the 1970s were more liberal ideologically than their male counterparts. Nevertheless, despite their marked presence on the legislative committees for education and social welfare and their support for social welfare issues, they were eager to distance themselves from any particular or special concern for women. They thought of themselves as elected to represent the needs of all their constituents, with no particular responsibility to women.

By the 1980s a number of changes were apparent in the women elected to state legislatures. To begin with, their numbers were growing, and the new occupational and educational opportunities opened to women began to show in the backgrounds of women leaders. Women legislators were now more likely to have had a background in business or management and to have had prior political experience before entering the legislature. Sue Thomas reports the following similarities between the 1970s and 1980s cohorts of women state legislators: "They reported liberal ideological stances in greater proportions than men, a gender gap on specific issues continued and their voting records reflected greater support for issues related to women, to families and to general social welfare concerns."[36]

Despite these similarities, however, a number of significant changes were apparent. In the late 1980s women in the state legislatures expressed a clear responsibility to represent "women." Moreover, they supported and worked for an agenda of women's concerns to a far greater extent than their male colleagues. Thomas concludes: "Women [legislators] of the 1980s developed dif-

ferent policy priorities than men. Issues of women, children and families went
to the top of their agendas. The differentiation that was not evident between
women and men [state legislators] in the 1970s has manifested itself in the
more recent era."[37]

Heightened attention to women's issues was also accompanied by a greater
sense of political efficacy among the women legislators surveyed in the 1980s.
They appeared to be more confident in their statehouse roles. Thomas notes
an important brake on their political involvement, however: "Greater access
to the public arena did not free them from their responsibilities in the private
one. For most women, their public sphere role was only half their job; they
continued to bear the major responsibility for home and hearth."[38]

Women state legislators in the 1980s report that while discrimination had
become less overt, covert discrimination continued and was felt most poi-
gnantly when women sought leadership positions within the legislature. Once
elected, women want committee assignments that allow them to shape and
pass the legislation they support. Women have begun to attain leadership positions within state legislatures, but all of the women Thomas studied remarked
that it had been a struggle.[39]

Nevertheless, despite the struggle to gain leadership positions, there was
clear evidence that female state legislators voted differently than their male
counterparts and had a different set of priorities. In short, their presence in
increasing numbers and growing experience made a difference. I hasten to
add that there is nothing inherently "essentialist" about the women legislators'
distinct priorities. Given women's continuing secondary status and their continued responsibilities for home and children, the need to address those concerns was readily apparent to female legislators. The important change in the
1980s was that women—despite party differences—saw the need to do so to a
far greater extent than their male colleagues.

*Leadership and Money: The Role of Women's PACs and Emily's List*

All political office seekers worry about fund-raising for their political campaigns. Women in particular seem to be at a disadvantage in their ability to
raise money. They do not have the same corporate ties as their male counterparts, and a tradition of women contributing to political campaigns did not
develop until the 1980s.

Women, and particularly feminist groups, set out to change this pattern
by establishing a group of fund-raising organizations to support women candidates. By 1989 there were over thirty groups focused on female candidates,
and by 1992 over forty-two. The Fund for a Feminist Majority, the Women's

Campaign Fund, and Emily's List are among the most successful groups. Emily's List is perhaps best known. The acronym stands for "Early money is like yeast—it raises the dough." The organization, founded in 1985 by Ellen Malcolm, represents an important change in women's political fortunes. Emily's List is both a fund-raising and political training organization. The need for such an organization underscores the centrality of fund-raising—money—to leadership in American politics.

But Emily's List and the other women's political action committees (PACs) also challenge the assumption that women candidates would not be able to raise money effectively or that women would not financially support the campaigns of female candidates. Women state legislators in the 1970s reported that fund-raising was a serious problem and that women had not contributed significantly to their campaigns. By the 1980s this had changed, and Emily's List had remarkable success supporting women for political office. In the 1990s it raised more money than the Democratic National Committee, and it was a force to be reckoned with in the 1992 elections. Emily's List alone raised more than $6.2 million in 1992 and donated to the campaigns of fifty-five women candidates.[40] To demonstrate the significance of the change in the 1992 election, consider this comparison: women candidates received approximately $2.6 million from PACs in 1990 and $11.5 million in 1992.

In addition to money, Emily's List provides hard-nosed assessment and training for its candidates. Support does not come automatically to any candidate who wishes funding. The funds are meant to support pro-choice female Democratic candidates. Furthermore, the candidate must have a reasonable chance of winning, which means a solid campaign organization. Candidates who wish support and endorsement are rigorously assessed. Money for political campaigns is always in limited supply, and Emily's List will not squander its resources on candidates who have no realistic chance of mounting a competitive campaign. Emily's List and the Women's Campaign Fund have also committed themselves to increasing the number of minority women in politics and have targeted their campaigns for support.

And what about the Republicans? They too have organizations to support Republican women candidates. The Wish List (Women in the Senate and House), similar to Emily's List, supports viable pro-choice Republican women candidates. Several PACs support pro-life Republican women, and RENEW (The Republican Network to Elect Women) was founded in 1992 to support Republican women candidates regardless of their position on abortion.[41] Susan Carroll points out that neither of the two major parties can ignore the initiatives of the other to include more women. Thus, the lead taken by women in the Democratic Party to push for equity has put pressure on the Republicans to follow suit.[42] The National Women's Political Caucus is a bipartisan group committed to electing more women regardless of party preference.

### The Political Context of the 1990s

In addition to a vastly improved funding network and substantially more funding for women candidates, a number of other factors converged in the early 1990s to create a political context that offered women new entrée to leadership. First, the end of the Cold War brought about a dramatic lessening in world tensions. While the Gulf War briefly rekindled support for a strong military and may have influenced the 1990 election, the overall tenor of the 1990s has been a cautious attitude toward military adventurism and lessened concern with military posturing. This helps undercut the claim that women are ill suited for political leadership because they lack the ability to direct the military.

Second, a series of political scandals surrounding corrupt practices in the House of Representatives led a number of members to resign rather than face the ire of the public for what was deemed inappropriate use of public monies. Also, new rules that restricted the use of campaign funds after 1992 led other sitting members of the House to retire. Resignations and redistricting based on the results of the 1990 census led to a record number of open seats.

Thus, 1992 was an exceptionally propitious year for women. It combined the structural and institutional changes that benefited female candidates— such as open seats—with a positive assessment of the female stereotypes. Far more open seats, the result of both reapportionment and resignations, lessened the number of incumbents and increased the number of districts in which women found an even playing field. Because it is difficult to defeat an incumbent and most incumbents are male, women have a better chance of election in years when they can compete for open seats.

In addition to open seats, in 1992 the stereotyped view of women as trustworthy, honest, and less open to corruption made them attractive candidates. Moreover, the stereotype that women are more pacific than men, less interested in and capable of using force, was not as limiting a factor in this post–Cold War environment. In a paradoxical fashion, stereotypes that in the past were disadvantageous to women appealed to voters in 1992.

But it is critical to remember that women could not have capitalized on the opportunities available in 1992 without the experience of the prior twenty years. The women who ran for the U.S. Congress in that election had been in the political pipeline, serving as state legislators and in local politics. They had the appropriate experience to present to the electorate. Patti Murray, who ran as "a mom in sneakers," a political "outsider," had actually served as a senator in the Washington state legislature.[43] In addition, women's organizations and PACs spent a great deal of effort getting ready for the 1992 elections. They helped identify candidates for the open seats and encouraged viable women to run.

Given the changes noted above, what can we say about women political leaders in the late 1990s? First, we know a great deal more about them. Knowledge about women in politics has burgeoned. Also, following the 1992 elections, there are now sufficient numbers of women in the U.S. House of Representatives to make that group the focus of survey analysis.

The Center for the American Woman and Politics (CAWP), a research center that has carefully tracked women's political behavior for the past thirty years, has completed an extensive study of the impact of women in the 103d Congress. *Voices, Views, Votes* (1995) builds on CAWP's pioneering work on women in the state legislatures. Those studies demonstrated significant differences between men and women in their political priorities and voting records. With the 103d Congress CAWP undertook a multifaceted project to assess the variety of ways in which women legislators made a difference across a range of policy issues. The study was based on interviews with congressional staffers as well as members of Congress and utilized extensive analysis of documents.

This rich and exhaustive study demonstrated that "even though they were a mere one-tenth of the membership and slightly more than half of them were freshmen, the Congresswomen found ways to have an impact."[44] The CAWP researchers broadened their analysis beyond a narrow focus on voting records and legislation sponsored. They sought instead a fuller and deeper understanding of how elected women leaders are able to shape and influence legislation by their presence in the Congress. Elected women were able to shape legislation in the committee structure to reflect an expanded range of concerns and ultimately to influence the fate of legislation.

As we have seen in studies of women in the state legislatures, the CAWP data indicate that women and men voted differently on bills. Moreover, with over twenty-five new members the Women's Congressional Caucus had new life and energy. The women of the 103d Congress felt a special responsibility to represent women and were able to advance a collective agenda. That agenda was in turn shaped by the continuing influence of women's pressure groups outside Congress and support from influential male colleagues. Women of course did not agree on every issue or on the priority that each issue should be assigned. There were important cleavages along party and racial lines. Nevertheless, the CAWP study notes that subgroups of women found ways to work together on common interests not necessarily shared by the larger group.[45]

These aggregate findings are impressive and tell us that it has made a difference to have women in the highest-level political positions in the United States. But this is only part of the story of women's leadership. The very small number of women in these positions, less than 15 percent of the House of Representatives and 9 percent of the Senate, raises questions about the women leaders themselves and the obstacles they have overcome.

One route of inquiry is to look at the psychological characteristics of women in political leadership. The study by Dorothy Cantor and Toni Bernay, *Women in Power: The Secrets of Leadership* (1992), profiles some outstanding women leaders, including Pat Schroeder, Ann Richards, Nancy Johnson, and Olympia Snowe. The authors set out to describe the common psychological traits of these leaders and the factors that allowed them to overcome considerable obstacles. As with the women state legislators in the 1970s and 1980s, the women studied by Cantor and Bernay all have very high self-esteem and a sense of competence, and they possess what the authors call "creative aggression" and a desire to have a positive impact on the world.

Beyond common psychological traits, women in the 103d Congress confronted barriers to their leadership that are built into congressional institutions, such as the rules of seniority in committee assignments and the expectations of party loyalty. Clara Bingham's study *Women on the Hill: Challenging the Culture of Congress* (1997) provides an insightful perspective on the political landscape of Congress and women's efforts to deal with those institutions and still remain effective agents for change.

The Class of 1992, the women elected during the much-acclaimed "year of the woman," saw themselves as much more committed to women's issues. They had come to Congress on the heels of the Clarence Thomas confirmation hearings. The treatment of Anita Hill, who charged Thomas with sexual harassment, by the all white male Senate Judiciary Committee, graphically brought home to women in America "that the Senate was largely a white male preserve where women's concerns were often trivialized or ignored."[46] Women ran for office and were elected to office in record numbers. When they arrived in Washington they intended to make changes, and they organized to accomplish their goal.

During their brief tenure, aided by a sympathetic White House, they had some notable successes. With the help of their male colleagues, they passed the Violence against Women Act and the Freedom of Access to Clinic Entrances Act, a major victory for pro-choice forces. They fought successfully for gun control and attempted unsuccessfully to lift the ban on the use of federal funds for abortion. They even managed to elect one of their number as president of the incoming congressional class. But even so, they were still only 47 out of a total of 435, and they still felt like outsiders.

They received a great deal of media attention, a factor that heightened public expectations that they would be able to achieve considerable change. But within the House their influence was limited by the weight of the seniority rules. Over half of the women were "freshmen," or first-term members of Congress. Consequently, they were at the bottom rung in the distribution of committee assignments. Nevertheless, their numbers were such that the presence of two or three women on several subcommittees had an impact on the formulation and fate of legislation.

They also organized and brought new life to the Congressional Women's Caucus. At the first meeting of the group in January 1993, Louise Slaughter (D-N.Y.), a veteran of the lean years for women, looked at the thirteen new faces around the table, breathed a sigh of relief, and remarked, "I feel like the cavalry has just arrived."[47]

From the perspective of feminists, the tragedy of the 103d Congress was that it was followed by the 104th. The Democrats lost control of the House and with that eight of the Democratic women. The survivors returned to a far more conservative and antifeminist House. The absolute number of women representatives remained constant, but the six newly elected Republican women did not support a feminist agenda and pointedly distanced themselves from the women's caucus.[48] Nevertheless, despite the defeats of 1994, there were those who argued that the impact of women on the Congress would not be lost. Bingham concludes her study: "When the Republicans took over in January, the Congress they had been elected to control was no longer the same place it had been two years earlier. Anita Hill's class of congresswomen had made their mark on the institution."[49]

But for some of the women leaders the culture of Congress had not changed, despite their long years of effort. Pat Schroeder (D-Colo.), the "dean" of congresswomen, commented during her last spring on the Hill (she returned to private life after the 104th Congress): "I can't get into the meetings where the decisions are made. . . . My being here is like parsley on a potato. I can be a voice but it is a voice in the wilderness." This was her assessment after over twenty years in Congress. She described what she faced in 1995 as follows: "It's twenty times more painful to watch everything you've built come under attack and watch sexist attitudes loom. It's a lot more painful because I thought we had moved beyond that, and in fact you only realize how far we still have to go."[50] Compounding the significance of Schroeder's disillusionment is that she was a leader with great seniority in Congress. It will be years before another woman has a comparable position.

## The Year of the Woman and Its Aftermath

One way to encapsulate our concerns is a consideration of the year of the woman in politics and its aftermath. The *New Yorker* cartoon reproduced here is prescient—though it might not have been perceived as such when it first appeared in late 1992. At a New Year's celebration, a rather unhappy man looks at his watch and proclaims: "Well, one more minute and the goddam year of the woman will be over." Perhaps meant to suggest a male sense of loss and vain hope that women's enhanced political leadership will be short-lived, the cartoon instead proved accurate when the gains of the 1992 election were called into question with the election returns from 1994. The "Year of the Woman" was followed by the "Year of the Angry White Male."

The results of the 1992 election led many to conclude that the gains women are likely to register in the electoral realm are transitory and vulnerable to the continuing biases and fluctuations in American politics. It also underscored the important differences among women. As noted above, the number of women in Congress remained the same, but the newly elected members represented a very different ideological position on women's rights, especially reproductive rights.

The results of the 1994 election galvanized many other women to rekindle their efforts to elect women, especially pro-choice women. They agreed that women's lower turnout rates in 1994 were a significant part of the defeat suffered by Democratic candidates. In 1996, following effective candidate recruitment and fund-raising efforts by a range of organizations, twelve new women were elected to Congress, and two more were added in 1998. In 2000, sixty-five women served in the 106th Congress, eighteen of whom were women of color. None of these figures approach the gains of 1992. Instead we see slow incremental gains, with most gains occurring in "open seat" elections.

In preparation for the 2000 election, Emily's List joined with the state Democratic Party committees of California, Florida, Kentucky, Michigan, Minnesota, Missouri, Montana, New Jersey, New York, Ohio, Texas, and Washington to promote a campaign entitled Women Vote 2000. These were key states for the presidential race and also for the election of women candidates to the Senate and House. The campaign was aimed at getting women to the polls in the November presidential and congressional elections. The

*"Well, one more minute and the goddam year of the woman will be over."*

Democrats counted on women's continued support for their party's nominees and women's heightened political interest to provide the measure of victory. As of August 2000, the gender gap had again emerged, with women's support for the Democratic presidential candidate even more marked than previously.

Will women's contribution to electoral victory bring with it new leadership in the Congress? If the past is any indication of the future, male legislators are loath to adapt their rules to share power with newcomers. The evidence from studies of the 103d Congress suggests that women had a substantial impact despite their newcomer status and small numbers. Nevertheless, given the power of incumbents, women simply will not have the numerical strength or seniority within legislatures to gain significant leadership for some time.

## Reassessing Women's Leadership: The Future

As we have noted above, there is no single women's point of view, even on women's issues. We would never expect a male representative to speak for all men, or for men to feel that every male congressman had to represent the "male perspective." Certainly American men have not been able to construct a political movement that bridges the differences of race, class, and region.

Nevertheless, the issue is raised for women because there has been so little female representation and leadership and there is so much inequity to address. Who, then, can speak for women? And who can represent women? The political challenge for the female leader is to bridge the differences in women's experience and interests to build a movement that recognizes and builds upon diversity. Moreover, it is clear that the presence of a strong women's movement, lobbying outside formal political institutions and pressuring lawmakers, governors, and presidents to support the legislation that enhances women's status, can advance a feminist agenda and strengthen the position of female legislators.

Women in Congress have been effective in advancing a feminist agenda. But given their small number, women must have the collaboration and cooperation of their male colleagues. Moreover, getting elected is only the first hurdle; once elected, women confront a whole new set of hurdles presented by the structure of Congress and the way a large legislature of 435 is organized to do its work. That work is done through committees, and the chairs of committees—determined by majority party according to seniority—hold tremendous power. Women as newcomers have little seniority, and women in the minority party have even less power. Thus, it should not surprise us that women are absent from the leadership in Congress. No woman has ever chaired a major congressional committee, and the highest leadership positions held by women in Congress are vice-chair of the party conference and deputy whip.

## The International Arena

We must not leave our discussion of women's political leadership without acknowledging the dramatic change in women's leadership internationally. This is critical not only because we live in a much more global community but also because it helps us appreciate the degree to which issues of concern to women have found their way to the international level through the organized efforts of women throughout the world. The international realm also underscores the importance of links between grassroots nongovernmental women's organizations and women in the formal governmental sector.

Under the auspices of the United Nations, the concerns of women have received international attention as never before. Moreover, a degree of global consensus has emerged about the necessity for change and the routes to improving women's status. Bridging the enormous differences in culture, wealth, and ideology and despite differences in race, ethnicity, and nationality, the past twenty-five years have witnessed a new global focus on women's status. Under the title "Equality, Development, and Peace" and encompassing five international meetings, a growing consensus is emerging on women's needs for reproductive freedom and bringing an end to all forms of discrimination against women. Women's rights as human rights have become a byword of the movement.[51] This consensus is emerging despite the continuing tendency of political leaders in many parts of the world to insist on traditional roles for women to protect the "cultural integrity" of the nation from the encroachment of "Western feminist" values. That women's subordination should be a hallmark of national independence is one of the many paradoxical situations confronting women in the international realm.

The international conferences—Mexico City 1975, Copenhagen 1980, Nairobi 1985, Beijing 1995, and New York City 2000—organized as governmental-level meetings with official delegates, have been accompanied by a flourishing grassroots movement of nongovernmental organizations attacking the sources of women's inequity. Women and the organizations they have created have been the key players in this international effort. The movement represents an important conjunction between those women in leadership positions in formal governmental institutions and those working in the nongovernmental, grassroots organizations. In many ways this exemplifies the range of leadership positions in which women are currently found and the synergism between these forms of power and empowerment. The broad coalition of groups working for women's rights would not exist without the support of women in high-level political leadership who share the goals of social change. Equity and peace cannot be pursued for all women without the actions of both governmental and nongovernmental organizations.

The most recent meeting, Beijing Plus 5, held in New York City in June 2000, reaffirmed the universal rights of women agreed to at Beijing by 180 nations in 1995. The significant victory of the Beijing Plus 5 conference was that opponents of women's rights were unable to reverse women's gains. On the other hand, many feminist groups were disappointed that they were unable to make more progress, and they criticized the role played by the Vatican and fundamentalist religious groups in the proceedings. The most contentious issue continued to be the proposition that "women have the right to decide freely and responsibly on matters related to their sexuality" and should be free to do so without "coercion, discrimination, and violence." On the positive side, strong stands were taken against the trafficking of women and girls, and strong planks were written that called for the punishment of domestic violence, including marital rape.[52]

## Concluding Remarks

Politics has been a field that has undergone profound change; nevertheless, there are still unresolved issues for women's leadership. The profession of political science has come to understand the importance of gender to the study of political life. From a tendency to ignore or dismiss gender—as late as the 1970s—the discipline now has gender on its agenda. But while the subject of gender is deemed worthy of serious study and academic debate, feminists in the profession of political science question the degree to which research on gender has restructured the study of politics. Some feminist scholars have emphasized the need to look beyond traditional institutions and the formal political arena. Women's participation and leadership are much more likely to emerge in grassroots organizations, geared more specifically to women's needs and concerns. They argue that differences in race, class, and ideology have been submerged in pursuit of a "least common denominator agenda," and that the compromise necessary in the current male-structured political system will never serve women's interests adequately. They conclude that for the interests of the most disadvantaged women to be served, a wholly new conception of politics will be necessary.[53]

Other feminist scholars stress the significance of the growth in women's numbers in the formal seats of political power and the influence women have had on the political agenda. They note that ideology and party affiliation matter—but so too do numbers. Often women legislators share a common agenda across party lines.

We are just beginning to appreciate the new lessons the study of women's leadership will teach us about political life. While women have made new claims for political leadership in American politics, feminist scholars continue to ask why the process is so slow and so vulnerable to reversals. They continue to ask about the role of the media in shaping our perceptions of women leaders, and they point out the special impact of motherhood on women candidates. The sexual division of labor in the household and the persistence of sex role stereotypes and expectations continue to constrain women's political opportunities.

At the same time, it is clear that women have organized to identify and support female candidates as never before. It is also clear that women are insisting on a broader definition of who is "electable" and what constitute the relevant criteria by which to judge a candidate. Will a new generation of women leaders emerge, and will they find their way to national political leadership in the House and Senate and ultimately the presidency? This essay suggests that if they do so, it will have to be with new understandings of how our homes and work can be organized, with new definitions of who can lead, and with more universalized and less stereotyped conceptions of the leadership abilities of both men and women.

# Notes

My thanks to Donna R. Divine and Marysa Navarro-Aranguren for their comments on an earlier draft of this essay.

1. While the focus of this paper is the United States, it is important to bear in mind the international context. Women's political leadership is well advanced in the Scandinavian countries, far outstripping the rest of the world in terms of numbers of women in the national legislatures and elected heads of state. A number of countries—including Argentina and Brazil—are experimenting with a variety of quota systems reserving for women a percentage of slots on party lists or seats in national legislatures. The most recent to take this step are the French with the adoption of *parité* in 2000. There is considerable controversy over many of these new mechanisms, but all of them recognize the need for visible and numerous female representation at the leadership level of government. For a discussion of the Latin American experience see Marysa Navarro and Susan C. Bourque, "Fault Lines of Democratic Governance: A Gender Perspective," in *Fault Lines of Democracy in Post-Transition Latin America*, ed. Felipe Aguero and Jeffrey Stark (Miami: North-South Center Press, 1998), 175–202; also Jane Jaquette and Sharon Wolchik, *Women and Democracy: Latin America, Central and Eastern Europe* (Baltimore: Johns Hopkins University Press, 1998).

2. To illustrate with one key example, consider the case of sex discrimination, which was legal in the United States until 1964. Title VII of the 1964 Civil Rights Act made sex discrimination illegal and established the Equal Employment Opportunity Commission to oversee compliance with the law. The inclusion of "sex" in the coverage of that act was due in large part to the political skill of Rep. Martha Griffiths (D-Mich.). Griffiths was one of only fourteen women in the U.S. Congress in 1964. Women's labor force opportunities dramatically broadened when sex discrimination became illegal. Moreover, the legislation played an important role in opening political leadership opportunities for women by widening access to law and business, traditional routes to political careers.

3. The figures are only slightly better at the local level, where women constitute

22 percent of the state legislators. Women of color constituted 28 percent of the women serving in Congress in 2000. Data and updates are available through the Center for the American Woman and Politics at www.cawp.rutgers.edu, or through www.wufpac.org. For international comparisons see www.ipu.org/wmn-e/world.htm.

4. Remarks of Ruth Mandel, director of the Center for the American Women in Politics, Eagleton Institute, Rutgers University, at the panel on "Choosing to Lead" of the annual meeting of the National Council for Research on Women, United Nations, New York, 9 December 1999.

5. Data from Women in National Parliaments as of 15 July 2000, www.ipu.org/wmn-e/world.htm.

6. Nancy McGlen and Karen O'Connor, *Women, Politics, and American Society*, 2d ed. (Englewood Cliffs, N.J.: Prentice-Hall, 1998), 154, 257–59, 275.

7. Ibid.; Deborah Rhode, *Speaking of Sex* (Cambridge, Mass.: Harvard University Press, 1997).

8. This finding occurs in Jeane Kirkpatrick's *Political Woman* (New York: Basic Books, 1974), based on the lives of state legislators in the 1970s, and again in Sue Thomas's *How Women Legislate* (New York: Oxford University Press, 1994), based on women state legislators in the 1980s.

9. The role of white women in the new American Republic was the creation of patriotic and democratic children. This enhanced the importance of women's role in the domestic sphere but also limited their political contributions beyond that sphere. See Mary Beth Norton, *Liberty's Daughters: The Revolutionary Experience of American Women, 1750–1800* (Boston: Little, Brown, 1980), 242–55, 297–99.

10. Raush et al. attribute George Allen's success against Mary Sue Terry in the 1993 Virginia gubernatorial race to Allen's skillful showcasing of his family in the media to contrast with Terry, who was a single professional woman. They also note that "Republicans conducted what became known as the 'whispering campaign' against Terry, spreading subtle and not so subtle rumors that Terry was a lesbian" (4); see John David Rausch Jr., Mark Rozell, and Harry L. Wilson, "Why Women Lose: A Study of Media Coverage of Two Gubernatorial Campaigns," *Women and Politics* 20, no. 4 (1999): 1–21.

11. The number of openly gay members of Congress is very small, and the preference for leaders with heterosexual credentials appears to be a "given" if unspoken criterion for high-level political leadership. There are exceptions, but they are just that—exceptions. Even political appointees are still subject to public scrutiny of their private lives.

12. See the study by Dorothy Cantor and Toni Bernay, *Women in Power* (Boston: Houghton Mifflin, 1992), as well as the theoretical work of Janet Flammang, *Women's Political Voice* (Philadelphia: Temple University Press, 1997); Joan Tronto, "Beyond Gender to a Politics of Care," *Signs* 12 (summer 1987): 644–63; Jean Bethke Elshtain, "Antigone's Daughters," in *Families, Politics, and Public Policies*, ed. Irene Diamond (New York: Longman, 1983), 300–311; and Kathleen Jones, *Compassionate Democracy* (New York: Routledge, 1993).

13. I have used Janet Flammang's term *transformational*, which she uses to distinguish the perspectives of feminist political scientists who hold this view of politics and power.

14. See Marcia Whicker and Hedy Isaacs, "The Maleness of the American Presidency"; Barbara Burrell, "The Governmental Status of the First Lady in Law and in Public Perception"; and Charles Tien, Regan Checchio, and Arthur H. Miller, "The Impact of First Wives on Presidential Campaigns and Elections," all in *Women in Politics: Outsiders or Insiders*, ed. Lois Duke Whitaker, 3d ed. (Englewood Cliffs, N.J.: Prentice-Hall, 1999).

15. See Rausch et al., "Why Women Lose," 3.

16. See Kim Fridkin Kahn, *The Political Consequences of Being a Woman* (New York: Columbia University Press, 1996).

17. The Clarence Thomas hearings before the Senate Judiciary Committee in 1991 are widely credited with underscoring women's absence from the U.S. Senate and serving as a catalyst for women's political mobilization. In contrast, the media's extensive interviewing of the very few female senators during the Clinton impeachment proceedings in 1999 tended to give a false impression of their numbers in the upper chamber.

18. Rhode, *Speaking of Sex*, 1–2.

19. Figures are from McGlen and O'Connor, *Women, Politics, and American Society*, 61–62. For a more sobering view, see Kathleen Dolan, "Gender Differences in Support for Women Candidates: Is There a Glass Ceiling in American Politics?" *Women and Politics* 17, no. 2 (1997): 27–41.

20. Cited in McGlen and O'Connor, *Women, Politics, and American Society*, 63–64.

21. Thomas, *How Women Legislate*, 157. Thomas notes that women were predicted to win a number of victories in the 1990 election until the Gulf War erupted. On this point, Thomas cites Celinda Lake, "Challenging the Credibility Gap," *Notes from Emily*, published by Emily's List, June 1991.

22. Recounted in Clara Bingham, *Women on the Hill: Challenging the Culture of Congress* (New York: Random House, 1997), 24–25.

23. Because this assertion was made on the basis of aggregate data, it was impossible to determine a household vote except by inference from shared SES. We simply do not know if this was the case, but we do know that from 1980 on there were distinct voting patterns by sex. See Susan C. Bourque and Jean Grossholtz, "Politics as an Unnatural Practice: Political Science Looks at Female Participation," *Politics and Society* 4, no. 2 (winter 1974): 225–66.

24. Angus Campbell, Philip Converse, Warren E. Miller, and Donald E. Stokes, *The American Voter* (New York: Wiley, 1964). For an extensive critique of *The American Voter* and the claims for female conservatism see Bourque and Grossholtz, "Politics as an Unnatural Practice."

25. Sandra Baxter and Marjorie Lansing, *Women and Politics: The Visible Majority* (Ann Arbor: University of Michigan, 1983), esp. 73–112.

26. Maurice Duverger, *The Political Role of Women* (Paris: UNESCO, 1955). Cross-culturally, claims for female conservatism have some historical and continuing significance. The power of this conservative characterization has led many a Latin American dictator to see women as worthy of enfranchisement, believing they would be a strong anticommunist voting block. Even today Chilean women appear to be more conservative voters than men. See Navarro and Bourque, "Fault Lines of Democratic Governance: A Gender Perspective," and Maria Elena Valenzuela, "Women and the Democratization Process in Chile," in *Women and Democracy*, ed. Jaquette and Wolchik, 47–74.

27. Rep. Shirley Chisholm (D-N.Y.) was the first African American to campaign for the presidency and a major party nomination in 1972. She received only 151 votes at the party convention.

28. For a fuller description of the various groups involved see McGlen and O'Connor, *Women, Politics, and American Society*, 47–49.

29. "What's It All About, Alpha?" *New York Times*, Week in Review, 7 November 1999, 1.

30. Sue Thomas, "Why Gender Matters: Perceptions of Women Office Holders," *Women and Politics* 17, no. 1 (1997): 54.

31. Kathleen Dolan, in "Gender Differences in Support for Women Candidates," notes the opposite trend in a 1989 survey of college students. Her findings indicate that college women are much more likely than college men to support women candidates for high-level political offices.

32. The term comes from Robert Darcy, Susan Welch, and Janet Clark, *Women, Elections, and Representatives* (New York: Longman's, 1987), cited in Thomas, *How Women Legislate*, 46.

33. Susan Carroll's work is especially insightful on this point. See her *Women as Candidates in American Politics*, 2d ed. (Bloomington: Indiana University Press, 1994).

34. Kirkpatrick, *Political Woman*, 222.

35. Ibid., 223.

36. Thomas, *How Women Legislate*, 63.

37. Ibid., 79.

38. Ibid., 81.

39. Ibid., 140.

40. McGlen and O'Connor, *Women, Politics, and American Society*, 53–56; Carroll, *Women as Candidates in American Politics*, 171.

41. McGlen and O'Connor, *Women, Politics, and American Society*, 56.

42. Susan Carroll argues that this is one of the most effective strategies for promoting women's candidacies among political parties; *Women as Candidates in American Politics*, 166–67.

43. Bingham, *Women on the Hill*, 166–67.

44. Debra Dodson et al., *Voices, Views, Votes: The Impact of Women in the 103rd Congress* (New Brunswick, N.J.: CAWP, Eagleton Institute of Politics, Rutgers University, 1995), 1.

45. Ibid., 1.

46. Ibid., 2.

47. As related in Bingham, *Women on the Hill*, 80.

48. Ibid., 247.

49. Ibid., 251.

50. Quoted in ibid., 257.

51. This is not to suggest total consensus or a lack of dispute. The Vatican and fundamentalist Islamic nations have challenged women's reproductive rights and changes in women's status. Many feminist groups have challenged the claims of the Vatican to governmental status during these international meetings. See *Conscience: A Newsjournal of Prochoice Catholic Opinion* 21, no. 1 (spring 2000), special issue on Beijing Plus 5.

52. Barbara Crossette, "Rights Gains Are Preserved at UN Forum on Women," *New York Times*, 11 June 2000, 4.

53. For the fullest treatment of this question, see Martha A. Ackelsberg, "Broadening the Study of Women's Participation," in *Women and American Politics: New Questions, New Directions*, ed. Susan Carroll (New York: Oxford University Press, forthcoming); Martha Ackelsberg, "Communities, Resistance, and Women's Activism: Some Implications for a Democratic Polity," in *Women and the Politics of Empowerment*, ed. Ann Bookman and Sandra Morgen (Philadelphia: Temple University Press, 1988). Also see the collection edited by Cathy Cohen, Kathleen Jones, and Joan Tronto, *Women Transforming Politics* (New York: New York University Press, 1997). For an excellent summary of the trends in feminist political science see Janet Flammang, *Women's Political Voice* (Philadelphia: Temple University Press, 1997), 3–34.

## Want to Learn More?

**Emily's List**

Emily's List was founded in 1985, when Ellen Malcolm and twenty-five friends decided to create a grassroots network of donors that would give women the credibility they needed to win elections. Emily's List is a donor network of fifty thousand members that raises money for pro-choice Democratic women candidates running for the House, for the Senate, and for governor; helps women candidates build strong, winning campaigns; and helps mobilize women voters through the Emily's List Women Vote! campaign.

Emily's List
805 15th Street, NW, Suite 400
Washington, DC 20005
Telephone (202) 326-1400
www.emilyslist.org

### The Center for American Women and Politics

The Center for American Women and Politics (CAWP) at the Eagleton Institute of Politics at Rutgers, the State University of New Jersey, is a university-based research, education, and public service center. Its mission is to promote greater understanding and knowledge about women's participation in politics and government and to enhance women's influence and leadership in public life.

Eagleton Institute of Politics
Rutgers, The State University of New Jersey
191 Ryders Lane
New Brunswick, NJ 08901-8557
Telephone (732) 932-9384
Fax (732) 932-0014
www.rci.rutgers.edu/~cawp

### The National Organization for Women (NOW)

NOW was founded in 1966. Its mission is to end the injustice and inequality women face daily. With over 500,000 contributing members, NOW is the largest feminist organization in the United States.

National Organization for Women
733 15th Street, NW, 2d Floor
Washington, DC 20005
Telephone (202) 628-8669
Fax (202) 785-8576
www.now.org

### The Feminist Majority and the Feminist Majority Foundation

Eleanor Smeal, Peg Yorkin, Toni Carabillo, Judith Meuli, and Katherine Spillar founded the Feminist Majority in the fall of 1987. The purpose of the Feminist Majority is to promote equality for women and men, nonviolence, social justice, and economic development and to enhance feminist participation in public policy. The mission of the Feminist Majority is to empower women, who are the majority, and to win equality for women at the decision-making tables of the state, the nation, and the world.

The Feminist Majority Foundation's mission is to create innovative, cutting-edge research, educational programs, and strategies to further women's equality and empowerment, to reduce violence toward women, to increase the health and economic well-being of women, and to eliminate discrimination of all kinds.

The Feminist Majority and Feminist Majority Foundation can be reached on either coast at:

Feminist Majority and Feminist Majority Foundation
1600 Wilson Boulevard, Suite 801
Arlington, VA 22209
Telephone (703) 522-2214
Fax (703) 522-2219
E-mail femmaj@feminist.org
www.feminist.org

*or*

8105 West Third Street
Los Angeles, CA 90048
Telephone (323) 651-0495
Fax (323) 653-2689
E-mail femajority@feminist.org
www.feminist.org

**Feminist Activist Resources on the Net**

Feminist Activist Resources on the Net is an online guide oriented toward connecting feminist activists to topics related to feminism. The site includes an index with topics such as communicating with other feminists, feminist issues, women's organizations, feminist resources, feminist news, general resources for political activists, feminist activist calendar, suggestions for current feminist action, and feminist fun and games.

www.igc.apc.org

**Women Under Forty Political Action Committee (WUFPAC)**

In January 1999 a group of young women representing diverse political, ethnic, and geographic backgrounds gathered together in Washington, D.C., to discuss the role of young women in politics. Recognizing that political capital is built by political tenure and frustrated by the relatively low number of women currently holding political office, they created WUFPAC to support the efforts of young women running for the U.S. Congress and state legislatures.

www.wufpac.org

**GenderGap.com**

The goal of this website is to provide the facts and figures that document unequal opportunity and treatment based on gender, the analysis that puts it in context, and the ideas useful in eliminating it. This is a one-woman project developed by Marilyn Brown. The site contains useful and up-to-date data and details on candidates and electoral races.

www.gendergap.com

# 4

## Leadership, Sport, and Gender

**Mary Jo Kane**

■ BACKGROUND

I have always been committed to the notion that women should be given an opportunity to have an impact locally and nationally on the important areas of public life, to have the ability to influence the public agenda, and to have a significant voice in the political and economic arenas. As a result, I've been concerned about the multiplicity of barriers that prevent women from having a public impact. One of the greatest areas of opportunity, and simultaneously one of the greatest barriers, has been the dearth of women in leadership positions.

My own area of scholarship is sport sociology, and sport is one of the most important sites in this culture where women can learn about and nurture their leadership: leadership skills not just for sport, but skills that have an impact far beyond the playing field. I want to understand and critique what attitudinal and structural barriers have prevented women's leadership in sport. As a scholar I know that to understand any phenomenon adequately I must explore the empirical data—and the theoretical issues related to those data—that have been generated by both academics and professionals in the field. In the case of women's leadership in sport, I have sought such evidence from the numerous investigations that have been conducted as well as from case studies of women who should have been highly successful leaders. In the latter instance, I wanted to study their personal experiences to gain greater insights regarding the wider structural and ideological patterns that limit women leaders. In the cases I write about, I have tried to understand why a woman who was highly successful in all the ways we are trained to define that term would meet not with congratulations but with strong, and in some cases fierce, opposition. Across all four case stud-

ies I have tried to address the various reasons why women leaders face
such systematic and active resistance. In doing so I have been able to identify
many of the remaining obstacles to women's leadership in sport and how
those obstacles can be overcome.

T HIS essay focuses on a significant political, social, and economic enterprise that has resisted changing notions of leadership and gender perhaps more than any other American institution—sport. The social
construction of gender and its relationship to leadership is embedded throughout this culture. Nevertheless, some of the most extreme examples of oppressive stereotypes concerning gender and leadership are found in sport. In the
information that follows I argue that this is because of the historical interconnections among sport, gender, and leadership. As we shall discover, if there is
any area where we need to alter our popular images and practices of leadership
and rethink what women can contribute in this regard, it is in the world of
sport. And if there is any arena where attempts at such change will be (and
are) met with fierce resistance, it is in one of the few male bastions remaining
after the sweeping changes brought about by feminism and its transformative
notions of women, power, and leadership.

## Sport, Leadership, and Gender

Dynamic. Forceful. Risk taking. Confident in oneself and possessing the
ability to inspire confidence in others. Grace under pressure. These are some
of the characteristics typically associated with great leaders. They are also attributes that are synonymous with great athletes. But effective leadership is not
simply about individual loners at the top. It is also about getting individuals
working together toward a common goal. These conceptions of individual and
group effort may explain why we have always believed there is a "natural"
connection between sport and leadership. In fact, the history of sport is replete
with anecdotes regarding one of its most important outcomes: that is, sport
builds leaders. It is important to remember, however, that sport has another
history. Sport didn't build leaders in any generic or universal sense. Sport built
*male* leaders.

The so-called natural connection between sport and male leadership has
recently been challenged in the wake of one of the most significant pieces of

federal legislation in this country's history, Title IX of the Education Amendments Act of 1972. This landmark legislation, designed to prohibit gender discrimination within our educational institutions, signaled an explosion of
women's involvement in sport and physical activity over the last three decades.
For example, 2.5 million females participate in interscholastic sports on a nationwide basis, compared to only 300,000 before Title IX.[1] According to the
National Sporting Goods Association, millions of young girls and women participate in organized sports, physical fitness activities, and recreational pursuits;
these activities range from exercise walking (80.8 million participants) to basketball (29.6 million), and from soccer (13.2 million) to canoeing (7.3 million).[2]
In addition to widespread participation increases, women have excelled in
sports at the highest levels. In the 1996 Summer Olympic Games, U.S. women
brought home the gold in basketball, gymnastics, softball, and soccer. In the
wake of such success a new professional basketball league for women, the
WNBA, was launched. And in the summer of 1999 an entire nation was caught
up in the frenzy over the U.S. women's soccer team's winning the world championship on an international stage. What these statistics and accomplishments
make clear is that an arena once considered the "natural" and exclusive domain of men has been directly challenged by the ever expanding presence of
females.

This challenge has not gone unnoticed or uncontested. As I have argued
elsewhere, because sport has served as a vehicle for reproducing and maintaining male power, the dominant group is certainly not eager, nor willing, to lose
its ideological basis of control. Yet enough women have penetrated this exclusive domain—and continue to do so with increasing frequency—that historical
questions of whether women should participate in sports are now moot. This
in no way means to suggest that power struggles over who controls sport, and
who are considered the most important athletes, have ceased to exist. If we
accept the argument that sport is an arena where men have been able to demonstrate their apparent natural supremacy over women and that it continues
to function as one of the last male strongholds, we shouldn't be surprised to
discover that "an influx of strong, competent, powerful women . . . constitutes
an assault on this stronghold."[3] Nowhere has an assault on men's power in
sport been more evident than in leadership roles. As numerous scholars have
pointed out, even with the explosion of participation rates, which one would
assume would be accompanied by an increase in leadership opportunities, the
reality is that Title IX has resulted in a dramatic *decrease* in leadership roles
for women in women's sports, with virtually no gains for women in leadership
of men's sports. For example, before the passage and implementation of Title

IX, 90 percent of all head coaches in women's intercollegiate athletics were female; more recent figures indicate that it is only 47 percent nationwide.[4] And even though the overall number of head coaching jobs in women's sports has increased by approximately 1,000 since the mid-1980s, "women gained only 333 more jobs than they had 10 years before, while men gained 670 more jobs."[5]

The picture for women in administrative positions is even bleaker: whereas before Title IX women occupied the vast majority (over 90 percent) of all athletic director positions, that number today is approximately 16 percent.[6] It is also worth noting that 32 percent of all intercollegiate programs for women in this country do not employ a single woman in an administrative position. We should also remember that these figures are confined to women's athletics: it has been almost thirty years since the passage of Title IX, yet in men's intercollegiate athletics women continue to occupy less than 1 percent of all head-coaching positions.[7] These figures make it undeniably clear that with respect to leadership opportunities, men have fared far better under Title IX than have women. This is particularly troubling given the spirit and intent of Title IX—to increase opportunities for women in *all* sports. How ironic that women not only have failed to gain admission into leadership roles in men's sports but have actually lost ground in their own domain. When it comes to one of sport's greatest hallmarks—preparing our nation's leaders—a rather significant component appears to be missing: that of preparing half of the population to occupy positions of leadership in one of this country's most influential and all-pervasive institutions.

How and why did this happen? These are two of the most frequently asked questions regarding sport, gender, and leadership. On its face it seems to make no logical sense that, given the great social change that has swept over sport in the last three decades, women would have significantly fewer opportunities for achieving leadership positions. The following example illustrates this point. A commonly held belief is that one important qualification for becoming a leader in sport (e.g., coach or athletic director) is past playing experience. Indeed, Fitzgerald et al. discovered that with respect to career patterns of intercollegiate athletic directors, competing at the college level was one of the most critical variables for attaining the position of athletic director.[8] Before Title IX women had very little formal sport experience; this lack of experience would seem to result in a relatively small pool of qualified women. Yet before and in the early stages of Title IX, when women had virtually no formal playing experience (particularly at the college level), leadership positions were filled overwhelmingly by females. At the same time, the pool of qualified women candidates (in terms of competing at the high school and college levels) has grown exponentially in the wake of Title IX. This ever expanding pool of experienced (and thus qualified) women candidates has had little if any impact, however, because women are not occupying key leadership positions, not even in women's sports.

I would suggest that what has happened to women with respect to leadership roles has very little to do with logic, or women's qualifications, and everything to do with power. As stated earlier, men have an enormous investment in constructing sport in ways that maintain their status and privilege. Therefore, what becomes key to any analysis of gender and leadership in this new post–Title IX world order is to examine how the dominant group struggles to retain its position, and the ways in which the subordinate group challenges this attempt at power maintenance.[9]

## Sport as a Site of Empowerment for Women

Men have long cherished the sport experience. This is something that, until recently, has been denied to women on any large-scale basis. But as we have discussed, women are participating in a greater variety of sports in unprecedented numbers. Sport scholar Mary Duquin argues that women are discovering how involvement in sport can become an important tool for gaining a sense of mastery and competence; in short, sport can be an ideal setting for establishing and experiencing feelings of self-worth and empowerment.[10] Through the physical, social, and intellectual challenges found in sport, women, like men, learn about their own physical potentials, test their own ambitions, goals, and dreams, and realize their ability to create their own destiny. It is precisely because of sport's liberating potential that scholars such as Catherine Mackinnon, Leslie Heywood, and Iris Young have argued that women have been systematically excluded from sport.[11] Indeed, patriarchal culture requires that females see and experience their bodies as weak and disabled because when women become physically active, "it has meant claiming and possessing a physicality that is our own . . . [the] physical self-respect and physical presence that women can get from sports is antithetical to femininity. It is our bodies as active rather than as acted upon."[12]

Numerous scholars have provided theoretical and empirical support for the argument put forth by Mackinnon. Much of this work has focused on alternative sport forms—woman-controlled organizations, feminist and lesbian sport teams and leagues—because more mainstream, so-called men's sports often promote values and practices that are hostile to women.[13] In this vein,

Nancy Theberge has suggested developing alternative models of women's sports that are closely linked with a "feminist vision of power"—one that includes a sense of community and empowerment rather than patriarchal models that subjugate women.[14] One example of this strategy involves women's softball. Drawing on feminist theory and a cultural studies approach, Birrell and Richter interviewed feminist athletes participating in a summer recreational league. Reflecting on the relationship these women saw between their feminist consciousness and the practice of sport, they rejected the values embedded in men's sports such as an overemphasis on winning, hierarchy, elitism, exclusivity (e.g., heterosexism), disparagement of one's opponents, and an ethic of endangerment. They opted instead for a "form of softball which is process oriented, collective, inclusive, supportive, and infused with an ethic of care."[15]

More recently, research has been conducted inside mainstream sports with women intercollegiate athletes. Blinde, Taub, and Han interviewed Division I athletes and found that sport participation enhanced the development of individual empowerment such as bodily competence, a sense of self-worth, and a proactive approach to life.[16] Based on these findings, the authors argued that sport can serve as a vehicle for personal liberation. They also examined whether sport can empower women at a group or societal level. Their findings revealed that sport facilitates female bonding, the development of a group identity, and a strong commitment to achieving common goals. Time and again throughout the interviews female athletes voiced themes that evoked images of future leaders: "You have a common goal so you learn to work together and you know a lot of times, you have conflict with personalities. But you learn to deal with it because you are on the same team." These athletes were also aware they were dispelling harmful stereotypes about women's abilities by challenging traditional notions that women could not, for example, be mentally and physically strong. They thus knew they were serving as role models for future generations and expanding the boundaries of what women can accomplish, not just in sport, but in a larger social context: "Team work is going to teach you a lot of those life lessons . . . it is hard to get that outside of sport."[17] One of the life lessons these female athletes were acutely aware of was how they were disadvantaged compared to male athletes; they made numerous comments about their unfair treatment regarding budgets, facilities, practice time, and marketing and promotion.

If we accept the argument that empowerment fosters the advancement of women into positions of decision making and authority, and if we further accept that this advancement can be threatening to those who already hold power, then women's involvement in sport can indeed be seen as problematic for traditional gender relations both inside and outside of sport. This is an environment that must be carefully managed if patriarchal relations of power are to be maintained. Interestingly, Blinde et al. discovered that in some respects this was already happening. According to the authors, most of the "women athletes . . . lack a critical understanding of the underlying ideology that perpetuates their disadvantaged position. Further, most athletes disavow the feminist label . . . and do not engage in activism associated with women's issues." The authors offer various reasons for this finding, from the overall conservative nature of sport to an environment so concerned with winning that activism would rarely be tolerated, and to a desire on the part of many females to distance themselves from feminist labels because open identification with feminism may "intensify the already present lesbian labeling of women athletes."[18]

In spite of this latter finding, it was quite clear that these female athletes were empowered by their sport experience. Females, like males, can gain valuable experiences and lessons from sport, particularly as they relate to leadership. The irony for the female athlete is that while she is gaining the experience she needs to qualify for a leadership role, she is also learning an all-too-familiar lesson in the post–Title IX era: in spite of her playing experience (and the empowerment that can bring her) she will be significantly less likely than her male counterparts to attain leadership status in two of the most important positions in sport—head coach and athletic director.

## Locked Out of Leadership

One of the most examined topics in the post–Title IX era is gender and leadership. Moving from descriptive data in the early 1980s that alerted scholars, educators, and administrators about the dramatic loss in leadership positions in the wake of Title IX, to a more recent theoretical analysis of how and why this is happening, numerous studies have focused on the various factors that have affected this employment trend.[19] For example, scholars have investigated why women may enter, stay in, or leave coaching; how female head coaches are recruited, selected, and retained; different administrative structures under which women coaches are hired; career patterns of athletic directors; and the relationship between the sex of the person doing the hiring and the sex of the person being hired.[20] One thing all of these studies have in common is they either explicitly or implicitly state that the loss of women in leadership roles, and their continued underrepresentation, is not desirable.

A second common theme throughout much of this research has been attribution of blame—who and what are responsible for this pattern of employment and how can this trend be reversed? To answer these concerns, studies have typically focused on either a micro (individual variables) or a macro (structural variables) level of analysis. In the former instance, scholars have sampled individual coaches and athletic administrators and gathered data on what made them enter, stay in, or leave sport leadership roles. In the latter instance, researchers have taken a more global approach and examined structural variables such as occupational sex discrimination or tokenism. Regardless of the approach, four themes have emerged from these investigations: (1) Why aren't women being recruited and hired? (2) Why aren't women staying once hired? (3) Even when women are in leadership roles, their impact may be severely limited. (4) What specific action can be taken to reverse these occupational employment trends? The following section highlights the research in each of these thematic areas. Although each area is presented here as a static, discrete category, they operate interchangeably in a highly dynamic process.

## Why Aren't Women Being Recruited and Hired?

In a groundbreaking nationwide study from the late 1980s, Acosta and Carpenter asked those most responsible for recruiting and hiring college head coaches—athletic directors—to list the reasons for the diminishing number of women coaches. Their findings indicated that male athletic directors perceived the four most important reasons to be: (1) lack of qualified female coaches; (2) failure of women to apply for job openings; (3) lack of qualified female administrators; and (4) time constraints due to family obligations.[21] It was particularly important to investigate the perceptions of male athletic directors because they make up approximately 85 percent of all athletic directors in intercollegiate athletics. (I will take up the responses of the female athletic directors, and their significance to this area of study, momentarily.) Hasbrook et al. empirically tested the validity of male athletic directors' beliefs that fewer women than men are hired because women are less qualified, and that women are more constrained by time as a result of family obligations.[22] The authors discovered that in fact: (1) female coaches were more qualified than their male counterparts in terms of coaching experience with female teams, professional training, and professional experience; and (2) male rather than female coaches experienced more time constraints due to family responsibilities.

What these findings reveal is that the perceptions of male athletic directors are woefully inadequate, not to mention inaccurate, when offering explanations for the underrepresentation of women in coaching positions. Perhaps more important, however, "is that the beliefs expressed by male athletic directors appear to be based more on a gender-stereotypic bias about female competence than on any objective data."[23] In an earlier and related investigation examining coaches' qualifications and backgrounds, Anderson and Gill also discovered that in terms of objective data, female coaches more than held their own.[24] Focusing on the occupational socialization patterns of female and male interscholastic basketball coaches, the authors found that female coaches of women's teams had more extensive professional qualifications (e.g., prior basketball involvement and achievement) than did male coaches. Despite this, almost 90 percent of the women's teams in their study were coached by men.

The findings from these studies suggest that it is not women's lack of ability or credentials that stand in the way. We therefore need to avoid a "blame the victim" approach in which individual women are viewed as responsible for their continued underrepresentation in leadership positions. It seems safe to assert, however, that the male athletic directors in the Acosta and Carpenter study took precisely this view. By emphasizing the inadequacies of women (e.g., their perceived failure to recruit and travel and their perceived lack of competence), the male athletic directors blamed the employment decline on individual women rather than on any institutional factor, even though these explanations were not based on any accurate, objective data. A more fruitful perspective would be to examine more global, structural variables such as occupational discrimination. Knoppers has convincingly argued that in order to understand adequately how women have been, and continue to be, kept out of the coaching profession, we need to "look at some of the structural and institutional factors which may interact to keep many women out [of coaching]."[25] One such structural variable that has been particularly useful for exploring women's underrepresentation in leadership roles is *homologous reproduction*.

This is a term employed by Rosabeth Kanter in her work on gender and leadership in the corporate sector. Homologous or homosocial reproduction is a process whereby those in positions of power (e.g., management) are most likely to hire and promote those who possess physical and social characteristics most like themselves because "those who run [things] often rely on outward manifestations to determine who is the 'right sort of person.' Managers tend to carefully guard power and privilege for those who fit in, for those they see as 'their kind.' "[26] This process of recruiting, hiring, and promotion is particularly salient for the issues we are discussing because in the study referred to earlier by Acosta and Carpenter, women athletic directors believed that the loss of leadership roles was a function of the success of the "old boys' network" and the parallel failure of the "old girls' network." Implicit in this line of reasoning is the perception that there is a direct link between the sex of the person doing the hiring (athletic director) and the sex of the person being hired (head coach). To empirically test this perception, Stangl and Kane examined employment patterns in women's interscholastic athletics in relationship to early Title IX (1974–75), ten years after passage (1981–82), and 1988–89 employment trends. They discovered that a significantly higher proportion of female head coaches were hired under female athletic directors and that this pattern was true regardless of the Title IX time frame under consideration.[27]

Stangl and Kane's findings have been replicated in ways that support the notion of homologous reproduction as an explanatory variable for employment trends in women's athletics. Pastore discovered that women administrators in two-year colleges and universities hired more female head coaches than their male counterparts. The most recent data from Acosta and Carpenter revealed that under female administrators, 51 percent of all head coaches were female, compared to 46 percent under male administrators. In a related study, Lovett and Lowry surveyed over one thousand secondary schools in Texas and found that homologous reproduction was operating for both genders and that "the greatest percentage of female versus male coaches came in the administrative models with a female athletic director."[28] This statement reveals one critical aspect of leadership opportunities for women in sport. While it appears to be the case that women administrators are committed to hiring female coaches, there are so few female administrators that their overall impact is minimal. For example, in Stangl and Kane's study, only 5.2 percent of all high school athletic directors were female. The figures for the Lovett and Lowry study were equally troubling: over 90 percent of all of the schools they surveyed had a male athletic director. And even though female administrators were able to reproduce themselves successfully, the "shocking difference is that the all-female model [an administrative structure consisting of a female principal and athletic director] represents a total of 30 coaches while the all-male model represents a total of 4,301 coaches."[29] As the authors point out, the good old girls' club is ineffective not because women administrators are uncommitted to hiring female head coaches but because so few administrative structures have female personnel in decision-making roles.

Homologous reproduction offers a powerful competing explanation for why women are not being hired. As the studies above strongly suggest, women's absence in leadership positions is not about their lack of credentials, nor the failure of the old girls' network. It is about choosing and promoting the "right

kind of person." Given the current makeup of athletic administrative structures, it seems clear that the dominant group is continuing to reproduce itself
systematically in its own image. In this made-to-maintain-the-status-quo power
structure, those who do not possess the "right stuff" are often perceived as
different because they are not carbon copies of the dominant group. In recruitment, hiring, and promotion, lacking the right stuff should not be underestimated. If a subordinate is considered different—that is, does not possess
common physical and social characteristics that reflect those of the dominant
group—then she or he is, by definition, outside the loop of homologous reproduction. To break this cycle of power and advance within the organizational
structure, subordinates must have extraordinary qualifications, or at the very
least, better qualifications than those colleagues who possess characteristics
similar to the dominant group.[30] This may help explain the earlier findings by
Hasbrook et al. that even though male athletic directors believed women were
less qualified than men, the empirical data indicated just the opposite. It may
also help explain why even though female head coaches were more qualified
than their male counterparts in the Anderson and Gill study, only 10 percent
of all head coaches were women.[31]

## Why Aren't Women Staying?

A number of studies have examined why female and male coaches leave
the profession and whether there are gender differences in this regard. The
studies indicate that numerous factors contribute to female coaches' reasons
for leaving, such as burnout, inadequate coaching abilities, time and family
commitments, and gender discrimination.[32] In an early study, Caccese and
Mayerberg discovered that female head coaches were significantly more likely
to experience burnout than male head coaches.[33] Almost a decade later, Pastore and Judd examined levels of burnout among head coaches in two-year
colleges.[34] They found that female coaches reported significantly higher levels
of emotional burnout than did male coaches. Pastore also found gender differences in a related study: female coaches rated the factors "increased intensity
in recruiting" and "burden of administrative duties" significantly higher than
did their male counterparts.[35] Although these findings could be interpreted as
women's inability to handle the pressures of coaching, Lovett and Lowry offer
alternative explanations such as lack of support or job discrimination: "The
recognition, facilities and psychological and financial rewards that are associated with female sport programs are increasing but are still far short of those
for most male sport programs. As women compare their coaching environment

to that for coaches in the male programs, they find few reasons for being satisfied."[36]

Pastore's 1992 study finds evidence of such an environment. None of the
male coaches in her study cited "discriminatory practices by administrators"
as a reason for leaving coaching, while female coaches cited it frequently.
Similarly, twice as many women as men cited "lack of support by administration" as a reason they would consider leaving the coaching profession.

What seems apparent from much of this research is that women often find
the job climate chilly at best and hostile at worst. This is particularly important
because job climate has an enormous impact on one's ability to lead. For
example, research findings from the world of education indicate that students
with high levels of achievement satisfaction and leadership attainment also
have high levels of environmental support.[37] The world of sport is no different.
Examining the effects of leadership behavior and organizational job climate,
Snyder discovered that the "degree of consideration shown by the athletic director had a strong effect on satisfaction with work and supervision."[38] Snyder
also found gender differences in factors related to job satisfaction: female
coaches were much more likely to indicate that consideration from the athletic
director helped them feel integrated into the department and supported by the
administration.

Gender differences are also present in another factor related to the job
satisfaction of female coaches. These differences are closely linked to gender
role stereotypes about women's capacities to lead, particularly in occupational
areas deemed more appropriate for males. Parkhouse and Williams polled female and male high school basketball players regarding their attitudes toward
hypothetical male and female basketball coaches. Both male and female players indicated they would prefer to play for a male coach.[39] In a follow-up study,
these same authors found that male and female athletes rated female and male
coaches equally. However, these ratings happened during a time period when
the athletes played for a female coach with a winning team and a male coach
with a losing team.[40] Commenting on such negative attitudes toward women
coaches, Lovett and Lowry suggest that "if this negativism is experienced in
real life situations, it could serve as a cause for the female coach leaving the
profession for good."[41] One interesting phenomenon in this literature is the
equivocal finding regarding the influence of time and family commitments.
Pastore and True discovered that females were often inclined to leave coaching
because of these two factors. Yet other scholars have found that women were
no more likely than men to leave coaching because of these outside pressures.
And Hasbrook et al. noted that it was men, rather than women, who cited

time constraints due to family obligations as a reason for quitting coaching.[42] Explanations that have been offered for these conflicting results have a common theme—women who feel more (or less) constrained owing to family and time commitments are influenced by gender role stereotypes more so than men. Lovett and Lowry suggest that women feel more pressure in this area because "society still expects women to fulfill the roles of the traditional wife and mother, which could possibly interfere with the pursuit of a successful coaching career. By contrast, society does not expect the man to choose between family and career."[43]

I would suggest an additional reason for these contradictory findings. For female coaches who are married or have children, time constraints and family obligations may indeed be a major barrier in terms of pursuing a career, particularly given traditional expectations of a woman's role toward her family. But this assumes that many of the coaches in the above studies were married or in a committed relationship and that this type of family arrangement was distributed evenly across both sexes. What the Hasbrook et al. and the Fitzgerald et al. studies indicate, however, is that the overwhelming majority of male administrators were married; this was not the case for women.[44] While on the surface single women with no children may be more attractive job candidates because they are often less constrained by family obligations, this profile can actually be damaging to these women because "single, never married" is often interpreted as "lesbian." What I am suggesting is that the equivocal findings around this issue appear to be directly related to the marital status of female and male coaches. Marital status may also explain why it was men (most of whom were married) rather than women (many of whom were not) who felt pressures owing to family commitments in Hasbrook's study. It may also help explain why women are often in a no-win situation when attempting to become sport leaders. If they are involved in traditional relationships that constrain them because of gender role expectations, they may be less likely to pursue a coaching career or more likely to leave it. But if they are free enough from family obligations (because of their single status) to pursue the pressure-cooker world of athletics, they may also be perceived as undesirable owing to the long-standing and deep-seated effects of homophobia.

## Women's Limited Impact as Leaders

The analysis above is not meant to suggest that women are unable to make significant contributions as sport leaders. Indeed, we have seen how the old girls' network, though limited in scope, can be effective in employing females as head coaches. But it would be a mistake to assume that simply occupying coaching and administrative positions gives women equal status and power. It would also be a mistake to believe that increasing the number of female athletic directors alone would solve the problem of women's underrepresentation in leadership roles. In this section I outline the reasons for these arguments.

Rosabeth Kanter was one of the first scholars to note that gender is a "very important determinant of who gets what in and out of an organization."[45] Similarly, Knoppers, Meyer, Ewing, and Forrest have argued that because organizational structures are gendered, even when women are employed in leadership roles they are often marginalized; this in turn limits their access to power.[46] Studies from business indicate that women have less access to resources and are less likely to receive favors and timely information from managers.[47] The notion of marginalization has also been addressed in sport. In a study focusing on men's high school athletic programs, Kane and Stangl found that even though some women were occupying head coaching positions, they were confined to the lesser-prestige sports: of the 7,325 head coaching positions analyzed in the sample, only 92 were occupied by females.[48] It should also be noted that there was never one instance where a female served as a head coach of a boy's football, basketball, baseball, or ice hockey team. These findings buttress arguments put forth by Fishwick, who states that "it is assumed that males are automatically able to coach women, but unthinkable that a woman would attempt to coach a men's team."[49]

A second way that women's influence may be limited even when they occupy leadership roles is related to the post–Title IX power struggles referred to earlier in the essay. Clearly, there are some instances where women aren't marginalized, where they occupy the same job position or title that men do. Head coach and athletic director immediately come to mind. We cannot assume, however, that putting women into "equal" positions within an occupation means that they will have equal power. As Reskin has insightfully argued, "neither sex-integrating jobs nor implementing comparable worth will markedly improve women's employment status because men can subvert these mechanisms or even change the rules by which rewards are allocated."[50]

Reskin also cautions us to remember that viewing women as equal to their male counterparts when they hold the same job classification ignores the reality that men have enormous incentives to maintain their advantages such as access to resources and power. They also have the ability to protect these advantages by establishing the very rules and mechanisms that distribute awards. A specific example of how this process works in sport was discovered by Knoppers et al. Analyzing the extent to which sport type (revenue versus non-revenue) and gender of head coach affected three dimensions of power—access to support, information, and supplies—the authors found that "female coaches of non-revenue sports were most limited while male coaches of revenue sports had the most power."[51] What is particularly relevant for our discussion is an additional finding from the study: although both men and women in revenue sports had the greatest access to power, the only sport that women coached where this was happening was women's basketball. The authors also emphasized that none of the women coached a men's revenue sport, while 32 percent of the women's basketball teams were coached by a male.

A final way that women's impact may be limited is through tokenism. According to Kanter, women (or any minority group) can be considered tokens when they occupy less than 15 percent of a particular occupation.[52] Using Kanter's theoretical framework, Kane and Stangl addressed the issue of tokenism in a sport context. The authors examined the number of women head coaches in men's athletics and whether their presence had increased in relationship to Title IX. They discovered that there were significantly more women head coaches in the late 1980s versus the mid-1970s. A caveat, however, is in order. Even with this increase, women still represented less than 2 percent of the overall number of head coaches. As Kane and Stangl noted, "Given this finding, it seems safe to assume that even during the time period when women made the greatest inroads, they continued to represent only a 'token' percentage of all head-coaching positions."[53]

What is particularly insidious about tokenism is that it gives the impression that the system is open and egalitarian. Yet tokenism often results in a system that is anything but open. By hiring and promoting a limited number of women, the organization (or profession) can accomplish a number of interrelated tasks that ultimately maintain men's privileged position. As Code observes: "One woman's token presence is more often presented as proof that the hiring or admission practices of a particular firm or institution are in order, that the 'woman question' has been settled, and that no more women will be admitted."[54]

By "settling the woman question" tokenism provides another "bonus" based on gender role stereotypes. If we see that some women are being hired and thus can assure ourselves that the system is indeed open, we can then attribute the continued underrepresentation to the fault of individual women. In a study of Canadian sport organizations, Hall, Cullen, and Slack found empirical evidence for this line of thinking. Individuals polled within these organizations did acknowledge that women were mostly absent from leadership positions. However, they also indicated that competent and well-qualified women would rise to the top. Thus, women's absence was considered the result of a personal deficiency (they're less qualified) or to some social factor (a family obligation) that was beyond the control and the responsibility of the sport organization.[55]

## Reversing the Trend

I stated earlier that women's ongoing struggle for greater equality in sport has not gone unnoticed or uncontested. But neither has the loss of women in leadership roles. Over the last twenty years there has been a concerted, nationwide effort to reverse the employment trends in women's sports since the passage of Title IX. One such strategy has been to develop clinics and workshops designed to increase the number of women coaches and administrators through practical experiences, networking, mentoring, and exposure to educational materials on such topics as sport medicine and sport psychology.[56] Although I will not discuss this approach in great detail, there are some important concerns that need to be raised regarding such efforts, not for their goals, but for how those goals may be misinterpreted. My first concern relates to the primary purpose of many of these programs, which is to improve the employability of potential women coaches. If our efforts focus on this approach too heavily, we may ignore larger structural variables discussed earlier (e.g., tokenism, marginalization) that have an enormous influence on occupational employment trends.

An article outlining the efforts of a program at the University of Oregon highlights my concerns. Sisley, Weiss, Barber, and Ebbeck point to programs around the country designed to "address areas that have been considered weaknesses in women's coaching to build a pool of qualified women coaches."[57] Sisley et al. also discuss techniques for developing competence and confidence in novice women coaches. Although certainly well intentioned, one major assumption underlying these coaching workshops is to improve the so-called weaknesses and inadequacies of individual women coaches. My intent here is not to criticize the efforts of these programs. Many of them emphasize women's strengths as well as weaknesses and also stress the importance of networking and career development. In addition, these programs teach practical strategies for pursuing coaching and administrative assignments. However, one potential harm is that these programs may unwittingly provide a rationale for assuming that the continued underrepresentation of women in leadership positions ultimately lies with women. The following example underscores this point. A primary purpose of the coaching workshops is to improve women's coaching skills so as to create a qualified pool of female coaches. Implicit in this approach is that women are less qualified and that this is one major reason why women are not being hired as often as are men. But in terms of objective data, studies have consistently indicated that female coaches are often as qualified as or more qualified than their male counterparts. This contradiction is a powerful example of how a dominant group maintains power: women's continued underrepresentation in leadership roles is framed entirely in terms of female competence (or lack thereof). As a result, the issue of male competence is rarely if ever questioned. Yet the data indicate that it is men's qualifications, not women's, that should be the focus of attention.

A second approach to reversing employment trends has to do with recruitment. In a study conducted with NCAA Division I coaches, Pastore and Meacci found that these coaches "selected *active recruitment* by administrators as the most important strategy for recruiting and retaining female coaches." Examining how coaches of NCAA Divisions I, II, and III are recruited, hired, and retained, the authors also discovered that female and male coaches and administrators believed that formal recruiting methods (e.g., advertising, interviews) were the least important factors when seeking to employ women coaches. At the same time, they found that women rated informal methods of recruiting more favorably than did men. As the authors note: "It is conceivable that females believe a better informal network of recruiting is necessary to encourage females to enter into coaching positions. This issue may be resolved by future studies that identify the specific strengths and weaknesses of the 'old girls' club network' as compared to its male counterpart."[58] While I certainly applaud such efforts, I would also encourage women to use the old boys' network as well because, as the data clearly indicate, male athletic directors, because of their larger numbers, make many more hires and have far more to say about who gets hired than do female athletic directors.

The strategies outlined above may prove to be helpful in reversing the employment trends in women's athletics that have occurred in the wake of Title IX. However, such strategies must also be analyzed within the broader framework of gender and power relations. Many women are already enormously qualified; their competence is not what should be at issue. We need to keep in mind that a major reason why women continue to be underrepresented in leadership positions in both women's and men's athletics is because men benefit from such arrangements. As Knoppers has argued, when the pool of potential (and current) women coaches is limited, the competition for coaching positions is, by definition, reduced.[59] At the same time, because the coaching profession in women's sports is becoming increasingly filled with males, the status of the position is inflated, which in turn attracts more males. We should not underestimate men's desire to co-opt and control women's sports. For example, the NCAA vigorously resisted the passage and implementation of Title IX. But once it passed, and more women's athletic programs were developed and received greater respect and larger budgets, men became increasingly interested in coaching and administering them. As these same authors point out: "Is there any wonder that women are losing ground in the professional field they created and nurtured?"[60]

## Backlash and Women's Resistance

I have argued throughout this essay that in order to adequately analyze the relationships among gender, sport, and leadership, we must examine the power struggle that is taking place in the aftermath of Title IX. Despite the persistence of gender role stereotypes that limit women's leadership potential, women are nevertheless making remarkable inroads and significant contributions to sport. When they do so, however, they often experience various types of backlash, including "fear of success" and homophobia. Much of the information provided up to this point has come from research literature. The purpose of this section is to supplement these scholarly findings with the faces and voices of women who have experienced this backlash in their everyday lives and careers.

### Fear of Success

The fear of success I am referring to is not based on Matina Horner's theoretical proposition that women are afraid to succeed.[61] Rather, the fear of success I refer to here has to do with men's fear of women's success, particularly in areas traditionally associated with males. To illustrate my argument, I will profile four courageous women who experienced backlash yet continued to persevere while making their mark in sport. Their careers and contributions represent the vast spectrum of the sporting enterprise from professional athlete to coach to sport promoter. But they all have one thing in common: a pioneering spirit that broke down barriers and created a path for others to follow. In sum, they are all great leaders.

In 1990 Rick Pitino, then head coach of the men's basketball program at the University of Kentucky, hired Bernadette Locke to become the first assistant head coach of a men's basketball team at a Division I school. This historic precedent was met with a less-than-enthusiastic response in some sport circles. A sportswriter from Nashville, Tennessee, weighed in with this assessment of the historic move:

Nobody has figured out what Kentucky basketball coach Rick Pitino is up to in his hiring of female assistant coach Bernadette Locke. As one Kentucky writer pointed out after last week's hiring: "If the 'Cats are down by a point with 10 seconds left and Pitino calls time out, you can bet he's not going to look down his bench and say 'OK, Bernadette, what do we do now?' " Rather than coaching, Locke's real responsibility is thought to be helping players with job placement.[62]

Apparently Locke's qualifications as a former college player (the University of Georgia's first woman All-American) and assistant coach (with the women's team at her alma mater) would not enable her to suggest, for example, that they set a screen and get the ball into the hands of their best shooter.

Demonstrating great leadership, Locke refused to let such open hostility limit her effectiveness. She expanded her role each new season and often contributed scouting reports. Pitino stated that without her efforts, Kentucky would not have been able to recruit some of its star players. As one of the Kentucky players remarked: "[No one on the team] looks past her. We don't disrespect her. The things she tells you [about coaching fundamentals] are true."[63] Bernadette Locke Mattox made the most of her leadership opportunity. She has since been promoted to head women's basketball coach at the University of Kentucky where, in 1998–99, she recorded her first twenty-win season and led her team to their first NCAA tournament appearance in eight years.

Another woman who also met great resistance in her pioneering efforts was Kate Bednarski, the mind behind Nike's hugely successful and groundbreaking ad campaign that cornered the women's sports shoes and apparel market. Even though her promotional scheme increased Nike's share of the market from 8 percent to 26 percent, Bednarski discovered that her success was seen not as something to be rewarded but as a threat to Nike's existing power structure. For example, she had her motives questioned by a male supervisor who accused her of trying to run a feminist movement instead of a business venture.[64] Apparently women's success at Nike was equated with their gaining power in ways that unsettled traditional gender relationships. Thus her feminist label.

As the example above indicates, a successful woman can equal too powerful a woman. Indeed, according to Bednarski, the "discomfort level [among male executives] began to rise" when Nike ads depicted women as "powerful, capable people and [addressed] the issue of what it feels like always to be told you can't do something simply because you're a woman." The theme of women-as-powerful-human-beings was so provocative that the Nike ads were featured on *The Oprah Winfrey Show* and discussed in magazines and newspapers nationwide. And even though Bednarski had been brought in specifically to increase the company's share of the women's athletic shoe market, and the mostly male management team supported her ideas in theory, "many seemed to fear that growing the women's business would somehow undermine the company's image and decrease its appeal to men."[65] Like Bernadette Locke Mattox, however, Bednarski would not be defeated. In response to her supervisor's insistence that she was, in spite of his warnings, still running a feminist movement, Bednarski would "just smile and say thanks" and continue to make her mark in women's sports. To date, it has been quite a mark. After leaving Nike, she was vice-president of marketing for Avia and in 1997 was named president of Ryka, Inc., which is the only footwear brand that focuses exclusively on women, a marketing niche with a 29 percent sales growth at roughly $20 million. Bednarski left her management position with Ryka in 1999 and is currently working with the marketing department of Holy Names College in the San Francisco Bay Area. She also continues her work in the sports marketing field: as a marketing consultant, she serves as Ryka's spokesperson on QVC, a cable network that sells products directly to its customers and reaches approximately 60 million households.

Another pioneering woman who experienced great backlash is Merrily Dean Baker, former athletic director at Michigan State University. Baker has been a sports administrator for thirty years and, until recently, had the distinction of being one of only two female athletic directors to head a combined men's and women's athletic program. Baker was thus in charge of men's basketball and football. The record indicates that from the beginning of her tenure, she was faced with hostility from a "little group of guys that tried to get me out from the day I got here. . . . I was dealing with more fires than any human being should have to deal with." She further stated that there was no question that many of the barriers she faced resulted from being a woman, and that "It was the little boys' club wanting things to be the way they were [when men were in charge]."[66]

Under Baker's leadership there were renovations to athletic facilities totaling $600,000, a $1.5 million contract with Coca-Cola, and the development of a student athlete advisory board to the athletic department. Baker also points out that she raised $2.2 million per year, which was equivalent to what was raised per year before she arrived. Even in the face of these accomplishments, Baker said, she was aware that her early departure from Michigan State could signal that a woman can't do a "man's" job. Her response? "The truth is I wasn't allowed [to succeed], and that's very different." In spite of her experience at Michigan State University, Baker remains confident: "I know what Merrily Baker can do [and I] look forward to more exciting endeavors."[67] Baker left Michigan State University in 1995 and in 1997 had a brief stint as president and CEO of Women's World Cup soccer. From that post, she served as interim athletic director at Florida Gulf Coast University. In the summer of 2000 she retired from athletic administration and is currently living in Florida.

The last woman to be profiled is Martha Nause, a professional golfer who recently retired after twenty-two years on the LPGA tour. Over that span, Nause won three titles (including one major) and earned nearly $1.5 million. Her career illustrates much of what we have discussed in this essay: men's resistance to women's success, women's resilience in the face of such resistance, and in the end, a triumph that signals how far women have come in the wake of Title IX.

Martha Nause grew up in Sheboygan, Wisconsin, in the 1950s and 1960s, before Title IX. Nause, who "loved sports more than anything," was the classic tomboy who played all kinds of sports with the neighborhood boys. In high school she showed great promise as a golfer by winning, among other tournaments, the Wisconsin State Junior title. As she entered her senior year some of her classmates suggested she try out for the boys' team—there was no girls' team—where she clearly would have been a top player. But this ahead-of-its-time idea was quickly squelched when word got back to Nause that if she tried out for the team all the boys would quit. She didn't push the issue because she "wasn't used to having [sport] opportunities anyway" and didn't "want to make myself even more weird."[68]

The lack of support and active resistance Nause encountered did not prevent her from pursuing her dream of becoming a professional athlete, as her success on the LPGA tour demonstrates. Indeed, her sporting accomplishments were recently recognized by her induction into the Wisconsin Sports Hall of Fame. Nause is also the first woman to be inducted into the Sports Hall of Fame at St. Olaf College, her alma mater. And in an ironic twist— "poetic justice," in her words—Nause was recently named the head coach of the men's golf team at Macalester College, a Division III liberal arts institution in St. Paul, Minnesota. In sharp contrast to the career trends of most women who seek head coaching positions, Nause is one of only seven women nationwide who is coaching men's golf at the intercollegiate level.

Martha Nause is a leader whose career path represents the spirit and intent (not to mention the reason) for Title IX. In the early days, her golfing abilities were so threatening to her male classmates that they exhibited the classic signs of men's fear of women's success. But Nause's determination, and the opportunities afforded her as Title IX took hold, created an environment where her experience and knowledge are now "respected by my [male] players." Poetic justice indeed.

### Homophobia in Women's Sports

A particularly effective weapon used against women to limit their power and constrain their leadership opportunities is homophobia. Many deeply entrenched myths surround the historical connection between women's sport involvement and homophobia. For example, there is a long and inglorious history of seeing sport participation as "problematic" for females because of the various societal concerns such involvement has typically aroused. These concerns range from fears that women's participation will harm their reproductive capacity—and thus make them unable to fulfill their "appropriate" roles as wives and mothers—to claims that athletic involvement will turn females into men because sport is a supremely masculine endeavor.[69] One implicit (and in some cases explicit) manifestation of this latter concern is that female athletes, particularly those who engage in so-called masculine sports, are (or will become) lesbians. The Blinde et al. study provides empirical evidence for this line of thinking. The authors' interviews with Division I female athletes on basketball teams made it clear that a "majority of athletes felt the lesbian label commonly associated with women athletes detracted from their accomplishments."[70]

Scholars are becoming increasingly aware of how much the fear of lesbians' presence in sports—reflected in and perpetuated by homophobia—serves to deny all female athletes recognition, power, and respect. If we accept earlier arguments that the connection between gender and leadership reflects a power struggle in which sportswomen are relegated to the category of second-class citizenship, homophobia becomes an effective (not to mention oppressive) tool for keeping all athletic females in that category, regardless of any particular individual's sexual orientation. This is because to be pejoratively labeled a lesbian is to be stigmatized as abnormal or deviant and to be threatened with the loss of employment, career, and family.[71] Helen Lenskyj conducted one of the few research studies that specifically addresses homophobia in women's sports and how it affects women's lives and careers. She found that the sport and physical education climates were so hostile, not only to lesbians but to women in general and feminists in particular, that the vast majority of lesbians, regardless of their status as players, coaches, administrators, or faculty, remained invisible for reasons of survival.[72] One powerful example that supports Lenskyj's findings occurred in 1992, when the head women's basketball coach at Penn State University, Renee Portland, created a national firestorm by de-claring that lesbians were not welcome on her team and that she would revoke any players' scholarship if she discovered they were lesbians. Penn State has since instituted a university-wide policy banning discrimination on the basis of sexual orientation, yet Portland has never been censured by the university.[73]

There is some suggestion that as women gain more power and acceptance in sport, tactics such as lesbian baiting are on the rise. Although not specifically addressing the connection between women's sport and lesbianism, social activist and author Suzanne Pharr delineates how lesbians are seen as a threat to the established order, and how that threat is dealt with in ways that marginalize all women labeled as lesbians. Pharr's words seem particularly relevant for female athletes: "If lesbians are established as threats to the status quo, as outcasts who must be punished, homophobia can wield its power over all women through lesbian baiting. Lesbian baiting is an attempt to control women by labeling us as lesbians because our behavior is not acceptable . . . to be named as lesbians threatens all women, not just lesbians, with great loss. Any woman who steps out of [a stereotyped] role risks being called a lesbian."[74]

Adrienne Rich points out that an additional consequence of lesbian baiting, or accusing females of being deviants, is that women's power is contained because such labeling fragments women and discourages their resistance.[75] To return to the Blinde et al. study, the authors' findings echo Rich's analysis: even though female athletes bonded with their teammates, and even though they felt empowered by their sport experience, the lesbian label was frequently mentioned as a "factor leading to divisions and conflicts among athletes . . . and the phrase 'don't act like a dyke' was used to discourage stereotypical lesbian behavior."[76]

Moving beyond research findings, the following example of how lesbian baiting is used to control sportswomen, irrespective of sexual preference, puts an individual face and a voice on this deeply entrenched mechanism of oppression in women's athletics. Sanya Tyler is in a leadership role in women's sport. She is the head basketball coach at Howard University in Washington, D.C. In the early 1990s she began advocating for greater equity between the women's and men's programs, and shortly thereafter a smear campaign was begun against her.[77] Among other things, she was accused of stealing money from the sports program and of trying to get Howard University investigated by the NCAA. But according to Tyler, the rumors that were most damaging involved claims that she is a lesbian: "Homosexuality is an incredibly damaging label in this business."[78] Donna Lopiano, director of the Women's Sport Foundation and former athletic director of the women's sports program at the University of Texas at Austin, makes similar claims. She says the lesbian label is something most sportswomen live in fear of because it is used to discredit and disqualify individuals, from athletes to coaches to administrators. Lopiano is not alone in her beliefs. A study conducted by the NCAA in the late 1980s indicated that three out of four female administrators and coaches believed that being labeled a lesbian served as a barrier for recruiting and retaining women in leadership roles.[79] In addition to keeping women out of important positions of authority, women's ability to gain greater equity in sport is also affected by lesbian baiting. According to Pat Griffin, women who want to advocate for change often keep quiet for fear of being associated with the career-ending label of lesbian.[80]

Sanya Tyler's experience certainly lends credence to Griffin's claims. But like the four pioneering women profiled above, Tyler did not give in to attempts to silence and control her: she was awarded $1.1 million in a sex discrimination lawsuit that she filed against Howard University.[81]

## Conclusions and Recommendations for the Future

Wenner has argued that no long-term and lasting change will take place in sport without addressing its core values.[82] Throughout this essay, I have suggested that one core value at the center of gender, sport, and leadership is power. Any recommendation that attempts to bring about social progress in this area must therefore consider its overt and covert manifestations.

The notion of power lies at the heart of analyses regarding women taking charge in the political realm. I would suggest that one critical arena for training in power is sport, because central to the sport experience is competition against oneself, others, and the environment. In sport, women can actually experience the agony and ecstasy of combat, of exercising power with themselves as well as with and against others. Using competition to push oneself to the limit and to expand one's own boundaries is one of the many ways in which sport can serve as a site of empowerment for women.

With this background in mind, there are a number of specific recommendations at both the theoretical and practical levels that have been suggested to help develop and nurture future sport leaders. The first has to do with practical experience. Acosta and Carpenter stated that in addition to the development and implementation of workshops and clinics, we should push for more internships and graduate assistantship programs designed to prepare women as coaches.[83] As part of this approach, formal mentoring relationships could be developed between current women coaches and aspiring coaches. Those serving in head coaching positions could not only share their experience but also serve as important role models; younger women could see the embodiment of their visions in such legendary individuals as Pat Summitt and Vivian Stringer. While serving as role models, women coaches could also actively encourage females to pursue a coaching career. We should not underestimate the significance of coaching experience to the advancement of women in sport leadership roles. As Fitzgerald et al. discovered, coaching experience at the intercollegiate level was the most common predictor for becoming a college athletic director.[84]

A second recommendation involves recruitment. As the research cited earlier in the essay clearly indicates, unless there is an aggressive attempt on the part of athletic administrators to actively recruit women, today's employment trends will remain relatively unchanged. A part of this recruitment process should be an extensive use of informal as well as formal networks, because both coaches and administrators say this is a critical factor when recruiting females. In a similar vein, women themselves must be more active in applying for coaching opportunities. As Lovett and Lowry suggest, "by aggressively seeking positions as coaches and athletic directors and by informing and recommending other qualified females for similar positions, women can become their own best friends rather than victims of the good ol' boy system."[85]

A third recommendation is to provide strong networks of support once women are hired so that they will be retained. Previously cited research indicates that women coaches suffered higher burnout rates, were more concerned with discrimination on the job, and felt a much greater need for support and consideration from athletic directors than did their male counterparts. If women are to be truly effective in leadership roles, chilly and even hostile climates must become more welcoming. For example, we should send the message that there will be a "zero tolerance" policy when it comes to bigotry in any form. Acknowledging this situation, the NCAA has implemented a series of workshops and seminars designed to "help athletic departments deal with issues of diversity, including sexual orientation."[86] This is a step in the right direction because attempts at changing the climate for women must specifically address the enormous damage that homophobia has wrought.

Additional strategies can involve making the media at both the national and local levels aware of the issues involved. As part of a national media campaign, individual states around the country could, for example, declare a certain month "Celebration of Women Sport Leaders Month." This in turn could be used to educate the general public about the continued underrepresentation of women in sport leadership roles while simultaneously sharing information about how this trend can be reversed. Finally, at the federal level, we could establish a task force that will provide resources to implement many of the above recommendations on a nationwide basis.

The history of women's sport involvement has been a history of overcoming challenges. There was a time when our popular images of sport leaders were exclusively male. But in the wake of Title IX, and the recent accomplishments of sportswomen at all levels of competition, some of those images now include Mia Hamm, Cynthia Cooper, Jackie Joyner-Kersee, and Pat Summitt. As we begin the twenty-first century, women will continue to face and defeat the next round of challenges. This is because women have always made significant contributions as warriors and leaders. Their contributions in sport have been, and will continue to be, no exception.

# Notes

1. Melpomene Institute for the Minnesota Coalition of Organizations for Sex Equity in Education, *Title IX: Providing Equal Opportunity for Girls* (St. Paul, Minn.: Author, 1998).

2. National Sporting Goods Association, *Sport Participation Study* (Mount Prospect, Ill.: Author, 1998).

3. L. Disch and M. J. Kane, "When a Looker Is Really a Bitch: Lisa Olson, Sport, and the Heterosexual Matrix," *Signs: Journal of Women in Culture and Society* 21 (1996): 278–308; M. C. Duncan, "Sport Photographs and Sexual Difference: Images of Women and Men in the 1984 and 1988 Olympic Games," *Sport Sociology Journal* 7 (1990): 40.

4. R. V. Acosta and L. J. Carpenter, "Women in Intercollegiate Sport: A Longitudinal Study: Twenty-Year Update," unpublished manuscript, Brooklyn College, Brooklyn, N.Y., 1998. See also J. S. Fink and D. L. Pastore, "Diversity in Sport? Utilizing the Business Literature to Devise a Comprehensive Framework of Diversity Initiatives," *Quest* 51 (1999): 310–27; D. J. Lovett and C. D. Lowry, "Women and the NCAA: Not Separate, Not Equal," *Journal of Sport Management* 9 (1995): 244–48; D. L. Pastore, S. Inglis, and K. E. Danylchuk, "Retention Factors in Coaching and Athletic Management: Differences by Gender, Position, and Geographic Location," *Journal of Sport and Social Issues* 24 (1996): 427–41.

5. Fink and Pastore, "Diversity in Sport?," 311.

6. Acosta and Carpenter, "Women in Intercollegiate Sport."

7. M. P. Fitzgerald, M. A. Sagaria, and B. Nelson, "Career Patterns of Athletic

Directors: Challenging the Conventional Wisdom," *Journal of Sport Management* 8 (1994): 14–26.

8. Ibid.

9. M. J. Kane, "Fictional Denials of Female Empowerment: A Feminist Analysis of Young Adult Sports Fiction," *Sociology of Sport Journal* 15, no. 3 (1998): 231–62; M. J. Kane and H. Lenskyj, "Media Treatment of Female Athletes: Issues of Gender and Sexualities," in *MediaSport*, ed. L. Wenner (London: Routledge, 1998), 186–201.

10. M. E. Duquin, "The Importance of Sport in Building Women's Potential," in *Sport in Contemporary Society*, ed. D. S. Eitzen, 3d ed. (New York: St. Martin's Press, 1989), 357–62.

11. Catherine Mackinnon, "Women, Self-Possession, and Sport," in *Feminism Unmodified: Discourses on Life and Law*, ed. C. Mackinnon (Cambridge, Mass.: Harvard University Press, 1987), 117–24; Leslie Heywood, *Bodymakers: A Cultural Anatomy of Women's Body Building* (New Brunswick, N.J.: Rutgers University Press, 1998); Iris M. Young, "Throwing Like a Girl: A Phenomenology of Feminine Body Comportment, Motility, and Spatiality," in *Throwing Like a Girl and Other Essays in Feminist Philosophy and Social Theory*, ed. I. M. Young (Bloomington: Indiana University Press, 1990), 141–59.

12. Mackinnon, "Women, Self-Possession, and Sport," 121.

13. M. J. Kane, "Resistance/Transformation of the Oppositional Binary: Exposing Sport as a Continuum," *Journal of Sport and Social Issues* 19, no. 2 (1995): 191–218; M. J. Kane and L. Disch, "Sexual Violence and the Reproduction of Male Power in the Locker Room: The Lisa Olson Incident," *Sociology of Sport Journal* 10, no. 4 (1993): 331–52; H. Lenskyj, "Sexuality and Femininity in Sport Contexts: Issues and Alternatives," *Journal of Sport and Social Issues* 18 (1994): 356–76.

14. Nancy Therberge, "Reflections on the Body in the Sociology of Sport," *Quest* 43 (1991): 129.

15. S. Birrell and D. M. Richter, "Is a Diamond Forever? Feminist Transformations of Sport," *Women's Studies International Forum* 10 (1987): 395.

16. E. M. Blinde, D. E. Taub, and L. Han, "Sport Participation and Women's Personal Empowerment: Experiences of the College Athlete," *Journal of Sport and Social Issues* 17 (1993): 47–60.

17. E. M. Blinde, D. E. Taub, and L. Han, "Sport as a Site for Women's Group and Societal Empowerment: Perspectives from the College Athlete," *Sociology of Sport Journal* 11 (1994): 54.

18. Ibid., 54, 57.

19. Acosta and Carpenter, "Women in Intercollegiate Sport"; C. A. Hasbrook, B. A. Hart, S. A. Mathes, and S. True, "Sex Bias and the Validity of Believed Differences between Male and Female Interscholastic Athletic Coaches," *Research Quarterly for Exercise and Sport* 63, no. 3 (1990): 259–67; M. J. Kane and J. M. Stangl, "Employment Patterns of Female Coaches in Men's Athletics: Tokenism and Marginalization as Reflections of Occupational Sex-Segregation," *Journal of Sport and Social Issues* 15, no. 1 (1991): 21–41.

20. H. Barber, "Examining Gender Differences in Sources and Levels of Perceived Competence in Interscholastic Coaches," *Sport Psychologist* 12 (1998): 237–52; Fink and Pastore, "Diversity in Sport?"; V. Krane, "Homonegativism Experienced by Lesbian College Athletes," *Women in Sport and Physical Activity Journal* 6, no. 2 (1997): 141–63; S. Wellman and E. Blinde, "Homophobia in Women's Intercollegiate Basketball: Views of Women Coaches Regarding Coaching Careers and Recruitment of Athletes," *Women in Sport and Physical Activity Journal* 6 (1997): 63–82; D. L. Pastore, "Male and Female Coaches of Women's Athletic Teams: Reasons for Entering and Leaving the Profession," *Journal of Sport Management* 5 (1991): 128–43; D. J. Lovett and C. D. Lowry, " 'Good Old Boys' and 'Good Old Girls' Clubs: Myth or Reality?" *Journal of Sport Management* 8 (1994): 27–35; Fitzgerald et al., "Career Patterns of Athletic Directors"; J. M. Stangl and M. J. Kane, "Structural Variables That Offer Explanatory Power for the Underrepresentation of Women Coaches since Title IX: The Case of Homologous Reproduction," *Sociology of Sport Journal* 8 (1991): 47–60.

21. R. V. Acosta and L. J. Carpenter, "Perceived Causes of the Declining Representation of Women Leaders in Intercollegiate Sports: 1988 Update," unpublished manuscript, Brooklyn College, Brooklyn, N.Y., 1988.

22. Hasbrook et al., "Sex Biases."

23. Stangl and Kane, "Structural Variables," 49.

24. T. W. Anderson and K. S. Gill, "Occupational Socialization Patterns of Men's and Women's Interscholastic Basketball Teams," *Journal of Sport Behavior* 6, no. 3 (1983): 105–16.

25. A. Knoppers, "Coaching: An Equal Opportunity Occupation?" *Journal of Physical Education, Recreation, and Dance* 60, no. 3 (1989): 40.

26. Rosabeth M. Kanter, *Men and Women of the Corporation* (New York: Basic Books, 1977), 48.

27. Stangl and Kane, "Structural Variables."

28. Pastore, "Male and Female Coaches"; Acosta and Carpenter, "Women in Intercollegiate Sport"; Lovett and Lowry, "Good Old Boys," 32.

29. Lovett and Lowry, "Good Old Boys," 33.

30. Kanter, *Women and Men of the Corporation*.

31. Hasbrook et al., "Sex Biases"; Anderson and Gill, "Occupational Socialization Patterns."

32. A. Knoppers, "Explaining Male Dominance and Sex Segregation in Coaching: Three Approaches," *Quest* 44 (1992): 210–27; Lovett and Lowry, "Good Old Boys."

33. T. M. Caccese and C. K. Mayerberg, "Gender Differences in Perceived Burnout of College Coaches," *Journal of Sport Psychology* 6 (1984): 279–88.

34. D. L. Pastore and M. R. Judd, "Gender Differences in Burnout among College Coaches of Women's Athletic Teams at Two-Year Colleges," *Sociology of Sport Journal* 10 (1993): 205–12.

35. D. L. Pastore, "Two-Year College Coaches of Women's Teams: Gender Differences in Coaching Career Selections," *Journal of Sport Management* 6 (1992): 179–90.

36. D. J. Lovett and C. D. Lowry, "The Role of Gender in Leadership Positions in Female Sport Programs in Texas Colleges," *Journal of Sport Management* 2 (1988): 114.

37. L. R. Offerman and C. Beil, "Achievement Styles of Women Leaders and Their Peers: Toward an Understanding of Women and Leadership," *Psychology of Women Quarterly* 16 (1992): 37–56.

38. C. J. Snyder, "The Effects of Leader Behavior and Organizational Climate on Intercollegiate Coaches' Job Satisfaction," *Journal of Sport Management* 4 (1990): 59.

39. B. L. Parkhouse and J. M. Williams, "Differential Effects of Sex and Status on Evaluation of Coaching Ability," *Research Quarterly for Exercise and Sport* 57, no. 1 (1986): 53–59.

40. J. M. Williams and B. L. Parkhouse, "Social Learning Theory as a Foundation for Examining Sex Bias in Evaluation of Coaches," *Journal of Sport and Exercise Psychology* 10 (1988): 322–30.

41. Lovett and Lowry, "The Role of Gender," 114.

42. Pastore, "Male and Female Coaches"; S. True, "Coaching: Study Evaluates Reasons behind Declining Number of Women Coaches," *Interscholastic Athletic Administration* 12 (1986): 18–19, 21; Acosta and Carpenter, "Perceived Causes"; B. A. Hart, C. A. Hasbrook, and S. A. Mathes, "An Examination of the Reduction in the Number of Female Interscholastic Coaches," *Research Quarterly for Exercise and Sport* 57, no. 1 (1986): 68–77; Hasbrook et al., "Sex Biases."

43. Lovett and Lowry, "The Role of Gender," 114.

44. Hasbrook et al., "Sex Biases"; Fitzgerald et al., "Career Patterns of Athletic Directors."

45. Kanter, *Men and Women of the Corporation*, 34.

46. A. Knoppers, B. B. Meyer, M. Ewing, and L. Forrest, "Dimensions of Power: A Question of Sport or Gender?" *Sociology of Sport Journal* 7 (1990): 369–77.

47. A. Harlan and C. Weiss, "Sex Differences in Factors Affecting Managerial Career Advancement," in *Women in the Workplace*, ed. P. Wallace (Boston: Auburn House, 1982), 59–100.

48. Kane and Stangl, "Structural Variables."

49. L. Fishwick, "Where Have All the Women Coaches Gone? Placing the Question in Context," unpublished manuscript, University of Illinois, Champaign, 1986, 7–8.

50. B. Reskin, "Bringing the Men Back In: Sex Differentiation and the Devaluation of Women's Work," *Gender and Society* 2 (1988): 58.

51. Knoppers et al., "Dimensions of Power," 369.

52. Kanter, *Men and Women of the Corporation*.

53. Kane and Stangl, "Structural Variables," 31.

54. L. Code, "Tokenism," *Resources of Feminist Research* 16, no. 3 (1987): 46.

55. M. A. Hall, D. Cullen, and T. Slack, "Organizational Elites Recreating Themselves: The Gender Structure of National Sport Organizations," *Quest* 41 (1989): 28–43.

56. Barber, "Examining Gender Differences"; Pastore, "Male and Female Coaches."

57. B. L. Sisley, M. Weiss, H. Barber, and V. Ebbeck, "Developing Competence and Confidence in Novice Women Coaches: A Study of Attitudes, Motives, and Perceptions of Ability," *Journal of Physical Education, Recreation, and Dance* 61, no. 1 (1990): 61.

58. D. L. Pastore and W. G. Meacci, "Employment Process for NCAA Female Coaches," *Journal of Sport Management* 8 (1994): 117 (emphasis added), 126.

59. Knoppers, "Coaching."

60. Lovett and Lowry, "The Role of Gender," 115.

61. In the late 1960s Horner developed an achievement motivation construct labeled fear of success (FOS), which dealt with an individual's motive to avoid success. Horner theorized that FOS "is much more common in females than in males and is especially evident in women who have the capability of success" (D. L. Gill, *Psychological Dynamics of Sport* [Champaign, Ill.: Human Kinetics, 1986], 89). According to Gill, subsequent research has cast serious doubts on Horner's measures and constructs.

62. L. Woody, "Phil's Saga May Shuffle Off to the Movies," (Nashville) *Tennessean*, 18 June 1990, D1.

63. R. Finn, "An Aide with a Different Image," *New York Times*, 30 December 1992, B7–8.

64. K. Bednarski, "Convincing Male Managers to Target Women Customers," *Working Women*, June 1993, 23–28.

65. Ibid., 24, 23.

66. M. Kaufman, "Baker Learned Pettiness, Sexism at Michigan State," *St. Paul Pioneer Press*, 27 May 1995, 1C, 7C.

67. Ibid., 7C, 1C.

68. Martha Nause, phone interview, July 2000.

69. P. Griffin, "Changing the Game: Homophobia, Sexism, and Lesbians in Sport," *Quest* 44 (1992): 251–65; P. Griffin, *Strong Women, Deep Closets: Lesbians and Homophobia in Sport* (Champaign, Ill.: Human Kinetics, 1998); Kane and Lenskyj, "Media Treatment"; Krane, "Homonegativism Experienced by Lesbian College Athletes"; M. J. Veri, "Homophobic Discourse Surrounding the Female Athlete," *Quest* 51 (1999): 355–68.

70. Blinde et al., "Sport as a Site," 55.

71. J. Cart, "Lesbian Issue Stirs Discussion," *Los Angeles Times*, 6 April 1992, C1, C12; H. L. Schwartz, "Out of Bounds," *The Advocate*, 18 March 1997, 56–62.

72. Helen Lenskyj, "Unsafe at Home Base: Women's Experiences of Sexual Harassment in University Sport and Physical Education," *Women in Sport and Physical Activity Journal* 1 (1992): 19–33.

73. Cart, "Lesbian Issue."

74. S. Pharr, *Homophobia: A Weapon of Sexism* (Little Rock, Ark.: Chardon Press, 1988), 19.

75. Adrienne Rich, "Compulsory Heterosexuality and Lesbian Existence," *Signs: Journal of Women in Culture and Society* 5, no. 4 (1980): 631–60.

76. Blinde et al., "Sport as a Site," 54.

77. D. Blum, "College Sports' L-word," *Chronicle of Higher Education*, 9 March 1994, A36.

78. Tyler, as cited in Blum, "College Sports' L-word," A36.

79. Blum, "College Sports' L-word," A36.

80. Pat Griffin, *Strong Women*.

81. Part of the award ($54,000) included damages related to defamation of character against Tyler. Howard is appealing the lawsuit (Blum, "College Sports' L-word").

82. L. A. Wenner, "Drugs, Sport, and Media Influence: Can Media Inspire Constructive Attitudinal Change?" *Journal of Sport and Social Issues* 18, no. 3 (1994): 282–92.

83. Acosta and Carpenter, "Women in Intercollegiate Sport."

84. Fitzgerald et al., "Career Patterns."

85. Lovett and Lowry, "The Role of Gender in Leadership," 116.

86. Blum, "College Sports' L-word," A36.

# Want to Learn More?

### Gender Equity in Sports

Gender Equity in Sports is designed to serve as a resource for any individual investigating the state of affairs in interscholastic or intercollegiate sports. The content and data are primarily based on an ongoing project being maintained by Mary C. Curtis and Dr. Christine H. B. Grant at the University of Iowa. Because changes are taking place every day, from the institutional level to the legislative level, this document will be updated on a regular basis. These reports have been collected from newspaper articles, the Women's Sports Foundation, and personal references.

Gender Equity in Sports
Women's Intercollegiate Athletics
340 Carver-Hawkeye Arena
Iowa City, IA 52242
Telephone (319) 335-9247
bailiwick.lib.uiowa.edu/ge

### The National Association of Collegiate Women Athletic Administrators (NACWAA)

The National Association of Collegiate Women Athletic Administrators' intent is to preserve and enhance opportunities for leadership and career development of women athletic administrators and to strengthen collegiate athletic programs, particularly as they relate to women. NACWAA is committed to providing opportunities for the formulation of new ways of confronting the issues and challenges affecting collegiate athletic programs.

National Association of Collegiate Women Athletic Administrators
4701 Wrightsville Avenue
Oak Park D-1
Wilmington, NC 28403
Telephone (910) 793-8244
Fax (910) 793-8299
www.oit.virginia.edu/nacwaa/nacwaa.home

### The Women's Sports Foundation

The Women's Sports Foundation is a national nonprofit, member-based organization dedicated to increasing opportunities for girls and women in sports and fitness through education, advocacy, recognition, and grants. Established in 1974 by Billie Jean King, its founder; Donna de Varona, a founding member and its first president; and many other champion female athletes, the foundation seeks to create an educated public that encourages females' participation and supports gender equality in sport. Its goal is to improve the physical, mental, and emotional well-being of all females through sports and fitness participation.

Women's Sports Foundation
Eisenhower Park
East Meadow, NY 11554
Telephone (800) 227-3988 or (516) 542-4700
www.lifetimetv.com/WoSport/index.htm

### Empowering Women in Sports

The *Empowering Women in Sports* report is a publication of the Feminist Majority Foundation's Task Force on Women and Girls in Sports. It profiles women athletes and administrators who have paved the way and offers "Strategies for Change" that women and girl athletes, coaches, administrators, and parents can take to make school and college athletics more equitable.

Feminist Majority and Feminist Majority Foundation
1600 Wilson Boulevard, Suite 801
Arlington, VA 22209
www.feminist.org/research/sports2.html

### The Tucker Center for Research on Girls & Women in Sport

The Tucker Center for Research on Girls & Women in Sport is dedicated to exploring how sport, recreation, and physical activity affect the lives of girls and women. The first of its kind in the country, it is an interdisciplinary center leading a pioneering effort on significant research, education, community outreach, and public service.

Tucker Center for Research on Girls & Women in Sport
University of Minnesota
203 Cooke Hall, 1900 University Avenue SE
Minneapolis, MN 55455
Telephone (612) 625-7327
Fax (612) 626-7700
E-mail info@tuckercenter.org
www.tuckercenter.org

*Part* II

CASE STUDIES

# 5

## Knowledge Is Power:
## *Our Bodies, Ourselves* and the Boston
## Women's Health Book Collective

**Barbara A. Brehm**

### ■ BACKGROUND

I have been a fan of *Our Bodies, Ourselves* since I first saw it in the early 1970s when I was in college. As a young woman, I loved its wild and free spirit and its high-energy message that if we work together, anything is possible. As much as I appreciated the written message and the great information, I think what I loved even more were the photos and total presentation, and the anonymous group voice that urged me to open my eyes. And over the years, I have admired and envied the women of the collective for their ability to work together over such a long period of time and to be so productive in their work.

I began thinking about the work of the collective again just a few years ago, when I started work on a teen health project. This project grew out of a perceived need for a health curriculum that appealed to and addressed the needs of adolescent girls. A group of us from Smith College and the YWCA of Western Massachusetts decided to enlist the help of teen girls in designing, writing, and editing a book that addressed their issues and concerns. Like the writing of *Our Bodies, Ourselves*, the process was essential for our product. Generously interspersed with the writings of the adult "experts" are personal stories from the girls themselves. It is truly the words of the girls themselves, in stories and quotations from the focus group transcripts, that make the book come alive.

The girls created a title for the project: *Our Health, Our Futures: A Project by and for Adolescent Girls*, which of course sounds very similar to *Our Bodies, Ourselves: A Book by and for Women*. Like the women in the Boston Women's Health Book Collective, those of us involved in *Our*

*Health, Our Futures* hope that the written information will be useful but know that it is not nearly as exciting or interesting as getting women and girls together to talk about their experiences. Visit our website (written by the girls, of course) at www.smith.edu/ourhealthourfutures.

The essay that follows discusses the evolution of the Boston Women's Health Book Collective, how it illustrates women's ways of working and knowing, and the effects it has had on the women's health movement and on health care in general.

*Real change in the modern age requires not the seizure of power, the revolutionary's dream, but the dispersal of power.*

— F. LEWIS, editorial, *New York Times*, 8 August 1990

THROUGHOUT history women with no inherent "authority" and with no leadership training or experience have worked at the grassroots level to solve social problems by educating themselves and others. One of the most successful and inspiring examples of this type of work is seen in the Boston Women's Health Book Collective, which more than thirty years ago began the work that led to the creation of the best-selling women's health book *Our Bodies, Ourselves.*[1] This essay examines the early years and the subsequent development of the collective. It looks at how these remarkable women worked together in the collective and as part of the larger women's health movement to create a new vision of leadership and authority. It also shows how the work of the collective, along with that of numerous other people and groups, has had and continues to have an enormous impact on the health information explosion, the doctor-patient relationship, and health care delivery in the United States, with important consequences for all consumers, both women and men.

The collective's work began in May 1969 when a group of women met in a discussion group called "Women and Their Bodies" at a women's liberation conference at Emmanuel College in Boston. The conference was sponsored by an early women's movement group in the Boston area called Bread and Roses. The women's movement of the 1960s comprised primarily white, middle-class women in their twenties and thirties. Most were fairly well educated, having completed high school. Many had completed some college as well.

The discussion in the Women and Their Bodies group was a heated one, as participants told stories of the frustration and anger they had experienced as patients in the health care system. Many participants, later referred to as the "doctor's group," decided to continue meeting after the conference, with the goal of creating a list of "good doctors" to distribute to other women living in the area.[2] They defined a good doctor as one who listened to what patients had to say; respected their opinions; clearly explained procedures, medications, and treatment options; and treated women as intelligent, responsible adults.[3] As they continued to meet and share their experiences, these women concluded that no such list was possible. For every good experience with a particular doctor, another woman had a story of frustration. As the women talked, they realized that in many instances they didn't know enough about their bodies to evaluate the quality of the medical care they had received. A drive to learn more about their bodies and the health issues they were facing set in motion the work that provided the foundation for *Our Bodies, Ourselves*.

## Powerless as Women and Powerless as Patients

To appreciate the passion these women brought to their work, we must transport ourselves back in time to the 1950s and 1960s, when these women were growing up. At this time, the medical system was at the height of its glory in conquering many infectious diseases, thanks to the discovery of antibiotics in the late 1940s. These new wonder drugs gave physicians great power over some of the leading killers of that time: pneumonia, tuberculosis, syphilis, and other infectious diseases. The use of antibiotic therapy typified the approach of the medical establishment: treatment of a disease state through a therapy aimed at the biological cause. This approach to healing, which focuses primarily on biological causes while underplaying the importance of social and environmental factors, is often referred to as biomedicine. I will say more about the changing face of health care later in this essay, as it has expanded its focus on health and disease to include a more holistic outlook. But in the 1950s and 1960s, a doctor's primary focus was on treating the disease, not the patient.

In the 1950s and 1960s, when a need for health care sent you to a doctor, he was most likely a white male, educated at a medical school whose curriculum focused on biomedical approaches to illness. This curriculum had grown almost entirely out of clinical work on men, except in the areas of reproduction, where little research was done at all. In medical textbooks, women's bodies were described primarily in comparison to male functioning; women were variants of "normal" (i.e., male) physiology.[4] Many women's health care problems such as premenstrual tension and dysmenorrhea (painful menstrual periods) received little attention. On the other hand, some female phenomena such as pregnancy, childbirth, and menopause were seen as health problems requiring expert medical intervention. Women of child-bearing age were rarely included as participants in studies of medical treatments, so treatments de- signed for men were often less successful for female patients. During the 1960s and early 1970s, the white, middle-class women who formed the foundation of the women's movement were angry about many medical issues, including the following: the prescription of the then high-dose estrogen birth control pills with no information regarding the possibly dangerous side effects; unnecessary and unauthorized hysterectomies and sterilizations; and childbirth practices, such as inducing labor, that accommodated the doctor but interfered with the process of labor and often led to unnecessary and painful interventions.[5]

What particularly angered women such as those in the doctor's group was the condescension they felt from doctors. In 1969 doctor knew best. Women exchanged stories of asking the doctor for information about their medications, only to be told, "Don't worry, dear." Women were often treated as emotional, irrational, unpredictable creatures who suffered from raging hormones.[6] Doc- tors usually made health care decisions with minimal input from patients, and patients received little information about the treatments they were receiving. Although many women were experiencing similar treatment, women individu- ally often felt isolated and confused. To those women who were to become the collective, the medical establishment represented a perfect microcosm of a larger political system in which power remained in the hands of a select few who did not always have your best interest at heart. This exclusion from deci- sion making, lack of respect, and lack of information struck a raw nerve in many women, for it typified what they perceived as their treatment by society in general. Biology was destiny, a destiny with limited possibilities for women and exclusion from economic and political power.[7]

Some of this anger is apparent in the last chapter of the first edition of *Our Bodies, Ourselves*, published in December 1970. The three-page chapter is titled "Women, Medicine, and Capitalism," and the following quotation is from a section called "The Ideology of Control and Submission":

> [In the medical system, h]ealth is not something which belongs to a
> person, but is rather a precious item that the doctor doles out from
> his stores. Thus, the doctor preserves his expertise and powers for
> himself. He controls the knowledge and thereby controls the patient.
> He maintains his status in a number of ways: First, he and his col-
> leagues make it very difficult for more people to become doctors. . . .

Second, he sets himself off from other people in a number of ways, including dressing in whites. . . . Another much more important way doctors set themselves off from other people is through their language. . . . Thirdly, doctors insulate themselves from the rest of society by making the education process (indoctrination) so long, tedious, and grueling that the public has come to believe that one must be superhuman to survive it. (Actually, it is like one long fraternity "rush" after which you've made it and can do what you like. Only members of the club get to learn the secret, which is that doctors don't know much to begin with and are bluffing a good deal of the time.)

And in a later section, "Alienation":

Doctors' blatant ignorance about sex stands in stark contradiction to the fact that they are considered the only legitimate person to consult about any sexual problem. Thus, we bring all our awkwardness and ignorance about sex to a doctor who cannot understand that his own ignorance and arrogance are the epitome of male chauvinism. (Add any man's standard portion of male chauvinism to the whole mind set and life style of the man who controls knowledge and thereby people "for their benefit" and we come up with the doctor of our society.)[8]

## Raising Consciousness

Consciousness-raising groups were a mainstay of the women's movement during the late 1960s and early 1970s. The women's liberation movement encouraged these groups as a vehicle for raising women's awareness of sexism in their daily lives. Increased awareness was seen as an important first step toward inspiring a desire for change and eventually, as women became inspired to work together, toward changing an unjust system that worked for a privileged few at the expense of many.[9]

Consciousness-raising groups generally comprised about ten women who met on a regular basis to share experiences, ideas, dreams, and problems in their lives as women. Analysis and criticism were an important part of the group dynamic. Women shared self-doubts and problematic issues in their personal lives and responded to the observations, suggestions, and criticism of others in the group. Often they found that a problem they thought only they faced, or for which they blamed themselves, was actually something many women experienced, something with social, political, and economic roots, which they could work together to address. Strong bonds often grew among group members as they supported each other in their efforts to express themselves and overcome the confines of gender role stereotypes.[10] This exchange of personal experiences was the vehicle through which consciousness-raising groups hoped to achieve their goal: "to make the personal political; to create awareness (through shared experiences) that what were thought to be personal deficiencies and individual problems are common and shared."[11]

Understanding the communication dynamics of these early consciousness-raising groups provides great insight into the workings and writings of the Boston Women's Health Book Collective.[12] In almost all of their writings, the collective speaks as a group; although individual voices are heard, the overall impression is that the writings are a product of conversations among a group of women, a group in which each individual is accorded equal respect and input. Much has been written about female communication styles and ways in which women make health care decisions.[13] Surely one of the primary reasons women have been drawn to the various editions of *Our Bodies, Ourselves* for over thirty years is the writing style, which fits perfectly with Belenky et al.'s descriptions of women's preferred ways of learning and knowing:

> [Educators help women most when they emphasize] connection over separation, understanding and acceptance over assessment, and collaboration over debate; if they accord respect to and allow time for the knowledge that emerges from firsthand experience; if instead of imposing their own expectations and arbitrary requirements, they encourage students to evolve their own patterns of work based on the problems they are pursuing.[14]

The writing in *Our Bodies, Ourselves* emphasizes the connection among all women while at the same time presenting an understanding acceptance of the diversity of individual experience. The explanatory text is richly illustrated with personal stories from thousands of women, with several personal stories or reflections appearing on almost every page. Use of the first and second person throughout the book draws the reader into the discussion. The reader feels as though she has become a part of the consciousness-raising group itself as she reads the stories of others and feels her own thoughts become part of the discussion.

## Women and Their Bodies

Conceptions about the female body have served to justify limiting women's access to power in many cultures throughout the ages. We laugh today that people once thought education and exercise diverted the "vital energies" necessary for women's reproductive functions.[15] In the 1950s and 1960s, however, women were still routinely excluded from many sports and occupations on the basis of conceptions about the female body. For such reasons, women have struggled for years to change restrictive ideas regarding their bodies. The work of the collective formed an important part of this struggle.

Western culture has long regarded our physical bodies and their functions (particularly sexual activities and childbirth) as the most animal-like part of the self and therefore something to be controlled and hidden, something to be ashamed of. In the 1950s the dictates of modesty discouraged frank discussions of sexual anatomy and function, and many mothers found (and still find) it difficult to discuss sex with their daughters. In schools, girls were usually taught a minimal amount about the menstrual cycle, with a focus on hygiene. Pregnancy and childbirth fell into the medical domain, and women generally knew little about these topics. Because people's limited knowledge of human physiology was often combined with a great deal of myth and superstition, it was no wonder that many women found learning about their bodies an enlightening and liberating experience.

The health concerns embraced by the early women's health movement reflect the situations of the women themselves. In 1969 many women active in the women's movement were concerned about reproductive health issues. Many of the women who were to become members of the collective had just had babies, some the result of unplanned pregnancies. A few had full- or part-time jobs. Some were currently home with their young children. Some did volunteer work in the community and were active in the antiwar movement. All were white and middle-class and ranged in age from mid-twenties to late thirties. They and their friends had been through abuses associated with hospital childbirth and were concerned about women's limited access to birth control (many doctors would not even prescribe a diaphragm for unmarried women). Abortion, which was then still illegal in the United States, was one of the pivotal issues that drew many women together in the late 1960s. Many women were outraged at stories of girls and women becoming ill or even dying from illegal abortions.

When the women composing the Women and Their Bodies discussion group met, there was plenty to discuss. As "the doctor's group" continued to meet during the summer following the conference, they decided to acquire the knowledge they needed to become more active participants in their own health care and to campaign more effectively for health care reform. Each woman researched and wrote a paper on a health topic of personal interest. Topics included menstruation, pregnancy, childbirth, postpartum depression, abortion, sexuality, and birth control. The women gathered knowledge about their topics by exchanging information among themselves and with other friends; talking to doctors, nurses, and friends who were medical students; and conducting research in medical and other libraries. While all of the women had some college education, none had medical or health-related training, so plowing through medical books and journals required the constant companionship of dictionaries and reference notes. As the women grew more excited and empowered by their research, they felt a strong desire to share the learning and experience with other women. They decided to teach a course on women and their bodies in the coming winter.[16]

Throughout the fall the women brought the fruits of their research back to the group at their weekly meetings. Their research blossomed with excitement and meaning as it became illuminated by the personal stories of the researcher and of other women in the discussion group. This was education at its best. Two of the group members later wrote:

> When we brought the factual information back to the group, we discussed the topics out of our own experiences of them in our own lives. In this way, the textbook view of childbirth or miscarriage or menstruation or lovemaking, for instance, nearly always written by men, would become expanded and enriched by the truth of our actual experiences. . . . We saw quickly the power of this kind of health and sex education. The weaving together of facts and feelings made the information useful to us in a new way, and putting our stories together helped us see ways we were all receiving inadequate treatment, allowed us to begin to build up an effective critique of a medical system that had heretofore kept us isolated from each other.[17]

In January 1970 the women gave their first course, called "Women and Their Bodies," several times. Each course continued for about ten to twelve weeks, meeting in the evening in any free space the women could find, including their homes. The women's research papers were incorporated into extensive group discussions in a lively atmosphere of learning and discovery for both "teachers" and students. After teaching the first course, the women decided to

revise their original papers and mimeograph them so copies could be distributed. At the end of each course, interested women were encouraged to teach
a course of their own, using the mimeographed papers.

As demand for the course and the papers continued to build, the women
decided to get them printed and bound in an inexpensive newsprint volume,
published by an alternative press, the New England Free Press.[18] This printing
of five thousand copies cost fifteen hundred dollars and was financed by several
of the women. The title of the first printing, released in December 1970, was
*Women and Their Bodies*, and it sold for seventy-five cents. Authorship was
attributed to the Boston Women's Health Course Collective, although individual authors' names were listed for each chapter. Demand for the book was
overwhelming, and in April 1971 a second printing of fifteen thousand copies
followed quickly on the heels of the first. Profits from the first printing were
used to bring the price of the book down to forty-five and then to thirty cents.
By the second printing, the women decided to change the title to *Women and
Our Bodies*, and then to *Our Bodies, Ourselves*. The office of the New England
Free Press was inundated with orders for the book, as women in Boston sent
copies to friends all over the country. Twenty thousand copies were printed in
September 1971, and twenty-five thousand in December 1971. The topics listed
in the table of contents are as follows:

1. Course Introduction
2. Anatomy and Physiology
3. Sexuality
4. Some Myths about Women
5. Venereal Disease
6. Birth Control
7. Abortion
8. Pregnancy
9. Prepared Childbirth
10. Post Partum
11. Medical Institutions
12. Women, Medicine, and Capitalism

A note added to the table of contents reinforces the notion that the book
and the course were rapidly evolving works-in-progress:

> The first printing sold so fast we haven't had time to revise the printed
> course. We are working on revisions which we hope will be ready for

the 3rd printing. We want to add chapters on menopause and getting older and attitudes to children (child rearing alternatives, single women having children, adopting, *also* not having children). We want to expand existing chapters to include more on monogamy, homosexuality, women's diseases and hysterectomies, the relation between mental and physical health, nutrition, etc., etc.

Would you like to make suggestions, write up your own experience, or otherwise work on the course? Please write us. The course is what all of us make it.[19]

At this point in the life of *Our Bodies, Ourselves*, the book was seen primarily as a vehicle for bringing women together to learn about their bodies and discuss their experiences. In fact, in the "Course Introduction" the writers state,

The papers in and of themselves are not very important. They should be viewed as a tool which stimulates discussion and action, which allows for new ideas and for change. . . . [In our experience with the course,] it was more important that we talked about our experiences, were challenged by others' experiences (often we came from very different situations), raised our questions, expressed our feelings, were challenged to act, than that we learned any specific body of material.[20]

As time went by, however, the book itself came to be seen by many readers as an authoritative source for women's health information. The research was thorough, the perspective broad, and the approach holistic. It was a book that women across the country, and indeed, around the world, had been wanting for many years.

## Acquiring Authority

Much of the power of medicine rests in knowledge. And medical knowledge is not only the basis for the authority of health care professionals but also primarily what consumers are buying when they pay for a visit to a provider. Patients want access to the provider's knowledge, knowledge acquired from years of training, knowledge that will presumably help patients improve their health. Back in 1969, entering the realm of medical knowledge probably felt much like entering forbidden territory to the women preparing the "Women and Their Bodies" course. Not that nonmedical people weren't allowed to read medical books and journals, but it just "wasn't done." It was assumed (and the assumption was widely reinforced by researchers and doctors) that common folk just wouldn't understand matters that had taken the researchers and doctors years of education to understand themselves. The terminology and scholarly writing style of these books and journals were inaccessible to most people. While the women in the group had no medical education, their college educations and intelligence certainly served them well as they learned to decipher medical writings. So did their persistence, their willingness to ask for help, and their belief in their abilities to understand how their bodies worked.

As the women who were involved in the Boston Women's Health Course Collective acquired medical knowledge, they also began to acquire authority. This authority felt strange at first, as it was at odds with societal conceptions regarding the capabilities of women in general, and in particular women with no medical training. Their authority certainly differed from the authority carried by traditional "medical experts." The idea that they were "authorities" also clashed with their political notions that "authorities" tended to be socially oppressive forces, holding power *over* others by virtue of their knowledge and authority. The women in the group wanted none of this type of authority; indeed, the primary purpose of their research, writing, and teaching was a dispersal of power and authority through dispersal of knowledge, empowering women to take charge of their bodies and their lives.

In the introduction to the original collection of papers published by the New England Free Press, the writers described the personal transformations they experienced as they began to become authorities, as they began to research, discuss, and then teach about women's health issues:

> The process we developed in the group became as important as the material we were learning. For the first time, we were doing research and writing papers that were about us and for us. We were excited and our excitement was powerful. We wanted to share both the excitement and the material we were learning with our sisters. We saw ourselves differently and our lives began to change. . . . By the fall, we were ready to share our collective knowledge with our sisters. Excited and nervous (we were *just* women; what authority did we have in matters of medicine and health?), we offered a course to sisters in women's liberation.[21]

## The Authority of Lived Experience

The women involved in the project felt strongly that authority beyond medical knowledge was required for a true understanding of women's health. For them, medical facts acquired meaning only in the context of lived experience. The women teaching the "Women and Their Bodies" course believed that more important than the authority they had acquired through their medical research, they had the authority to teach about women's health by virtue of their years of personal experience as women. This authority of lived experience was especially important because almost all of the medical knowledge about women's experiences had been written by men. Hence, the pictures that had been painted of such things as menstruation, orgasm, pregnancy, childbirth, and menopause were incomplete and often erroneous.

In the traditional biomedical model, the experience of individual patients counted for little. Experience that did not match the medical model was discounted or labeled diseased or abnormal.[22] It has been said that there is power in numbers. As women began to share their experiences with various health issues, they found authority in numbers. If so many women had so many similar experiences with childbirth, few of which matched the medical model, could this medical model really be a true representation of what was "normal"?

In addition, the view of biomedicine was decidedly limited with its focus on the physical body. For the Boston Women's Health Course Collective, for readers of *Our Bodies, Ourselves*, and indeed for growing numbers of people and groups across the country and around the world, health was more than the state of the physical body. You couldn't know everything about a person's health by looking at her body. She might be "healthy" in terms of having no measurable symptoms of illness, but she might be overwhelmed with fear because her children were in danger of being harmed by her partner. Only by including her thoughts, feelings, and lived experiences in your consideration could you find out about her state of health. In this way, the Boston Women's Health Course Collective added a voice to the growing demand for a more holistic view of human health, a view that included not only physical but also psychological, economic, and social well-being, a view that was also at the heart of many other health care reform movements of the 1960s and 1970s.[23]

## Ourselves as Leaders

For the first two years of research and discussion, group membership was somewhat fluid. Collective member Wendy C. Sanford wrote in 1979 that the group's initial turnover probably contributed greatly to its subsequent stability.[24] Because the group's focus for the first two years was on research, writing, and teaching the course, interested members had time to get to know each other and develop relationships based on a strong personal interest. The women grew together as women, teachers, writers, and friends. By November 1971 a core group of twelve women had emerged. Most of these women were from the original doctor's group, while a few women from the courses had joined along the way to help with research, writing, and teaching.

After two years, over 200,000 copies of *Our Bodies, Ourselves* had sold with no advertising beyond word of mouth. Colleges and women's centers bought and distributed copies, and women bought copies for their friends. The office of the New England Free Press could not keep up with the flood of orders, and the collective could not find a nonprofit publisher or women's press big enough to handle the printing and distribution demand. Consequently, the collective decided to allow the book to be published commercially. In order to sign the contract with Simon and Schuster, the twelve women became a legal entity known as the Boston Women's Health Book Collective in 1972. Initially bitterly divided over the issue of commercial publication, the women hired a lawyer to bargain with the publisher over the conditions of publication. Simon and Schuster agreed to meet several important demands. First, royalty money from the book would go to support women's health education projects; and second, the collective would control layout, advertising, editorial, and other important decisions. In addition, the publisher agreed that the book could be sold to health clinics and other organizations at a 70 percent discount. Since its original publication, *Our Bodies, Ourselves* has sold over 4 million copies and has been translated into nineteen languages.[25]

The emerging organizational structure of the Boston Women's Health Book Collective makes for an interesting study of collective leadership. Power and leadership were consciously shared as equally as possible among all group members, and all decisions were made by group consensus. This structure contributed great strength to the ability of the collective to speak and act in a unified manner. It also presented many challenges as conflict invariably arose from time to time among group members. Nevertheless, this sharing of leadership, power, and authority was a conscious response of the women's movement to women's longtime experiences of being overlooked and ignored. As Norsigian and Sanford wrote, "We are among the women who want to let our longtime experience of being the ones without power shape a vision that challenges the existing power structures themselves. Instead of our own piece of the pie, in other words, we want to change the recipe."[26]

This vision of shared leadership was tremendously important to the women in the collective. Sanford wrote in 1979:

> Our experiences in giving the course reinforced the group's growing sense that we operated with the most energy, effectiveness and authenticity when our decisions were based on the shared ideas of every member. This conviction has become stronger over the years. We know that a powerful creative energy flows when each of us holds responsibility for the way the group or project goes. To release that energy, each of us has to know that she can air any ideas, disagreements or uneasiness. Our experience together has reaffirmed something that women have perhaps always known: our feelings about a given subject are as important as the factual information about it, and any project or decision that leaves out feelings is not whole. . . . Personal confrontation and careful listening often make the process of coming to a consensus as meaningful as the decision itself.[27]

Learning to function as a nonhierarchical group often had its problems. For example, some members invariably did more work at certain times than others. During their first ten years together and after much discussion about shared leadership and group dynamics, the women eventually began to accept the fact that all groups have leaders, and that the important thing was how the leaders led. They also grew to understand that power dynamics exist in any group, but that power was not necessarily a bad thing. Power can exist without dominance, without "power over." As Sanford wrote, "Different members of the group will have power or exercise leadership at different times, in the form of expertise or initiative, energy or personal dynamism or some special responsibility, but standing as they do on our base of mutuality and self respect, they exercise power with, not over, all of us."[28]

The structure and functioning of the group gradually changed over time, as the collective's workload began to grow. In 1974 members decided to begin to pay themselves for their work, which included giving workshops, researching and writing, and administration of a rapidly growing number of projects. Conflicts invariably arose from time to time as the idealism of the early women's movement was forced to confront the everyday realities of spending money and running a workplace; the members of the collective became employers, not only of themselves and each other, but of a growing number of "non-group" women.

One of the most challenging problems that faced the collective during the first ten years was finding the right balance of work time and personal time in their weekly meetings. Urgent deadlines and mountains of exciting projects often crowded out the time for sharing personal feelings, concerns, and experiences, a sharing that was the spark igniting the collective's work when they first began. Although meetings focused increasingly on business, the women made time to be together in various other ways, including day-long retreats and informal gatherings outside of business meetings.

## Ourselves Working with Others

The scope of *Our Bodies, Ourselves* has greatly expanded over its thirty years in print, as has the scope of the Boston Women's Health Book Collective. Throughout the years, the collective has actively sought to diversify the voices heard in *Our Bodies, Ourselves*. While the original content reflected the personal interests of a group of young, white, middle-class women, even as the first set of mimeographed papers were going to press, the women realized that their course and their papers had only touched the tip of the women's health iceberg. The collective was quick to respond to criticisms levied by other groups that, like the women's liberation movement, their focus reflected not the health issues of all women but the health issues deemed important by women of their age, class, and race. For example, while white, middle-class women were concerned about the medicalization of childbirth, working-class white women and many women of color wished for more access to health care during childbirth. While white women struggled for the right to safe home births, low-income women had no desire for "out-of-hospital births," too often the only type of birth they could afford. Salient health issues for women of color included racial oppression and poverty, violence, and the health of the men in their community.[29] Male unemployment, not just depressed female wages, were seen as depriving women of color of access to an economic base sufficient to maintain healthful living conditions. Many women of color saw poverty and racism, not sexism, as the real problems.

Like the women's movement of the times, the collective strove to listen to these other voices and, in response to these criticisms, to broaden the coverage of women's health care issues in their workshops and writings. New topics and chapters were added to each new edition of *Our Bodies, Ourselves* and to subsequent books coauthored by individual founding members of the collective, including *Ourselves and Our Children: A Book by and for Parents* (1978), *Ourselves Growing Older: Women Aging with Knowledge and Power* (1987), and a book for teens, *Changing Bodies, Changing Lives* (1981).[30]

Idealism is rarely achieved in the daily operations of an organization, and the Boston Women's Health Book Collective is no exception. As the work of the collective grew, new staff members were hired, and the collective was no longer technically a collective. The original members ("founders") became the "board," as did some of the staff members. As new staff was hired, the collective sometimes experienced growing pains as the way in which workers made decisions, assigned work, and completed tasks was challenged by the changing organizational structure. Some of the frustrations cited by both workers who stayed and those who left the organization evolved from an organizational structure that, in its effort to reject "status quo" organizational models, left some workers with a perception that there was no organization at all, but an informal and unclear power structure. The collective has worked in many ways to address worker concerns, including charges of racism.[31] In 1995 workers at the collective decided to unionize. The founders continue to work with the union to clarify the many matters that confront daily operations in any organization.

Accommodating diverse voices, concerns, and opinions is not always an easy task, yet the collective has continually worked to remain true to its mission of representing and reaching out to all women. Feminist health activists, including women in the collective, have increased national awareness of the diversity of women's health issues. Some of these include health issues of African American, Latina, and Asian American women, women with disabilities, and lesbians, as well as health issues related to various other life circumstances and life cycle stages.[32] Throughout the years, the Boston Women's Health Book Collective has often joined forces with other women's health organizations to promote awareness of women's health issues. For example, in 1994 they wrote a position statement on childbirth policy in conjunction with the National Black Woman's Health Project, the National Women's Health Network, and the Women's Institute for Childbearing Policy.[33] In all of its work, acquiring knowledge has been the vehicle to dispersing power back to readers.

It's impossible to say exactly how much of which changes in our culture and in the health care system over the past thirty years are a direct product of the collective's work, because the work of the collective is interwoven with the work of so many other groups and cultural forces. Suffice it to say that *Our Bodies, Ourselves* has made its way into the hands of millions of men and women around the world. It has been used as a textbook for courses in medical schools and in college health classes.[34] It has been endorsed by doctors and handed out in countless health care clinics.[35] Many of the ideas promoted by the collective have been echoed in many different ways. One example is the self-help movement of the 1980s, in which consumers were urged by both consumer groups and health care providers to play a more active role in preventing illness and managing chronic health problems.[36]

Our Bodies, Ourselves has been part of an explosion of health information. Indeed, one of the primary goals of the women's health movement has been the dispersal of power through a dispersal of information to the people, the consumers of medical services.[37] Today, health information aimed at the consumer abounds. Newsletters on every conceivable health care issue are published each month. Doctors' offices and clinics' shelves are overflowing with pamphlets and handouts on hundreds of health topics. Some writers on health issues have called the 1990s the decade of the consumer.[38] Health care organizations have responded to some consumer demands, especially demands for more information about illnesses, medications, and treatments.

The Boston Women's Health Book Collective, along with political organizations such as the National Women's Health Network, has raised national awareness of many important women's health issues. (Judy Norsigian, of the collective, has been an active member of the latter organization from its founding.) In 1990 activists helped to initiate a U.S. General Accounting Office investigation that acknowledged that women had been left out of health research. This led to the creation of the Office of Research on Women's Health, which was established within the National Institutes of Health. The office has since launched a number of nationally funded health research projects on a number of women's health issues that are beginning to inform many health care and treatment decisions.

Perhaps one of the most important effects of the collective, along with the women's health movement in general, has been a growing awareness that patients should be partners in their health care. While we do not see this awareness in every doctor's office, health clinic, or segment of society, we see it much more than we did thirty years ago. And while we still have a long way to go, we do see increased attention to accommodating diversity in our research and health care institutions. As one researcher wrote recently, "Health and health care are no longer the preserves of specialists. . . . Researching the people's health means attending to many voices and making use of multiple perspectives."[39] We see a blurring of the distinction between "the people" and "the professionals."[40] After all, we are all health providers, taking care of ourselves and, at various times, family members and friends. And we are all the people: doctors get sick, too, and seek the same quality of care we all yearn to receive.

## The Collective Today

In 1995 the Boston Women's Health Book Collective formed an organizational development committee, composed of collective members and staff, who worked with two consultants to revise their mission statement and develop a new management structure. An administrative director joined the collective in January 1996, staff was expanded, and projects were set in motion to address needs to further diversify the collective. In 1997 the collective identified several pressing issues: how to bring new leadership into an organization that had been led for so long by its founders; how to further diversify this historically white, middle-class organization; and how to create an organizational structure that was fiscally sound, effective, and fair to all workers. The following year, the collective completed the transition from a board of directors that included only the founders of the collective and staff to a community-based board that includes women from diverse racial and cultural backgrounds. The collective currently is directed by a management team consisting of a program director, Judy Norsigian, who has been with the collective since it began, and a financial/administrative manager who joined the organization in 1998. With these changes, the Boston Women's Health Book Collective hopes to achieve its vision of a collaborative, multicultural workplace.[41]

## Notes

Thank you to Claudine Mussuto, Judy Norsigian, Jane Pincus, and Wendy Sanford of the Boston Women's Health Book Collective for your feedback on my manuscript and for digging through your archives and memories to verify the facts and dates contained in this essay.

1. Boston Women's Health Book Collective (BWHBC), *Our Bodies, Ourselves for the New Century* (New York: Touchstone Books/Simon and Schuster, 1998); Boston Women's Health Book Collective, *The New Our Bodies, Ourselves: A Book by and for Women, Updated and Expanded for the 1990s* (New York: Touchstone Books/Simon and Schuster, 1992); Boston Women's Health Book Collective, *Our Bodies, Ourselves: A Book by and for Women* (New York: Simon and Schuster, 1973); and Boston Women's Health Course Collective (BWHCC), *Our Bodies, Ourselves* (Boston: New England Free Press, 1971).

2. BWHCC, *Our Bodies, Ourselves.*

3. J. Norsigian and W. C. Sanford, "Ten Years in the 'Our Bodies, Ourselves' Collective," *Radcliffe Quarterly*, December 1979, 16–18.

4. A. B. McBride and W. L. McBride, "Theoretical Underpinnings for Women's Health," *Women and Health* 6 (spring/summer 1981): 37–55.

5. B. Eaton, "A Decade of Healthy Feminism: The Boston Women's Health Book Collective," *New Roots*, September/October 1979, 38–40; J. Norsigian, "The Women's Health Movement in the United States," in *Man-Made Medicine: Women's Health, Public Policy, and Reform*, ed. K. L. Moss (Durham, N.C.: Duke University Press, 1996); S. B. Ruzek, A. E. Clarke, and V. L. Olesen, "Social, Biomedical, and Feminist Models of Women's Health," in *Women's Health: Complexities and Differences*, ed. S. B. Ruzek, V. L. Olesen, and A. E. Clarke (Columbus: Ohio State University Press, 1997).

6. B. Beckwith, "Boston Women's Health Book Collective: Women Empowering Women," *Women and Health* 10, no. 1 (1985): 1–7.

7. L. Doyal, "Women, Health, and the Sexual Division of Labor: A Case Study of the Women's Health Movement in Britain," in *Women's Health, Politics, and Power: Essays on Sex/Gender, Medicine, and Public Health*, ed. E. Fee and N. Krieger (Amityville, N.Y.: Baywood, 1994); E. Fee and N. Krieger, "Introduction," in *Women's Health, Politics, and Power: Essays on Sex/Gender, Medicine, and Public Health*, ed. E. Fee and N. Kreiger (Amityville, N.Y.: Baywood, 1994); Norsigian, "Women's Health Movement"; Ruzek et al., "Social, Biomedical, and Feminist Models of Women's Health."

8. BWHCC, *Our Bodies, Ourselves*, 134, 135–36.

9. S. E. Hayden, "Twenty-three Years of *Our Bodies, Ourselves*: Individualism, Community, and Social Change in the Work of the Boston Women's Health Book Collective," Ph.D. diss., University of Minnesota, January 1994.

10. H. Marieskind, "The Women's Health Movement," *International Journal of Health Services* 5, no. 2 (1975): 217–22.

11. K. K. Campbell, "The Rhetoric of Women's Liberation: An Oxymoron," *Quarterly Journal of Speech* 59 (1973): 79.

12. S. Hayden, "Re-claiming Bodies of Knowledge: An Exploration of the Relationship between Feminist Theorizing and Feminine Style in the Rhetoric of the Boston Women's Health Book Collective," *Western Journal of Communication* 61, no. 2 (spring 1997): 127–63.

13. See, for example, M. F. Belenky, B. M. Clinchy, N. R. Goldberger, and J. M. Tarule, *Women's Ways of Knowing: The Development of Self, Voice, and Mind* (New York: Basic Books, 1986); M. Bond and P. Bywaters, "Working It Out for Ourselves: Women Learning about Hormone Replacement Therapy," *Women's Studies International Forum* 21, no. 1 (1998): 65–76; and M. Rothbert, G. Padonu, M. Holmes-Rovner, J. Kroll, G. Talarczyk, D. Rovner, N. Schmitt, and L. Breer, "Menopausal Women as Decision Makers in Health Care," *Experimental Gerontology* 29 (1994): 463–68.

14. Belenky et al., *Women's Ways of Knowing*, 229.

15. B. A. Brehm and J. G. Iannotta, "Women and Physical Activity: Active Life-

styles Enhance Health and Well-Being," *Journal of Health Education* 29, no. 2 (1998): 89–92.

16. BWHCC, *Our Bodies, Ourselves*; and W. C. Sanford, "Working Together, Growing Together: A Brief History of the Boston Women's Health Book Collective," *Heresies* 2, no. 3 (1979): 83–92.

17. Norsigian and Sanford, "Ten Years in the 'Our Bodies, Ourselves' Collective," 16–17.

18. Sanford, "Working Together, Growing Together"; BWHCC, *Our Bodies, Ourselves*.

19. BWHCC, *Our Bodies, Ourselves*.

20. Ibid., 2.

21. Ibid.

22. M. Lock and P. A. Kaufert, eds., *Pragmatic Women and Body Politics* (Cambridge: Cambridge University Press, 1998).

23. D. B. Ardell, "The History and Future of the Wellness Movement," in *Wellness Promotion Strategies; Selected Proceedings of the Eighth Annual National Wellness Conference*, ed. J. P. Opatz (Dubuque, Iowa: Kendall/Hunt, 1984).

24. Sanford, "Working Together, Growing Together."

25. Press release from the Collective's Resource Center, Somerville, Mass., 1999.

26. Norsigian and Sanford, "Ten Years in the 'Our Bodies, Ourselves' Collective," 18.

27. Sanford, "Working Together, Growing Together," 86.

28. Ibid., 97.

29. S. B. Ruzek, A. E. Clarke, and V. L. Olesen, "What Are the Dynamics of Differences?" in *Women's Health: Complexities and Differences*, ed. S. B. Ruzek, A. E. Clarke, and V. L. Olesen (Columbus: Ohio State University Press, 1997).

30. Boston Women's Health Book Collective, *Ourselves and Our Children: A Book by and for Parents* (New York: Random House, 1978); P. B. Doress, D. L. Siegal, and the Midlife and Older Women Book Project, in cooperation with the Boston Women's Health Book Collective, *Ourselves, Growing Older* (New York: Touchstone/Simon and Schuster, 1987); Ruth Bell and other coauthors of *Our Bodies, Ourselves* and the Teen Health Project, *Changing Bodies, Changing Lives: A Book for Teens on Sex and Relationships* (New York: Times Books, 1981).

31. Alba Bonilla, April Taylor, Mayra Canetti, and Jennifer Yanco, "An Open Letter to the Board of Directors, Boston Women's Health Book Collective," in *Sojourner: The Women's Forum* 23, no. 4 (December 1997): 4; The Board and Founders of the Boston Women's Health Book Collective, "Response from the Board and Founders of the Boston Women's Health Book Collective," in *Sojourner: The Women's Forum* 23, no. 4 (December 1997): 5; and Shelley Mains, "Our Feminist Institutions, Ourselves: International Crisis at the Boston Women's Health Book Collective," in *Sojourner: The Women's Forum* 23, no. 4 (December 1997): 10–12, 25.

32. Boston Women's Health Book Collective, "Disability and the Medical Sys-

tem," *Ms.*, September/October 1992, 36–37; M. Bayne-Smith, "Health and Women of Color: A Contextual Overview," in *Race, Gender, and Health*, ed. M. Bayne-Smith (Thousand Oaks, Calif.: Sage, 1996); Ruzek et al., "What Are the Dynamics of Difference?"

33. Boston Women's Health Book Collective, National Black Woman's Health Project, National Women's Health Network, and Women's Institute for Childbearing Policy, "Excerpts from Childbearing Policy within a National Health Program: An Evolving Consensus for New Directions," in *Women's Health: Readings on Social, Economic, and Political Issues*, ed. N. Worcester and M. H. Whatley (Dubuque, Iowa: Kendall/Hunt, 1994).

34. R. W. St. Pierre and M. E. Taylor, "The Role of Women's Health in Health Education," *Health Education* 19, no. 2 (April/May 1988): 39–41.

35. C. T. Massion, "Our Bodies, Ourselves" (book review), *Journal of the American Medical Association* 269, no. 20 (1993): 2680–81.

36. A. Withorn, "Helping Ourselves," in *The Sociology of Health and Illness: Critical Perspectives*, ed. P. Conrad and R. Kerns (New York: St. Martin's Press, 1986).

37. T. K. Landwirth, "The Women's Health Movement: An Information Based Phenomenon," *Serials Librarian* 12 (1987): 89–95; C. S. Weisman, *Women's Health Care* (Baltimore: Johns Hopkins University Press, 1998).

38. J. Popay and G. Williams, "Researching the People's Health: Dilemmas and Opportunities for Social Scientists," in *Researching the People's Health*, ed. J. Popay and G. Williams (London: Routledge, 1994).

39. Ibid., xii.

40. M. Stacey, "The Power of Lay Knowledge: A Personal View," in *Researching the People's Health*, ed. J. Popay and G. Williams (London: Routledge, 1994).

41. Judy Norsigian and Claudine Mussuto, BWHBC, personal communication, April 2000.

## Want to Learn More?

### Internship Ideas: Women's Health

Many organizations with an interest in women's health have already established internship positions for which you can apply. Some are paid, but most are unpaid. Some of these positions are fairly structured, while others may be shaped by your suggestions and ideas, especially if you are volunteering your time. Here are some options to consider if you are looking for an internship experience:

• Contact local chapters of girls' and women's organizations such as the YWCA, Girls, Inc., Girl Scouts, or Planned Parenthood. You might find their addresses and phone numbers in your telephone book.

- You might find or create an internship at a local emergency shelter, food pantry, nursing home, or hospital.
- Many schools have after-school programs; maybe you could work with an after-school course on a health-related topic. Some schools have special programs for pregnant and parenting teens.
- Is there a particular aspect of women's health you would like to learn more about? You might be able to shadow a physician, physician's assistant, nurse, or midwife.
- If you are near Boston, contact the Boston Women's Health Book Collective. They are a great resource to find out about local and national women's health projects. Their address is: 240 A Elm Street, Somerville, MA 02144. Their telephone number is (617) 625-0277.

These national organizations may also be able to give you helpful information:

**National Asian Women's Health Organization**
250 Montgomery Street, #410
San Francisco, CA 94104-3401
Telephone (415) 989-9747

**National Black Woman's Health Project**
1211 Connecticut Avenue NW, Suite 310
Washington, DC 20005
Telephone (800) 444-6472

**National Clearinghouse on Women and Girls with Disabilities**
Educational Equity Concepts, Inc.
114 East 32d Street
New York, NY 10016
Telephone (212) 725-1803
www.onisland.com/eec

**National Latina Health Organization (NLHO)/Organizacion Nacional de la Salud de la Mujer Latina**
P.O. Box 7567
Oakland, CA 94601
Telephone (510) 534-1362 or (800) 971-5358

**National Women's Health Network**
514 Tenth Street NW, Suite 400
Washington, DC 20004
Telephone (202) 347-1140

# 6

# From Beijing to Atlanta and Beyond: The International Challenges for Women in Sport

**Christine M. Shelton**

■ BACKGROUND

I had the privilege to be trained as an athlete in the 1960s. I spent my adolescent years training as a field hockey and basketball player during the winter so that I would be in shape to begin the summer junior tennis circuit that was offered in the mid-Atlantic states. My male tennis coach gave me a vigorous training schedule of lifting free weights, running distance and sprints, and spending endless hours on the tennis courts to prepare for tennis competition that would earn me a national ranking. This accomplishment would not earn me a sport scholarship because when I started college in 1966, no scholarships were available for women. I had to win an academic scholarship, not a sport scholarship, to be able to attend James Madison University. From that time in my life, it has been my dream to live in a world that rewarded and embraced women's involvement in sport.

After completing my undergraduate degree I became a Peace Corps volunteer, working for two years in Venezuela and then for a few more years as a cross-cultural trainer for the Peace Corps. I began to see that there were ways to connect my sport experience and my training as a physical educator to my interest in and love of Latin America. I have worked as a volunteer in the international sport arena, and this work has paralleled my career as a physical education teacher, as a college coach and athletic administrator, and currently as an associate professor and co-director for the Project on Women and Social Change at Smith College.

I could not give my background without including the importance of Title IX in my life. I was part of a group of four female coaches who filed one of the first Title IX suits in Fairfax County, Virginia, in 1972. This single action and the inflammatory outcome helped to direct, frame, and inform my involvement in the women's sport movement for the past twenty-eight years.

Finally, I was privileged to have wonderful female mentors who encouraged me to get involved in professional service. I have been privileged to serve as president and executive director of the National Association for Girls and Women in Sport (NAGWS) (1983–86); chair and one of the founding members of the Latin American Project, which is now the International Committee of NAGWS (1980 to present); member of the International Committee for the Women's Sports Foundation (1992 to present); representative for North America to the International Working Group (1998 to present); and vice-president for the International Association of Physical Education and Sport for Girls and Women (IAPESGW).

I N some countries of the world there are a rising number of men and women who take for granted the accomplishments and advances of women in sport; in many other countries, culture, religion, and law limit and at times prohibit public participation for women in sport. The international women's sport movement attempts to develop policies and practices that speak to these issues as it promotes women's access to sport. The movement strives to embrace the issues and concerns of all women: working-class women, women of different sexual orientation, disabled women, Muslim women, indigenous women, and aging women. A wide range of educational and sporting interests are included, such as outdoor adventure, experiential learning, and physical education, as well as individual, dual, and team sports. The level of participation includes organized youth sport, recreational, elite, Olympic, and professional sport.

The international women's sport movement parallels other feminist and international women's movements. Initial work was accomplished at the grassroots level and emphasized consciousness raising, demonstrations, and projects to promote women's inclusion in sport. As it has sought to become broader and more inclusive, it has created an international network with strategic plans, as well as a declaration of principles that includes women's rights in sport and a call for international action at the governmental level.

In recent years the opportunities for women's participation in sport and physical activity have continued to increase. However, gender inequality still remains a significant problem. Sport leadership and participation are still dominated by men. Far fewer women than men participate at all levels, from recreational activity to elite and Olympic sport. There are far fewer females in decision-making positions such as sport leaders, officials, coaches, and media personnel. Women's sports still receive much less media coverage and much less financial support at all levels than do men's sports. In some countries, physical education classes provide the only opportunity girls have to participate in any physical activity.

In the past two decades increasing numbers of initiatives have been designed to improve the status of girls and women in sport and physical activity. These initiatives have been at the global, regional, national, and local levels and are diverse in their origins and implementation. Special women's sports units have been added to ministries of sport, departments on women and sport have been added by governments, and separate women's committees and commissions in sports federations and in sport organizations such as the International Olympic Committee (IOC) have also been established. There has been a sharp increase in the number of women's sport conferences, books devoted to women in sport, articles about women in sport in both professional and trade journals, and increased magazine production.

In the United States we measure much of women's success in sport from the passage of Title IX in 1972 to the present in two ways: the increased opportunities for participation for girls and women in sport, and the financial resources that are allocated to reversing discriminatory practices. Internationally, similar factors are part of the pattern of change. Federal legislation in the United States ensured that gender equity was a goal in sport in educational institutions receiving federal funds; internationally, women's access to sport has been improved through legislation and the elaboration of policies that promote gender equity in sport. Norway, Canada, and the European Sports Commission have all passed legislation to ensure equal treatment for women in physical education programs, in industrial sport leagues and clubs, and in national sport federations. Moreover, these groups are tracking the outcome of increased participation by women.

Similarly, access to increased funding to support women's teams has been a critical aspect of change at the international level. Funds may come from the IOC, the European Sports Commission, national governments and ministries, or the national and international governing bodies for individual sports.

The link between women's sport and the international women's movement was forged through new appreciation of the importance of physical activity and the health of women. The U.N. Beijing Conference on Women in

1995 marked a new era of mutuality and coalition building between the two movements. This was reinforced and furthered at the United Nations' Beijing Plus 5 meeting in June 2000.

International competitions in sport also have an impact on national interest and pride. U.S. women's basketball, soccer, and softball reached new levels of public appeal after producing gold medal teams in the 1996 Olympics. That public appeal was renewed during the 1999 soccer World Cup championships, as demonstrated by the dramatic increase in the numbers of spectators and television viewers. Credit for the success of the American women's teams was widely attributed to the girls' and women's improved access to sport accomplished through Title IX.[1] The public's renewed interest in watching women athletes has meant the success of a professional basketball league in the United States, the Women's National Basketball Association (WNBA), and the emergence of women's ice hockey as one of the fastest-growing women's sports. Corporate America has not been blind to the significant growth in women's sports and is rethinking strategies to capitalize on this important market.

Dramatic as these changes have been in the United States, international changes have been equally important. In fact, a "quiet revolution" is occurring in women's participation and leadership in international sport. At long last the international women's movement and the IOC have begun to recognize the importance of sport in women's lives. Even more important, the "women and development" community is beginning to explore the role that sport might play in increasing women's status and improving their access to and control over resources. In both cases the emphasis on women in sport represents significant institutional change and signals a new direction for the role of women's sports in development efforts and for the role of women's sport at the international level.

At the fourth U.N. Conference on Women, an understanding of the relationship between women's sport and development was actualized. Four platform statements were designed and adopted to encourage the participation of girls and women in physical education and sport. The IOC has begun to recognize the importance of including women's voices in the leadership of the Olympic movement, with new mandates to include women on the national Olympic governing committees by 2000. Both of these events, one occurring in Beijing in September 1995 and the other in Atlanta in 1996, are part of a greater set of changes taking place both nationally and worldwide.

This essay is divided into three sections. The first introduces the reader to the background and context for the international women's sport movement, tracing the evolution from the May 1994 conference in Brighton, England,

"Women, Sport, and the Challenge of Change" to the most recent meeting of the European Women Sport committee in Helsinki, Finland. The second section explores the critical issues facing the movement, with selected examples of the struggles and successes. The final section considers the challenges that lie ahead and the magnitude of this global initiative that declares that physical activity and sport is a human right and the right of every girl and woman.[2]

Between 1994 and 1998, over two hundred organizations throughout the world, from international governments to national nongovernmental women's groups and sport federations, have adopted a positive statement of principles on women and sport set forth in the Brighton Declaration (www.iwg-gti.org/e/ brighton.htm). These actions taken by many individuals and organizations have helped place women's issues on national sporting agendas and have helped define the contributions that sport makes to the wider women's agenda. Most importantly, the Brighton Declaration links women's sport opportunities to the efforts of the international women's movement with specific ties to the Platform for Action set out by the United Nations in the 1995 Fourth World Conference on Women.

## Background and Context

In 1994 there were significant developments taking place for women and sport throughout the world. Progress was being made in Europe through the European Women and Sport Movement, and plans were being made to include more women's events in the 1996 Atlanta Olympic Games. There were efforts within governmental and nongovernmental organizations (NGOs) in Australia, Canada, New Zealand, the United States, and many other countries to expand opportunities for women in sport. National and international organizations worked to promote opportunities for girls and women in sport: for example, the National Association for Girls and Women in Sport (NAGWS) in the United States, the International Association for Physical Education and Sport for Girls and Women (IAPESGW), Women's Sport International (WSI), and the Canadian Association for the Advancement of Women and Sport and Physical Activity (CAAWS).[3] Nevertheless, there was no venue in which these groups and governments could come together to share ideas and experience.

### The Brighton Conference
In May 1994 a conference entitled "Women, Sport, and the Challenge of Change" took place in Brighton, England, organized and hosted by the former British Sports Council and supported by the IOC. At this conference, 280

international delegates from both governmental and nongovernmental organizations, representing eighty-two countries, met to address the issue of how to accelerate the process of change that would redress the imbalances women face in their participation and involvement in sport.

The conference itself was instrumental in initiating change because it established three important outcomes:

1. The launch of the International Strategy on Women and Sport
2. The Brighton Declaration (www.iwg-gti.org/e/brighton.htm)
3. The creation of the International Working Group on Women and Sport (www.iwg-gti.org)

The Brighton Declaration outlines ten principles to assist those involved in sport in the development of appropriate policies, structures, and mechanisms to increase women's access to sport. Each of these principles builds on extensive research that identifies the obstacles to women's participation in sport. The Brighton Declaration both identifies these obstacles and suggests mechanisms for their elimination. They are delineated as follows:

1. Equity and equality in society and sport. Equal opportunity to participate and be involved in sport, whether for the purpose of leisure and recreation, health promotion, or high performance, is the right of every woman regardless of race, color, language, religion, creed, sexual orientation, age, marital status, disability, political belief or affiliation, and national or social origin. Resources, power, and responsibility should be allocated fairly and without discrimination and should redress any inequitable balance in the benefits available to women and men.

2. Facilities. Women's participation in sport is influenced by the extent, variety, and accessibility of facilities. The planning, design, and management of these should appropriately and equitably meet the particular needs of women in the community, with special attention given to the need for child care provision and safety.

3. School and junior sport. Research demonstrates that girls and boys approach sport from markedly different perspectives. Those responsible for sport education, recreation, and physical education of young people should ensure that an equitable range of opportunities and learning experiences that accommodate the values, attitudes, and aspirations of girls is incorporated in programs to develop physical fitness and basic sport skills of young people.

4. Developing participation. Women's participation in sport is influenced by the range of activities available. Those responsible for delivering sporting

opportunities and programs should provide and promote activities that meet women's needs and aspirations.

5. High-performance sport. Governments and sports organizations should provide equal opportunities to women to reach their sports performance potential by ensuring that all activities and programs relating to performance improvements take into account the specific needs of female athletes. Rewards and support should be provided fairly and equitably to both women and men.

6. Leadership in sport. The underrepresentation of women in leadership and decision-making positions has been well documented.[4] Policies and programs should be designed to increase the number of women coaches, officials, administrators, and sports personnel at all levels, with special attention given to recruitment, development, and retention.

7. Education, training, and development. Those responsible for the education, training, and development of coaches and other sports personnel should ensure that education processes and experiences address issues relating to gender equity and the needs of the female athlete. In addition, they must take into account women's leadership experiences, values, and attitudes.

8. Sport information and research. Those responsible for research and providing information on sport should develop policies and programs to increase knowledge and understanding about women and sport and ensure that research norms and standards are based on research on both men and women.

9. Resources. The allocation of resources is critical to developing women's sports. Support is needed for programs, research, policy implementation, and education and coaching.

10. Domestic and international cooperation. Governmental and nongovernmental organizations should incorporate the promotion of issues of gender equity and the sharing of examples of good practice in women-and-sport policies and programs within the domestic and international arenas.

In the four years from 1994 to 1998, over two hundred national and international organizations adopted the Brighton Declaration. These include key government groups such as the Caribbean and Commonwealth Heads of Government, the European Ministers of Sport, and the Supreme Council for Sport in Africa. In addition, organizations that address the disciplines within physical education and sport studies have adopted the Declaration, including the International Council for Health, Physical Education, Recreation, Sport, and Dance (ICHPER-SD) and the International Council of Sport Science and Physical Education (ICSSPE).

The Brighton Declaration acknowledges that physical education, sport, and sporting activities are an integral aspect of the culture of every nation, but it also highlights the inequalities that exist in participation levels and opportunities for women and girls compared to men and boys. It also acknowledges that women are still underrepresented in management, coaching, and officiating, particularly at the higher levels. Without women leaders and role models for girls, equal opportunities for women and girls will not be achieved.

The Declaration is addressed to all governments, public authorities, organizations, businesses, educational and research establishments, and women's organizations. Additionally, it addresses individuals who are responsible for or who directly or indirectly influence the conduct, development, or promotion of sport or who are in any way involved in the employment, education, management, training, development, or care of women in sport. It is meant to complement all sporting, local, national, and international charters, laws, codes, rules, and regulations relating to women or sport.[5]

While the distance between a declaration of principle and the achievement of those goals is considerable, the importance of governmental recognition of the values attributed to sport should not be underestimated. There has been a long-standing tendency to deny any significant value of sport to women and to claim that, given the vast inequities that women face, sport equity should be low on the list of priorities. Moreover, groups such as the IOC have claimed that the conditions that impede women's progress in sport fall under the province of national governments, not the Olympic movement. Thus, national government support for the Brighton Declaration is critical on a number of fronts.

The International Strategy on Women in Sport, which was an outcome of the Brighton Conference in 1994, aimed to coordinate work on issues of women and sport in the international arena. This strategy promoted the sharing of model programs and successful initiatives among national and international sporting federations and accelerating change in the sport culture worldwide. The International Working Group on Women and Sport (IWG) was formed to help oversee the implementation of the strategy. The IWG is composed of senior decision makers from sport on all continents. From 1994 to 1998 the IWG was co-chaired by the minister of Land Rehabilitation and Resettlement of the Republic of Namibia, Pendukeni Iivula-Ithana, and the director of Development for the English Sports Council, Anita White, with the secretariat provided by the U.K. Sports Council.

The aims of the IWG are to:

• Monitor the adoption of the Brighton Declaration by countries and national and international organizations worldwide

- Act as a contact and reference point focusing on international developments on women and sport and facilitating the exchange of information
- Act as a liaison with international federations and multisport organizations
- Assist in the development and coordination of regional groupings on women and sport
- Act as a forum for these regional groupings and international women and sport organizations to review status reports and strategies and disseminate information
- Seek the inclusion of issues relating to women and sport on the agendas of major international conferences and to provide advice on the content of international conferences that address issues of women and sport

Another outcome of the Brighton Conference and part of the International Strategy on Women and Sport was the decision to hold a second conference on women and sport in a developing nation. The 1998 conference was called "The Challenge of Change" and took place in Windhoek, Namibia, 19–22 May 1998. Over four hundred delegates, representing seventy-four countries, attended. The major outcome of the conference was the adoption of the Windhoek Call for Action. This document builds on the Brighton Declaration and stresses the need for linkages with other international instruments such as the Beijing Platform for Action and the Convention for the Elimination of All Forms of Discrimination against Women (CEDAW). The Windhoek Call for Action moves from statements of principle and raising awareness to positions of action.

While significant progress has occurred internationally for women in sport, a number of challenges still lie ahead. The challenges take the form of concerns about the health of women athletes, the complexity of gender verification programs, and the ongoing concerns with sexual harassment and abuse in sport. There are also larger questions about the appropriate models for women's participation in sport and long-standing concerns about the advisability of a program of female sport that looks remarkably similar to that of men and carries with it the same potential for abuse and corruption. Finally, there are complex religious and cultural constraints related to women's participation in sport. As women in Islamic societies make choices about how to pursue sport in their cultural context, a number of vexing issues are raised for the international women's sports movement and its organizations.

There are two central ways to trace the international shifts in support for women in sport. First, one can trace the treatment of women's sport issues at the United Nations' world conferences for women, which since 1975 have been the key international arena for focusing on issues of concern to women. Second, one can examine the response of the IOC. This heavily male institution has the power to redistribute the funds raised every four years during the Olympic competition for promoting future Olympic competition. These funds amount to millions of dollars that are placed in the Olympic Solidarity Fund, which is distributed every four years.[6]

In addition, the IOC is the body that makes the rules governing international competition and thus decides which sports will be included in the Olympic Games. The IOC also makes the rules that govern who may compete and under what circumstances; therefore, drug and gender testing fall under their mandate.

Important and significant changes for women have resulted from both the U.N. conferences and IOC decisions before and after the Atlanta Olympics. As a result of these meetings, more leadership opportunities for women were created, dialogue about the treatment of women in all areas of their lives (including sport) was expanded, and new links between government, NGOs, and sport organizations were forged.

### Beijing and Atlanta: The U.N. and IOC Initiatives

It was truly a twenty-five-year battle to get the international women's community to understand the importance of sport and physical activity in the lives of all women. Many people followed the proceedings of the U.N. Fourth World Conference on Women in Beijing and the parallel NGO forum, "Looking at the World through Women's Eyes," in August and September 1995. What many may not have realized is that, while women's health has been an important issue in all of the world conferences on women, sport and physical activity have been absent from the platforms from Mexico City, Copenhagen, and Kenya.

The Platform for Action from Beijing contained three items that encouraged nations to:

1. Pay attention to the importance of physical activity and sport in the lives of girls and women
2. Pay attention to the need for increased opportunities for participation for girls and women in sport
3. Ensure that there are more women in leadership positions in sport

These proposals helped influence the International Olympic Committee and led it to respond to the need to include more women in its leadership and improve women's participation in the Olympic movement. The IOC made overtures to renew its commitment to opening more opportunities for girls and women in sport.

At its September 1995 meeting, the Executive Board of the IOC, having heard a report of the chairman of the Study Commission of the Centennial Olympic Congress, committed itself to promoting the presence of women within sport and its technical and administrative structures. Specifically, it agreed to the following:

1. National Olympic Committees must reserve to women by 31 December 2000 at least 10 percent of the offices in all their decision-making structures, in particular all legislative or executive organizations. This proportion should reach 20 percent by 31 December 2005.
2. The International Federations, the National Federations, and the sports organizations belonging to the Olympic movement are strongly invited to fill at least 10 percent of the positions in all their decision-making structures with women.
3. The subsequent stages needed to reach a strict enforcement of the principle of equality between men and women shall be determined by the year 2001.
4. The Olympic charter will be amended to take into account the need to achieve and maintain equity between men and women.

The IOC passed these proposals before the Atlanta Olympics. Following Atlanta, the IOC has called two international meetings allowing leaders of women's sports from around the world to engage in a dialogue with the IOC about changes that are needed for women to gain parity in the Olympic family. The first meeting was held in Lausanne, Switzerland, in 1996. In the opening session, Juan Antonio Samaranch, the president of the IOC, said, "Sport, whether for competition or simply for enjoyment, has become a powerful social force with major effects on the structure of our society. But the problem of low participation by women in sport is fundamentally linked to the social challenges which they face, and therefore cannot be solved by the Olympic Movement alone."[7] He went on to claim that sport has not been a priority among the many issues that concern women. Women, he said, have had other vital areas of concern: health, education, and the eradication of poverty and violence. It is the responsibility of governments, not the IOC, to address these issues. Similarly, Samaranch emphasized the responsibility of national governments to develop sport policies to enhance women's participation and to increase the budget for women's sport.

Women representatives attending the conference often had a very different perspective. Nawal El-Moutawakel, the 1984 Olympic Champion in the four-hundred-meter hurdles and a member of the IAAF Council, commented, "As we approach the third Millennium, this first World Conference on Women and Sport was organized with the objective of reflecting together and identifying the goals which must be attained in order for women to play a leading role in all of the professions in the Olympic Movement."[8]

In the industrialized countries, the advent of the woman athlete often went hand in hand with economic development. In developing countries, which were seriously lacking in areas such as infrastructure, and where sports activity was regarded as a useless occupation or a leisure pursuit for the economically privileged, sportswomen were a rare commodity. In some societies, precarious conditions (including problems of health and education) did not encourage women to practice sport. In addition, there was such a chronic lack of infrastructure in rural areas that for a woman to succeed in these conditions was a real achievement. Nonetheless, the 1980s had seen the rise in Africa of elite women athletes, a phenomenon that was attributed to several factors, including training, motivation, access to sport infrastructure, and family background (above all, parental support). The life of a woman athlete is not easy, as she must be prepared to defend herself and move into areas where she has never dared to venture before.

By the second IOC Conference on Women and Sport, "New Perspectives for the Twenty-first Century," held in Paris in March 2000, Samaranch and the IOC's perspective had shifted. During the four years between conferences, the IOC had attended and supported some major international grassroots events—the Windhoek women and sport conference, the international conference on sport for all, the Berlin meeting on the world crisis in physical education, and the UNESCO meeting of all sport ministers in Punta del Este, Uruguay, to name a few. It now appears that the IOC is moving outside of its tight-knit family to join forces with other groups and organizations that deal with issues of gender, disability, physical education, and grassroots sports.

Attending the second IOC World Conference on Women and Sport were the women of National Olympic Committees newly appointed under the 10 percent rule, in addition to other international sport leaders. The purpose of this conference was to assess the progress made on the issues concerning women and sport and to set out the future challenges. Although many of the issues were similar to those addressed during the first conference, this time a new dynamic was present. Those who had been working in the international women's sport movement for quite some time were meeting the newly anointed women who are now part of the IOC family. Merely because the new IOC sport leaders are women does not mean that they will have gender high on their list of concerns. It will be interesting to observe how the gap between the old and the new is closed. Will there be an interest on the part of the new female IOC members in what has gone before them? Will some of the women's associations that formed outside of the IOC be allowed to continue? Will there be a unified voice of concern for women and sport within the international Olympic movement?

## Critical Issues for the Women's International Sport Movement

### HRT, Drug Testing, and Gender Verification

One of the fastest-growing sport phenomena in recent years has been the development of the Masters Games and the participation of Masters Athletes at all levels of competition. This growth is reflected in the numbers of women who participated in the recent World Masters Games—eight thousand women! As in any international competition, regular drug testing is undertaken. One of the banned performance-enhancing substances is testosterone, a drug that is regularly prescribed for women who are on hormone replacement therapy (HRT). HRT potentially affects any woman over the age of forty. To date there is no international policy covering this potentially difficult situation. Currently, competitors on prescribed HRT containing testosterone are presented with two options: go off their HRT or risk being disqualified in a drug test. This situation has the potential to close the door on thousands of female participants in Masters events, but equally, if not more importantly, removing the motivation of many mature women to participate regularly in physical activity.[9]

Since the 1930s there have been media reports that individuals who once competed as female athletes subsequently appeared to be men. The results of the medical and genetic examinations were almost never reported, and many of the alleged cheaters may have been individuals with disorders of sexual differentiation. As early as 1960 the International Amateur Athletic Federation (IAAF) began establishing rules of eligibility for women athletes. Initially, the test was a physical examination. The female athletes were subject to a physical inspection that required them to parade more or less naked in front of a panel of physicians. When this test was first used in the European Track and Field Championships in 1966 in Budapest, all participants passed the test, but the resulting humiliation was widely resented. Physical inspection was repeated at the Pan American Games in Winnipeg, Canada, and at the Commonwealth Games of 1966, in Kingston, Jamaica, manual examination of the external genitalia was conducted on all women athletes by a gynecologist. Because many athletes who had to be subjected to this inspection were outraged, sports authorities sought alternative methods for gender verification. This led the IOC to introduce the buccal smear test at the Mexico City Olympic Games in 1968.

The advantages of this test are that no physical exam or blood sampling is required. If the buccal smear test proves negative or questionable, however, a full chromosome analysis should be conducted on a blood sample. This test is no longer endorsed by geneticists because it can easily give a false positive result.

In the mid-1980s a number of scientific bodies submitted petitions urging the IOC to abandon the femininity testing because the method used was not scientifically adequate and therefore not ethically acceptable. These initiatives did not result in action, perhaps because the group most deeply concerned, the female athletes, did not object to being tested. Not even objections by French scientists before the Albertville Games or the Spanish scientists before the Barcelona Games gave rise to a reaction or open debate. Even more puzzling is the fact that the incidents in Lillehammer passed in silence. Norwegian scientists refused to conduct the test, and a foreign group had to be brought to Norway to do the testing.

In May 1992 the International Amateur Athletic Federation decided to abandon femininity testing. Other sport organizations have done the same, and today only five Olympic sports federations conduct such testing. Why, then, do some female athletes not object to being tested at the Olympic Games? They may believe that the test prevents men from competing as women, or perhaps they are unaware that the test is scientifically inadequate and can produce false results.

Deviations from the general sex chromosome pattern are not uncommon. There are men with the female pattern (46XX) and women with the male pattern (46XY) or some other chromosomal difference. There are, for instance, women who are XXY and are physiologically, psychologically, and socially normal women. Women who have tested positive with the buccal smear test have been barred from competition, with devastating effects on their lives.

If the sole purpose of the test is to prevent men from masquerading as women, it seems unnecessary today considering the scrutiny of athletes by the media and the fact that women may be asked to provide a urine sample under the observation of the female doping control officer.

For the Sydney Olympic Games, gender verification was suspended. The IOC placed, for the foreseeable future, a moratorium on gender verification testing owing to the lobbying efforts of many involved with the women's sport movement. This was a major advocacy victory. It followed a very hard debate on this matter at the First IOC Conference on Women after persuasive debates from many of the women present. Many men and women sport medicine professionals were contributors as well.

The Australian Sports Commission has argued that the current genetic screening for gender is scientifically inadequate:

> While the philosophy behind gender verification is to prevent female athletes from being disadvantaged, questions remain. Why use a test that is inaccurate, does not really test what officials are trying to test for and has the potential to subject some women who "fail" the test to unwarranted stress when the number of men who would be attempting to compete as women in international competition would be negligible and ethically unacceptable. (www.ausport.gov.au/partic/wsgend.html)

### Sexual Harassment

Over the last decade, we have seen a growing public awareness of the problem of sexual harassment in the workplace, on university campuses, and in the community in the United States and in many other nations in the world. For the majority of girls and women, physical activity offers personal fulfillment, fitness, and fun. However, there is increasing evidence that for others the experience of sexual harassment is negating the many positive benefits sport has to offer.

Sexual harassment is usually defined as unwanted sexual attention, but in its extreme manifestations it includes sexually abusive and pedophile behavior that may involve significant others in whom the athlete has placed her trust. In addition to the obvious moral and ethical issues raised by such behavior, there is the worry that innocent coaches, who also deserve protection, might become unwittingly involved in what might be termed unprofessional behavior.

Prior to the Fourth U.N. Conference on Women in Beijing, 1995, the NGO Forum on Women "Looking at the World through Women's Eyes" was held in Hauiro, China. Among the thousands of workshops held at the forum were several on sport. These were conducted by organizations as diverse as the All China Sports Federation, the Women's Sports Foundation USA, Kenyan Sports Administrators, Atlanta Plus, and the National NGO Association of Zimbabwe. Although few in number, the workshops provided the opportunity for discussion and debate and highlighted how much work needs to be done, particularly in the developing world, before we can say that women are treated equally and fairly in sport and physical activity.

One particularly significant workshop was convened by Orie Rogo Mandoli and Betty Nyawade from the Sport Administrators and Ladies Hockey Association of Nairobi, Kenya.[10] Mandoli reported that very young girls were being abused at the hands of head coaches, assistant coaches, and managers. She said that often the girls were so young that they didn't understand how they got pregnant or by whom. This has led to great fear among the mothers of girls who want to do sport. The mothers hold their daughters back because they fear their daughters will be sexually abused. The Kenyan women asked the IOC, members of which attended the session, to help provide more training for women to be coaches so the problem of sexual abuse would be reduced and girls would have a better chance to stay in sport.

The extent to which sexual harassment exists in the sport community is difficult to assess accurately. More research is needed in this area, such as the study conducted by international sport sociologists Kari Fasting (Norway) and Celia Breckenridge (England). They have begun reporting on their research on sexual harassment and have shared the difficulty of doing this research with those attending the IAPESGW Conference (1999) and at the recent European Women and Sport Conference in Helsinki, Finland (June 2000).[11] Educational materials must be developed to assist athletes, coaches, and parents to understand the nature of the problem.

### The Female Triad

The female triad—disordered eating, amenorrhea, and osteoporosis—is a frequent result of an overemphasis on weight loss and can lead to long-term health problems for the athlete and in some cases even death.

Powerful pressure is placed on young female athletes to maintain a low body weight and present a feminine body image in order to secure lucrative sponsorship deals or media exposure. Sometimes athletes will enter into a cycle that may begin with dieting but progress to anorexia or bulimia and then to amenorrhea and osteoporosis. The incidence of what has been called the female athlete triad is hard to estimate accurately, as eating disorders and the behaviors associated with them are often well hidden even from those as close as the athlete's family, coach, or medical doctor. However, sufficient evidence now indicates that far greater numbers of female athletes, first estimated to be at risk of becoming involved in the cycle, are already affected by it. Estimates range from between 15 and 62 percent of female athletes, depending on the activity. Athletes who compete in what have been called the "performance sports," such as gymnastics, ice skating, diving, and tennis, are at particular risk. Much is now known about the elements of eating disorders in sport and their detrimental effects, which may involve more serious consequences such as amenorrhea or oligomenorrhea and bone loss.

### Religious and Cultural Constraints for Women's Participation in Sport

At the IOC's first world conference on women and sport in Lausanne, Switzerland, in 1996, Fazeh Hashemi, daughter of Iran's past president Ali Akbar Rafsanjani, asked the IOC to do more to promote sports for Muslim women. She called on the IOC to be attentive to the issues of Muslim women if their goal is truly to increase sports in Islamic societies. Hashemi noted that several Muslim nations had no women athletes on their teams at the 1992 and 1996 Olympic Games. She stated that there are 500 million Muslim women in the world, one-fourth of the world's female population, who cannot do sport in existing conditions.[12]

The first Muslim women's games, held in Iran in 1993, are an example of recent developments in Muslim women's sport practice, participating in sport in ways that are consistent with their religion and culture and also with the Olympic Charter. Similarly, in Atlanta, Iranian shooter Lida Fariman was allowed to compete, but wore the traditional Islamic robe.

On the other hand, there are examples of continuing resistance to women's participation in the Olympic Games in some Muslim countries. Hassiba Boulmerka of Algeria won the fifteen-hundred-meter race at the 1992 Olympics, wearing running shorts and a shirt. She later received death threats, became an outcast, and could not return to her country. Similarly, at the 1992 Olympic opening ceremonies, Iran refused to let a woman volunteer carry the national placard for the team.

Josefina Bauzon, chairwoman of the Philippines Women's Sport Foundation, also talked about religious barriers to women's participation in sport: "Barriers to change could become carriers of change."[13] She gave examples of sport activities designed in the Philippines to take account of Muslim women's traditional dress.

Pakistan sent no women to the 1996 games. Women's sports were neither given recognition nor organized in Pakistan, whose prime minister, Benazir Bhutto, was then fighting discrimination against women. To promote women's sports, Pakistan has since established a separate women's sports board and in 1997 hosted the Second Islamic Countries Women's Solidarity Games. Prime Minister Bhutto believed that this effort will be backed by a movement that will create a cadre of female technical officials, referees, judges, and organizers who will have the ability to sustain this movement in the future. She concludes: "The value of sport lies in the unlimited opportunities which they provide for developing human abilities, both physical and mental. . . . Participation in sport teaches understanding and tolerance more effectively than any other area of education because humility in victory and grace in defeat are the two fundamental principles of sports education."[14]

## Examples of Good Practice

### The Colombian Women in Sport Association

Since 1994 there have been various national and regional efforts to replicate the international women and sport conference held in Brighton, England. One successful example was in Colombia, where a national conference was organized and subsequently the Colombian Women in Sport Association (La Asociación Colombiana de Mujer y Deporte, or ACMD) was formed in 1996. Coldeportes (the Colombian National Sport Federation) and the Colombian Olympic Committee (COC) supported the first Colombian conference and selected Clemencia Anaya Maya, director of the Olympic Education Academy of the COC, to organize the conference "Mujer y el Deporte" in Bogota, Colombia, November 1996. This meeting was attended by more than two hundred men and women from all areas of sport, recreation, and physical education. Anaya Maya began the opening session with a challenge to all: "Sport as it relates to culture is an integral aspect of the culture of each country. Women are represented in the most minimal form in areas of decision making and leadership in Colombian sport. How can we change this so that women are integral to the culture of sport in our country?"[15]

At the end of this conference ACMD was formed as a nongovernmental organization (NGO), officers and executive board were elected, and initial meetings were scheduled with the Ministry of Education to begin plans for programs that would expand girls' opportunities in physical education and sport. Clemencia Anaya Maya was invited to be a member of the international working group (IWG) to represent South America. In addition, she was invited by the IOC to give a presentation at the IOC meeting in Lausanne, Switzerland, in October 1995 about the ACMD and how it functions as an NGO between two governmental organizations (Coldeportes and the COC).

To date, ACMD members from Antioquia University in Medellin have conducted interesting research on gender and sponsored programs to demonstrate how sports activity can be used to combat drug-related violence in Colombian communities.[16] The association has organized a total of three conferences on women in sport. The second was in Medellín, Colombia, in March 1998 and the third in Cali, Colombia, in December 2000. There have been international participants at all three of these conferences from Venezuela, Mexico, Panama, Cuba, and the United States. The network for women in sport is spreading throughout Latin America, and slowly more women sport leaders are being identified and empowered through their involvement with sport NGOs such as the ACMD.

### Mathare Youth Sports Association (MYSA)

The Mathare area in Kenya is one of the largest and poorest slums in Africa. Several hundred thousand people live there. The majority of the population is children who have few chances to play and little space for sport activities. The attitudes toward women's and girls' participation in sport in Kenya in general are summarized by Tegla Loroupe, who owned the women's marathon world record: "I come from Kenya, where they don't put much effort into women. . . . They think that women are only to stay with their family. But, yes, I believe we are catching up. Women have strong ability of doing hard chores. They have stronger will than men."[17]

The MYSA started in 1987 as a small self-help project to organize sports and cleanup activities in areas designated as slums. By 1988 the Mathare football team (male) had won its first national championship, and in 1992 they won the Youth Football Games sponsored by Pele during the 1992 Earth Summit in Rio de Janeiro, Brazil. However, there was still no provision for girls' participation in the soccer leagues. In mid-1992 MYSA started the first leagues for twelve- and fourteen-old girls and the league faced major constraints. The MYSA leaders, all male, found that organizing a league for girls was far different and more difficult than for boys because young girls had overwhelming domestic responsibilities (e.g., caring for younger brothers and sisters, helping with cooking and laundry, and carrying water). There was also the challenge of changing traditional views and attitudes: the boys believed that girls could not play soccer, and the girls believed that they must play netball rather than soccer. Finally, the most difficult obstacle was the attitude of parents who felt that girls should not play soccer because they were needed at home and that their participation in soccer was frivolous and offered no skills training for their future lives. In addition to these negative attitudes about girls' participation, a lack of coaches, equipment, organizers, and funding created further difficulties.

One of the lessons learned by the MYSA organizers was that they needed to find a way to have child care for the younger brothers and sisters near the fields while the older sisters were playing soccer. In addition, the MYSA Executive Council helped parents understand that soccer was only part of the MYSA's activities, and that their daughters would get a chance to develop their leadership and organizational skills in other Methare community service programs. Finally, the Stromme Memorial Foundation, a Norwegian NGO specializing in help for self-help organizations, joined with the MYSA to secure funds from the Norwegian Agency for Development Cooperation (NORAD) to expand the girls' soccer leagues.

## Challenges for the Future

The international women's sports movement has had considerable success in the past decade and has broadened the discussion of women's equity in sport to include many nations in the developing world. At the same time, it faces important challenges in making its leadership more representative and inclusive of women in these developing countries. This is a challenge faced by many women's organizations as they struggle to maintain their ties to grassroots organizations and still remain connected to international forums. It is not surprising that the leadership of many international women's sports organizations relies heavily on women from the advanced industrialized nations—indeed, the former colonial structures have often provided the framework for new organizations dedicated to women's sport equity. Just as the international feminist movement has struggled to be more representative of the majority of the world's women, so too has women's participation in sport been challenged.

Thus, the legacy of colonialism can still be perceived in the leadership of the Commonwealth nations. Women in sport face the same challenges articulated for NGOs and government leaders as outlined at the Beijing conference and most recently during the Beijing Plus 5 proceedings. How can one keep the link to grassroots organizations and the agenda consistent with the needs of all women if the skills needed to operate effectively in the international forums are imparted primarily to the privileged?[18] There is no denying that the difficulty of building such bridges is not confined just to women or women's sport organizations. Similar problems face the emerging indigenous sport movement.

Nevertheless, in the United States we have experienced firsthand the impact of federal legislation since the passage of Title IX. The increases in participation and funding have changed programs and dramatically improved opportunities for women. Only dreamers might have foreseen the popularity of women's team sports such as basketball and soccer prior to Title IX. The thought of women's expanded sport career opportunities were not part of our collective consciousness regarding women in sport, or women and physical education. If this has been the case in the United States, it is important to ask the same questions comparatively. It is important that international programs are designed so that women's needs, concerns, and opportunities are taken into account. Sport must be seen as an important career and participation option for girls as well as for boys.

Cross-cultural differences will always be significant factors, especially because of sport's close association with the physicality of the human body. This should not deter us but rather lead us to view those differences as important points of comparison. It is already the case that women in Islamic societies have constructed culturally acceptable ways to compete in sport through separate organizations.

As we enter the new millennium, it is becoming clear that one of the greatest challenges facing leaders is how to address social and economic development. The international women's sport movement must be able to articulate clearly the contribution that sport can make to the lives of girls and women, but more importantly, it must convey sports' importance to the broader social and development issues.

Long-standing issues such as poverty, illiteracy, food and water scarcity, aging populations, and disease are all being confronted by forces such as technology, globalization, urban population concentration, and increasing demands for human and political rights. These forces are reshaping the development terrain, and each issue could have a potentially harmful or positive effect on human welfare.[19]

The value of sport and physical activity to social and sustainable economic development, particularly with respect to gender issues, has not been well understood and has often been undervalued. Women remain the subjects of discrimination in sport; however, there is an increasing awareness that participation in sport is both a human right and an instrument for social change and sustainable development. This has been evident in the ways that policy makers and governments in most societies have given sport and physical activity low priority; however, the situation has begun to change. There is greater knowledge of the benefits of sport and physical activity for girls and women with regard to sport's impact on health, social, and psychological development and empowerment. In addition, there is evidence that sport and physical activity can have an economic impact on nations in three key areas: improvement in work performance, saving on health expenditures, and direct economic contributions to a nation's economy through employment, sales of clothing, equipment, advertising, media, admission fees, and related areas such as sports tourism.

The future efforts of scholars and activists can make these links clear to policy makers and parents throughout the world. The future of women's empowerment has much to do with their future in the world of sport.

## Notes

Susan C. Bourque provided invaluable assistance throughout the development of this paper. I am especially grateful for her suggestions and insightful comments throughout the process.

1. The paradoxical story of Title IX is best told in the account of Joyce Gelb and Marian Lief Palley, *Women and Public Policies* (Princeton, N.J.: Princeton University Press, 1982). In brief, legislation that was intended to secure gender equity in all public school programs soon became associated primarily with redressing equity in access to athletics.

2. In fact, the women's sport movement historically was slow to join with the feminist movement of the 1970s and 1980s. See M. G. McDonald, "The Marketing of the Women's National Basketball Association and the Making of Postfeminism," *International Journal of Sport Sociology* 35, no. 1 (March 2000): 35–47.

3. Internet links for each of these organizations can be found in the "Want to Learn More" section of this essay.

4. R. V. Acosta and L. J. Carpenter, "Women in Intercollegiate Sport: A Longitudinal Study: Twenty-Year Update," unpublished manuscript, Brooklyn College, Brooklyn, N.Y., 1998; K. Fasting, S. Scraton, G. Pfister, and A. Burruel, *The Experience and Meaning of Sport and Exercise in the Lives of Women in Selected European Countries*, technical report prepared for the International Olympic Committee, Lausanne, Switzerland, 1999.

5. These descriptions of the Brighton Declaration are taken directly from the document *Women and Sport: From Brighton to Windhoek: Facing the Challenge* (London:

RQA, for the International Working Group on Women and Sport and the United Kingdom Sports Council Publishers, 2000), 3–5.

6. J. Lucas, *Future of the Olympic Games* (Champaign, Ill.: Human Kinetics Books, 1992), 85–94. One way in which the IOC returns a small portion of the revenue generated from the Games is through the Olympic Solidarity Fund. This money is an effort to raise the level of elite sport, recreational sport for all, and athletic education in every country through grants to the National Olympic Committees (NOCs). Grant amounts were $25 million in 1991. The Olympic historian John Lucas states: "Solidarity grants have frequently made a difference in some countries' abilities to serve their athletes, administrators and young scholars of the Olympic Movement." There are factions within the international women's movement that would like the IOC to monitor how the Solidarity Fund is spent and encourage NOCs to use this money to help with gender equity.

7. *Preliminary Report* from the International Olympic Committee's First World Conference on Women and Sport, Lausanne, Switzerland, 14–16 October 1996, 4–5.

8. Ibid., 14.

9. J. L. Simpson, A. Ljungqvist, A. de la Chapelle, M. Ferguson-Smith, M. Genel, A. Carlson, A. Ehrhardt, and E. Ferris, "Gender Verification in Competitive Sports," *Sports Medicine* 16, no. 5 (1993): 305–15.

10. Participants in the workshop included representatives of the IOC (Fekrou Kidane, head of the International Cooperation Department, and Anita DeFranz, now vice-president of the IOC), Gunilla Lindberg (secretary general of the Swedish Olympic Committee), Sophia Raddock (Fiji Olympic Committee), Lu Shengrong (China/ president, International Badminton Federation), and Elizabeth Darlison (Australia). In addition, Dr. Sokoh Narob Jejad, a sport psychologist from Iran, and members of the delegation from the U.S. Women's Sports Foundation (Yolanda Jackson, Chris Shelton, and Marg Snyder) were present. These individuals attended and contributed to the outcomes from this session. Speakers in the workshop emphasized that issues of exploitation of girls, cultural and religious practices, and socialization of girls in sport as well as other areas of education must be addressed to enhance sport equity.

11. Kari Fasting, Norway, "Sexual Harassment in Sport," paper presented at the IAPESGW 50th Anniversary Conference on Physical Education and Sport in a Global Context, Smith College, Northampton, Mass., 7–10 July 1999.

12. *Preliminary Report* from the International Olympic Committee's First World Conference on Women and Sport, Lausanne, Switzerland, 14–16 October 1996, 24.

13. Ibid., 23.

14. Ibid., 8.

15. Clemencia Anaya Maya, "Razones para Crear una Asociación Nacional de Mujer y Deporte," first national conference, "Mujer y Deporte," Bogota, Colombia, 23–24 November 1995.

16. Rubiela Arboleda Gomez and Elvia Correa, "El Projecto de Deporte Contra la Narcoviolencia," Second International World Conference on Women and Sport, "Reaching Out for Change," Windhoek, Namibia, 19–22 May 1998.

17. *Preliminary Report* from the International Olympic Committee's First World Conference on Women and Sport, Lausanne, Switzerland, 14–16 October 1996.

18. S. E. Alvarez, "Latin American Feminisms 'Go Global': Trends of the 1990s and Challenges for the New Millennium," in *Cultures of Politics, Politics of Cultures*, ed. S. E. Alvarez, E. Dagnino, and A. Escobar (Boulder: Westview Press, 1998), 293.

19. "World Bank Entering the Twenty-First Century," *World Development Report* 1999/2000. See www.worldbank.org/wdr/2000/.

## Want to Learn More?

### Australian Sports Commission

Included in the Australian Sports Commission home page is the section on the Women and Sport Unit. This page provides in-depth analysis and information about current international issues about women in sport, including gender verification. For more information contact:

Women and Sport Unit
Australian Sports Commission
P.O. Box 176
Belconnen ACT 2616, Australia
Telephone (02) 6214 1960
Fax (02) 6214 1224
www.ausport.gov.au/partici/wshist.html
www.ausport.gov.au/wspahome.html

### The Canadian Association for the Advancement of Women and Sport and Physical Activity (CAAWS)

The Canadian Association for the Advancement of Women and Sport and Physical Activity is a national not-for-profit organization founded in 1981. CAAWS works in partnership with Sport Canada and with Canada's sport and active-living communities to achieve gender equity in the sport community. CAAWS operates with a strong base of volunteers and a small team of effective and efficient staff.

Canadian Association for the Advancement of Women and Sport and Physical Activity
1600 James Naismith Drive
Gloucester, ON, Canada, K1B 5N4
Telephone (613) 748-5793
Fax (613) 748-5775
E-mail caaws@caaws.ca
www.caaws.ca

### Japanese Association for Women in Sport (JWS)

JWS is a nonprofit organization whose major mission is to create a more gender-equitable society by means of sports. The goal of JWS is to promote women's participation in sport and to increase the number of opportunities for women's leadership. Further, by improving the status of women in sport, it strives to enhance the quality of life and improve the status of women in society.

www.jws.or.jp/english/index.html

### International Association of Physical Education and Sport for Girls and Women (IAPESGW)

Founded in 1949, the International Association of Physical Education and Sport for Girls and Women, IAPESGW, supports its members working for women's and girls' sport and physical education, and provides opportunities for professional development and international cooperation. IAPESGW, which has members in all five continents and more than forty countries, publishes a yearly bulletin and holds scientific congresses every four years. The last conference was in 1997 in Lahti, Finland, and the next will be in Alexandria, Egypt, in 2001. The association also organizes a scientific program every four years at pre-Olympic scientific congresses.

www.udel.edu/HESC/bkelly/iapesgw

### International Olympic Committee (IOC): Women in the Olympic Movement

This site gives the history of women in the Olympic movement all the way up to the present day. There is current information about the IOCs, including the resolutions of the Second IOC World Conference on Women and Sport and the activities of the IOC's women's and sport working group.

Section for Women's Advancement
Department of International Cooperation
Mrs. Katia Mascagni Stivachtis
International Olympic Committee
Château de Vidy
1007 Lausanne, Switzerland
Telephone + 41-21-621-6419
Fax + 41-21-621-6354
E-mail katia.mascagni@olympic.org
www.olympic.org/ioc/e/org/women/women_intro_e.html

### International Working Group on Women and Sport (IWG)

The International Working Group on Women and Sport is an informal coordinating body consisting of governmental and key nongovernmental organizations with the overarching objectives of promoting and facilitating the development of opportunities for girls and women in sport and physical activity throughout the world.

Here you will find information about the conferences mentioned in this chapter: Brighton, 1994, Windhoek, 1998, and Canada, 2002.

Conference Secretariat
Department of Canadian Heritage (Sport Canada)
Secretariat IWG
8th Floor
15 Eddy Steet
Hull, Québec, Canada, K1A 0M5
Telephone (819) 956-8036
Fax (819) 956-8019
E-mail trice_cameron@pch.gc.ca
www.iwg-gti.org/e/index.htm

*Part* **III**

MATERNAL POLITICS

# 7

# Marching Along with Mothers and Children

**Myron Peretz Glazer and Penina Migdal Glazer**

## ■ BACKGROUND

Beginning in 1982, we spent six years studying sixty-four American whistle-blowers in government and industry. As social scientists, we were particularly interested in the values that propelled the whistleblowers to protest unethical and illegal activities. We emphasized the social networks that sustained them and provided publicity, legitimacy, and legal defense. We scrutinized the organizational retaliation mounted against them as they faced firings, isolation, and character assassination. We also highlighted the cultural significance of their victories, their impact on corrupted institutions, and their often-successful efforts to rebuild their shattered careers and lives.

After the publication of *The Whistleblowers: Exposing Corruption in Government and Industry* (1989), we decided to continue our study of the social and cultural foundations of courageous behavior. We interviewed scores of grassroots activists in the United States, Israel, and the former Czechoslovakia who would not remain silent when their air was polluted, their wells contaminated, and their children sickened by radiation or other hazardous substances. In continuity with the whistleblowers study, we approached a wide spectrum of environmental crusaders to understand their backgrounds, values, allies, and adversaries. We wanted to test and advance our theory that environmental crusaders, like the organizational whistleblowers, are on the front lines in exposing and demanding remediation for society's most serious problems. They often serve as bellwethers heralding crises just over the horizon. In addition, they act as moral exemplars who embody the society's highest ideals of concern for one's neighbors and community. Whistleblowers and crusaders for a safe environment constantly reassert the boundaries beyond which others, no matter how powerful, shall not pass without encountering serious and sustained resistance. In heralding these interrelated contributions, sociologists and historians help us understand the sources of a society's moral balance.

I N recent years, mothers' groups throughout the world have won public recognition for initiating movements on behalf of important social causes. From the Madres de la Plaza de Mayo, who regularly marched to protest the disappearance of their family members in Argentina, to the U.S.-based Mothers against Drunk Driving (MADD), mothers' groups have surfaced to demand attention for serious social problems. Scholars have referred to these activities as maternalist or motherist movements, meaning that women in these groups have claimed the special nurturing and caring qualities of mothers to justify their public roles in causes associated with children and families.[1] While some applaud women's ability to use their status as mothers to move beyond the private sphere of the home in order to engage in public discourse, other scholars are critical of women's tendency to define themselves as inherently different, possessing unique qualities limited to women.[2]

This essentialist argument, as it has come to be called, always runs great risks. While using the mantle of motherhood may initially garner support for women's entrance into political arenas from which they have traditionally been excluded, an emphasis on difference, the critics argue, also reinforces notions of inequality because it places women on a plane different from that of men. Further, this focus on mothers' special roles and qualities overlooks important differences between women of divergent class, race, or ethnic backgrounds and ignores the fact that mothers can be found on both sides of any controversial issue. In addition, an overemphasis on the unique role of mothers can have the effect of excluding men, as well as women who have no children, from their movements. Perhaps most challenging is the critics' observation that, even where successful, most of these mothers' movements are a flash in the pan, arising in periods of crisis and disappearing as soon as the immediate crisis ends, leaving men in the dominant political structures to continue business as usual.[3]

Despite these serious charges, feminist scholars who have looked most closely at the history of mothers' involvement in social movements have not denied the significance of women's attention to public activity that grows directly out of their maternal concerns for peace, child welfare, and elder care.[4] These scholars point to a long history in many countries of significant political activism by mothers. Antiwar organizations, rent and bread strikes, and other militant actions all began out of maternal concern but proceeded to politicize women and take them into the complex public arena. Some women activists use their maternal role because they believe it is the only one that the predominately male media and government officials will recognize. These men are willing to show women defending their sick children but rarely invite them to meetings to discuss serious analyses of the technical and political issues at hand. Recognizing this reality, feminist scholars such as Sara Ruddick and Ann Snitow argue that women must be careful not to accept oversimplified ideas about mothers' special qualities. While continuing to draw on their concerns for nurturing and caring, women must avoid a tendency to rely solely on their maternal role for legitimacy. They must not see a contradiction between their special experiences as mothers and the need to seek social justice based on equality for all people.

The community-based environmental movements from which women have protested dangerous health and safety conditions highlight both the advantages and limits of organizing as mothers. Since the 1970s women in the United States, Israel, and Czechoslovakia have expanded their traditional activities as wives and mothers when they believed that local and national policies endangered their families and communities. To fulfill their roles as caretakers and guardians of husbands and children, these women have overcome deeply ingrained cultural practices that limited their public activities to more traditional settings such as the school, the church, and benevolent associations. They had not been part of the feminist movement that encouraged women to move into nontraditional roles, but they were prepared to broaden their definitions of appropriate behavior for themselves and others concerned about health, safety, and the quality of life. They came together as neighbors and friends in comfortable and familiar settings to articulate shared problems and to force their issues onto the political agenda of their respective governments.

Relying on the sense of their unique vantage point as mothers, these new community activists developed initial confidence and eventually won acceptance for activity that might otherwise have been considered brazen or foolish. Yet as they created effective networks, women confronted questions from others about their ability to take care of their children. At times, initial approval from husbands, relatives, and friends turned sour as increased involvement took the women away from their traditional homemaking tasks. Accusations of child neglect or inadequate housekeeping often vied with earlier approval for their actions as concerned mothers. Women also became the target of criticism from government and corporate officials, who wanted to minimize their effectiveness in seeking remediation for environmental damage. For example, one consultant for the organization representing the industries that were being sued by a California group of environmental activists graphically described his ambivalence in dealing with Penny Newman, a determined and competent woman organizer (whose case is described in detail later in this essay). For her adversaries, every acknowledgment of Newman's effectiveness was offset by a question about her integrity or her "real" motives for threatening the status quo. The industry representative believed that there were two reasons that nearly all activists were women—the very reasons that made them vulnerable to severe criticism: "First, their home is threatened. I grew up in the cattle business, and if you really want to have your hands full with a mad cow, mess with her calf. But also, here was a chance for a woman to assert herself as an equal. And what we have discovered is that there are a lot of Penny Newmans in this world that are maybe just as competent as Governor Wilson [of California]. And they've discovered it. So you are not going to shut them up."[5]

The industry spokesman's grudging respect for Newman's competence was nevertheless compromised by his insistence that she was like a "mad cow"—irrational, insistent, and adversarial. He trivialized her political and environmental insights by reducing them to mere psychic tensions when he suggested: "As a matter of fact, Penny has made quite a career for herself here, but the problem is that these activists can't be reasonable. They have to be adversarial because, if they start being reasonable, industry will pat them on the top of the head and tell them to go home. So they really raise hell, and it turns out that it's a lot of fun to do that. It's very gratifying because suddenly people listen, but then you get to be a problem because, once people start taking corrective action and you are still screaming wolf, they want to skin the wolf."[6]

Mothers' groups, whether in the United States, Israel, or Czechoslovakia, had to confront this patronizing level of opposition in meetings, in the local media, and on the streets of their communities. They heard complaints from relatives as well as adversaries, in words that could be painful and stinging. To overcome the ridicule and put-downs, successful community groups had to go beyond legitimizing their actions as an extension of their traditional activities, because this simply provided ammunition for those who were attacking them for their naive approach to social problems. Would-be activists had to prove their seriousness by finding one or more committed and knowledgeable leaders and by developing a working core group, a cogent ideology, political savvy, and the resources for processing technical information. The central figures in the core group had to become sophisticated community organizers, able to build broad-based coalitions and develop strategies to negotiate with political leaders in their city or their nation's capital.[7]

Local mothers' groups sought and often received essential assistance in their endeavors from national environmental organizations. Where the neighborhood groups were able to create or join a broader-based political coalition, they had the greatest success in forcing officials to take remedial action. When they remained isolated, they could not sustain the ongoing effort necessary to prevent the issue from slipping onto a back burner.

While there are important political and cultural differences among the United States, Israel, and Czechoslovakia, all these women undertook new commitments as grassroots activists when they perceived serious environmental threats to their families. In this essay we highlight the personal transformation of several mothers whose experiences in their three societies exemplify varying degrees of transition from the private sphere to the public arena. They changed from concerned neighbors to formidable environmental activists, from devoted mothers to nationally recognized figures. Some retained this new identity only until an immediate crisis ended, while others never left the arena of political and social change.[8] They were captured by the enormity of the environmental and social problems facing their region, and by their own ability to function effectively in the political sphere.[9]

As in earlier cases, we emphasize their strategy of creating a culture of solidarity that provided them with meaning to undergird their fight and with emotional support to nurture and soothe them in moments of despair and dread. They also sought links with other groups engaged in comparable struggle, with journalists who could provide the necessary publicity, and with government officials willing to give them encouragement, credibility, and information. All of these groups and individuals helped the women form alternative networks of power, which carried them or their messages from their homes and small group meetings into high-level government offices or corporate boardrooms. As they pursued their cases and made contacts with others working on public safety issues, the women began to define their work as more than an isolated project. They came to believe that they were contributing to the democratic process, in which citizens help to shape the political agenda and to force accountability on their elected officials.

We underscore that this commitment to reinforcing or actually building democracy differed in the countries under study. In the United States, California activists fighting the terror of chemical wastes defined their organization as a reaction against the blatant disregard of government and corporations for the safety of their children and community. The residents organized as a form of self-defense and to secure their rights as American citizens. They insisted that as taxpayers they were entitled to the same services and concern for their health and property as others living in more affluent communities. These ideas were at the foundation of their understanding of democracy. Equality under the law also meant that all people were entitled to protect their homes from toxic wastes generated by powerful industries. They passionately believed that the system had failed them, and they were determined to reverse that by using every legal means they could find.

In Israel, activists based in Haifa, Israel's third largest city, demanded acknowledgment from responsible public and business officials that serious air pollution existed and that residents were at severe risk from daily exposure. As they organized for a long-term battle, they came to believe that their actions went well beyond concern for a local problem. They believed they were making a significant contribution not only to their city but also to their country at large. The leaders articulated this ideology by asserting openly that their time, energy, and financial contribution to their cause was a worthwhile investment in the future of their country. In an era when the vitality of early Zionist ideology in motivating citizens was fading, they reasserted and redefined its importance. They believed that their Zionist dream could best be realized by enlarging the issues to be addressed through Israel's democratic institutions. For too long, they argued, serious environmental problems had been ignored as the government attended to other priorities and citizens accepted the premise that the issue was "out of their hands." In building a grassroots environmental organization that challenged this passivity, these activists were true "civic innovators";[10] they drew on extant groups in the community and persuaded them to enter a new terrain to fight for cleaner air and better health.

In Czechoslovakia, the women who focused on environmental problems had long been political dissidents. Unlike their counterparts in California, they had no illusions that under the Communist government there was any right to protest against environmental degradation. Their actions were more akin to those practicing civil disobedience against unjust authority. They were willing to take the risk of state punishment because they believed in their cause and in an ideal of democracy that entitles citizens to act on behalf of the larger community. Unlike the women in Haifa, the women of Prague had no interest in strengthening either the ideology or the actuality of the existing state. On the contrary, they were harkening to a democratic tradition in Czechoslovakia that they believed the Communists had tried to destroy.

In all three countries, the mothers had to exhibit courage not only in confronting their environmental adversaries but also in overcoming the subtle and obvious challenges to women assuming leadership roles in protest politics. As they engaged seriously with the problems that they identified, their roles expanded into hitherto forbidden and foreboding areas of public life. They were easy targets for criticisms that they were just ignorant housewives, on the one hand, or neglectful mothers and wives on the other. Either explicitly or implicitly, critics raised questions about women's participation in public, male-oriented debates; ridiculed their political style; called into question their experience and technical competence; and emphasized their "emotionalism." Sometimes these coded comments were delivered with humor; in other cases the criticisms were purely vindictive. But in either case, the critics mounted an insidious attack on ordinary women's attempts to challenge established authority and traditional roles in the community, just because they were mothers concerned about their children's future. Their critics appealed to long-standing, if unspoken, assumptions that mothers had a prescribed arena in which they should operate—school, home, church—an arena that was not supposed to accommodate their roles as lead challengers demanding attention from the highest authorities.

The women activists did not always respond directly. In most cases, they insulated themselves against such attacks by building an identity that gave legitimacy to their new roles. Beyond defining themselves as mothers entitled to protect their families, they mastered all the technical vocabulary; they never missed an important public hearing or meeting; they learned to use the media and techniques of public demonstrations. They self-consciously articulated the issues in ways that could be easily understood by a larger public, whose support they needed. Whether they used folksy methods or sophisticated analyses, they understood the importance of building a sustaining organization that could push their agenda forward, no matter what the stance of the opposition.

The cases profiled below are representative of a widely noted phenomenon. Small women's groups have appeared throughout the United States to confront local environmental threats. The Citizens Clearinghouse for Hazardous Waste works with hundreds, if not thousands, of such groups. Our own interviews with dozens of women confirmed the finding of other scholars that women are heavily represented in membership and leadership of grassroots groups.[11] Although there are fewer such groups in Israel and Czechoslovakia, the Israeli and Czech women embodied a growing concern by citizens like themselves about environmental problems. Dozens of women in all three countries told us that they believed they must interrupt daily life as they knew it in order to demand action and remedy for serious problems of pollution, radiation, and other toxic hazards.

## From Community Volunteer to Citizen Activist

Penny Newman of southern California is a prime example of a shy housewife permanently transformed into a successful leader whose influence continues to permeate an entire region of the country. When Penny Newman and her family arrived in Glen Avon, California, in the early 1970s, she knew nothing of a site called the Stringfellow Acid Pits. Although it was located just a few miles from her new home, she, like most residents, had no idea that in 1956 the state of California had persuaded a local landowner, James Stringfellow, to let them use a high, arid plot of land as a depository for the growing industrial wastes in southern California. Neither Penny Newman nor her neighbors could have known that since then the accumulation of toxic chemicals had filled the pit to such a point that a period of heavy rains would send them overflowing into the community of Glen Avon just a few years later.

There were several long-term residents in the community who did express concern that they were living at the edge of a potential disaster. As president of the local PTA, Penny Newman felt obliged to look into the allegations that the pits posed a threat to the children of the community. Newman approached local and county water quality and health officials, who assured her that the site had been closed recently and that everything was under control. She trusted their competence and their integrity.

> And so I dismissed my concerns. I figured these people were the experts. They knew what was going on, and their job was to protect us. It was not until several years later, in 1978, when we had heavy rains, that I saw for myself there was foam in the water. And then the newspaper reported that the state had decided to release some of the chemical waste onto our town. There was a part of me that just could not believe that the state would release a million gallons of toxic chemicals into the community. They just let it flow with the rainwater in the areas where our kids were playing, into the school, which six hundred children attended. It seemed impossible, but from everything I could see, it was happening.[12]

Government officials claimed that the chemicals had been diluted by the rainwater and that this kind of deliberate release was preferable to the potential danger of uncontrolled flooding. Newman was profoundly disenchanted with what she felt was a breach of trust on the part of school officials. They were not faceless bureaucrats from Sacramento but men and women with whom she had worked for years, first as a teacher's aide, then as a volunteer, and finally as PTA president and special-education teacher. When she learned that the superintendent had decided not to inform parents that chemicals had leaked into the schools and that he had unilaterally decided to keep the school open, Newman was transformed into a bitter critic: "It was like having my best friend turn on me. Everything that I had believed all my life was just turned upside down."[13]

Newman's reaction captured the disenchantment that affected many of the women who were caught between the desire to believe that government and corporate officials knew what they were doing and direct evidence that their children had been endangered. Their daily lives reminded them that they were living with contaminated water, poisoned by toxic chemicals. At first, activist Sally Mehra explained, the mothers thought the problem was limited to the poisoned water that had run through the school. Then they realized that every rainy day might bring more chemicals onto their streets, and they felt they should keep their children home in bad weather. The final insult occurred when Mehra learned that her well water was contaminated; she had to rely on bottled water until the local residents could convince the state to develop an alternative community water supply: "I had a year-old daughter and didn't want to expose her any more than necessary to the chemicals and radiation. I bathed her in bottled water, washed her clothes out of the area, and had a diaper service for a year so that she wouldn't be exposed."[14]

This sense of daily danger led Newman, Mehra, and their fellow residents to form Concerned Neighbors, an organization to monitor events at Stringfellow Acid Pits. Newman's PTA and Junior Women's Club leadership led to her selection as co-chair of a meeting at which residents expressed their concerns and fears about Stringfellow. A dozen years later, she was still chairwoman of Concerned Neighbors, which had grown from a small neighborhood organization to one that sued state, county, and corporate officials on behalf of thousands of persons who claimed to have sustained harmful effects from the chemical releases.[15] Their significant social capital—membership in PTAs, service as Cub Scout den mothers, and other voluntary service—provided initial motivation and a social network to draw on. But the experience as concerned neighbors created a whole new set of opportunities and challenges that transformed the group into sophisticated agents of change, while they still retained their down-to-earth style as mothers and friends.

In part, the organization helped the mothers confront their guilt. Initially, when they saw their children suffer from asthma, skin rashes, headaches, and dizziness, the mothers had blamed themselves. As Penny Newman described it:

> Am I such a bad mother that I can't take care of my children? . . . It was years before we really connected their health problems with exposure to the toxic chemicals. I was feeling those things, along with many of the women in the community. We were the ones who were up all night with the kids. We were the ones taking them to the doctors day after day. On windy days you had kids throwing up everywhere from the chemicals coming down in the dust. All of this prompted the women of Glen Avon to join hands. We didn't know what we were going to do. But we knew we could not allow the flow of chemicals into our community anymore.[16]

The experience of caring for sick children was a classic motivation for neighborhood women to mobilize. Sharing their frustration and guilt was the first communal move, one that has been repeated in mothers' groups throughout the world.[17] When the feelings of pain and despair are converted into determination to do something about a problem, mothers take their first steps toward becoming community activists. At first, women's entrance into the political arena may be viewed as surprising and even refreshing. Historian Amy Swerdlow described the initial response of the media to Women Strike for Peace action when strontium-90 was found in cow's milk after nuclear testing. She quoted Newsweek's shock in 1961 that these mothers were "perfectly ordinary looking women with their share of good looks, the kind you would see driving ranch wagons or shopping at the village market, or attending P.T.A. meetings."[18] But this benign appearance was only one side of the coin. In fact, women had to move out of their ranch wagons and village markets and learn new skills.

Penny Newman's new responsibility as chair was different from anything else she had done. She had to gather and interpret technical reports, organize her neighbors, and confront local and state authorities, all the while balancing her family responsibilities. It proved to be a tough act. Her husband initially approved of her activism but came to resent the extreme demands it made on her time and energy. Like many women activists, she had to negotiate a set of principles that protected her marriage by enabling her family to maintain some semblance of a private life. It was not easy. Newman's name now appeared frequently in the media, and like many women activists, she had become the butt of local jokes and wisecracks, as well as the object of admiration and affection. Her involvement changed her sense of herself: "When I look back at how I was when I got married versus how I am now, I see two totally separate people. In the beginning I was going to be a housewife and just take care of the kids. I was very shy."[19]

This personal and emotional growth was enhanced by her group's growing political acumen. Initially, the women's techniques involved trial and error and unlimited determination. They did not like being labeled as hysterical housewives:

> We were consistently underestimated because we were women. The agencies didn't expect us to be able to do anything. After all, we weren't trained scientifically; we didn't have Ph.D.'s. So we began to think about calling on our experiences in running a family and taking care of children. We found that many of our skills fit perfectly into a campaign to influence policy. We found that if you treat bureaucrats like children, it works. We would ask them nicely the first time. If they didn't respond, there was a consequence.[20]

The "consequences," according to Newman, often meant targeting a middle-level bureaucrat and besieging him or her with pickets, petitions, memos, and then moving on to his or her superior.[21] Newman and the Concerned Neighbors learned to use the media effectively. They made sure that the local papers and television stations had pictures of every protest. They befriended reporters and invited them to meetings and demonstrations. As in so many other areas, their use of the media became increasingly sophisticated as they gained experience. One activist recalled the difference:

> Our demonstrations have gotten high-tech. It's not like the old days of walking with picket signs in the hot sun. We plan a demonstration and contact the press. We have always had good rapport with press, and they almost always show up if given notice. We do a press packet, walk up and down for the camera crews, pack up our stuff, and go home. That way we're on the news and have reached millions of people. It's important to know how to get publicity. You have to have something important to say or the press won't keep coming back.[22]

After a rocky start, the group also formed a close relationship with their congressman and his aides. In February 1983 George Brown promised Penny Newman that he would hold a field hearing so the public could express its views on Stringfellow. By the time of the meeting in April, Concerned Neighbors succeeded in bringing more than nine hundred people to the hearing. When the congressman cut Newman off after ten minutes, a near riot erupted. The crowd so shocked Brown's staff that the court reporter threatened to leave. Yet the public concern was clear. To Congressman Brown and Penny Newman's credit, they had breakfast the next day, cleared the air, and developed a strong working relationship.[23]

Initially, the only source of substantial funds for the Stringfellow cleanup was the state of California. When Concerned Neighbors wanted to lobby for an appropriation for Stringfellow, they had to go to Sacramento to meet with state legislators and officials. It was the first time that many of these women had ever been to Sacramento, and it became an occasion to learn how state politics worked. At first, they did not receive the full $11 million they had requested; nonetheless, they were placed on a priority list for some of the clean-water funds. Most important, they began to learn how to approach state agencies. All of this would serve them well in future negotiations with several California governors and with EPA officials. By working together, Concerned Neighbors figured out how to penetrate the political system. After getting the runaround, they no longer accepted benign expressions of concern that were not followed by concrete actions. Where cooperation failed, Concerned Neighbors sought other means. When, for example, the regional EPA failed to take action after several animals died suspiciously near a test well site in 1991, Newman and her neighbors demanded action. When persistent attempts failed to obtain a safety plan or an investigation of the animal deaths, the exasperated activists raised the ante. They explained their intentions to the regional director in very strong language: "Since cooperation with EPA has gotten us nowhere, we will no longer bother but will find other means for making our concerns known. We will also make sure that everyone knows that EPA does not have the trust, confidence, or cooperation of this community. This will continue until you can come to us with a resolution to the problems. Specifically, that you've developed a community safety plan. . . . EPA, not the polluters, are charged with protecting public health, and we aim to see that you do."[24]

As part of their struggle, the activists developed an ideology that focused on the necessity of community solidarity and empowerment. Penny Newman became an eloquent spokeswoman for the power of community involvement: "It really doesn't matter who's in office. You have to make it an issue that the public can understand and that the public appreciates. The ultimate lesson we learned is that outside help will come and go. But the people that you can count on, and the only people you can rely on, and the people that you worry about are those from the community itself. These are the people who are going to be there come hell or high water, because they all share the common problem."[25]

Although the women in Concerned Neighbors did not initially define themselves as feminists or political activists of any kind, they developed a keen understanding of protest politics. Maybe a small core group would do most of the ongoing work. But it was important to have strong community support, to be able to bring dozens of people to a meeting if necessary or sign hundreds on to a class action suit. Some of the core group continued to be surprised at the transformation of their personalities. Sally Mehra, a member of the steering committee in the suit against the state of California and the involved corporations, noted that "if you had seen me when I was younger, you would never have thought that I'd be in this position. I'm not the type of person to do this type of stuff. I was okay with PTA, Girl Scouts, and Little League, but this requires keeping up with technologies, processes, changes in government, and more."[26] Many of the citizen crusaders began as traditional housewives, sometimes working as secretaries, teacher's aides, or occasionally as professionals. They were active in community organizations ranging from the PTA to social service clubs. They had fairly traditional views about gender-segregated roles and accepted the major responsibility for maintaining their homes and caring for their children, but as a result of their experiences, they also sought greater influence in community affairs. They met other women who were organizing against environmental hazards and came to realize that women's roles had to be expanded if the quality of their lives was to improve. They seized the opportunity to control their own destiny by directly confronting powerful government and corporate entities. The most active among them no longer defined themselves exclusively as mothers. They had learned how to use the political process to further their own influence, and they were a substantial force to reckon with.

These deeply involved citizens were also influenced by the growth of a worldwide environmental movement that educated the public about the dangers of the degraded quality of air, water, and soil. Environmentalists reported on growing health hazards and insisted that the public could take action to reverse the discouraging trends. The women in Glen Avon soon had allies and supporters throughout the country. As Penny Newman became increasingly sophisticated in her organizing ability, she assumed the position of regional coordinator for a West Coast alliance, which gave her an office, a salary, and national recognition for her efforts to assist communities suffering from toxic waste all around the country. She developed close ties to her congressman, George Brown, and to his chief aide, Leannah Bradley, who facilitated Concerned Neighbors' participation in public hearings and served as a liaison to EPA and other federal agencies. Later, Newman's group joined with the Clearinghouse for Hazardous Waste, headed by Lois Gibbs, who had led the fight over Love Canal. This enabled Newman to bring her by-then-considerable expertise to parallel efforts on the East Coast.

Newman became an excellent public speaker and led the formation of a community coalition that sued the principal responsible parties, the state, and the county. The formerly shy mother was now a formidable political leader, able to face detractors as well as ardent supporters. After years of participating in every forum, hearing, protest, and citizens' advisory committee, Concerned Neighbors could point to significant victories. The state of California and the Environmental Protection Agency had spent more than $100 million to cap the Stringfellow Acid Pits and to contain the toxic wastes within the pits. The community successfully lobbied the state for money to install a safe drinking water system. The activists were also instrumental in the passage of a state Superfund law that phased out the disposal of liquid hazardous wastes into landfills. These victories became models for other communities in the Superfund program. Nevertheless, the local residents continued to worry about underground movement of the toxics and applied pressure for improved technologies that would continue to monitor and pump out deeply buried dangerous waste materials that could travel along a plume into the water supply of Glen Avon. Nine years of personal injury trials against the state of California, Riverside County, and eleven private companies that had dumped wastes in the Stringfellow Pits resulted in a series of settlements and verdicts that awarded Glen Avon residents more than $110 million.[27] Although pilloried by the lawyers for the defense, Penny Newman remained a folk hero to many members of her community. She continued her work as director of the Center for Community Action and Environmental Justice and coordinated Communities at Risk, a network of communities at contaminated sites.[28]

In contrast, one might see Concerned Neighbors as "culture menders." Faced with fear and despair over the toxic floods and damage in their small community of Glen Avon, they were able to build new bonds of trust, to invent new political strategies that would allow them to preserve the life they knew and cherished. Their activities were a strange mixture of traditional and radical, of cherishing the past while demanding political change. As mothers, they placed the future welfare of their children above all other priorities. As neighborhood women, they used emotional ties and bonds of friendship and caring to set the political style. One activist explained how important this style was in sustaining the group: "Because you are with these people so much, you're able to talk about things that aren't going well. Maybe somebody's illness has kicked up again, or maybe someone's child is having trouble. There's been a lot of true lasting friendships that have happened over this time that have held the community together to keep the fight."[29]

This gendered form of political action, however, was never exclusionary. In fact, the women wanted as many men to join them as possible, and one local art teacher was a contributing member of the group. "It didn't bother me that I was the only man involved with all those women. They tried to get men involved, but the women have been doing it for years and years. Some don't have jobs; one is an old activist who loves the work. I'm not a member of the core group, but I go to protests, make posters, attend community meetings."[30]

Some men were worried that protests would affect their property values or make their houses impossible to sell. But the women persisted. They called meetings, explained the problems, and critiqued the responses of officials. They worked with lawyers and kept the community advised about the intricacies of their class action suit. In combining barbecues and local celebrations with this demand for change in the power relationships, they maintained the allegiance and confidence of their followers and persuaded most people that there was hope for Glen Avon and its future.

## From Immigrant to Activist

Transformations such as Penny Newman's and the formation of core groups of activist mothers could be found in many places throughout the world. Several years after the toxic floods in Glen Avon, a serious environmental threat mobilized a woman and her neighbors to confront the powerful government and corporate officials of the city of Haifa, Israel. That experience transformed Lynn Golumbic from a recent immigrant absorbed in the daily life of family and work into an activist leading a community-based group that placed the issue of pollution control high on the list of social and political goals in Israel's third largest city.

Lynn Golumbic and her family immigrated to Israel in 1982. This was the fulfillment of a dream she had had ever since college, when she had spent a year in Israel. Golumbic's husband, Marty, went to work at the IBM research center in Haifa. Lynn, who had an MBA from Columbia University, worked in sales for IBM. They bought an attractive apartment high up on Mount Carmel in Haifa and proceeded to settle in with their two daughters. In addition to home and work, Lynn Golumbic was active in the Association of Americans and Canadians in Israel (AACI), and she and her husband were deeply committed to the country's development. They did not yet realize that their family's health would deteriorate because of Israel's neglect of its environmental problems.

The Golumbics knew that since the formation of the state in 1948, the major focus had been on defense, economic development, and absorption of immigrants, and that issues like pollution were viewed as the cost of supporting much-needed industrial development. They understood that young Israeli adults were challenged by the usual problems of study, work, and family. In addition, all Israelis served two or three years in the military, and after that men served in the reserve forces for at least one month a year for several decades. As a result, citizens and political leaders alike believed that they did not have time for issues like the environment, which they defined as "luxuries."

The Golumbics never intended to challenge these prevailing cultural values, but within a relatively short time after their arrival in Haifa, Lynn and Marty and their two young children were all suffering from asthma. Two more children were born, and they too suffered from unexpected respiratory problems. The Golumbics had been neither environmentalists nor political activists in the United States, but it became increasingly clear to them that Haifa was the most polluted city in Israel, and that its petrochemical industry and oil refineries created constant black smoke that produced serious health hazards. In their first apartment they would be visually reminded of the constant black cloud hovering over the city:

> We would face the city of Haifa, and see this black cloud just sitting in the middle of the city. We were in shock and had physical problems as well. We weren't environmentalists, but we knew that breathing black smoke was bad for us. If you look over the valley of industry, you see the problem. We have oil refineries; we have the Israel power plant, petrochemical industries, close to two thousand plants down there. So there is a lot of junk in our air. We didn't know that much then, but we soon got to know more about it.[31]

Subsequently, the Golumbics moved to one of the most desirable residential sections of the city. But even living high upon Mount Carmel no longer shielded the more affluent residents from the effects of the pollution coming from industries surrounding the port. A small group of activists had been trying to fight the pollution problem for decades, yet political and economic realities militated against them. Haifa was a progressive city with strong labor unions, but the issues of health and safety had not become part of the unions' agenda. Many people employed by the electric power company or in the oil refineries were afraid of losing their jobs. Air pollution data were impossible to obtain from either the companies or the government, so no one could prove that pollution posed a serious health risk to the city's residents. The offending companies were the only ones monitoring the amount of sulfur dioxide in the air, and they were unlikely to define the situation as a health hazard.

The activists' experience with public protest began in 1988. A group of workers from the oil refineries had been told that environmental fanatics were planning to meet and demand the plant's closure. Determined to save their jobs, the workers' committee organized busloads of workers to demonstrate against the environmentalists. When Lynn Golumbic and a few friends arrived at the demonstration to join the activists, they were immediately confronted by the workers and asked which side they were on. Golumbic responded that they were there to appeal for clean air for everyone's children, not to divide the crowd into us versus them: "After a half hour of vigorous arguing, they understood that we were not going to demand to close down the plant, merely demand that antipollution measures be taken, and then they decided not to interfere with our demonstration. They also gave us their megaphone to address the crowd, since no one from the environmentalists had brought one."[32]

Later that year, when the electric company announced that a new power plant would be built in Haifa, the level of concern and controversy grew among the residents of the city. A citizens' group, Enza, served as an umbrella organization for local residents. They consistently asked, "If present levels of pollution are unacceptable, what would a new plant do?" Golumbic, who had ceased working when her fourth child was born, was at a meeting of the AACI when an Enza representative urged the group to take advantage of the upcoming elections. This would be a propitious moment to challenge the existing pollution standards and the planned construction of a new power plant. Golumbic and a few friends agreed to devote themselves to this issue.

Lynn Golumbic was elected chair of the AACI air pollution committee and formed a coalition with Enza and the Haifa branch of the Society for the Protection of Nature in Israel (SPNI). Since 1988 was an election year, activists believed that they had the opportunity to influence politicians if they could mount a full-blown campaign to gain serious attention from the candidates.

First, the activists had to make air pollution an ongoing public issue. Golumbic and her core group used as many appeals as they could. Saving the children was a popular theme. In one instance, they decided to sit in on sessions of an ongoing court case involving the oil company. When they arrived at the courthouse, they learned that the trial was a closed session, so they held a demonstration of mothers and babies:

> We got there, and they wouldn't let us in because it was a closed session. So we decided to have a mini-demonstration right there. We bought posterboard and markers and made up five signs. We called the local paper and told them we were demonstrating in front of the city hall/courthouse. Our signs said things like "You're Choking Us to Death," or "Let Us Breathe." The policemen watching us were very uncomfortable with our impromptu protest. We told them, "Let us stay for five minutes, just until the reporter takes our picture." We were six or seven women and some children, so we decided to continue with it.[33]

These experiences were crucial educational opportunities for the women. By negotiating with the police and the reporters, they learned how to plan strategic demonstrations for maximum media impact. Their focus on mothers and babies reflected their understanding that this emphasis on family had an emotional resonance that would further their cause. In addition, the availability of several mothers who were working part-time or not at all enabled the women to devote themselves more fully to the cause. The emphasis on mothers and children was not their only approach. They invited men to join their activities and used the motto "Air pollution is destroying the city." The style they developed differed markedly from that of other longtime Israeli environmentalists, who did not understand or use direct public appeal. Golumbic, like many successful leaders, understood that social movements had changed. They now required a profound understanding and use of mass media. The message had to appeal not just to sympathizers but to an indifferent and even unsympathetic public. Therefore, effective messages had to be simple, direct, and free of complexity or ambiguity.[34] Despite some serious personality differences, Golumbic succeeded in holding together the loose coalition of the AACI air pollution committee, Enza, the original environmental group, and the Haifa branch of SPNI, Israel's largest nature conservation society. Sometimes more energy went into achieving consensus on appropriate tactics than actually went into the struggle with the electric and petrochemical companies, but in the end the coalition held.

Golumbic succeeded in getting her colleagues to take advantage of the forthcoming elections; at political rallies and meetings they questioned all candidates about their positions on building a new power plant in Haifa and on the pollution problem more generally. The activists contacted professors at the university, who advised them on technical issues and pulled together all available studies on the health effects of air pollution. Israel was not accustomed to this kind of focused and concerted effort on any environmental issue, and the novelty of the group's pointed, persistent crusade enabled them to receive good coverage from the local press as well as from radio and television.

When Lynn and Marty Golumbic arrived in Israel, they never thought that they could personally influence developments in their adopted country. In the course of Lynn's active involvement in the pollution issue, both husband and wife came to define her activism as their contribution to Israel: "What did Americans contribute to the struggle? We brought style and technique and a lot of perseverance. We basically came with the attitude that if we went about it in the right way, we would win. It may not be this year, and it may not be next, but if we go for it, justice is on our side. We understand that you need to have an issue, define it, bring it to the attention of everyone in the best way you can, and keep on this issue until something is done about it."[35]

This belief that they were making Israel a better place sustained them. They convinced themselves and others that they had an obligation to interrupt politics as usual. Citizen participation on behalf of the community may have been an American idea, but Israelis quickly adapted these techniques to their politics and culture. Gradually, Lynn Golumbic emerged as a nonpartisan leader who could articulate the growing popular concern about environmental problems. After years of intense effort, which included several lawsuits, Golumbic's coalition could point to serious changes. The electric company and the minister of energy recommended to the National Planning Authority that the new power plant be located elsewhere. The environmental group also initiated a court case in which Marty Golumbic served as the named injured party in an attempt to force lower thresholds for sulfur dioxide in the air. An elaborate legal procedure resulted in a negotiated settlement. The minister of the environment signed into law twenty-one new air pollution standards, eleven of them for pollutants that had never had standards before. As a result of these agreements, Haifa no longer exceeds acceptable standards for sulfur dioxide pollution; pollution levels are reported every day in the newspaper. These were major and unprecedented victories for the citizens and their allies, although concerns remained about peak days when pollution exceeded the legal limits.[36]

In some ways Lynn Golumbic's personal transformation parallels that of

Penny Newman.[37] Never previously an activist in the United States, Golumbic had nevertheless absorbed certain strategic skills in her college years that stood her in good stead as she and her colleagues began to organize a protest movement. As a marketing professional, she knew how to define an issue and mobilize a public effort by using petition drives, demonstrations, door-to-door campaigns, and children's contests in the schools. She learned to write effective press releases and to contact reporters in a timely way in order to maximize the coverage the group's actions would receive in the media.

As in Glen Avon, California, local groups in Haifa based on neighborliness and a sense of community used their social capital to bring crucial issues to the public, to demand accountability from local officials, and to effect changes in public policy. They acted together when disillusioned by the neglect of health hazards by the established political and industrial leaders. They thrived on strong leadership and the work of a small core group of activists, and they formed coalitions between traditional nature societies and newly formed grassroots environmental groups to maximize their influence.

The Glen Avon and Haifa cases also differ in significant ways. Penny Newman and the Concerned Neighbors were not content simply to raise consciousness and turn the remediation process over to the state. They aimed for a redistribution of power in which they would be party to the many decisions necessary to clean up the acid pits and monitor underground contamination of the water. For more than a decade, they continued to attend every hearing, give critical readings to every report, and file objections when they felt that the plans were deficient. They were also involved in a long-term legal suit to recover damages to their health and property.

The Haifa group, by contrast, was determined to stop the new plant and wanted to ensure continued monitoring of sulfur dioxide and other chemicals. But they did not insist on active participation in the monitoring and treatment of air pollutants. They did their service to society and assumed that the victories they had won would be honored by responsible officials. Lynn Golumbic described them "as a group of women with Western views of democratic participation who used their education and dedication to organize and push for environmental change."[38] They believed that they had successfully demonstrated the power of public participation. Writing in the *Jerusalem Post*, environmental activist and journalist Devorah Ben Shaul applauded the Haifa mothers' victories: "But the real gain here is more than just the lowered sulfur content in Haifa's air. There is also the renewed confirmation that the citizen does have something to say about the quality of the environment in which he or she lives and works, and that ordinary citizens, working together, can bring about change."[39]

By succeeding as agents of change and by proving that citizens' voices do matter, these activists enhanced democracy. They were perfect examples of civic innovators, engaged citizens seeking new strategies to resolve contemporary problems.[40] In both the Haifa and the Glen Avon cases, the mothers' concern about environmental damage spurred the women to move beyond their normal daily lives to confront new challenges. They were not willing to define environmental hazards as part of the natural order or as an acceptable price of economic progress. They believed that dangerous pollutants resulted from the conscious decisions of industrial and government officials, and that these poisons in the air and water could cause irreparable harm to human health. The political and economic order had to be challenged if their children and communities were to grow and prosper.

In the wake of these achievements, these mothers' domain could no longer be limited to the home and child-oriented activities. The traditional boundaries between the public and private spheres no longer made sense. As mothers, they were obligated to confront even the most powerful forces to reverse dangerous actions and protect their families. They were drawn to environmental activism over other political activities because it centered on an issue that directly threatened their families. They described their desire to protect their children as the primary motivation for joining a local group; children provided the essential ideological underpinning for demanding action and lent weight to their cause. They represented a socially acceptable reason for mothers to move outside their conventional roles to engage in sit-ins, stand on picket lines, miss dinner, and leave the house uncleaned. The protection of children was more than a public rationale. In private life as well, it legitimized mothers' new roles for other family members and for the women themselves.

For leaders like Penny Newman, the initial desire to protect their children continued to transform their lives long after their children had grown up. Their commitment to social change and community building remained their central priority. In contrast, Lynn Golumbic was drawn back into the orbit of a job and caring for her family. Although she remained on the AACI's National Environmental Task Force, it was difficult to sustain her previous level of activism once she went back to work. Professional commitments often compete for women's time and attention; in most societies, working women continue to take the principal responsibility for home management and child care, leaving few hours for other commitments. Therefore, many of the most active women in the maternal movements have historically been those who were not working or who had part-time jobs.[41] There is little doubt, however, that should the circumstances warrant it, should the environmental problems resurface, Lynn Golumbic would once again reassert her leadership. She has learned far too much over the years to settle back into a passive role.

Like many Israeli women and others in the United States and elsewhere, Lynn Golumbic represents that reserve army of women activists who have made a substantial contribution to social and cultural change and then have stepped back to attend to other responsibilities. While they have reduced their day-to-day involvement, they continue to value their activist ideology. They are remembered by their peers and by subsequent leaders for what they attempted, sought, and achieved. They become part of the history and folklore of the movement.

## From Dissident to Activist

Ja'ra Johnova became involved in the environmental movement in Czechoslovakia when her deep-seated disenchantment with the Communist government took a sharp personal twist with the oncoming birth of her first child in 1977. Until that time, like many people in Czechoslovakia, she had privately hated the Communists, who had seized power in 1948 in a political coup. They had been kept in power in 1968 when Soviet tanks crushed the popular reform movement known as Prague Spring, which had won public support on the promise of "socialism with a human face." By 1977 Ja'ra Johnova was fed up with the years of political repression. She knew that, at best, anyone who challenged the government faced the loss of a decent job and the right to adequate housing or a university education. At worst, dissenters faced the possibility of a long prison term.[42] Nevertheless, in 1977 Johnova's passive alienation became public dissidence when she decided to act on her belief that the debased environment in Prague was a direct threat to the health of her expected child.

The year 1977 was crucial in Czechoslovakian history. At the end of a decade of repressive rule that followed the Soviet invasion, a few hundred citizens denounced the Communist government for the first time. Led by writer and activist Vaclav Havel, the dissidents signed a statement calling for an end to government human rights abuses. Johnova and several members of her family decided to sign the Charter 77 document. This was a courageous act in which relatively few Czechoslovakians joined.[43] Johnova knew that she risked government censure and retaliation by participating in an open act of

defiance. Nevertheless, she believed that officials had to be put on public notice that Czech citizens held them accountable for the lack of human rights:

> In 1977 my daughter, Christina, was born. That year was important
> for me because I signed Charter 77. I wasn't really interested in poli-
> tics, but I wanted to say no to all the liars and all the lies. Many of my
> friends also signed. They were coal stokers and cleaners, musicians
> and students.
>
> For the first time, Charter 77 announced that all people had basic
> human rights. We supported the country's laws, but they were con-
> stantly being violated by the authorities. We were opposed to aggres-
> sion and violence.
>
> I knew, of course, that nothing would happen in the next year or
> two, but I believed that if we helped to do something, then there
> would be a long-term possibility of change. At least if I signed it, I
> would have the right to look my daughter straight in the eye.[44]

For Johnova and many women activists, children embodied the future.
Would there be a reasonable society in place for them? Activities that showed
no possibility of immediate gain became worthwhile because they might aid
the children in the future. Ja'ra Johnova's optimism did not bear fruit until
twelve years later, in 1989, when the Charter 77 dissenters and hundreds of
thousands of other Czechoslovakians forced the downfall of the Communist
regime in a bloodless confrontation known as the Velvet Revolution. Yet during
the intervening years of the late 1970s and 1980s, Johnova was not inactive.
Despite the government's efforts to crush the opposition by severely limiting
their employment options and by imprisoning their leaders, Johnova and her
friends focused their attentions on the environment.

Johnova knew that the air pollution was so serious that it scarred all the
city's buildings. The government exported the best coal and kept the inferior
soft brown coal as the domestic source of fuel, creating pollution that was so
debilitating that the residents of Prague suffered high rates of asthma and other
respiratory illnesses. The government's practice of removing children from the
harsh city air for a few weeks may have appeased some worried parents but did
nothing to alleviate the disastrous environmental conditions. Johnova was even
more disturbed by the government's effort to conceal incriminating data, and
by its continued insistence that the pollution problem was under control. She
and her husband were part of a small group of environmentalists, the Green
Circle, that met to discuss a wide range of environmental problems within

Prague and throughout the country. Their major goal was to penetrate government secrecy in order to obtain basic empirical data that would have been readily available in Western countries. They wanted information on dam construction, the operation of nuclear plants, soil contamination, and agricultural problems.

Although the Green Circle emphasized many environmental issues, Johnova herself continued to be most concerned with air pollution in Prague. In early 1989, ten months before the fall of the Communists, she met with several women who had organized themselves into a small group called the Prague Mothers (Prazskewe Matky). These women were searching for a way to make a statement without going to jail. They were troubled that in the winter, when the pollution was most heavy, their children were chronically ill with headaches, vomiting, allergies, and respiratory diseases. Anna Hradilkova, one of the initial founders of the Prague Mothers, described its origins:

> We had many good friends and spent hours talking about the situation. We were concerned about the health of our children, and this led my sister to write a petition in the form of an open letter to the government. We knew that we had to obtain as many signatures as possible, because the more people who signed, the smaller the danger would be. Many people would not sign it because they were afraid. But we managed to get five hundred signatures, one person passing it to another. Mothers were more prepared to sign because they were worried about the health of their children. We called it the petition of Prague Mothers because this was an emotional name. We never thought of forming an organization—it did not seem possible at the time.[45]

Anna Hradilkova and her friends circulated the petition to all the newspapers, but only one small environmental journal was willing to print it. The petition, mild by Western standards, defied the norms of Communist society by publicly challenging the government's assertions that there were no pollution problems. The petition demanded vital statistics about pollution and the impact on children's health, and went on to call for conversion from the highly polluting soft coal to gas as the principal means of heating buildings in the city.

In January 1989 the Prague Mothers submitted their petition to many city offices, including the main pediatric health officer of Prague, the Office of Hygienics, and city hall. The officials responded to their concerns by asserting that the government was beginning to take appropriate steps and that, with the program underway, the air would be more suitable by the year 2010. The Mothers were disgusted by this response. In their view, no one seemed to be accountable for conditions that were damaging to their children in the present. Vague talk of improvement twenty years in the future merely underscored the failure of the government to meet the pressing needs of Czechoslovakian citizens.

After some additional correspondence and a fruitless meeting with local officials, the Prague Mothers decided to organize one of the first environmental demonstrations ever to occur in Prague. This was a particularly daring act in a country known for citizens who held their tongue and kept their disapproval of public policy to themselves. Anna Hradilkova described the atmosphere in Czech society: "We lived in a society that had no ideas, that didn't believe in anything. Our generation just did not believe in community or anything else. People just tried to get the best without harming themselves. There was no responsibility to anything larger than your own family."[46]

Clearly, any idea of civic responsibility or individual responsibility for the common good went against the social norms. Yet the Prague Mothers and other environmental dissidents wanted to revitalize democratic traditions as much as they desired to protest environmental degradation. The Prague Mothers were determined but not reckless. They carefully chose to hold their protest the day that visiting environmental officials were in town, because they knew that foreign journalists would be there to cover the meeting. This lessened the likelihood of police interference and harassment. About thirty women and their children marched in the demonstration, carrying a banner demanding improvement of the Prague environment.

Many friends and acquaintances accused them of irresponsibility for taking their children to such a dangerous event. Here the concept of motherhood became a double-edged sword. Taking children on the march no longer symbolized nurturance and love of family; marching with children represented risk and a real question of responsible action. Anna Hradilkova was well aware of the danger and the paradox involved in their political activity: "I understand that there is really a question whether to take children to such a risky event, but I think it is a much bigger danger for the children and their parents to remain passive. I think it was especially important for the bigger children who already understood the situation and realized that some things are worth fighting for."[47]

The Prague Mothers' determination to defy societal norms against challenging the authorities, their willingness to risk substantial punishment, was based on a multifaceted concept of courageous behavior. The mothers had decided that they must act to protect their children from the effects of reprehensible official actions. To remain silent would give tacit support to policies they abhorred. They could no longer be complicit, precisely because so many of their compatriots seemed willing to remain silent in order to avoid any trouble. The Prague Mothers had earlier taken the first steps of protest, and a public demonstration seemed an appropriate follow-up to their petition, which had garnered attention but ultimately had been unsuccessful in evoking a positive government response. They realized that a carefully planned outward show of resistance would be most effective if the children were there to represent all young victims of environmental degradation. While such a presence entailed risks, it also would be a significant learning experience for the children. They would march hand in hand with their mothers and with other children and would imbibe a political philosophy that required citizen participation in public life. Such a socialization experience, the mothers reasoned, would pass important values from one generation to the next. Courage, the willingness to put oneself at risk for a principle, was a precious social resource that had to be taught to their children. To reinforce its significance required going beyond the mere mouthing of words. In this case, they were willing to expose their children to a short-term risk in order to achieve a long-term benefit for all youth in the city of Prague.

Ultimately, their action was successful. Foreign journalists covered the event, and police followed the protesters, but they did not break up the demonstration or disrupt their protest. An unauthorized political demonstration in a Communist country was so unusual that the Prague Mothers became an object of curiosity. Many bystanders gathered to watch and ask questions. Despite the dangers of participation in any act of dissidence, more than a hundred people in the crowd actually signed a version of their statement, which they delivered to several ministers just as the police arrived to confiscate it.

The Prague Mothers were exhilarated by the success of their public protest. The large number of signatures and interested bystanders reinforced their belief that they were acting on behalf of the larger community. Several women who had organized the demonstration continued to work together and remained involved in the growing dissidence against the government. In November 1989 things came to a climax when police responded to a student march with massive brutality. By this time the government was no longer able to count on a quiescent population that would look the other way. Hundreds of thousands of citizens assembled in the main square of Prague. The Civic Forum, the umbrella group of the opposition, demanded the resignation of the party leadership and free elections. Strikes and demonstrations developed throughout Czechoslovakia to support these demands. On 10 December 1989 the Communist Party leaders agreed to turn over power to the Civic Forum and its counterpart in Slovakia. Free elections were held for the first time in almost half a century, and Vaclav Havel was elected president.[48]

Initially, the Prague Mothers were thrilled by the realization of their dream. Although it was unclear if long-standing problems would necessarily be resolved, the mothers decided to pursue their goals and become an official organization. They began to hold regular meetings and to invite others to attend. Both Anna Hradilkova and Ja'ra Johnova were important members of this new effort, but they found that the transformation from a small dissident group to an effective political pressure organization was not easy.

Ja'ra Johnova remembered the frustration of those early days and their need to refocus: "In the beginning we tried to do too much, and it was a mess. We soon began to specialize, and we decided our main activity would be to focus on air pollution. Nowadays, we have quite a lot of information on it."[49]

Major problems continued to confront them. Even in the new regime, government officials argued that qualified experts should make environmental decisions, not mothers pressing for cleaner air. They wanted the Prague Mothers to return to taking care of their children. Although they themselves held many traditional ideas about gender roles and family obligations, Johnova and Hradilkova and their friends totally rejected the view that they should be excluded from public discourse about the environment. Their earlier experiences as dissidents and environmental activists had persuaded them that responsible motherhood required them to remain concerned about environmental issues that affected the lives and health of their families and the entire society. They were less sanguine about the means by which to make the most effective contribution in this new regime. The Prague Mothers were disheartened by a raging new public desire for more cars, appliances, and household goods. This yearning for a consumer society only promised more air pollution in an already crowded Prague. The enemy was no longer visible in the form of corrupt, self-serving Communist bureaucrats.

The Prague Mothers found that environmental issues quickly lost the center stage they had held during the first days of the Velvet Revolution.[50] The new government began defending policies that gave priority to economic development over protecting clean air and water. The Prague Mothers wanted to continue fighting for their cause and believed that their revolution could be successful only if citizens took personal responsibility for the common good.

As Johnova explained: "Prague Mothers cannot just organize lectures; we have to engage in serious political activities."[51]

The difficulty encountered by mothers' groups in maintaining their effectiveness during a transition from authoritarian to democratic government has occurred in other countries as well. The Madres de la Plaza de Mayo in Argentina demonstrated formidable courage when they marched weekly to protest the disappearance of their children during the military dictatorship of the 1970s and 1980s. The Madres became a symbol of morality, credited with inaugurating a new politics of mothers by breaking down earlier barriers against women's participation and against any form of public protest criticizing the military regime.

Yet the Madres had difficulty remaining effective once a democratic government was elected. Despite their attempts to maintain a unified moral voice resisting amnesty for military leaders, they lacked the political know-how needed in the new political atmosphere. One student of Argentine politics described the new requirements that the Madres seemed to lack: "To be effective, women had to master the armed forces' budget, convince the committee of defense in the legislature of their demands, and analyze the potential effects of any hurried move on the political chessboard. To be effective in this new environment required more than principled commitment; it required political acumen and technical know-how."[52]

The Prague Mothers recognized that organizing in a postcommunist society required different organizational strategies and skills on their part. It was no longer effective to show that environmental degradation resulted from the corruption of the government and the bureaucrats' lack of concern for its citizens. Ironically, the end of the Communist government, which the Prague Mothers had long yearned for, also brought great difficulties. The enemy of environmental progress became time, money, and concern for economic development. Former friends and fellow dissenters scattered. People worked longer hours and had less free time. The Prague Mothers felt caught between the need to spend time with their children and their fight for a decent environment, which was so essential for their children to thrive.[53] There was limited precedent for voluntary organizations and public participation in democratic politics in the new republic. The emergent political culture left the Prague Mothers somewhat frustrated but determined to figure out the next steps.

## The Transformation of Mothers

The confrontation between mothers and the authorities in Czechoslovakia was the most adversarial and dangerous of the three cases we have presented.

But in all three countries, women activists came to realize that straightforward appeals to local officials did not result in the desired actions, and they felt betrayed. They lost trust in the idea that the established institutions would be able or willing to deal with the serious environmental problems that profoundly and personally threatened them and their children. These women were not moved by officials' explanations that repairs would take time, were too costly, and could threaten local industry. Because they had never had political power, women activists were less invested in the traditional institutions and were well placed to take on leadership in new groups such as Concerned Neighbors or the Prague Mothers. Angered by the platitudes intended to pacify them, women formed neighborhood networks to confront local conditions that affected their families. These new groups became the archetypes of what Alberto Melucci and Enrique Laraña and others have described as the "new social movements."[54]

As Melucci and Laraña have noted, these mothers' groups did not organize around traditional class issues. While not speaking with a Marxist vocabulary of class conflict and proletarian revolution, they did quickly see their battle as confronting powerful and often wealthy adversaries. The groups emerged in response to a concrete threat and were founded on the belief that conventional authorities overlooked their needs. Their ideology was diffuse and emphasized grassroots involvement in decisions affecting their communities. The social structure of the organizations was nonhierarchical despite the rise of well-known leaders. Decisions were largely made by consensus, which made sense for women whose primary allegiance had been to the family and the neighborhood. Propelled forward by their strong identity as mothers, these women crusaders took on new activist roles to reinforce their maternal obligations. But in so doing, those who became leaders and core-group activists permanently changed their own identity and the character of their families. Inevitably, some conflicts arose.

Often, what began as a jointly approved attempt to protect the family later produced severe familial tensions. Some husbands and children resented the incessant meetings, constant phone calls, missed dinners, and kitchens filled with organizational literature. The intense level of activity could easily undermine the very family stability and harmony that the women had initially set out to preserve. Some women responded by renegotiating familial expectations and limiting their political participation. They maintained their activist commitments but agreed to limit calls during dinner, to remove files from the kitchen, or to preserve certain days or hours for uninterrupted family time. Others could not renegotiate and withdrew from their new lives as reformers when they realized that the disruption of their old patterns was too threatening. In a few cases, particularly in the United States, where divorce is more common, the strains were too deep, and marital relationships disintegrated.

This new form of activism for mothers had some resemblance to mothers' groups formed by earlier generations of women to address a range of crises. But the new grassroots organizers had some critical differences. For one thing, they had the advantage of a worldwide environmental movement that had paved the way by raising consciousness, establishing precedents, and supplying information and advice. Mothers were concerned with the impact of environmental degradation on their children and felt compelled to take action, but they recognized that these problems were political and required more than just maternal concern. They insisted that industry and government acknowledge that environmental and health damage was not the result of an act of God or the consequence of misguided but innocent policy makers. They demanded that officials admit that their policies were responsible for serious problems and that they take appropriate remedial action.

The struggle for changing local and national policies transformed these mothers and their communities. Years of dedication often involved them with officials from the Environmental Protection Agency, the Department of Energy, the Environmental Ministry of Israel, the Czech police, and others whom they had never believed they would encounter. Women learned how to organize their activities for widespread press coverage and recruited technical advisers to assist them in the face of official criticism that they did not understand the technicalities of the issues involved. They quickly realized that their most important asset was widespread community support backed by a core group of committed workers who made the cause their first priority. In some instances in the United States and in Israel, groups turned to the courts to sue those who were responsible for community damage. These complex, lengthy class action suits required extensive interaction with lawyers and grueling trial preparation. Even when they were victorious in their legal battles, difficult questions arose about administering the settlements fairly and not allowing monetary gains for some to derail the larger quest for repairing the environmental damage.

As important as the "mother role" was in motivating political action, the most effective leaders knew that they had to learn new skills of organizing, gain mastery over technical information, and reject often painful criticism that they were neglecting their families. A smaller group of leaders went beyond the push for a single neighborhood-improvement goal. For them, the experience of community organizing opened new possibilities for long-term engagement in pursuing social change and environmental safety. To gain leverage in their political systems, they used grassroots methods: building broad coalitions, developing appropriate expertise, and engaging in ongoing negotiations with officials throughout the corporate and government hierarchies.

Those who had to negotiate with the maternal activists understood the power they had developed. One Department of Energy official at the Fernald nuclear bomb factory in Ohio described somewhat enviously the effectiveness of Lisa Crawford, the leader of FRESH, the community-based Fernald Residents for Environmental Safety and Health: "Lisa's a good leader. She does her homework, strikes good chords with the media. They know they can call her and get a quote. She knows where the sensitive spots are, how to pour salt into open wounds to get action. As a result of all her work, she's nationally known. She can call the secretary of energy and get a response. She's talked to the secretary, while I never have."[55]

This determination to be heard and get results led the mothers' groups to achieve unconventional but formidable power. With unconventional protest strategies and traditional gendered behavior that emphasized close personal relations, they forced attention from officials. By developing a sophisticated understanding of legal and technical issues, the women introduced new forms of civic engagement into their communities. As "civic innovators" they worked hard to maintain widespread public support that gave credence and political clout to their demands. The activists often served as "culture menders" in communities that were threatened both environmentally and psychologically. They demanded attention to hazards that had serious health implications and that demoralized the community. In resurrecting public morale, the citizen crusaders became a driving force for maintaining and building a democratic society.

# Notes

This essay originally appeared in *The Environmental Crusaders: Confronting Disasters and Mobilizing Community* (University Park, Pa.: Pennsylvania State University Press, 1998), 61–97. Copyright © 1998 by The Pennsylvania State University. Reproduced by permission of the publisher.

1. Evelyn Nakano Glenn, "Social Constructions of Mothering: A Thematic Overview," in *Mothering: Ideology, Experience, and Agency*, ed. Evelyn Nakano Glenn, Grace Chang, and Linda Rennie Forcey (New York: Routledge, 1994), 22–24.

2. Linda Rennie Forcey, "Feminist Perspectives on Mothering and Peace," in ibid., 355–75; Seth Koven and Sonya Michel, "Introduction: 'Mother Worlds,' " in *Mothers of a New World*, ed. Seth Koven and Sonya Michel (New York: Routledge, 1993), 1–42; Ann Snitow, "A Gender Diary," in *Rocking the Ship of State*, ed. Adrienne Harris and Ynestra King (Boulder, Colo.: Westview Press, 1989), 48–52; Sara Ruddick, "Mothers and Men's Wars," in ibid., 75–92. For an empirically based analysis of the similarities and differences between women and men on a significant emotional response, see Robert Wuthnow, *Learning to Care* (New York: Oxford University Press, 1995).

3. Amy Swerdlow, "Pure Milk, Not Poison," in *Rocking the Ship of State*, ed. Harris and King, 226.

4. Forcey, "Feminist Perspectives," 372. For an analysis that emphasizes the central role of women throughout the developing world, see Bron Taylor, Heidi Hadsell, Lois Lorentzen, and Rik Scarce, "Grass-Roots Resistance: The Emergence of Popular Environmental Movements in Less Affluent Countries," in *Environmental Politics in the International Arena*, ed. Sheldon Kamieniecki (Albany: State University of New York Press, 1993), 69–89.

5. Interview, 17 January 1992.

6. Ibid.

7. Resource mobilization theorists have defined in great detail how social movements must accumulate certain resources to promote their causes. In these new, informal groups, resources have to be integrated with close friendships, intimate ties, and informal organizational strategies. See, for example, Doug McAdam, John D. McCarthy, and Mayer N. Zald, "Social Movements," in *The Handbook of Sociology*, ed. Neil Smelser (Newbury Park, Calif.: Sage, 1988); Enrique Laraña, Hank Johnston, and Joseph R. Gusfield, eds., *New Social Movements: From Ideology to Identity* (Philadelphia: Temple University Press, 1994); W. A. Gamson, B. Fireman, and S. Rytina, *Encounters with Unjust Authority* (Homewood, Ill.: Dorsey Press, 1982). For a critique of resource mobilization, see Alberto Melucci, *Nomads of the Present: Social Movements and Individual Needs in Contemporary Society* (Philadelphia: Temple University Press, 1989), 21–23.

8. In her study of Women Strike for Peace in the 1960s, Amy Swerdlow points out that "the key women of WSP maintained that they had left their homes only to save the children and that when the political emergencies, such as the nuclear threat and the Vietnam War, were resolved they would return to full-time homemaking. Yet most of the women of WSP never did go home, because when the Vietnam War was over they no longer perceived the home as the center of their lives or responsibilities" (*Women Strike for Peace* [Chicago: University of Chicago Press, 1993], 239).

9. Ann Swidler, "Culture in Action: Symbols and Strategies," *American Sociological Review* 51 (April 1986): 273–86, shows how important culture is in supplying a set of strategies of action. In unsettled periods, when old strategies no longer work, new ideologies came into play to compete with older, more accepted ideas and actions.

10. Carmen Sirianni and Lewis Friedland, "Civic Innovation and ᴅ mocracy," *Change* 29 (January–February 1997): 14–23.

11. The significance of women has been noted by many. See, for example, las Freudenberg and Carol Steinsaper, "Not in Our Backyards: The Grassroots ᴇ ronmental Movement," in *American Environmentalism: The U.S. Environmenta Movement, 1970–1990,* ed. Riley E. Dunlap and Angela G. Mertig (Philadelphia: Taylor and Francis, 1992), 29–30. In their study *No Safe Place: Toxic Waste Crisis and Childhood Leukemia in Woburn, Massachusetts* (Berkeley and Los Angeles: University of California Press, 1990), 45, Phil Brown and Edwin J. Mikkelsen point out that the leaders in most toxic-waste-site organizations are working-class or lower-middle-class women at home with their children. Thus, they both have time and are likely to know about neighbors' health problems.

12. Interview with Penny Newman, 14 January 1992.

13. Ibid. The breach of trust was a fundamental factor in the rise of many community resistance groups. For an astute analysis, see Bernard Barber, *The Logic and Limits of Trust* (New Brunswick, N.J.: Rutgers University Press, 1983), and Francis Fukuyama, *Trust* (New York: Free Press, 1995).

14. Interview with Sally Mehra, 13 January 1992.

15. Tilly alerts us that the development of such indigenous social movements is most likely to occur in opposition to state authorities that claim to represent local citizenry; Charles Tilly, "Social Movements, Old and New," in *Research in Social Movements: Conflicts and Change,* ed. Louis Kriesberg and Bronislaw Misztal (Greenwich, Conn.: JAI Press, 1988), 1–18.

16. Penny Newman, "Making the State of California and Major Corporations Pay for Environmental Pollution," paper delivered at a conference entitled, Education at the Grassroots: Women and the Struggle for a Safe Environment, Smith College, Northampton, Mass., 9 April 1995.

17. Neighborhood groups provide crucial ties and support for the formation of protest and resistance efforts. For a discussion of "affinity groups," see William Gamson, "Social Psychology of Collective Action," in *Frontiers in Social Movement Theory,* ed. Aldon D. Morris and Carol McClung Mueller (New Haven, Conn.: Yale University Press, 1992), 53–76.

18. Swerdlow, "Pure Milk," 227.

19. Penny Newman, "Making the State of California and Major Corporations Pay for Environmental Pollution."

20. Ibid.

21. For an analysis of the development of social movement strategies and tactics, see Mayer N. Zald, "The Trajectory of Social Movements in America," in *Research in Social Movements,* ed. Kriesberg and Misztal. Charles Tilly's analysis of social movement actions against adversaries reveals how nonviolent and nonconfrontational Concerned Neighbors and other grassroots environmental groups were ("Social Movements, Old and New").

22. Interview with Linda Spinney, 15 January 1992.

23. Interview with Leannah Bradley, aide to Congressman George Brown, 16 January 1992.

24. Unpublished letter from Penny Newman to David Jones, EPA Region 9, 17 January 1991.

25. Interview with Penny Newman, 14 January 1992.

26. Interview with Sally Mehra, 13 January 1992.

27. *Riverside Press Enterprise*, 16 September 1993.

28. Penny Newman, personal correspondence, 22 July 1996.

29. Interview with Sally Mehra, 13 January 1992.

30. Interview with Paul Strain, 15 January 1992.

31. Interview with Lynn Golumbic, 23 March 1992.

32. Lynn Golumbic, personal correspondence with authors, 9 July 1996.

33. Interview with Lynn Golumbic, 23 March 1992.

34. See Ron Eyerman and Andrew Jamison, *Social Movements: A Cognitive Approach* (University Park: Pennsylvania State University Press, 1991), 138–40.

35. Interview with Lynn Golumbic, 23 March 1992.

36. In 1985 sulfur dioxide concentrations in the air averaged 104 micrograms per cubic meter. By 1995 major improvements, including the burning of low-sulfur fuels, had lowered that number to 11; Janine Zacharia, "Smoke Gets in Your Eyes," *Jerusalem Report*, 8 August 1996, 22.

37. Anthony Oberschall and Hyojoung Kim, "Identity and Action," *Mobilization* 1, no. 1 (1996): 63–85, for a discussion of links between political action and personal transformation.

38. Lynn Golumbic, personal correspondence with authors, 9 July 1996.

39. Devorah Ben Shaul, "Taking on Haifa's Polluters," *Jerusalem Post*, 1 April 1991.

40. Sirianni and Friedland, "Civic Innovation and American Democracy."

41. Many studies show that working women in Western countries continue to do more housework and child care than their husbands, even when they work full-time. In Israel, as in Europe and the United States, the overarching belief has been that a mother, above all, is responsible for her family. The "double day" of a job and home management become very time consuming. See Judith Lorber, *Paradoxes of Gender* (New Haven, Conn.: Yale University Press, 1994), 188–89; Swerdlow, "Pure Milk," 227; Marilyn J. Boxer and Jean H. Quataert, eds., *Connecting Spheres: Women in the Western World, 1500 to the Present* (New York: Oxford University Press, 1987), esp. 199–201.

42. The possibilities for dissent in different social systems are discussed in Zald, "The Trajectory of Social Movements in America," 19–41.

43. From 1971 to 1989 only 1,864 citizens signed Charter 77, and of those, half signed on in 1989, when the government was weak and the danger seemed less ominous; Tina Rosenberg, *The Haunted Land* (New York: Random House, 1995), 29.

44. Interview with Ja'ra Johnova, 7 May 1992.

45. Interview with Anna Hradilkova, 4 May 1992.

46. Ibid. Rosenberg, *The Haunted Land,* 30–31, points out that in Poland one of every two adults was a member of Solidarity, the principal opposition group. In Czechoslovakia, in contrast, the average citizen had his or her basic needs met and was "willing to forgo living in truth as Havel put it."

47. Interview with Anna Hradilkova, 4 May 1992. Such a redefinition of meaning in oppressive regimes occurred in other countries as well. For a discussion of resistance in Poland, see Helena Flam, "Anxiety and the Successful Oppositional Construction of Societal Reality: The Case of Kor," *Mobilization* 1, no. 1 (1996): 103–21.

48. Rosenberg, *The Haunted Land,* 33–34.

49. Interview with Ja'ra Johnova, 7 May 1992.

50. The problems confronting the Prague Mothers affected environmentalists in all the countries of the former Soviet Bloc. Although they had been deeply involved in opposing the Communist regimes, the environmental activists soon understood that problems would not be resolved quickly. Barbara Jancar-Webster, "Eastern Europe and the Former Soviet Union," in *Environmental Politics in the International Arena,* ed. Sheldon Kamieniecki (Albany: State University of New York Press, 1993), 199–221.

51. Interview with Ja'ra Johnova, 7 May 1992.

52. Maria del Carmen Feijoo, "The Challenge of Constructing Civilian Peace: Women and Democracy in Argentina," in *The Women's Movement in Latin America,* ed. Jane S. Jaquette (Boston: Unwin Hyman, 1989), 84. Martha Ackelsberg and Mary Lyndon Shanley, in "From Resistance to Reconstruction: Madres de la Plaza de Mayo, Maternalism, and the Transition to Democracy in Argentina," a paper delivered at the Latin American Studies Association, Los Angeles, September 1992, argue that the resistance to engaging in "normal" party politics has not ended the Madres' political engagement. They continue to challenge the state with their unique form of political discourse and participation. But the experience of the Prague Mothers seems to confirm Feijoo's analysis that a different form of knowledge is required in a transition from police state to democracy.

53. Interview with Anna Hradilkova, 9 June 1994; interview with Ja'ra Johnova, 11 June 1994.

54. Melucci, *Nomads of the Present;* Laraña, Johnston, and Gusfield, eds., *New Social Movements.*

55. Interview with Pete Kelly, 2 March 1992.

# Want to Learn More?

Here are some mothers' organizations working for social change. Check on the Internet or write to them for more information. If there is a local chapter in your community, try to interview one or more of the participants. Attend a meeting to learn about their activities and goals.

### Mothers Against Drunk Driving

Mothers Against Drunk Driving (MADD) is an organization of moms, dads, young people, and other individuals determined to stop drunk driving and to support victims of this violent crime. They're real people, trying to make a difference.

Mothers Against Drunk Driving
P.O. Box 541688
Dallas, TX 75354-1688
www.madd.org

### Mothers & Others for a Livable Planet

Mothers & Others is concerned about the impact of the environment's deterioration on the health and well-being of children. It works to promote consumer choices that are safe and ecologically sustainable for this generation and the next. Mothers & Others aims to harness consumer demand for a shift to farming methods that are safe, sustainable, and environmentally responsible by rebuilding alliances between consumers and those who produce and market food and by stimulating consumer activism in the marketplace. By providing strategies that can reduce individual and community consumption of natural resources, and by mobilizing consumers to seek sustainable choices, it aims to effect lasting protection of public health and the environment.

Mothers & Others for a Livable Planet
40 W. 20th Street
New York, NY 10011
Telephone (212) 242-0010
Fax (212) 242-0545
www.mothers.org

### Mothers' Voices

Mothers' Voices is dedicated to fighting AIDS and promoting sexual health through advocacy and education. It exists to connect mothers to information and is a movement of mothers united to end ignorance, discrimination, and apathy in the struggle against AIDS.

Mothers' Voices
165 W. 46th Street, Suite 701
New York, NY 10036
Telephone (212) 730-2777
Fax (212) 730-4378
www.mvoices.org

### Safeguarding Our Children–United Mothers (SOC-UM)

Safeguarding Our Children–United Mothers is dedicated to awareness, prevention, and providing a resource to those who have been wounded by childhood abuse.

Their website has information on topics ranging from Kids in Danger to a Letter Writing Campaign.

Safeguarding Our Children–United Mothers
1878 W. 11th Street
Tracy, CA 95376
Telephone (209) 832-5703
www.soc-um.org

## Million Mom March

The mission of the Million Mom March is to prevent gun death and injury and to support victims of gun trauma. It is advocating gun control laws to keep children and families safe and to counter the strong lobbying of the "gun lobby."

www.millionmommarch.com

# 8

# Mothers as Leaders:
# The Madres Veracruzanas
# and the Mexican Antinuclear Movement

**Velma García-Gorena**

## ■ BACKGROUND

My first exposure to the Madres Veracruzanas and the Mexican antinuclear movement happened quite by accident. I had been in Mexico in the late 1980s doing research on a peasant movement in Veracruz in the 1920s when a friend told me that she was heavily involved in the emerging antinuclear movement, which was attempting to convince the government to close the Laguna Verde nuclear power plant. She told me that she had cofounded a mothers' group and that the participants were using the Madres de la Plaza de Mayo of Argentina as their model. As she explained more about Mexico's first nuclear power plant and the opposition of the Madres and the antinuclear movement, I became more fascinated.

I quickly dropped my previous project and turned my attention to studying the Madres Veracruzanas and the Mexican antinuclear movement. A Ford Foundation postdoctoral fellowship allowed me to spend many months with the Madres in 1989–90. I had never really thought much about mothers and political participation, but I found the issues in this case—the uses of high technology, the protection of the environment, the mobilization of mothers, and the struggle for democracy in the Mexican context—to be quite compelling. The Madres have not been successful in convincing the Mexican government to close down the plant, but they have emerged as legitimate and respected political actors, which is a new phenomenon in Mexico.

N UMEROUS mothers' organizations have emerged recently in various contexts throughout the world; generally, the members of these groups seek to extend their nurturing roles from the private into the public arena. While perhaps the most famous of these groups is the Madres de la Plaza de Mayo of Argentina, mothers' groups have sprung up in other contexts pursuing different goals throughout Latin America and beyond. Following is a discussion of a mothers' group in Mexico, the Madres Veracruzanas, who have been part of the Mexican antinuclear power movement since 1987. The Madres, like many other mothers' groups, argue that they have extended their roles as protectors of children beyond the private domain of the household into the public and political arena. The Madres Veracruzanas argue that they want to protect their children from the dangers of nuclear technology by demanding that the Mexican government close down the Laguna Verde nuclear power plant, located just off the coast of the port of Veracruz in the Gulf of Mexico.

The rise of mothers' organizations has spurred a debate among feminist scholars about the meaning of such groups. Some feminist theorists argue that mobilization based on an identity of motherhood is a dead-end strategy, merely reinforcing old stereotypes of sex role differentiation. Other scholars have challenged these assumptions, arguing that the use of maternal imagery need not be inherently nonprogressive. My argument, based on the Mexican case, is that while mothers' mobilization may seem traditional and not "progressive," the Madres Veracruzanas' participation has evolved over time and the group has actually challenged old gender and public/private boundaries. In addition, I argue that feminist theorists should differentiate among different types of mothers' groups: some mothers' groups have been amenable to incorporating women of different classes, but in Mexico the Madres Veracruzanas have remained an upper-middle-class group, often actively protecting their class interests even as they struggle to protect the Mexican environment. Mothers' groups thus should not be romanticized—many of these groups are as divided along race and class lines as are other organizations and movements.

This essay provides an overview of feminist theory's view of mothers' movements as well as a brief history of the Laguna Verde nuclear power plant and of the Mexican antinuclear power movement before proceeding to an analysis of the Madres Veracruzanas.

## Mothers' Movements and Feminist Theory

What is feminist theory's view of the political mobilization of women based on their identities as mothers? Scholars' opinions vary, echoing the equality/difference debate.[1] Some feminist scholars have deep reservations about mothers' organizations. Micaela di Leonardo, for example, has identified several problematic tendencies in mothers' movements. Mothers' organizations often make essentialist arguments about men and women based on differing reproductive functions: men are inherently warlike, while women are "naturally" peace-loving. This is part and parcel of "moral mother" imagery, in which women are viewed as inherently more protective of life.[2]

This maternalist imagery is not new. "Through the manipulation of images of women as morally superior mothers and wives, nineteenth and early twentieth century feminists claimed the right to enter the public world as moral reformers and 'social housekeepers.' "[3] These movements' participants thus maintained that they were preserving the sexual division of labor—they only attempted to enter the male, public, political sphere in order to correct a particular problem.

Di Leonardo proposes three arguments against the use of moral mother imagery by female activists. The first is that while this imagery may be appealing in the beginning, "these newly mobilized women then have no reason to become feminists." Moreover, such imagery essentially precludes a thorough analysis of military processes. "The Moral Mother argument is a poor organizing tool: it does not challenge us to think in complex ways about the sources of military threat, nor about women's own consciousness and social activity."[4] Second, moral mother imagery privileges heterosexual mothers while casting aside childless women, lesbians, and antimilitarist males. Finally, moral mother imagery is vulnerable to empirically based counter arguments: in real life women are not necessarily peaceful or moral, and many women in fact are now joining the military in record numbers.

Maria del Carmen Feijoo, writing about the Madres de la Plaza de Mayo of Argentina, has similar reservations. The Argentinean mothers argued that their intention in the 1970s and early 1980s was to protect their disappeared children by extending their roles as mothers into the political arena. The Madres' actions were an "extension of the sexual division of labor in Argentina, which gives mothers the responsibility of defending and protecting their sons and daughters."[5]

Feijoo believes that while the Madres de la Plaza de Mayo served an important function in confronting the military government's human rights abuses and in developing new political practices, the Madres' strategy ultimately was self-limiting.[6] The mothers were admired throughout the world for their courageous confrontation with the military government, something that no other groups in Argentina were willing or able to do. In addition, the Madres developed novel political practices, such as the weekly protests in the main plaza of Buenos Aires and the wearing of white handkerchiefs, which came to symbolize their resistance to the regime's policies.

Yet Feijoo identifies at least two problems with the Madres' political strategy. First, their organizational style, which responds well to crises, subsequently is ill suited to working within the democratic institutions that were erected under President Raúl Alfonsín. "The Madres as a group had a weak institution with minimal functional differentiation; they rely heavily on strong personal leadership and are held together by gender solidarity, not organizational sophistication." The second problem concerns the fact that mobilization behind the banner of motherhood ultimately serves to reinforce the traditional sexual division of labor and does not challenge women's subordinate position in society. "Linking the possibility of change to feminine emotionality constitutes a paradoxical 'vicious circle.' Doing politics based on emotions . . . ends up making altruism sacred."[7]

Nevertheless, other scholars have countered these arguments about mothers' movements. Amy Swerdlow, in her study of the U.S. organization Women Strike for Peace, defends the notion of women's mobilization as mothers. This group, which was especially active throughout the 1960s and early 1970s, challenged both the United States and the Soviet Union to end the nuclear arms race; eventually, the organization also opposed the Vietnam War. Swerdlow argues that the women had little choice but to mobilize as mothers—the participants had been raised in the 1940s and 1950s, during a time when women had been socialized to believe that motherhood was the most important aspect of a woman's identity.

The organizers used maternal imagery for at least two reasons. First, the women were "expressing their own sense of male betrayal of the agreement they, as women, had made with society to sacrifice their own personal interests and career goals in favor of raising the next generation." Because male political leaders were putting much of the world's population at risk by pursuing a nuclear arms race, it was up to women as nurturers to step into the public sphere to save the world. Second, these women were mobilizing as mothers because "they were also trying to speak to the American people in a language they believed would be understood by the American people." The women also were fearful that if they mobilized as anything other than as mothers they would be dismissed or attacked for reasons of sexism. Swerdlow is careful to state that though the women of WSP mobilized as mothers, they never claimed to be more "peaceful" or more "nurturing" than men.[8]

In sum, feminist theorists have identified several reasons for questioning the utility of women's mobilization using maternal imagery. First, this imagery reinforces, rather than questions, the traditional sexual division of labor in society. Second, moral mother imagery also promotes an essentialist view of men and women, with men perceived to be inherently warlike and aggressive while women are construed to be morally superior and nurturing. Finally, maternalist mobilization, in the case of the Madres de la Plaza de Mayo, can work well during the initial stage of mobilization but can be noticeably ineffective at working with democratic institutions in the long run.

Ultimately, the debate about mothers' movements reflects the current debate about equality and difference in feminist theory. During the late 1960s and 1970s, feminist theorists were primarily interested in exploring women's unequal status in society. Theorists influenced by materialist approaches attributed women's subordination to their simultaneous oppression by capitalism and patriarchy. For many feminist scholars during this time, the private sphere of the family was viewed as an important site of women's oppression. Subsequently, some feminist theorists began to change their perspective, giving the category of gender the most important (if not the only) position in their analysis. Scholars such as Sara Ruddick began to study and to espouse "maternal thinking."[9]

The equality theorists have viewed motherhood as one of the *causes* of women's subordination: women's responsibilities in the private sphere have meant that their participation in the public sphere has been curtailed, thus leading to inequality. These theorists, then, often criticize mothers' movements because they reinforce the traditional sexual division of labor—this division of labor is presumed to be at least partially responsible for women's subordination and "should" be challenged rather than reinforced. Those scholars exploring "difference," on the other hand, have moved gender to the center of analysis; they do not treat gender as a derivative category. The theorists concerned with "difference" have begun to embrace those traditionally undervalued female traits usually associated with mothering. Ruddick, perhaps the most explicitly pronatalist writer, bases her argument not on the biological underpinnings of motherhood, however, but on the work mothers actually do. That is, "maternal thinking" emerges not from hormones but from the perspective of caring for and nurturing a human being, which gives mothers (they can be male if they also perform this work) a different political agenda. Below, I shall examine the case of the Madres Veracruzanas in light of this theoretical debate.

## The Laguna Verde Nuclear Power Plant

Mexico's nuclear energy program began in 1965, during the administration of President Gustavo Díaz Ordaz. During the late 1960s and early 1970s, the Mexican government was enthusiastic about nuclear power for several reasons. First, Mexico had not yet discovered its largest oil fields, and the government was concerned with finding alternative sources of energy. In addition, nuclear power experts predicted that nuclear energy would be cheaper than energy produced from other sources. Finally, Mexican government officials were anxious to keep up with advancing technology.

Originally, the Mexican government had planned to construct a nuclear plant on the U.S.-Mexican border as a joint Mexican-American venture in order to provide electricity to Arizona, California, Sonora, and Baja California. The site of the proposed plant was later changed to Laguna Verde in Veracruz after the Mexican government had consulted with its own Instituto Nacional de Energia Nuclear, the Banco de Mexico, and the Stanford Research Institute, a North American consulting firm. After a bidding process in 1972, the Mexican government awarded General Electric a contract to build the two nuclear reactors to be contained in the Laguna Verde plant. Yet other companies have also been involved in various aspects of the plant's construction. These companies, from various different countries, include Bufete Industrial, Burns and Roe, Bechtel, and EBASCO. Overall, the Laguna Verde plant took twenty-three years to build: four presidential administrations and some forty companies and groups were involved.

## The Mexican Nuclear Power Movement

The antinuclear movement in Mexico began in 1986 in response to two events—the accident at Chernobyl and President Miguel de la Madrid's state of the nation address on 1 September 1986, when he announced that the Laguna Verde project would be completed and that the plant would be put into operation. In 1986 and 1987 numerous groups emerged in response to these

events; they range from the Grupo de los 100, a group of Mexico's most prominent artists and intellectuals, to local peasant organizations.

The most intense antinuclear sentiment emerged in the state of Veracruz,
the area that would be most affected by a nuclear accident. People from every
social class spoke out against the plant. For example, hotel owners such as
Abraham Orozco Quintero, owner of the Hotel Prendes, worried that the plant
would hurt tourism in Veracruz.[10] Catholic bishops in Veracruz used the pulpit
to express their opposition to nuclear power, arguing that Laguna Verde would
intensify, rather than solve, Mexico's problems. And poor peasants and farmers
joined the movement because they feared that their crops and animals would
become contaminated by nuclear waste.

The antinuclear groups expressed their opposition to Laguna Verde for
numerous reasons; many of these arguments have also been used by antinuclear activists in the United States and Europe.[11] First, the opponents claim
that the plant's technology is poorly designed and is already obsolete. In addition, one of the two vessels in the plant was damaged shortly after its arrival
from the United States, making Laguna Verde especially susceptible to an
accident. Second, the plant's opponents argue that Laguna Verde is located
near a fault line and a volcano, making the plant susceptible to danger in case
of an earthquake or a volcanic eruption. Third, the antinuclear activists maintain that even when a nuclear power plant is operating "normally" it emits low
levels of radiation, which can harm living beings and the environment. A
fourth argument against Laguna Verde concerns the fact that at the present
time there is no safe way to dispose of nuclear wastes. In addition, the villagers
of Palma Sola discovered that the emergency evacuation procedure for the
Laguna Verde region was deeply flawed.[12] Finally, the plant's opponents claim
that the electricity generated by Laguna Verde will be twice as expensive as
electricity produced by conventional power plants.

The antinuclear activists have used a variety of tactics to express their
opposition to Laguna Verde. During the last several years they have staged
numerous marches; many of these demonstrations inevitably end in Xalapa,
the state capital, where opponents stand before the Governor's Palace. In addition, the cattlemen of the village of Palma Sola organized three blockades of
traffic along Mexico's main coastal highway, which cuts through the town.
The last blockade, in June 1988, lasted three days and was finally broken up by
state and federal military forces. Moreover, in the city of Cordoba, Veracruz
residents have periodically organized voluntary blackouts in the evenings as a
dramatic gesture. Finally, many residents of Veracruz have scribbled notes of

protest on their electricity bills, and some have threatened to withhold their electricity payments until Mexico abandons its nuclear energy program.

The antinuclear groups' criticisms of the plant are not based merely on uninformed fears of nuclear technology. The environmental group Greenpeace has verified many of the criticisms of the Laguna Verde plant. A Greenpeace publication explains that Laguna Verde's main problem lies in its faulty design; the Mexican plant is one of several General Electric Mark II boilingwater reactors that have been criticized for their faulty containment systems. In an internal report made public in 1975, several G.E. engineers advised that the Mark II BWRs should be taken off the market. Subsequently, "several utilities" sued General Electric, accusing the company of knowingly selling flawed reactors.[13] In the case of Laguna Verde, Mexican officials decided to proceed with the construction of the plant regardless of public criticism of the plant's design.

Despite all of the criticism, certain groups in Mexican society have continued to support Mexico's nuclear energy program. During the last few years the most vocal of these groups has been SUTERM, Mexico's electrical workers' union. SUTERM has threatened a national blackout if the Mexican government suspends its nuclear program. In addition, the Federal Electricity Commission (CFE) supports nuclear energy. But most important of all, the leaders of Mexico's dominant political party, the PRI (Institutionalized Revolutionary Party), support nuclear energy; PRI party officials have consistently portrayed the opponents of nuclear energy as enemies of technological progress.[14]

## The Comité Antinuclear de Madres Veracruzanas

The Madres Veracruzanas organization was founded in early 1987 to inform mothers throughout the state of Veracruz about the danger that nuclear energy poses for their children and for the population at large. The mothers' main demand is that the Laguna Verde plant be shut down permanently. The organization has chapters in the port of Veracruz, in Xalapa, and in Cordoba, Veracruz. About two hundred women belong to the group. The Xalapa chapter, the largest and most active of the three, was founded in February 1987 by several concerned women. In the beginning, these women, the majority from upper-middle-class backgrounds, decided to educate themselves about nuclear energy. They persuaded an engineer from the Universidad Veracruzana to give them private classes on nuclear issues. Then, armed with this knowledge, they proceeded to organize protest activities against the Laguna Verde nuclear power plant.

The members of the Madres Veracruzanas view themselves primarily as mothers defending their children from imminent harm. The Madres argue that their group is not political. When asked how their group can be apolitical, given that they have to use the political process in order to achieve their goal, they respond that politics is a dirty, corrupt, and male business and that they want no part of it. They have been forced to participate in order to protect their children. Once they achieve their goal they intend to withdraw from the political arena.[15]

The mothers' protest activities reflect their status as upper-middle-class women and mothers. Consciously copying the tactics of the Mothers of the Plaza de Mayo of Argentina, the mothers from Veracruz have staged protests every Saturday morning in Xalapa's main plaza—in front of the Governor's Palace—for the last nine years. The members maintain a dignified profile— they wear white, feminine clothing while holding their protest signs as they explain their opposition to Laguna Verde to interested passersby. The women have adopted red ribbons as their symbol and have persuaded merchants and residents throughout Xalapa to display red ribbons in their homes and businesses.

Though only one of the members had had any previous political experience, the women have shown to be quite adept in the political arena. Representatives of the Madres Veracruzanas have met with such high-ranking politicians as Manuel Bartlett Díaz, Manuel Camacho Solis, and Carlos Salinas de Gortari, the president of Mexico from 1988 to 1994.

The members have also participated in events sponsored by other antinuclear groups. In the beginning they were especially close to the cattlemen from the village of Palma Sola, and representatives from the Madres Veracruzanas joined in the blockades of traffic in that village. In October 1988 the mothers also joined other antinuclear groups at the Chamber of Deputies in Mexico City, where they tried to persuade the deputies to vote against Mexico's nuclear program. The mothers, along with other members of the antinuclear coalition, turned their backs on the PRI delegates who spoke in favor of operating the Laguna Verde plant.

Until mid-October 1988 the mothers had been relatively satisfied with their strategy and with the antinuclear coalition in general. Once the government announced that the plant would begin operating and that several more plants would be constructed, however, everything changed. First, the mothers had to face the fact that they had lost a crucial battle. Further, once the government began operating the plant even more citizens and organizations joined the opposition movement. Many of these new groups included labor unions and grassroots lower-class organizations, whose demands include higher salaries, better working conditions, and better housing in addition to their opposition to nuclear energy.

This provoked a crisis for the Madres Veracruzanas. The group recognized that the coalition had to maintain its unity if the antinuclear movement was to be successful. Yet because they see themselves as upper-middle-class mothers forced to participate in the "dirty" business of politics, they were deeply ambivalent about the other groups' goals. As one mother explained, "I'm only in this because I'm against Laguna Verde. I don't like other groups who shout 'higher salaries and no to Laguna Verde!' or 'better housing and no to Laguna Verde!' "[16] Clearly, the mothers were (and remain) deeply uncomfortable with the working-class groups' goals, yet they did not wish to provoke confrontations with them for the sake of the antinuclear movement's coherence and unity.

The movement reached its peak in late 1988, immediately before and after Laguna Verde was put into operation. In October and November 1988 there were daily demonstrations in Xalapa, the state capital, with thousands of participants in the days following the federal government's actions at the village of Palma Sola; the villagers had protested the plant's presence, and the government responded by calling out the military and putting the area in a state of siege.[17] Other antinuclear activists also experienced repression: a university professor was beaten by police officers and many others received threatening phone calls. The Madres Veracruzanas were spared, however.

The government gave no indication that it planned to shut down the plant. By 1989 the movement had lost momentum: many participants were scared away by the government's use of coercion in Palma Sola. At that point, the activists' tactics changed somewhat, given that it became more difficult to mobilize large masses of people. The Madres Veracruzanas decided that their new strategy should focus on meeting with top officials. Their plan was to arrange for a meeting with President Salinas to explain their position. The Madres believed that if they could convince the president about the severity of the problems at Laguna Verde, he would close the plant.

The plan was not far-fetched in that the Madres had already met with Salinas during his presidential campaign. Through the intervention of the governor of Veracruz, Dante Delgado Rannauro, the Madres were granted an interview to be held in November 1989. After a somewhat contentious selection process, the group sent eight of the members to meet with Salinas. During the half-hour meeting the Madres presented their views; each representative explained different aspects of the danger posed by the plant. One of the representatives, a physician, explained the dangers of radioactivity for the population's health; another representative, a psychologist, explained the psychological and social harm that could occur after an accident. The president, along with the governor of Veracruz, listened intently, though he interrupted often. In the end, Salinas responded by saying that technical consultants had told him that a conversion of a nuclear plant to a combustible plant was not feasible. Ultimately, however, he promised them that Laguna Verde would be subject to an independent review. Moreover, the nuclear plant's fate would be decided by the results of that study. The Madres, though disappointed that Salinas had not agreed to close the plant immediately, were nevertheless pleased with the notion that the plant would be investigated by outside technical experts.[18]

The president never gave an explicit timetable as to when the review would take place, however, and no more was heard about the study until February 1990. At that time the director of the plant, Rafael Fernández de la Garza, declared that he had every confidence in the plant and that it would be running at 100 percent capacity by 1993. In response, the governor of Veracruz declared that the president had informed him that the study would take place before the ultimate fate of the plant was decided.[19]

By early March 1990 the Federal Electricity Commission (CFE) began to outline the procedure for the selection of the body that would conduct the review promised by the president. The director of the plant announced then that the independent review, in order to be considered honest, should be conducted by an independent panel of experts with no connections to Laguna Verde.[20] This independent body would be selected through an international competition. No further details were announced—it was not clear who would select the winners, for example.

As the antinuclear activists anxiously awaited the results of the international competition, a scandal developed. A fax, sent by the director of the CFE to the governor of Veracruz and leaked to the media, indicated that the study would be rigged, essentially to ensure a positive review so the plant could keep operating. "A formal competition would have been too complicated," it stated; instead, it was decided that it would be better to hire a U.S. consulting firm, selected ahead of time, taking the necessary steps so it would appear that this firm had won through competition, "with the object of eliminating possible criticisms."[21]

The newspaper *Política* revealed that the fax, which was supposed to have been sent to the governor's office, was sent by mistake to a wrong fax number. The recipients of the fax decided to make the information public and personally delivered the document to the newspaper's offices. These individuals told

*Política* that they were motivated by a desire to protect the interests of the people of Veracruz. They decided to remain anonymous.

According to *Política*, the actions of the various bureaucracies involved with the plant did indeed seem to be rigging the study. The CFE picked four companies and "invited them [to do the study] through a simple description of the work to be done." Further, *Política* made clear that the governor of Veracruz, along with the heads of such important agencies as SEMIP, SEDUE, and the CFE—very high levels of government—were involved.[22]

The antinuclear activists were outraged by this news, but they still held a faint hope that the study might reveal the plant's flaws. The Madres recommended two engineers who might be included as part of the investigative team. They suggested Robert Pollack of the United States, along with Marco Antonio Martínez Negrete of the National Autonomous University of Mexico (UNAM), both known for their antinuclear views. In the end, however, the government announced that a Spaniard, Manuel López Rodríguez, would head the group that would conduct the study.[23]

Though all of the antinuclear groups sought to meet with government officials to express their displeasure with the selection process, only the Madres Veracruzanas were granted such an audience. The Madres met with Governor Dante Delgado at the Governor's Palace, where they indicated that they had little confidence in the review's credibility. During the meeting, the Madres proposed that four foreign technical specialists be included in the investigative team. But this suggestion simply "hung in the air."[24]

Nevertheless, the governor assured the Madres that the plant was not operating commercially, something that the antinuclear activists insisted should not happen without guarantees that the plant was safe. The governor insisted that he would be the first to protest the plant's operation "behind the back of my government."[25]

In the end, the government chose the investigative team. The eleven members included, along with Manuel López Rodríguez, several Spanish engineers with experience at the Lemoniz and Vandellos nuclear power plants in Spain. The antinuclear activists argued that all of the team members were strong proponents of nuclear energy. López Rodríguez was especially undesirable for the antinuclear activists, given his connection to Laguna Verde. López is a friend of Juan Eibenshutz, a Mexican engineer known as the "father of Laguna Verde."[26] López Rodríguez is also closely connected to Hidroélectrica Española, S.A., one of the companies involved in the construction of the plant. The team (which called itself the "Equipo Xalapa") took eleven days to do its work, at a cost of 350 million pesos ($120,000).[27] The independent review turned out to be superficial; it was not the thorough inspection that the antinuclear activists had wished.

Once the investigation was completed, in mid-August 1990, the final results were released quickly, though access to the report was restricted. Members of the press were allowed to read the report but were not allowed to photocopy it. The document began by explaining that "given the number of audits and inspections that have already been done, there was no reason to undertake yet another one."[28] Instead, the investigators focused on particular aspects of the plant's operation. The report indicates that the team visited the plant just once, interviewed personnel of particular sections of the plant, and reviewed documents pertaining to the plant's operation. Yet, overall, many of the details of the team's investigation were not made public. Indeed, except for the team's leader, not much was known about the rest of the engineers involved in the study. The investigative team concluded with the statement that they were "conscious that our work is not complete and that there will be issues that will escape us." Nevertheless, the team concluded that the plant should be allowed to operate.[29]

The antinuclear activists were outraged once again. Pedro Lizárraga, of CONCLAVE, the Coordinadora Nacional Contra Laguna Verde, declared that the investigation had been a farce and that the Mexican government was succumbing to various national and international pressures: "The obstinacy of operating a nuclear plant that is eighteen years old, obsolete, dangerous, with two acknowledged radioactive leaks and with exceedingly high production costs and unrecoverable investments, responds to financial and industrial interests, to technical sectors of power, and certainly, to very strong global economic interests."[30]

At a subsequent meeting with President Salinas, the Madres complained about the contents of the leaked fax: they also believed that the inspection was a farce. They showed the president a copy of the fax, and he responded by saying that their demand would be investigated, but nothing further was heard. Nevertheless, Sara González of the Madres Veracruzanas vowed to continue the struggle. "With the operation of Laguna Verde the ecological groups suffered a profound disappointment, the struggle did not have an effect, but now [the groups] are prepared to fight more aggressively because they have a time bomb a few kilometers from their homes."[31] Some of the activists were pessimistic, however. Thomas Berlin, author of a book condemning the plant, declared that "only an accident will stop the project."[32]

To add insult to injury, not only did the conclusion of the independent review allow the government to proceed unimpeded with its plans for Laguna

Verde, but only a few weeks later government officials made an announcement concerning Unit 2 of the Laguna Verde plant. Laguna Verde had been operating on only one of its two units. The second was yet to be completed. The head of the plant's Center for Information, Vinicio Serment, announced that the federal government had earmarked $350 million more to enable Unit 2 to begin commercial operation in two years, in 1993. Only Unit 1 had begun operation in October 1988, and Serment announced that that unit was operating at 80 percent capacity, providing 4 percent of the nation's electricity. The spokesman also maintained that the results of the independent study were trustworthy. "The results are reliable, despite the ecologists, who are never content."[33]

In the end, the Madres Veracruzanas were successful in securing meetings with President Salinas, just as they had already been successful in obtaining audiences with other important officials, such as the governor of Veracruz. No other antinuclear organization has had such free access to important government officials. Further, the Madres extracted an important concession from President Salinas—the promise of an independent investigation of the plant in order to end speculations about the plant's deficiencies. However, the Madres, along with the rest of the movement, were disappointed with the results. They were convinced that the review had been a sham, and they promised to continue with the struggle to close the Laguna Verde plant.

## The Madres Veracruzanas in the 1990s

By 1991 many of the antinuclear groups had ceased to exist. Almost three years had passed since Laguna Verde had gone on line, and many of the movement participants were disillusioned with the government's indifference to their arguments. Only the Madres Veracruzanas remained as active as before: they continued to hold their Saturday protests in Xalapa's main square and insisted on meeting with more government officials. Other groups, including CONCLAVE, could count on only a few members' participation.

During the early to mid-1990s, those antinuclear activists still participating had grown more cynical. The activists no longer believed that Laguna Verde would be shut down in the near future: they realized that their struggle would take years. Nevertheless, they continued to attempt to expose the plant's flaws, and they continued to question the government's credibility. In addition, many of these participants blamed the movement's decline on certain leaders' defections. These leaders now held positions in the government and had given up their antinuclear activities.

For the Madres Veracruzanas especially, this last period of movement activity was characterized by a desperate search for a successful strategy to close the plant. This search now included running for political office, even though the Madres had always insisted that they would stay away from political parties. The Madres' opportunity to run for office came in 1994, when the antinuclear activists had turned their attention to the presidential succession.[34] Cuauhtémoc Cárdenas of the Partido de la Revolución Democrática (PRD) once again announced that he would run for the presidency, against Ernesto Zedillo of the PRI (after the assassination of Luis Donaldo Colosio in March 1994) and Diego Fernández de Cevallos of the Partido de Acción Nacional (PAN). Cárdenas reiterated his position against Laguna Verde, promising that he would close the plant if he were elected.

At this point, after seven disappointing years of participating in the antinuclear movement, some of the Madres decided to change one of the most fundamental principles of their struggle—keeping their distance from political parties. Cuauhtémoc Cárdenas approached the Madres, asking if one of their members wished to run for the Senate as a candidate of the PRD. After much deliberation, Mirna Benítez decided to accept his offer. The Madres were divided on the issue; some continued to argue that the group should remain steadfast in keeping political parties at bay. Others, however, maintained that they had to take advantage of this opportunity ("aprovechar la coyuntura") because it might lead to further antinuclear mobilization. The decision was not an easy one for the Madres. Because there was no consensus, Benítez decided that she would withdraw from the group during her campaign.[35] In addition, the Madres allowed Benítez to run only after getting reassurances from the PRD that they were keeping their autonomy: they were by no means joining the party en masse.

Pedro Lizárraga, a fellow antinuclear activist, believed that this new strategy had both positive and negative elements for the Madres. On the one hand, joining the PRD would spread the anti–Laguna Verde message further. This was important because, as time had passed, the antinuclear issue had lost much of its urgency for the general population. Yet by running under the PRD bannerhead, the Madres could also risk closing certain doors—especially because the PRI has traditionally won most of the important elections in Mexico. According to Lizárraga,

> In Mexico, where the entire administrative apparatus is controlled by the government, that is to say the PRI, surely the new nexus of the Madres Veracruzanas will close even more doors for them regarding

their demands for an impartial technical review and regarding possible [future] conversations and negotiations. But if the candidacy of Mirna Benítez ends the amiable treatment [that they have received], it also ends the governmental hypocrisy.[36]

Mirna Benítez, like Cuauhtémoc Cárdenas, lost the election, and the Madres now have had to reexamine future strategies for participation. Benítez believes that her bid for the Senate helped the movement, however. Throughout the campaign, crowds gathered at Xalapa's Plaza Lerdo once again: many of these people carried antinuclear banners. Laguna Verde was once again an important issue. However, after the election—held on 21 August 1994—the mobilization died down once again.

During the mid to late 1990s, the Madres Veracruzanas have devoted themselves to reminding Mexican society of the effects of the Chernobyl accident in 1986. In April 1996 the Madres joined Mexican and international members of Greenpeace in recalling that event. As the Greenpeace ship *Moby Dick* arrived at Laguna Verde on 26 April 1996, the Madres were waiting on the beach to lend their support.[37] The Greenpeace members then blocked the entrance to the plant for one hour as they, along with the Madres, held photographs of Ukrainian children born with deformities after the Chernobyl accident.[38]

At the present time (2000), the Madres continue to demand that the Mexican government sponsor an unbiased review of the Laguna Verde plant. In addition, they continue to perform an important watchdog role. During the last few years they have revealed that Laguna Verde has experienced minor accidents, that earthquakes have struck in the plant's vicinity, and that workers have been exposed to high levels of radiation. In each case, the government had initially denied that these problems existed but subsequently admitted that these indeed had occurred.[39]

## Feminist Theory and the Madres Veracruzanas

How do feminist theorists' criticisms of mothers' movements fare in the case of the Madres Veracruzanas? Do the Madres reinforce the Mexican sexual division of labor? Do they make essentialist arguments? And have the Madres shown an inability to work in the long term with Mexican political institutions?

First, the Madres Veracruzanas are definitely working within the traditional paradigm of sex role differentiation. The Madres do believe that in Mexican society women are ultimately responsible for the care and nurturing of infants and children. They have been clear that their motivation for joining the antinuclear struggle has everything to do with their role as protectors of children; they argue that they are merely extending that role from the private into the public sphere. Indeed, the Madres have often carried pictures of their children during the weekly protests in Xalapa's main square: the pictures serve to remind government officials and the public at large that the Madres wish to protect their children from the dangers of nuclear technology.

Moreover, since the group's formation in 1987, the Madres have tended to make essentialist arguments. Most of these have reflected their belief that many politicians and CFE officials have become so enamored of advancing technologies that they have forgotten about the general welfare of the society as a whole, and of children in particular. The Madres argue that it is up to mothers, as the nurturers of children, to remind politicians and engineers that not all new technology is desirable because of the dangers that it may pose for humans and the environment.[40] The Madres' motto is "porque amamos la vida" ("because we love life"). Thus, the Madres believe that their unique role as nurturers gives them a special insight into what is good for children and for society in general, and that they sometimes have to transcend the domestic sphere in order to perform their duties.

Yet while the Madres consistently use maternal imagery in their mobilizational efforts, this imagery is not one-dimensional. Their identity as mothers not only reflects their view of the sexual division of labor but also symbolizes their disdain for Mexican politics in general and for the authoritarianism of the dominant political party, the PRI, in particular. The Madres often speak of their disapproval of authoritarianism; they believe that politicians, as well as many individuals who are involved in politics, are interested only in achieving political power and economic gain. The Madres believe that while women generally are less interested in achieving power over others, this is not always the case. Both women and men, they believe, are vulnerable to co-optation. In fact, the Madres Veracruzanas work hard to maintain their image as being "above politics" and as having no interest in economic gain. They believe this so strongly that the group has expelled two important members over this issue. One member, who had been the informal leader at the time, was expelled because her husband, an engineer, accepted a political post as head of public works in the nearby town of Coatepec, Veracruz. Because the Madres believed that the government was attempting to co-opt the member through the husband, the group summarily expelled her.

The Madres have stated repeatedly that they do not necessarily respect politicians and that they want Mexican society and the government to understand that they do not wish to participate in normal political practices, including bargaining, compromise, and co-optation. They argue that nuclear energy is so dangerous that they will back down only after Laguna Verde is closed. The Madres Veracruzanas believe that there is no room for compromise, and they insist that group members have to be disciplined in order to avoid co-optation by a corrupt political process.

Not only is maternal imagery a means to protest against authoritarianism, but this imagery is also not static. While maternal imagery can portray women as self-sacrificing and meek, this imagery in the case of the Madres Veracruzanas has evolved, and many of the members now view themselves as empowered. The Madres argue that they have changed a great deal as a result of their experiences in the movement. In the beginning, the women regarded themselves as mere housewives, but now, years later, they think nothing of confronting top government officials. Moreover, they are also comfortable dealing with the media: they are often asked for their views about nuclear energy and the environment in general. And most importantly, this sense of efficacy has carried over into their personal and professional lives. Carolina Chacón, a schoolteacher, says that she is no longer submissive in her interactions with colleagues and superiors in her professional life. She and several of the mothers say that they have "awakened"—they now question all aspects of the status quo.[41] Thus, while initially these women may have based their mobilization on traditional sex roles, they are now in the process of renegotiating those sex role boundaries.

Nevertheless, the Madres have not been as successful in breaking down class barriers. The vast majority of the members of the organization are from middle- to upper-class backgrounds. The Madres have been careful to construct the term *mother* in a particular way. For example, the Madres' political tactics have been carefully calculated to preserve their pure, dignified image. In their words, they want to be perceived to be "above politics." The mothers despise the tactics of the working class (including working-class women), which they say include the use of obscene language and sometimes violent behavior. They also disapprove of the tactics of feminist groups from the United States and Western Europe. Mercedes Solé, a forty-three-year-old housewife, says: "I remember seeing pictures of antinuclear women in England chained to fences. Mexican women are not like Europeans. The Madres would never chain themselves to anything—they would lose their dignity and respect from Mexican society, and our group would fail in its mission."[42]

The mothers also explain that their age range helps their image. The mothers range in age from their midthirties to midfifties. They believe that this works to their advantage because the media and Mexican society in general do not view them as mere young sex objects who are participating in the movement only to attract attention to themselves. Instead, the Madres say that they are regarded as serious, concerned mothers who are interested in protecting their children's welfare.

The Madres Veracruzanas are attempting to define the terms *woman* and *mother* (they use the two interchangeably) in a way that reflects not only their gender but also their own class backgrounds. For example, when Mercedes Solé, in her comment above, says that Mexican women as a whole are not like English or European women in that Mexican women would never resort to such extreme tactics as chaining themselves to fences, she is really only referring to Mexican women of the middle class. In reality, she and the other Madres Veracruzanas are aware that lower-class Mexican women in organizations, including antinuclear organizations, do often use such tactics. Yet the Madres have shaped the terms *woman* and *mother* in such a way as to refer only to middle-class women.

The following example serves to illustrate class issues in the Madres Veracruzanas' mobilizational strategies. The Madres' attempts to construct the terms *woman* and *mother* have precluded the participation of lower-class and other women in their group. As I have noted above, the Madres insist on group discipline—on a certain type of "feminine" attire, on not using harsh or obscene language, and on not taking over public buildings, for example.[43] These are precisely some of the tactics that many lower-class women use in the antinuclear and other movements in Mexico.[44] Yet the Madres are truly concerned about recruiting more women, of all backgrounds, for their organization. The members have expressed a great deal of concern about the fact that the movement and their organization are not growing.[45] They believe that this could be problematic if the government perceives that the Mexican public is no longer concerned about the nuclear debate.

Yet the Madres refuse to change their approach, and often they seem unaware of the concerns of lower-class women. During the spring of 1990, for example, the antinuclear organizations received some disturbing news from a fishermen's cooperative located near the Laguna Verde plant. The fishermen reported that tests by Laguna Verde personnel indicated the presence of high levels of strontium-90, a carcinogen, in the waters surrounding the plant. The fishermen had begun an investigation as to why the number of shrimp had declined in the area, and their research pointed to nuclear waste dumped illegally in the waters surrounding the plant. Moreover, the Laguna Verde plant's analyses of water samples and shellfish from the area indicated that the shrimp had absorbed unusually high levels of strontium-90. The mothers decided to exploit this information in order to mobilize more women in the fight against Laguna Verde. They decided to hand out leaflets in downtown Xalapa during their regular Saturday morning protests. The leaflets announced the fishermen's results about the contaminated water and shrimp and concluded by asking, "Are you willing to serve your family this shrimp during the current Lenten season?" The leaflets then encouraged women to join the movement. In the end, no new female members joined.

Ironically, the Madres had not considered that perhaps the majority of Mexicans may not be terribly concerned about the contamination of a food that they are not in the habit of consuming. Shrimp is expensive in Mexico, and most Mexicans are poor. The country has been experiencing an economic crisis during most of the last decade — many foods consumed by Mexicans (beans, for example) have skyrocketed in price. Thus, the news about a carcinogen in shrimp did not prove to be an effective tool for the mobilization of the general population.

The construction of concepts and terms has implications for political mobilization. The Madres' attempts to define the terms *woman* and *mother* narrowly may make them more acceptable to government officials, but these attempts have also prevented them from recruiting women of lower-class and other backgrounds.

Finally, the literature on mothers' movements has indicated that while mothers' groups may excel at raising society's consciousness about particular issues, they are noticeably ineffective in working with established political institutions. The Madres de la Plaza de Mayo, for example, have been "more prepared to respond to a crisis than to institutionalize a durable model of participation" owing to the group's informal organization.[46]

Is this also a valid critique of the Madres Veracruzanas? I would argue that it is not. The Madres Veracruzanas, together with the larger antinuclear movement, have been unable to close the Laguna Verde plant. But their failure cannot be attributed simply to an organizational problem within the Madres Veracruzanas' organization. Indeed, the Madres have exhibited a high degree of sophistication in their many meetings with government officials such as President Salinas, Governor Dante Delgado, and other politicians. If Laguna Verde is still operating, it is because the executive branch of the Mexican political system has refused to budge on this matter, despite the vehement protests of the antinuclear movement. The Mexican political system, despite recent reforms, remains authoritarian.[47]

*J*

## Conclusion

Feminist theorists have found mothers' movements to be problematic: while many have been successful in mobilizing women around particular issues, these movements also have often reinforced the traditional sexual division of labor in society. In addition, the Madres de la Plaza de Mayo have been criticized for their inability to engage in "normal" politics after democratic institutions were revived in Argentina.

The case of the Madres Veracruzanas in Mexico serves to illustrate the strengths and weaknesses of these arguments. The Madres Veracruzanas have indeed reinforced the traditional sexual division of labor in Mexico. They have argued that they are in the political arena to fulfill their role as protectors of children and of society. They believe that the Laguna Verde nuclear power plant is dangerous for their children, and they have ventured into the political arena to convince politicians that the plant should be shut down. Yet the Madres have also renegotiated these gender boundaries. The Madres believe that it is now appropriate for mothers to question the authoritarianism of the government and of technocratic elites who have made decisions about issues such as nuclear energy without consulting civil society. Moreover, the experience of meeting with important government officials and movement activists has given them a new self-confidence, which has spilled over into their professional and private lives. Thus, while the Madres continue to justify their political participation on the Mexican sexual division of labor, this division of labor has evolved into something new.

The case of the Madres Veracruzanas ultimately helps to answer the question of why some women would choose to mobilize politically as "mothers" rather than as just "citizens" or "feminists." The Madres Veracruzanas argue that Mexican society is more likely to listen to women who call themselves "mothers" rather than "feminists." Thus, these women were constrained by societal forces: the women who founded the group believed that maternal imagery was most likely to be effective in their mobilizational efforts. And structural factors were also at play. One of the members says that she joined the Madres Veracruzanas because she believed that this group would be sympathetic to her busy schedule as a full-time mother. She is one of the most active members, yet there are times when family demands interfere with her participation; she believes that the Madres understand these pressures better than the other antinuclear organizations.

The case of the Madres Veracruzanas also indicates that mothers' movements are not necessarily one-dimensional. The Madres Veracruzanas' mobilization as mothers not only serves to make a statement about the sexual division of labor but also symbolizes the members' rejection of the PRI and of "normal" political processes in Mexico. The Madres believe that the Mexican political system is corrupt and authoritarian, and they choose to confront it as mothers with pure motives interested only in what is good for children and for society—closing the Laguna Verde plant. The Madres want to be perceived to be "above politics" because they believe that political processes are corrupt and compromised.

Moreover, maternal imagery is not necessarily static. The Madres Veracruzanas have changed as a result of their participation in the group and in the larger environmental struggle. Mirna Benítez, one of the members, explains how this has happened for the women.

> Each of the mothers has become politicized in her own way. Irma, the doctor, has come to realize through her participation that she is against aggressive technology. She is not against technology, but she is against destructive technology that the government has pursued only because it is considered new and modern. Irma favors technology that is not destructive to people and the environment. Margarita Castellanos lives out in the country, and she has grown to love her land and the vegetation on it. Her motivation for joining the group, and her political analysis, is rooted in this love for the land and the countryside. Each woman's position and analysis is thus rooted in her own personal experience. . . . [The mothers'] participation has been steady. Initially, the mothers didn't see much beyond their own homes, then Xalapa; now they've grown to understand the political system and how it affects the nuclear industry in Mexico.[48]

Thus, while mothers' movements may appear to be purely traditional in that they reinforce the sexual division of labor, they have the potential to change and to become multidimensional.

The Madres and the rest of the antinuclear movement have not achieved their goal, but it would be wrong to suggest that the Madres and the movement have had no effect. At the present time the Madres are playing an important watchdog role, warning Mexican society of problems at the Laguna Verde plant. This watchdog role is especially important in the Mexican context, given that the Federal Electricity Commission and the Mexican government have not provided the Mexican public with much information about the plant. Thus, despite all of the obstacles presented by the government, the Madres

Veracruzanas continue to work to rid Mexico of Laguna Verde and of nuclear energy in general.

Finally, the Madres gained credibility and became leaders in the Mexican antinuclear movement by monitoring their pure, dignified image carefully. They maintain that they are "above" politics and have even expelled members whom they believed might compromise the group politically. Yet these tactics have also served to erect class and racial barriers that have prevented the group from recruiting working-class and other women. The Madres' dress, demeanor, and political tactics have reflected their middle- to upper-class and mestizo status, and this has prevented the group from recruiting large numbers of non-middle-class and indigenous women. Clearly, mothers' organizations should not be romanticized: they, like many other groups, are divided along racial and class lines.

## Notes

This essay originally appeared as "Mothers' Movements and Feminist Theory: The Case of Madres Veracruzanas," in *Mothers and the Mexican Antinuclear Power Movement*, by Velma García-Gorena. Copyright © 1999 by The Arizona Board of Regents. Reprinted by permission of the University of Arizona Press. Research for this paper was funded by a Ford Foundation Postdoctoral Fellowship for Minorities. All interviews were conducted in Spanish in Mexico. All translations of quotes from interviews are mine. For an overview of the Mexican antinuclear movement, see Velma García-Gorena, *Mothers and the Mexican Antinuclear Power Movement* (Tucson: University of Arizona Press, 1999).

1. See Linda M. Blum, "Mothers, Babies, and Breastfeeding in Late Capitalist America: The Shifting Contexts of Feminist Theory," *Feminist Studies* 19, no. 2 (summer 1993): 291–311.

2. Micaela di Leonardo, "Morals, Mothers, and Militarism: Antimilitarism and Feminist Theory," *Feminist Studies* 11, no. 3 (fall 1985): 599–617.

3. Ibid., 602.

4. Ibid., 612.

5. Maria del Carmen Feijoo, "The Challenge of Constructing Civilian Peace: Women and Democracy in Argentina," in *The Women's Movement in Latin America*, ed. Jane Jaquette (Winchester, Mass.: Unwin Hyman, 1989), 77. For a more sympathetic account of the case of the Mothers of the Plaza de Mayo, see Marguerite Bou-

vard, *Revolutionizing Motherhood: The Mothers of the Plaza de Mayo* (Wilmington, Del.: Scholarly Resources Books, 1994).

6. Feijoo, "Challenge," 78.

7. Ibid., 78, 88.

8. Amy Swerdlow, *Women Strike for Peace: Traditional Motherhood and Radical Politics in the 1960s* (Chicago: University of Chicago Press, 1993).

9. Sara Ruddick, *Maternal Thinking: Towards a Politics of Peace* (New York: Ballantine Books, 1989).

10. Guillermo Zamora, "Todas las clases sociales de Veracruz contra Laguna Verde," *Proceso*, May 1987, 18–19.

11. See David de Leon, *Everything Is Changing: Contemporary U.S. Movements in Historical Perspective* (New York: Praeger, 1988), esp. chapters 1 and 2.

12. Interview with Antonio Bretón, treasurer of the Asociación de Ganaderos, Palma Sola, Veracruz, 21 July 1988. Bretón explained to me that the evacuation procedure's map is not accurate. For example, entire villages are missing and the major evacuation routes are, in reality, barely passable dirt roads. For a detailed critique of the evacuation plan, see Alejandro Nadal and Octavio Miramontes, "Análisis crítico: El plan de emergencia radiológica de Laguna Verde," *La Jornada*, 16 October 1988, 15–18.

13. John May, *The Greenpeace Book of the Nuclear Age: The Hidden History, the Human Cost* (New York: Pantheon Books, 1989), 334.

14. The Partido Revolucionario Institucional has been in power in Mexico since its inception in 1929, a few years after the end of the Mexican Revolution of 1910–20.

15. Interview with the Madres Veracruzanas, 15 October 1988, Xalapa, Veracruz.

16. Interview with Margarita Castellanos, 18 October 1988, Xalapa, Veracruz.

17. Guadalupe H. Mar, "Soldados en Palma Sola: Antinucleares exigen que sean retirados," *Política*, 25 October 1988, 1.

18. Interview with Sara González, 23 November 1989, Xalapa, Veracruz.

19. Regina Martinez, "L.V.: Primero, la auditoría," *Política*, 26 February 1990, 1.

20. "L.V.: Habrá auditoría," *Política*, 1 March 1990, 1.

21. Angel L. Gutierrez, "Laguna Verde: Auditoría Simple," *Política*, 14 March 1990, 1.

22. SEMIP, SEDUE, and CFE stand for Secretaría de Minas e Industria Paraestatal, Secretaría de Desarrollo Urbano y Ecología, and Comisión Federal de Electricidad, respectively.

23. Regina Martínez, "Laguna Verde: España auditará," *Política*, 14 March 1990, 1.

24. Claudia Gutiérrez, quoted in ibid.

25. Ibid.

26. Alma Sámano Castillo, "Laguna Verde, la nucleoeléctrica más peligrosa del mundo," *Revelación*, 10 September 1990, 15.

27. Rodrigo Vera, "Sólo un simulacro de revisión, hecha por un amigo, se hizo para abrir la planta," *Proceso*, 20 August 1990, 7.

28. "Revisión técnica de la seguridad de la Unidad I de la Central de Laguna Verde," quoted in ibid.

29. Vera, "Sólo un simulacro," 7.

30. Pedro Lizárraga, quoted in ibid., 14.

31. Sara González, quoted in ibid., 18.

32. Thomas Berlin, quoted in ibid.

33. "Destina el Gobierno Federal más de 350 millones de dólares," *El Dictamen*, 18 September 1990, 1. Unit 2 actually began operating in 1995.

34. Presidential elections are held every six years in Mexico.

35. Interview with Mirna Benítez, 23 March 1996, Xalapa, Veracruz.

36. Pedro Lizárraga, "Las Madres Antinucleares en la Contienda Electoral," *Política*, 1 June 1994, 1.

37. Interview with Mirna Benítez, 23 March 1996, Xalapa, Veracruz.

38. "Urge Auditoría a Laguna Verde: Greenpeace," *La Jornada* (Internet version), 27 April 1996.

39. See García-Gorena, *Mothers and the Mexican Antinuclear Power Movement*.

40. Unlike Sara Ruddick (*Maternal Thinking*), the Madres Veracruzanas believe that only women can mother.

41. Interview with the Madres Veracruzanas, 15 October 1988, Xalapa, Veracruz.

42. Interview with the Madres Veracruzanas, 22 July 1988, Xalapa, Veracruz.

43. "I'm not taking the [Governor's] Palace. I'll withdraw. We're here because of our families. We can't take such a risk. And we have to say this to the press. We have to avoid a situation in which the movement takes over the palace and everyone blames the Madres"; interview with Rebeka de Labastida, 21 October 1988, Xalapa, Veracruz.

44. "Lower-class people fight hard; in a sense we're reaping what they've sown. And lower-class women fight hard; the men often put them out in front during demonstrations to discourage repression. But these women are in danger"; Claudia Gutiérrez, during an interview with the Madres Veracruzanas, 22 July 1988, Xalapa, Veracruz.

45. Interview with Mirna Benítez, 8 December 1989, Xalapa, Veracruz.

46. Feijoo, "Challenge," 78.

47. During the movement's early years, many antinuclear groups demanded that the government hold a referendum on the Laguna Verde issue. The government refused. The Japanese government, by comparison, recently decided to hold a referendum on nuclear energy after local groups demanded it.

48. Interview with Mirna Benítez, 8 December 1989, Xalapa, Veracruz.

# Want to Learn More?

**Greenpeace**

Greenpeace is an organization working at the national and international levels on environmental problems.

www.greenpeace.org

## American University

This website at American University in Washington, D.C., provides information on environmental activities around the world. The destination cited below provides information on Mexico's environmental problems.

www.american.edu/projects/mandala/TED/hp213.htm

## The Latin American Network Information Center

The Latin American Network Information Center at the University of Texas, Austin, includes a wealth of information on Latin American history, politics, and economic development.

lanic.utexas.edu

## Mexico's Green Party

This is the official site for Mexico's Green Party. The site includes information on Mexico's most important environmental challenges.

www.prem.org.mx

## Mothers of the Plaza de Mayo of Argentina

This is the website for the Mothers of the Plaza de Mayo of Argentina, who challenged the disappearance of their children during Argentina's "Dirty War" of the 1970s.

www.madres.org

## Latino On-Line News Network

The website of the Latino On-Line News Network includes up-to-the-minute news from Latin America and the Latino community in the United States.

www.latnn.com

*Part* IV

## PROFESSIONAL ENCLAVES

# 9

# Women in Veterinary Medicine: Past Achievements and Future Challenges

**Miriam Slater**

## ■ BACKGROUND

My study of women in veterinary medicine grew out of two sources, one scholarly, the other personal. My scholarly work on the history of women in the professions in the late nineteenth and early twentieth centuries reflected a long-standing interest in women's experience in the professions. I also had personal reasons for focusing on veterinary medicine. My daughter, Margaret, had always wanted to become a veterinarian. But when she was growing up I was uncertain about whether I should in good conscience encourage her in that direction, because so few veterinary colleges accepted any women applicants. In fact, they did not open their doors to women until some years after the human medical schools had gone beyond token numbers in the mid-1960s. By the time she came to Smith College for her undergraduate training in the late 1970s, the veterinary colleges were beginning to accept women in somewhat larger numbers, but the competition for entrance was very keen. She was fortunate to have received excellent preparation at Smith for graduate work, and she was accepted as one of the pioneering women veterinary students of that period. She is now a professor of veterinary epidemiology on the faculty of a veterinary college. She and I were both aware that she has been a beneficiary of the women's movement's efforts to open up opportunities for women. I was interested in finding out whether the paths of pioneers like her were going to be different from those of the first wave of feminist professionals whom my colleague, Penina Glazer, and I had previously written about. Moreover, veterinary medicine is a profession unlike the others that we had studied. It was to become the first traditionally male profession to become predominately female. As such, it was a case study that was especially intriguing and became the focus of my next work. I am delighted that it is to find a wider audience in this volume.

Veterinary medicine has historically been attractive to women as well as men. But until the second wave of feminism in the 1960s and 1970s, veterinary medicine was a historically male preserve, as were human medicine, law, the ministry, and other professions. Women were not given admission to veterinary colleges except in a handful of extraordinary cases. The few tokens who earned the DVM degree faced discrimination from clients who preferred "real," that is, male, veterinarians to treat their animals. Even fewer women were admitted to graduate work in order to become professors of veterinary medicine, and even today, women professors are still a small minority among the tenured ranks in veterinary colleges.[1] If women made it into the ranks of the professoriate, they were seldom promoted or tenured. In sum, before the 1960s, those women veterinarians who by dint of extraordinary talent, prodigious devotion, and sheer luck made it into the profession as practitioners or professors were definitely there on sufferance.

Dr. Elizabeth A. Lawrence, who was trained in the 1950s, recently summed up the experience of such pioneers. In a speech before the Association for Women Veterinarians, she recollected that "in the sexist atmosphere of the 1950s, both professors and male students could say or do whatever they wished with impunity. Men made it clear that women did not belong, that we should be at home raising children, and that we were unsuited to handling and treating animals; they saw us as misfits."[2]

This discriminatory treatment of women was similar to their experience in other professions at that time. What makes modern veterinary medicine distinctive, however, is that it is the first traditionally male profession of the twentieth century in which women are becoming predominant. Women veterinary students are the majority in most veterinary colleges and are expected to be half of all practitioners in the field by the year 2004.[3] This represents a remarkable increase unmatched by the professions of law or human medicine.[4]

This unprecedented gender shift in veterinary medicine presents a historically new pattern of development for women in the professions. It offers a case study that should be instructive in testing established ideas about the effects of

women's participation on professional development as well as pointing to barriers to their professional leadership, recognition, and reward. The study of
women's experience in veterinary medicine can also highlight the more subtle
obstacles to professional equality that exist beyond the need for numerical pre-
dominance.

Any number of historical and sociological studies have documented the
importance of numbers, of having a sufficient presence in a profession, as
critical to the achievement of equal recognition and reward for groups that
previously had been excluded.[5] Common sense would also confirm the notion
that a larger presence of women should enhance their prospects. My research
on women in veterinary medicine certainly confirms the importance of numbers as one guarantor of equality of treatment. But this study also suggests
that large numbers are not a sufficient buttress against complex patterns of
discrimination. The thorough integration of any out-group is certainly contin-
gent on having more than a token presence in the profession, but the experience of women in veterinary medicine indicates that full inclusion is not
identical with full acceptance. Other obstacles having to do with private rather
than professional life need to be examined critically if behaviors and attitudes
prejudicial to women are to be eliminated. The history of veterinary medicine,
as in the other professions, confirms that merit alone, that is, superior performance, is merely a prerequisite to admission to the bottom rungs of the profession. To reach positions at the top with their concomitant recognition,
financial rewards, and control of the entry gates, future veterinarians need also
to concern themselves with the connections between successful professional
engagement and the cultural values and attitudes of the larger society regarding women's place in private as well as professional life. This is an angle of
vision rarely entertained by scholars of either private life or the professions,
who generally tend to examine these developments separately.[6]

The profound changes in women's education, life goals, and opportunities
in the second half of the twentieth century will have significant consequences
for their career aspirations in the twenty-first. Since these trends are not likely
to reverse themselves, I would like to examine both the social and professional
changes that affect women in veterinary medicine and especially the ways in
which paths to their equable treatment have been created, as well as some of
the shifts in values and attitudes toward women that this has entailed.

I chose to examine veterinary medicine not because the profession has
responded less well to women than human medicine or law. On the contrary,
it has moved from a tradition of exclusion on the basis of sex to one of inclusion
on the basis of merit more quickly and in greater numbers than any of the

traditional professions. I chose it because of its unique development in becoming predominately female in gender composition and its attraction for increasing numbers of scientifically educated women. These are women whose training and abilities offer them a spectrum of professional options, but who choose veterinary medicine undaunted by its challenging training because they care profoundly about animals. They see it as offering the rewards, recognition, and status of other professions with the added satisfaction of working with and helping animals as well as expanding our knowledge about them. That is a very compelling assessment for many talented and idealistic young women.

For the historian, veterinary medicine offers a real-life experiment in the effort to gain equal treatment according to merit in a highly competitive field. Its present treatment of women is rooted in historical circumstance, shifts in political and economic demands, and changes in ideas about family life and expectations. At the same time, changes in the practice and technology of veterinary medicine also have shaped women's experience as particular drugs and animal-handling mechanisms made practitioners' body strength irrelevant. In trying to uncover and understand the remaining barriers to women's present empowerment and leadership in this profession, which has welcomed them most generously, I will examine the wider shifts that account for their numbers and acceptance as well as the challenges they still face in achieving leadership roles as a majority presence in a traditionally male profession.

To get a better sense of the lived experience of women in the profession, I also interviewed more than a dozen women veterinary academics in two widely separated geographical areas of the country. Because women veterinary academics are a small minority of the professoriate in veterinary graduate colleges, any individual in my small sample might be easily identifiable. I promised them that they could speak freely on condition of anonymity, so I shall not name them or their institutions. They are all tenure track or tenured professors at their respective institutions. They all hold advanced degrees beyond the Doctor of Veterinary Medicine, such as M.A. or M.S. and Ph.D. In addition, depending on their area of expertise, a number of them are board certified in their specialties, a process involving several additional years of training and passing the board examinations. They have all published scientific papers and are the teachers of future generations of veterinarians. In addition, some specialties involve them in running teaching clinics in the hospitals of their institutions. In sum, they are at the cutting edge of producing scientific knowledge and designing curricular and teaching methods to transmit that knowledge to future professionals, most of whom will become practitioners and some of whom will become academics and researchers in various settings. They also generously shared with me their private life experiences as well as their sense of the place of their professional engagement and its connection to personal life choices of marriage, children, singlehood, and so on. When I have quoted from this interview sample I have done so without specific attribution.

## The History of Women's Entrance into Veterinary Medicine

Women's interest in animal health has a long history that can be traced back to the Middle Ages in Europe and to colonial times in the United States. With the emergence of professional veterinary care in the nineteenth century, as was true in the other professional developments of the period, women were excluded from professional training on the basis of gender. The typical attitude toward women of the period who wished to become veterinarians was expressed in an editorial in 1897 that observed that "no lady . . . would like to perform those operations which are the almost daily work of the veterinary practitioner . . . [unless she] is prepared to unsex herself completely."[7]

Cultural values such as these and the practices that bolstered them ensured that even as late as 1963, just as the women's liberation movement was beginning to gear up, there were only 277 female veterinarians in the United States. In the same year, the American Veterinary Medical Association published a study that predicted that the next couple of decades would require twice the number of practitioners.[8] This was a bid for expansion of veterinary medicine education, but neither the association nor the veterinary colleges anticipated that this expansion might be filled by women. Their numbers did increase dramatically from the mid-1970s onward, and women make up an increasing proportion of the ranks of veterinary students and practitioners.[9]

## Political and Legislative Changes

A major influence in opening the doors to women was the women's movement and its organized political demand for equal access of all kinds. Women's pent-up demand for places in veterinary colleges was satisfied by a shift in the political climate and especially by the enactment of federal legislation. At the same time, a pool of talented women existed whose fascination with science had been nurtured in undergraduate education that increasingly provided them with the necessary scientific training. When that training was afforded to women who had an abiding interest in animals, they formed a pool of eligible applicants. Congressional action produced a series of laws and agencies supporting women's efforts to break down formidable and long-standing barriers, and these educated women were ready. Those who wished to enter veterinary medicine were the beneficiaries of society's expanding commitment to undergraduate female education and, in this case, especially of women's successful political organization and its consequent legal changes.[10]

Whoever said that laws cannot change attitudes and behaviors has not studied women's entrance into veterinary medicine. Whatever the biases that remained in the inner reaches of their souls, the formidable opposition long maintained by male educators and fostered by institutional arrangements dissolved with startling rapidity on the passage and enforcement of a raft of congressional acts, starting with the Federal Equal Pay Act of 1963 (977 Stat. 1409 29 USC 206), Title VII of the Civil Rights Act of 1964 (78 Stat. 253 42 USC 2000E), the 1965 repeal of the 1870 law that permitted discretion in offering equal pay to female federal employees (79 Stat. 9875 USC 33 Section 165), and perhaps most keenly felt by women in a range of fields, the Equal Employment Opportunity (EEO) Act of 1972 (86 Stat. 103 42 USC 2000E). The last-named act meant that federal agencies were also required to think about and formulate affirmative action plans and submit these to the Civil Service Commission annually. Additionally, the President's Commission on the Status of Women had issued its final report in 1963, as well as subsequent executive orders prohibiting sex discrimination in federal contracts and federal employment.[11]

Two pieces of legislation that were particularly significant for women who wanted to enter the veterinary colleges were the Educational Amendments of 1972 and the Women's Education Act of 1974.[12] Together these acts put pressure on institutions of higher learning that wished to receive federal funds and grants to establish admission policies based on the merits of the individual rather than on physical characteristics. As these political and legislative enactments indicate, monumental changes had to come from the federal government to redress discriminatory practices.

## Women's Participation and the Modernizing of the Veterinary Profession

All of this legislation, along with directives, relevant studies, and commission reports, was taking place against the background of a perceived need for future expansion on the part of the veterinary profession. This was a fortuitous conjunction of events for women's prospects. Furthermore, as women's experiences of prejudicial treatment were aired in public forums as well as in Congress, old myths about their unsuitability to do science or engage in professional work, and even their disadvantageous physical stature and strength, came to be questioned. Such previous reservations faded considerably when placed against the possibility of the expansion of professional training as well as the modern buildings, facilities, and technology that federal monies would provide. In fact, several new colleges were brought into being at this time, bringing the number of veterinary colleges to an unprecedented twenty-seven. As one woman, now a senior academic, put it, "the flood gates opened and we moved in" on what was then untested waters.[13]

Furthermore, changes in the nature and practice of veterinary medicine itself helped to assuage fears about women's participation. Large animal and farm animal practices remained important, but increasingly in modern times companion animals—dogs, cats, birds, and so on—have become the focus of veterinary practitioners. Even in the treatment of equine or food chain animals, modern technology and tranquilizing drugs made the strength of practitioners increasingly irrelevant. The confluence of all these legal, social, and scientific changes served to open opportunities for academically talented women and men in greater numbers than ever before. Entrance requirements were upgraded, and placement in entering classes became highly competitive. These changes provided novel opportunities for talented women's entrance into the profession.

This unprecedented expansion had come after a long period of exclusion. As late as the 1950s, only 139 women were graduated from veterinary schools in the United States during that entire decade. But these numbers climbed quickly, more than doubling in the next decade and reaching into the thousands in the 1970s and 1980s.[14] The latter decade also saw entering classes of future practitioners begin a shift in gender composition that crossed the 50 percent mark and resulted in the unprecedented 70 percent female gender composition that characterizes most veterinary colleges in the United States today. But one should also remember that most practitioners in the field are still male, with women constituting only one-third, a reflection of the relative recentness of their admission to professional training as well as their distance from equity in the professional power structure.[15]

Some sense of the rate of attitudinal change can be gathered from this observation by a male practitioner who had graduated in 1963. During the 1970s, when women veterinarians were still a rarity, he hired one in his practice. One day a couple came to his "mixed animal practice and found a woman practitioner working alone. The wife turned to her husband and said, "There are no doctors here, it's just her."[16] Another woman, a 1977 graduate of Cornell, presently a professor who is board certified in surgery, suggested how she had seen attitudes change over time. "There was [in the late 1970s], perhaps, suspicion or lack of confidence that women could do the job." At that time, one of her fellow students still believed "it was a man's job." But fifteen years later she observed that this same man "hires only women. He thinks they do a better job."[17]

## How Much Do Women's Numbers Count?

Still, with the realistic expectation that women practitioners will outnumber men early in the twenty-first century, future practitioners and the public should know what barriers to women's full participation in the profession remain, barriers that numbers alone have not been sufficient to overcome. The latest figures, though impressive, cast something of a shadow on too much optimism. While enrollments at veterinary programs in the United States and the four Canadian colleges for 1996–97 continued to increase, old fears and myths continue to resurface. Women constituted 67 percent of U.S. students in 1996.[18] Women's increasing presence in the profession at these numbers evoked fears and claims that the so-called feminization of the veterinary profession would lead to declining standards. This is one of several myths that were widely bruited as women's participation climbed and that the Association for Women Veterinarians (AWV) continues to challenge in print and at meetings. Another myth maintained that women would only establish practices that centered on small animals, that is, they would be cats and dogs practitioners, and that other specializations and highly technical fields would languish.[19]

In fact, as veterinary scientific knowledge has expanded in recent decades, women have entered all specialties. Moreover, they have led the way in some of the newer specialties and also participated in newly created specialty areas such as oncology, cardiology, dentistry, and epidemiology. Many of these newer specialties and diplomates have actually been created or expanded in recent decades, precisely those times marked by women's increased presence in graduate training.[20] In addition, during these decades of expansion of veterinary research and sophistication, many more graduates of veterinary colleges have sought a range of residency training often combined with masters and even doctorate degrees.[21]

Even though the training of recent graduates, men and women, is more scientifically rigorous and challenging, and veterinary education and required courses are almost identical at each year of training for the DVM irrespective of gender, upon graduation females nevertheless find themselves at a distinct disadvantage. It is a truism that women still earn less than men in the United

States generally. This disparity is usually explained away by suggesting that gross earnings or averages do not get at the real reasons, which, it is claimed, have less to do with discrimination against women than with female performance, career choices, or reproductive realities regarding maternity and child care. Veterinary medicine is a particularly good field for analysis of the validity of such causes for the differential treatment of men and women. The training of newly minted veterinarians is remarkably similar within colleges. Their pre-vet requirements at the undergraduate level are also similar. Applicants to veterinary colleges are ordinarily college graduates who have strong science backgrounds, along with documented, long-standing interest in animals. Their subsequent four-year DVM training prepares them to be practitioners without regard to gender. But when they apply for their first jobs, usually working for other established veterinary practices, the male graduates receive more employment offers, greater salaries, and usually larger benefit packages than their female counterparts for full-time employment.[22]

When the research first showed that women received fewer offers and smaller salaries and anticipated less attractive bonuses, this was explained away by the fact that many more women than men entered small animal practices. In fact, in every specialty—small animal, large animal predominant, large animal exclusive, mixed practices, and so on—mean starting salaries for men were larger than for women.[23] All but equine practice favored men, from a differential of $1,326 for small animal practice to over $3,000 for other types. Although salary differences were admittedly small, this difference could be considerably compounded by the usual practice of making subsequent salary increases a percentage of base salary. This differential in reward is also reflected in women's generally smaller benefits and anticipated bonuses.

The pay differential is one that women veterinarians share with women in many other professions. Similarly, women are still seen as inferior prospects, or at least problematic ones, for promotion and leadership positions primarily because many women want to marry and have families. However, this kind of personal decision does not usually work against their male counterparts even though, increasingly in modern times, husbands and fathers do share in family and child-rearing responsibilities. This particular "myth" that women will not, or cannot, participate fully in professional life because they will become wives and mothers persists. Unsurprisingly, at a meeting of women veterinarians as recently as 1997, at a symposium celebrating the fiftieth anniversary of the Association for Women Veterinarians, Dr. Billy E. Hooper, of the Oklahoma State University College of Veterinary Medicine, believed it necessary to attack this myth in his remarks to the association. He also cited recent research by others that compared women's professional activity, hours worked per week, time out from the profession, and so on, and noted that men and women show little difference in work force participation.[24]

But these studies generally also show that women have a harder time combining family and career, and for good reason. As historical scholarship has repeatedly demonstrated, modern professional life has been predicated on older, traditional models of the male life course in which men were the professionals and their wives were helpmates who took care of private life, including child rearing. The modern professions developed in the United States and Europe at a period when women were excluded from postgraduate training and middle-class women were not expected to work outside the home. This legacy still haunts contemporary views about women professionals. Today, and in the foreseeable future, the lines separating public and private life for men and women will be much more permeable, especially as the work force participation of women meets that of men.[25] Women veterinarians have virtually achieved that pattern of equal, full-time professional work.[26]

## The Problem of Family and Work

Women veterinarians, as well as their counterparts in other professions that require years of postgraduate training, need to plan their professional as well as their reproductive lives with great care. The academic women whom I interviewed were all in agreement on this point. One married professor with two children spaced her children widely. She had her first child at a point in her graduate career when her laboratory responsibilities made that a possible combination. She said that she had held off on having a second child "for seven years so that she could get some publication out" for promotion to associate professor. In this way she received tenure by age forty but had her second child in her late thirties. Since she had always "planned to be tenured by forty," she was justifiably satisfied with the success of this arrangement. Another professor said she "waited till she was forty" to marry and subsequently had two children. Both women reported that their husbands were very supportive.

Modern women are considerably helped in this kind of career and family planning by their capacity to control fertility. But if they wish to have children, they still work against the biological clock. These two women were fortunate in that regard, in that their reproductive delays did not affect their fertility. They were also fortunate in their choice of husbands and in the fact that they are both women of enormous stamina, organizational ability, and professional performance quite beyond the threshold of mere competence.

For those who are merely competent, or less physically strong and fertile, the picture is not as rosy. The established patterns of professional career, shaped as they still are around male needs, fit poorly with maternal needs. Veterinarians typically finish their DVM degree in their midtwenties and begin as practitioners in their late twenties, or even later if they began their postgraduate training after a hiatus between undergraduate work and the DVM, a not uncommon pattern. In fact, on the basis of anecdotal evidence, one professor suggested that veterinary students at her university seem to be taking "time out" during their training, a pattern that would make their professional engagement arrive even later in the life cycle.

After graduation, in the early phase of a career as a practitioner, is the time when a woman is least likely to have personal autonomy or flexibility of time commitment on the job. For the first few years out of veterinary college, new practitioners typically work in someone else's practice, usually one with fewer than three veterinarians. This means that the newer, nonowning members of the staff are likely to take the most after-hours emergency calls.[27] It is also not uncommon for practitioners to work at least fifty hours per week. When she is ready to open her own practice, a formidable financial investment, lending institutions tend to be much more chary of female borrowers.[28] Female practitioners also have special needs during pregnancy and when they are trying to conceive. Certain animal diseases threaten the human fetus, and there are other exposures that should be avoided. Women also experience different vulnerabilities in late-night emergencies than men do.[29]

Requesting special consideration during these relatively short periods of the life cycle is complicated for women. Historically speaking, there have been two major strategies for dealing with gender differences, especially in male-dominated fields. They could be denied, ignored, or somehow overcome, for instance, avoiding marriage or, if married, forgoing children. In particular, pioneers in the field found this strategy most attractive. They were understandably insistent on denying any difference in the abilities of men and women to perform the work. In earlier periods, women professionals made good on this insistence by seldom marrying. For this relatively small group of educated women, singlehood was not a difficult choice, and it had the added advantage of demonstrating the depth of their calling to public life by their sacrifice of motherhood. But that was a century ago.[30]

The second strategy was to admit the differing needs of women and men and to lower their sights by choosing careers that were less demanding, prestigious, and rewarding. Women of today, however, see equality of opportunity in terms that emphasize the expansion of life choices rather than the narrowing of them. Increasingly, they are developing the confidence and sense of entitlement that their educational achievements, shifts in familial values, and economic realities have afforded them. More women today are prepared to address the differences between men's and women's needs rather than denying that any exist. This strategy is more constructive for both sexes in that professional achievement based on merit, as measured by objective standards of training and performance, is ideally the same regardless of gender, but now it is no longer necessary to deny any variation in gender needs. Previously, women's belief in merit worked to make them predisposed to deny differences and to compensate for these differences by heroic effort and personal sacrifice to perform as well as men, even when they were not afforded equality of condition caused by the discriminatory practices against them.[31] Today they are finally able to acknowledge that commitment to merit standards need not be incompatible with acknowledging differing needs at specific points in the life cycle for men as well as women.[32]

Women's track record in the veterinary profession suggests no diminution of quality by their participation, and scholarly studies make the same point. It is now possible to think in new ways about the achievement of parity of treatment, ways that permit our acknowledging differences without sacrificing opportunities for advancement or standards of excellence. Specifically, this path should afford solutions that are more suitable to the needs of modern social, economic, and family life. Moreover, an appropriate acknowledgment of the differing needs of both men and women can become a source of enrichment to the professional as well as the family life of both sexes.

## Paths to Equality: Acknowledging Differences

A few examples in other fields can give some specificity to this acknowledgment of differences. I want to examine one of these in some detail to suggest that change from traditional ways and policies is possible and often beneficial to the individual as well as the institution. In a fascinating study of the U.S. Merchant Marines' efforts to integrate women and minorities into a largely white, male enclave, Jane P. Brickman, professor of history and head of the department of humanities at the Merchant Marine Academy, told of her experiences. In "No Androgynous Officers" she describes what changes she had made as a counselor and adviser to the academy in the 1980s. Women had been admitted in token numbers in 1974, but the attrition rates were 40–50 percent and sometimes higher almost ten years later, when she began her efforts at instituting policies and procedures to integrate previously excluded groups.[33]

Professor Brickman had a particularly difficult challenge in trying to change what has been called the "chill" factor in previously all-male enclaves. This term is shorthand for the receptiveness of the work environment to out-groups or the visibly different. The "chill" usually manifests itself in petty tyrannies of various kinds, sexual jokes, disparaging remarks, and exclusion from casual conversation, informal informational networks, study groups, and so on. She realized that the "chill" factor had to be eliminated or reduced in order to allow talented and motivated women a better chance at completing the training. Completion of the course at the Merchant Marine Academy was an entrée to a career in the maritime industry. Graduates were eligible to receive a B.A. degree, a Coast Guard license, or a third assistant engineer license. Unsurprisingly, many young women looked on training at the academy as an attractive opportunity.

Professor Brickman made a number of changes. Because she knew that numbers matter, she advised the academy to admit women in sufficient numbers to form a cohort of support, rather than accepting only a few tokens at a time. To combat the "chill," she introduced peer counselors as well as seeing to the appointment of female role models and mentors. Women were appointed to some positions of leadership and given administrative posts at the Merchant Marine Academy. These changes in the power structure provided the female cadets with female mentors who offered daily, highly visible proof that women could succeed. This served to increase the female cadets' self-esteem, and their completion rates increased dramatically.

In addition to making the environment more friendly, a further challenge to equal treatment in this case was the daunting necessity of having to train young men and women cadets, many of whom had not left their teens, during months at sea in their sophomore and junior years. With the new policies aimed at lowering female attrition rates, women cadets were sent aboard ship in pairs, and their treatment at sea improved. Professor Brickman also instituted sensitivity training for faculty as well as emphasizing the importance of institutional research as an important mechanism for monitoring continued progress in creating equality of condition. After these changes were instituted, not only did attrition rates drop precipitously, but in 1997 a female cadet graduated second in a class of 218. In the same year, the academy could point to eight women faculty members and two female department heads and know that their institution provided appropriate role models for its applicants.[34] The

Merchant Marine Academy's efforts to make these changes illustrated its willingness to acknowledge that different groups have differing needs. In accommodating those differences, the academy provided for equality of condition and humane treatment for all cadets as well as ensuring its strength and prestige as an inclusive modern institution for the twenty-first century. The Merchant Marine Academy also will enjoy the advantage of drawing the best candidates from a wider pool of possibilities in the future.

## Obstacles to Professional Equality

Although women in veterinary medicine, owing to their numbers, have a much easier path to integration, they have not quite achieved parity with men. One of the ways equality is measured is by examining the producers, that is, the graduate school professoriate of a profession, those who prepare and teach the future generation of professionals, decide on and research the important questions, and control the standards of admission and licensing of the profession. The sample of women veterinary academics whom I interviewed provided some insights into women's status in the veterinary profession. This group of highly trained women were fully credentialed, and all held veterinary medicine degrees and advanced degrees in particular areas, such as anatomy, cell biology, and ophthalmology. In addition, in recent years, as medical and scientific knowledge has advanced, veterinary specialties have flourished. Many professors are now expected to be board certified in a specialty. This involves years of further study, passing the board examinations as well as research and publication in the area of specialization. Obviously, the opportunity costs of this lengthy training are considerable for men and women; but the personal costs—in terms of professional dedication as well as the need to carefully carve out a private life and a possible family life—fall differentially on men and women.

The situation is complicated for women veterinary academics because the climb up the academic ladder from assistant professor to associate professor and finally to full professor is an arduous and often lengthy one—for those in clinical specialties particularly so, because they are expected to teach graduate students, pursue their own research, and publish, often while they are preparing for board certification. And clinical specialists are also expected to run the clinics in the teaching hospitals of the veterinary colleges. This means that the months when they are "on clinics" they have an additional load. Assistant professors on the first rung of the professional career ladder are often precisely at the time in their lives when young professionals of either sex might marry and have children. For women this means that life choices need to be carefully plotted. They know that throughout academe women have yet to reach parity with men in salary, tenure ranks, and positions of leadership in administration.[35] For veterinary academics, who were admitted relatively recently, the picture is not very different, although it varies from institution to institution and even among particular departments of a given university.

The sample of women I interviewed helped to put a human face on these rather disappointing statistical realities. For example, these women all mentioned how important their senior professors were in their decision to continue in advanced training and opt for academic life. With few exceptions they were satisfied with that decision. They uniformly believed that the support of the department head or dean was crucial in helping or hindering their advancement up the ranks. The importance of mentoring has also been seen by some scholars "as the single most important contributor to building a career."[36] The same point has been made recently in Phyllis Larsen's compilation of the experience of women veterinarians, *Our History of Women in Veterinary Medicine: Gumption, Grace, Grit, and Good Humor.*[37]

Support from professional colleagues and networking are also necessary for a successful career either as a practitioner or in veterinary academic medicine. That kind of support can be garnered in women's separate professional organizations such as the Association for Women Veterinarians (AWV). Although women's presence in the primary professional organization, the American Veterinary Medical Association (AVMA), has increased in recent years, it is the AWV that has made a point of tracking women's progress in gaining positions of power in the profession. For example, they recently published their concern regarding the fact that there are no women deans of veterinary medicine in the United States and very few heads of departments.[38]

One of the difficulties in achieving full parity in academe has been women's continuing minority presence in high administrative posts. Inasmuch as mentoring by senior administrators has already been identified by scholars and practicing professionals as crucial to career advancement, the lack of female models at those levels in an increasingly female profession serves to slow the advancement of others in the lower ranks. We have also seen in the experience of the Merchant Marine Academy, as well as elsewhere, that this problem, though a long-standing one, is not insuperable.

The fuller explanation for women's absence or relatively poor numbers in the power structures of the profession is quite complex, however, and goes beyond lack of models and mentoring, although the latter are certainly significant. Women also share with their counterparts in other professions the difficulty of the double day. They are still burdened with primary responsibility for maintaining home life and child care. Our society still provides few structural supports for combining work and family.

For example, there is no national child care policy of the kind common in other industrialized countries. Arrangements for child care are always made individually and are usually patchwork and private. In this regard, the experience at one institution of veterinary medicine offers a not unusual scenario. Ten years ago, a group of women academics at this institution, one of the largest producers of veterinarians, began negotiations to establish on-site child care. After a decade of petitioning and pressuring, the ground was broken for the new facility. A woman faculty member who had been one of the original proposers of the child care center said that she stayed with the decade-long struggle even though in the year that they finally began construction her own children "were already in middle school and [the child care facility was] well past its usefulness to me."[39] The glacially slow institutional response that she received is not atypical. Corporate as well as educational institutions have been reluctant to face the requirements of modern professional and familial life or to acknowledge the linkage between them.[40]

In addition to lack of child care, few academic institutions are willing to slow the tenure clock to accommodate women's reproductive needs. In fact, several women I interviewed told me that they decided to forgo having children because, as one put it, "I could not figure out how to include them into the demands of my professional life." This woman was regularly working more than fifty hours a week, and frequently on weekends. She considered herself lucky to have found a husband who understood and was supportive of the demands of her professional commitments.

Admittedly, the pool of qualified women who might be considered for deanships or department heads is not as large as the comparable male pool, owing to women's more recent access to the profession and their consequently smaller numbers in the upper ranks. But the matter is further complicated by the fact that women academic veterinarians in the tenured ranks of the professoriate are usually among those who can fairly be defined as "super-achievers."[41] These are women who have persisted throughout their education in the sciences, scaled all barriers, and successfully overcome the washout phenomenon of the educational "leaky pipeline." The leaky pipeline refers to the phenomenon in which girls are weeded out of mathematics and science education starting at grade school and continuing at every educational level thereafter, always in greater numbers than the boys. In addition, "doctoral level jobs are at the end of the pipeline," where few women remain after that kind of culling. Given this reality, it is not surprising, for example, that "the number of [female] department chairs in [human] medical schools has not changed in the last 20 years" and that there are so few in veterinary medical colleges.[42]

When I asked the sample of women academic veterinarians if they had considered applying for administrative posts, few were enthusiastic about the prospect, despite their full understanding of the importance of mentors. Most were reluctant to consider a move to administration in part because they had to overcome so many obstacles to get to their present positions in research and teaching. As one professor, who had been offered an administrative post, put it, "I agonized over the decision" because it meant giving up most of her research engagement. She was also uncertain about how the demands of the new job would change the time available to spend with her family.

In general, the women's models of professional endeavor were based on their own (usually male) professors. These men's careers followed the traditional trajectories of utter devotion to science and research, and for them marriage and children presented little interference with career goals. In the women professors' lives, even in cases where both they and their husbands were professionals, they had most often accommodated to the demands of the husbands' careers, particularly in the early years of the marriage. In sum, as in other professions, the career track for men and women has not accommodated to the needs of familial life and is still predicated on outmoded, early-twentieth-century models in which the husband was the professional and his wife cared for home and children.

Given the difficulties of combining private and professional life, it is easy to understand why a successful woman would be loathe to leave a hard-fought position in the professoriate to become a dean or enter the ranks of administration at some other level. Such administrative work usually requires the woman to relinquish her self-image as a professional who is committed to scientific research and the production of knowledge. In addition, high-level academic administrative jobs often necessitate the kind of geographic mobility that few two-career couples can easily accommodate and that the hiring institution seldom can. It usually means finding two places to hire both spouses. Few institutions find that an appealing or feasible prospect when the available pool of mobile male candidates is larger. And few senior women candidates are willing to undertake the radical life changes such a move usually would necessitate.

In view of the nature of these complexities, it is not mere prejudice that keeps women out of positions of power, although that prejudice certainly exists; instead, it is the more formidable realities of structural and cultural barriers that militate against placing women in high places. But it is precisely because

leaders can shape institutional policies that women, who have a sharper understanding of the necessity for finding realistic solutions for addressing professional and familial needs, need to be encouraged to move into policy-making
positions. Experience has previously demonstrated how these barriers to wom-
en's empowerment can be overcome. Women in the veterinary profession already have the justification of numbers to assert their claim to positions in
the power structures of the profession. Other scholars have made a range of
suggestions that would serve to make the professional life of practitioners and
academics more humane and equable for both sexes.[43]

## The Attractions of Veterinary Medicine for Women

There is no consensus as to why veterinary medicine continues to draw
women despite the problems outlined above. It is clear, however, that many
find its continued attractiveness in the fact that it is a professional engagement
that allows those who love animals to make working with them the focus of
their life's work. Clearly the field is attracting fewer men, and the usual reason
that is offered for their waning interest is a financial one.[44] The length and cost
of training presumably draws them to more lucrative fields. But it costs women
just as much, and the indebtedness for either sex is commonly $60,000–
$100,000 at graduation.[45] This is the kind of expensive training that makes a
full-time career a sensible and, for most people, necessary option. The veterinary colleges have already begun to address the growing disparity between the
high cost of training and the future earnings of practitioners or academics.
Some have begun to advise graduates to negotiate with employers for salaries
that are commensurate with opportunity costs.

The veterinary colleges are understandably concerned with what appears
to be a continuing trend. Some in the profession express the fear that it is the
large numbers of women—the so-called feminization of the profession—that
accounts for the relatively declining incomes of practitioners. I find more persuasive the notion that structural changes in the nature of veterinary practice
are more likely to account in part for this gap between educational costs and
remuneration. In particular, the increasing scientific, epidemiological, and
technological expertise offered in the modern curriculum tends to make that
an expensive educational package regardless of the sex of the students.[46]

One should also note, however, that these changes in more sophisticated
and scientific training increasingly serve to enhance the value of veterinary
service as well as the demand for those services in the society at large. A growing range of the human population looks to veterinarians not only for treat-

ment for their pets but also for scientific management of the human and animal food supply, as well as for solutions to public health problems. This highly sophisticated veterinary training, though expensive, in the long run should enhance the attractiveness of the profession as one that is lucrative and also has great flexibility as a "steppingstone" career for those who want a range of work settings. With few exceptions, the women I interviewed believed that it was an excellent career choice and one that they would recommend to undergraduate women for its intrinsic satisfactions as well as for the opportunities veterinary education provided for careers in government, military, and corporate life as well as private practice.[47]

There are other reasons to be optimistic about women's future in the veterinary profession. On the one hand, many of the difficulties encountered by and biases against women in veterinary medicine are also true of women in other professions, including salary discrimination, slow promotions, workplaces unfriendly to family needs, and so on. On the other hand, many demographic and social developments are in their favor. More women, irrespective of marital or maternal status, continue to enter the work force full-time. Educated women tend to have few children close together in a narrow band of the life cycle. At the same time, women's life expectancies are lengthening. This means that although biological differences with men exist, women still bear the children, and fertility rates and patterns suggest that decades of women's lives will be spent in full-time, paid work. The situation is just the reverse of the earlier part of the twentieth century. At that time, women might or might not work, but they were expected to marry. Today just the opposite is true. Women may or may not be married all or part of their adult lives, but they will work. The prevalence of the female-headed household and the two-career family both document that reversal of values and expectations.

In the case of highly trained veterinarians, there is the additional impetus to work in order to make use of an expensive and arduous education in a field with a range of work settings and satisfactions. Neither is the preponderance of women in the field apt to reverse itself because of the lack of an eligible pool of candidates. Not only do women outnumber men in undergraduate colleges, but increasing numbers of them are majoring in the sciences.[48] This augurs well for the continuing growth of eligible and valued candidates for veterinary colleges. Under the circumstances, the unwarranted fears about the "feminization" of the profession and its presumed deleterious effects will fade into obscurity along with the previous myths about women's unsuitability. When the profession takes full cognizance of its increased societal and economic value, it will begin to find ways to ensure all its graduates the financial rewards they deserve, particularly if it wishes to sustain educated women's loyalty in the future.

There are also signs that the structure of veterinary health care delivery is changing in ways that may be beneficial to women and men. Recent corporate models of veterinary care in which large corporations offer walk-in veterinary services and pet products in shopping malls and similar areas point to one model for the future. This kind of veterinary care delivery offers practitioners the advantages of a known work schedule, an eight-hour day, no emergency calls, and employee benefits—in sum, a work profile that combines more easily with maintaining a social and familial life. At the same time, it relieves the practitioner from the financial risks and responsibilities of hospital ownership. Obviously, this is only one suggestive option for creating a more humane working life, but it does reflect the need for more imaginative solutions for an increasingly diverse population of professionals.

Whatever other solutions are offered in the future, several givens of the veterinary profession in the twenty-first century are already discernible. Women will constitute a significant part of the profession and will occupy places in all ranks of the power structure. This again is not a shift that is peculiar to veterinary medicine.[49] Women in other professions and corporate life have had wide experience of the glass ceiling, but they also have more knowledge and experience of breaking through it. They certainly have plenty of incentive to do so; considering the significance of shifts in demographics, familial life, and educational opportunities in their lives, they can hardly be expected to do otherwise. Inasmuch as none of these trends show signs of reversing themselves, women veterinary professionals can be optimistic about their prospects for the new millennium.

## Notes

1. Women are a minority of the professoriate in other professions and fields. See, for example, the recent figures on women on chemistry faculties of major universities; Mairin B. Brennan, "Women Chemists Reconsidering Careers at Research Universities," *Chemical and Engineering News*, 18 June 1996, 8–15. In fact, the Ph.D.-granting universities have the lowest percentage of women faculty, 8 percent. The good news is that women chemistry Ph.D.s have risen in the last twenty years to one-third of recipients in chemistry; ibid., 13.

2. "Veterinarian Recollects Gender Biases," *Journal of the American Veterinary Medical Association* (hereafter cited as *JAVMA*) 211, no. 7 (1 October 1997): 828.

3. B. C. Gehrke, "Gender Redistribution in the Veterinary Medical Profession," *JAVMA* 208, no. 8 (15 April 1996): 1254–55.

4. Lynette A. Hart and Patrick Melese d' Hospital, "The Gender Shift in the Veterinary Profession and Attitudes towards Animals: A Survey and Overview," *Journal of Veterinary Medical Education* 16, no. 1 (spring 1989): 27–30.

5. To cite just two examples, Rosabeth Kanter's groundbreaking study *Men and Women of the Corporation* (New York: Basic Books, 1977); P. Glazer and M. Slater, *Unequal Colleagues: Women's Entrance into the Professions* (New Brunswick, N.J.: Rutgers University Press, 1987). We argued that numbers were important in changing attitudes and behaviors toward newer groups. We also pointed out that token appointments of selected superachievers were ineffective in making places for future generations of women in the professions.

6. For a fascinating study of female executives by a psychologist that moves beyond individual psychology to the nature of corporate life to explain the reasons for women's scarcity, see Sue J. M. Freeman, *Managing Lives: Corporate Women and Social Change* (Amherst: University of Massachusetts Press, 1990). Professor Freeman argues persuasively that it is not women's psychology or personal deficits that explains their absence from the corporate power structure, but "structural obstacles and persistent, albeit subtle, discrimination" (5).

7. Susan D. Jones, quoted in "Women in Veterinary Medicine Overcoming Adversity, Achieving Acceptance," *JAVMA* 212, no. 8 (15 April 1998): 1178.

8. P. Rinesch, "Pioneer Women Veterinarians in European Society," *JAVMA* 212, no. 2 (15 January 1998): 182–84. It was well after World War II that even a trickle of extraordinary women pioneers were given entrance in the United States or abroad. See Sue Drum and H. Ellen Whiteley, *Women in Veterinary Medicine: Profiles of Success* (Ames: Iowa State University Press, 1991), xi–xii.

9. Ibid., xii.

10. In addition to the traditional professions of human medicine and law, other previously male preserves such as natural resource disciplines also fell under increasing government scrutiny. See Jesse Faupell, "Women in Natural Resource Disciplines: Attitudes toward Suitability and Acceptability," M.A. thesis, Utah State University, 1977.

11. Ibid., 28–29.

12. L. Brown, "Women in the Veterinary Profession Yesterday and Today," senior thesis, Hampshire College, 1987, 12–13. Dr. Brown, now a practicing veterinarian, did her excellent study under my direction. Her work is still being cited. See Drum and Whiteley, *Women in Veterinary Medicine*, xv.

13. Personal communication from a member of the sample.

14. Lynne Brakeman, "Myth-Busting: Women Will Enter Ownership Positions," *DVM: The Newsmagazine of Veterinary Medicine*, October 1997, 1.

15. B. C. Gehrke, "Geographic Distribution of Female and Male Veterinarians in the U.S. 1996," *JAVMA* 211, no. 8 (15 October 1997): 989–90. Women comprised 19,421 of 56,694 veterinarians in the United States in 1996. See also B. C. Gehrke, "Enrollment in Veterinary Medical Colleges, 1995–1996 and 1996–1997," *JAVMA* 211, no. 10 (15 November 1997): 1240–41.

16. Liz Swain, "Women in Practice: The Veterinary Profession and General Public See Benefits to the Increase in Female Veterinarians," *AWV Bulletin*, spring 1996, 4–9, quote from p. 5 (reprinted with permission from *Veterinary Product News*, January 1996).

17. Ibid., 5.

18. Most of this increase was in the United States, where just under nine thousand students were enrolled; Gehrke, "Enrollment," 1240–41.

19. For example, see notes 15 and 16.

20. Brakeman, "Myth-Busting," 26. This was also confirmed by personal communication from interviewees, a number of whom were themselves specialists, who noted women colleagues' participation in a wide spectrum of specialties.

21. Gehrke, "Enrollment," 1240–41.

22. B. C. Gehrke, "Employment of Male and Female Graduates of U.S. Veterinary Medical Colleges, 1997," *JAVMA* 212, no. 2 (15 January 1998): 208–9.

23. B. C. Gehrke, "Employment of 1995 Graduates of U.S. Veterinary Colleges: Analysis by Gender," *JAVMA* 207, no. 12 (15 December 1995): 1559–60.

24. Brakeman, "Myth-Busting," 1, 25.

25. Glazer and Slater, *Unequal Colleagues*, esp. chapter 6. On this point many scholars in family studies have made these changes abundantly clear. See, for example, Stephanie Coontz, *The Way We Really Are: Coming to Terms with the Changing America's Families* (New York: Basic Books, 1997); Stephanie Coontz, *The Way We Never Were: American Families and the Nostalgia Trip* (New York: Basic Books, 1992).

26. B. C. Gehrke, "Employment, Starting Salaries, and Educational Indebtedness of 1996 Graduates of U.S. Veterinary Medical Colleges," *JAVMA* 209, no. 12 (15 December 1996): 2022–23.

27. J. Karl Wise and Jih-Jing Yang, "Veterinary Issues Survey—Part II: Employment Prospects and Business Needs," *JAVMA* 204, no. 6 (15 March 1994): 886–87.

28. Anonymous, "Did You Read the Letters to the Editor in the October 1 *JAVMA*?" *Association of Women Veterinarians (AWV) Bulletin* 53, no. 1 (winter 1998): 8.

29. Ibid. Some women I spoke to felt this was somewhat exaggerated because often in their work during training, they build up some immunity to some of these diseases. No woman I spoke to volunteered concern about the safety issue. Several also told me that they took their own dogs on late-night calls to the clinic.

30. On the various strategies used by pioneering professional women, see Glazer and Slater, *Unequal Colleagues*, 209–22.

31. Glazer and Slater, *Unequal Colleagues*, chapter 6.

32. We discussed the shortcomings of total reliance on merit alone as a strategy

for professional success in M. Slater and P. Glazer, "Prescriptions for Professional Survival," *Daedalus: Journal of the Academy of Arts and Sciences,* fall 1987, 119–35.

33. Jane P. Brickman, "No Androgynous Officers," *Naval Institute Proceedings,* January 1998, 64–66.

34. Ibid.

35. This point has been widely documented. For a recent and enlightening analysis of women university faculty in the sciences and engineering, see A. N. Pell, "Fixing the Leaky Pipeline: Women Scientists in Academia," *Journal of Animal Science* 74 (1996): 2843–48.

36. Barbara P. Glenn, "The Role of Mentors for Women in Animal Science: Perspectives from the Government," *Journal of Animal Science* 74 (1996): 2855–59, quote on p. 2856.

37. Phyllis Larsen, comp. and ed., *Our History of Women in Veterinary Medicine: Gumption, Grace, Grit, and Good Humor* (Madison, Wisc.: American Association for Women Veterinarians, 1997). See especially S. D. Johnston and P. N. S. Olson, "Women Faculty Members and Leaders in Colleges of Veterinary Medicine," in ibid., 92.

38. S. D. Johnston and P. N. S. Olson, "Women in Veterinary Academic Leadership," *AWV Bulletin* 52, no. 4 (fall 1997): 8–9. Since this article was published, one woman has been appointed dean at the newest college of veterinary medicine.

39. Personal communication.

40. Stephanie Coontz, *The Way We Never Were* and *The Way We Really Are,* both offer careful documentation concerning what family life is like and the kinds of trends, such as working mothers, that she believes are here to stay.

41. Glazer and Slater, *Unequal Colleagues,* 211–12. As we suggested here, this strategy for achieving professional success has a long history and a high personal cost that, though effective for the extraordinarily talented, does little to assure future places for the next generation of professional women, most of whom, like their male counterparts, are likely to be merely competent.

42. Pell, "Fixing the Leaky Pipeline," 2844.

43. See, for example, Susan A. Harlander, "Breaking through the Glass Ceiling: An Industrial Perspective," *Journal of Animal Science* 74 (1996): 2849–54.

44. Hart and d' Hospital, "Gender Shift."

45. Student indebtedness at increasing rates has been a trend in veterinary medicine education. B. C. Gehrke, "Trends in Starting Salaries and Educational Indebtedness of U.S. Veterinary Medical Colleges, 1983–95," *JAVMA* 208, no. 2 (15 January 1996): 206–7; indebtedness has been increasing at a faster rate than starting salaries. See B. C. Gehrke, "Employment, Starting Salaries, and Educational Indebtedness of 1996 Graduates of U.S. Veterinary Colleges," *JAVMA* 209, no. 12 (15 December 1996): 2022–23; B. C. Gehrke, "Employment, Starting Salaries, and Educational Indebtedness of 1997 Graduates of U.S. Veterinary Medical Colleges," *JAVMA* 211, no. 12 (15 December 1997): 1519–20.

46. William R. Pritchard, "Some Implications of Structural Change in Veterinary Medicine and Its Impact on Veterinary Education," *JAVMA* 203, no. 3 (1 August 1993): 361–64. Dr. Pritchard was concerned here not with gender composition but only with structural changes in public demand and veterinary education.

47. Pritchard, "Some Implications of Structural Change," makes a similar analysis about the growing demand for veterinary medicine.

48. Glenn, "Role of Mentors," 2856.

49. Labor force composition is expected to become increasingly diverse in gender, race, and ethnic composition. See ibid., 2857.

## Want to Learn More?

### The American Veterinary Medical Association (AVMA)
The AVMA is aware of the change in demographics in the field of veterinary medicine. This site offers several press releases and other information on the topic.

www.avma.org

### Women in Veterinary Medicine
This short article touches on several issues surrounding the change in gender composition.

www.equinevet.com/vetcareer/womenvetmed.html

### Superwomen
This keyword will bring up several hits on how to balance career and family. A good starting place is the *Detroit News*.

www.detnews.com/STRAT/9712/29/super/super.htm

### Advancing Women
This page is designed to help women entrepreneurs keep abreast of news, networking, and strategies geared toward women. It addresses diversity issues and balancing work and home, and provides helpful articles, posting boards, and chat opportunities for women to express their ideas and learn from each other's experiences.

Advancing Women
Corporate Office
P.O. Box 6642
San Antonio, TX 78209
Telephone (210) 822-1103
Fax (210) 821-5119
www.advancingwomen.com

**National Partnership for Women and Families**

This nonprofit organization is geared toward heightening fair play in and out of the workplace. It has advocated for women and families since 1971 and currently has job opportunities and internships.

National Partnership for Women and Families
1875 Connecticut Avenue, NW, Suite 710
Washington, DC 20009
Telephone (202) 986-2600
Fax (202) 986-2539
www.nationalpartnership.org/publications/contentanalysis.htm

**The Fatherhood Project**

This site takes a unique position of advocating for increased father support in the family. It provides a fairly long list of links that touch on the same topics.

E-mail Jlevine@familiesandwork.org
www.familiesandwork.org

# 10

# Intersections: Women's Sport Leadership and Feminist Praxis

**Carole A. Oglesby**

## ■ BACKGROUND

The relative freedom of academe has afforded me the opportunity to construct and enact multiple professional identities. My contributions emanate from a primary identity as a social scientist working in the participant observer mode. Four observations interweave through the more than forty years of my work as a feminist scholar.

First, it was my contention that sport was neither inherently good nor bad (a crucial argument pre-1970s in sport science), neither inherently masculine nor feminine. I argued, in various publications as early as 1974, that sport was a "human construction" and that we shape its meanings and symbolism to our purposes, both conscious and preconscious. For me, it has been clear that the principal obstructions to women's involvement in sport and physical activity were limiting internalized notions of gender, held by men and women alike.

Second, progress in my life has been accomplished through both scholarship and leadership. I have served as commissioner of National Championships, Commission on Intercollegiate Athletics for Women, 1969–71; inaugural president, Association of Intercollegiate Athletics for Women, 1971–72; president, National Association of Girls and Women in Sport, 1977–78; United States member of the International Federation of University Sport, 1972–92; Board of Trustees, Women Sports Foundation, 1990–94; Board of Directors, United States Olympic Committee, 1992–96; president, Women Sport International, 1997 to the present.

In my leadership roles, I have always felt it crucial that bridges be built to cross the apparent "mind/body" divide and to mainstream sport into the general women's movement. I have always believed that American sport advocates had both an important role to play and lessons to learn from sport advocates around the world. Through presentation of scholarly papers and leading consultative workshops in eighteen countries and serving in administrative roles at international competition, I have sought to make clear to American colleagues that our work is contextualized in a global community. I have attempted to demonstrate to international colleagues that many American women stand ready to collaborate, not dominate, in international development efforts for women in sport. In my international work, I have come to realize that until we American sport feminists address racism (in our country, in our scholarship, in our sport, and in ourselves) we can never hope to collaborate with others with integrity. My students and colleagues of color at Temple University have shown me that simply "ending" one's own racist beliefs and actions are not enough. A "tithe of time" must be given over and over again to antiracist effort. This under-standing has led to scholarly publications and the development of profes-sional training on a host of social justice issues including sexism, racism, sexual harassment, and heterosexism.

Finding ways to facilitate resistance to create change consumes me still. During my years from age fifty to sixty, I completed a second doctoral degree in counseling psychology. This was a visible sign of the commitment I feel to "continue growing." When the growing stops, the giving stops and surely we die. I believe in life!

THERE is a lengthy history of women in leadership, in those "separate spheres" ceded to women's presumed gifts. Sport itself has been treated as a virtual "separate sphere," relatively unexamined in the general so-cial sciences until the last decade. For example, it is very rare to find sport (as here) a parallel topical theme in a general women's studies text. One other exception to this rule would be *The Knowledge Explosion: Generations of Femi-nist Scholarship*.[1]

Contemporary sport social science inquiry describes sport as a domain uniquely impervious to the inclusion of women.[2] Traditions of sport even teach males to beware of, and avoid, an attitude of respectfulness toward the tradi-tional qualities reflected by women.[3] This learned disdain for women and the traditional feminine, combined with exceptional adherence to hierarchical and linear systems, makes the assumption of sport leadership as daunting a challenge as that posed by any of the institutions addressed in this book.

Thus, in this essay, I address the most basic of questions: Why is the matter of women and sport leadership important to the intent of this book? Why is the "sport question" so problematic in the mainstream of feminist scholarship and praxis? I close with suggestions of possibility with regard to women's influences on culture, through leadership explorations conducted in the "field laboratory" of sport.

Why include sport leadership in analyses of women, leadership, and power?

Two types of explanations are offered here, owing to the dual planes of abstraction of the sport construct: the institutionalized "icon" status of sport, and the personal wholeness experiences of sport. In exploring what might be termed the "iconography" of sport, I identify examples of legendary women and women's events that seemed to serve a "boundary-breaking" function for women generally.[4] Contributing also to new and enlarged perceptions of women were institutionalized gains accomplished through purposeful sport feminist praxis. Examples of such gains are described. In the area of personal meanings, attention is given to the expanding range of health and capacity-building consequences of sport and physical activity involvement of "every woman." Finally, sport and women's physicality is drawn as one fundamental part of the mosaic of basic human rights and entitlement being envisioned for women's achievement of potentiality.[5]

## Icon Status of Sport

Jolie Sandoz and Joby Winans scoured the American literary scene to find women's writing about their own experience with sport. "What does sport mean to girls and women? The signal for life to begin," so characterized one of their writers. Sandoz and Winans also conclude that "Americans tend to use sport symbols and myths to help define and give life to shared cultural values."[6]

Brian Pronger emphasizes a similar theme in his assertion that the world of sport and physical education has a "profound effect on the experience of human embodiment for both men and women." He continues that sport is crucially involved in the cultural construction of gender. Similar ideas resound in virtually all the cited sport references in this chapter.[7]

There is much to find distasteful, even appalling, about institutionalized sport. Some of those aspects are addressed in the next section. More than twenty years ago, a few feminist sport scholars began a serious criticism of traditional sport.[8] These individuals combined their academic criticism with prolonged advocacy for the expansion of the place of girls and women in sport.

This was not professional split personality, although it may seem so to those who are uninvolved with the sport phenomenon.

This peculiarity may also be seen in an observation by Jim McKay, Michael Messner, and Don Sabo. They point out that during the last ten years of heavy critique of men's sport, the number of girls participating in high school sport was increasing exponentially (one of every twenty-seven girls in 1971 and one in every three by 1994). In 1972, 31,000 women participated in college sports, while by 1999 the figure rose to 120,000.[9] If sport is so bad, why do so many want to join in? While the question is overly simplistic, facts do lend themselves reasonably to a conclusion that: (1) the phenomenon of sport is sufficiently pervasive and ubiquitous that it requires attention within scholarly discourse on popular culture; and (2) the "sport question" is complex, ambiguous, and often paradoxical. It requires deconstruction and analysis with the care for contextualization, defining, and operationalizing consistent with scholarship in other areas of inquiry.

Let me now highlight selected women's sport events, achievements, political gains, and historic recognitions that transcended obstacles of silence, economics, and ignorance to function as icon events in public consciousness.

In 1978 an all-women climb of the Himalayan peak Annapurna I featured two women who became the first Americans to achieve the summit. Arlene Blum, the leader of the expedition, writes in the twentieth-anniversary edition of her account of the event of visiting the Dartmouth College campus and being shown the shell of the women's varsity eight, christened *Annapurna*. The student athletes told her, "Your book explained why we row—the hard work and the satisfaction of pulling together. Every time we see the name 'Annapurna' on our boat, we are reminded of what your team did and the extraordinary things we can do when we push ourselves and each other to and beyond our limits."[10] Blum says she has found such commentary to be a recurring theme over the years. Their climb "made a difference" by dispelling myths about the limitations of women.

Although there surely are limitless ways to dispel myths, examples of concrete physical and holistic questing are ancient ones. Another example comes out of my own life history. In 1978 the National Women's Conference was being held in Houston. A friend and mentor, Catherine East, detailed from the U.S. State Department as a ranking staff official responsible for the event, sought to find a dramatic way to illustrate the strengths, endurance, and capability of women. With a shared sense of women's history and the importance of demonstrating physicality, we created a project in which women would run a "torch of emancipation" from Seneca Falls, New York, to the Houston conference site. Dividing the distance of the trek by fifty-mile parcels, with a day coordinator for each day and state coordinators as intermediaries, the torch successfully made the trek. A picture of one of the runners made the official title cover for the report marking the conference. Without long words of explanation, the "marathon of emancipation" was captured by the torch run, with its inclusiveness of thousands participating in the run, some from far away and by merely buying the commemorative T-shirt.

A recent encyclopedia identified eight women and events as "boundary breakers" in completing a task or feat that irrevocably changed public perceptions of women. Certainly every one of us could compile her own (different) list, but these examples seem unarguably to qualify as reflecting icon status.

*The climb of Aconcagua*, a 23,000-foot peak in Chile, by a group of breast cancer survivors

*The climb of Annapurna I*, a 26,500-foot peak in the Himalayas; first ascent by Americans and by women

*Susan Butcher*, who won the grueling Iditarod Alaskan Dog Sled Race not once but three times

*Babe Didrikson*, Olympian and professional golfer, who has been recognized as the best all-around female athlete of the twentieth century

*Gertrude Ederle*, who set the world record for swimming the English Channel, besting men's records by hours, and who received the first ticker tape parade down Broadway for a woman athlete

*Janet Guthrie*, the first woman to qualify for the Indianapolis 500

*Billie Jean King*, winner of many grand slam championships in tennis and a women's activist

*Diana Nyad*, who swam from Bimini to the Florida coast, over one hundred miles in open ocean[11]

The potential for icon symbolism was implicitly understood by all these women. In writing an essay on the Aconcagua climb, Eleanor Davis stated: "Just as each woman had struggled to overcome her fear of death and made the journey to regain her health, each now joined to train to climb a mountain to bring a message of hope . . . for each woman, the mountain became a metaphor for her cancer experience."[12] This truism, that there is a special effect attendant to women's athleticism and achievement, seems somehow to be Teflon-coated, a lesson learned only to be quickly unlearned and relearned ad infinitum. Ann O'Hagan wrote an ode, which somehow sounds brand-new, to the athletic woman in the *Munsey Magazine* (a then popular women's journal) in 1901:

With the single exception of the improvement of the legal status of
women, their entrance into the realm of sports is the most cheering
thing that has happened to them in the century just passed. . . .

To whomsoever the athletic woman owes her existence, the
whole world of women owes a debt incomparably great. Absolutely
no other social achievement is so important or far-reaching in its result.[13]

Long before O'Hagan, Sandoz and Winans found evidence that women
had fought for their sports opportunities in print since 1790. Few, however,
seem to be aware of this history. Home Box Office (HBO) in the United States
created a 1999 television special "Dare to Compete."[14] Imagine my surprise,
as a sports scholar since my Ph.D. in 1969, to learn (and in fact see) that two
women athletes had received solo ticker tape parades down Broadway before
midcentury: Gertrude Ederle and Althea Gibson.

Icon status may also be inferred from a variety of successes influencing
national and international recognition of the importance of women's sport.
During the last decades, power and leadership have been asserted at the highest levels of government by the global women's sports advocacy community.
In a 1999 international presentation, U.N. Commission on the Status of
Women chair Patricia Flor stated, "For over two decades, the international
community confirmed time and again, explicitly in UN documents, that the
principle of non-discrimination encompasses the right of all women and girls
to engage in sport, physical and recreational activities, on an equal basis with
men and boys."[15]

Other examples of governments being moved to offer new health and
education-building efforts for girls' and women's physical activity and sport
may be seen in the Philippines, Trinidad and Tobago, Australia, New Zealand,
and South Africa.[16] A report by Women and Sport South Africa (WASSA)
states: "It is time that the integral role which sport plays in nation-building is
fully recognized. Sport is an investment. It is an investment in the health,
vitality and productivity of one's people. It is secondly an investment in the
future. The social benefits include an overall improvement in the quality of
life and the physical, mental and moral well being of a population."[17]

The 1995 Beijing Platform for Action, developed and approved through
the fourth United Nations Conference on Women, contained for the first time
in these contexts three references to sport, exercise, and physical activity. As
the noted feminist Wilma Scott Heide affirmed, institutional changes occur
neither by accident nor by the simple passage of time.[18] These language inser-

tions in U.N. documents were the result of women's sport advocates' research, strategic planning, and lobbying among both governmental and nongovernmental networks, as well as the investment of human and material resources at appropriate times and places. All these steps were repeated in an effort to maintain and build on the inclusion of these important issues in the context of the "Final Outcomes and Actions Document" of the 2000 U.N. Beijing Plus 5 deliberations.[19] This document includes a paragraph on sport and physical activity (no. 128) and several references throughout to the importance of provisions for "healthy, active aging." Sport advocates believe the inclusions have been influenced by the work of our advocacy community.

These are all examples of hard-won successes. When sport leadership is included as a part of all matters that affect the study and enhancement of women and their lives, sport feminists are enabled to share experiences with others whose interests and concerns have not yet been fully explicated. Additionally, the eradication of gender discrimination in sport and physical recreation is exceedingly complex, and many challenges are resistant to solution. There appears to be a necessity for wide-ranging "partnerships," collaborations that in governments are referred to as "intersectoral."[20] Efforts to mainstream gender equity concepts and strategies across considerations of health, politics, business, education, and sport will be needed. Isolated efforts, no matter how brilliantly conceived, will not succeed.

Within the world of sport, probably the "icon" experience most available to women has been the Olympic Games. It is not as administrator, coach, or elected officer that women have made their mark at the games, but as athlete. Looking at the steady but agonizingly slow progress in expanding the areas of the program open to women, one can discern the near-invisible successes of advocacy.

Table 1 shows the numbers of women who have actually competed in the Olympic Games, with the 2000 games in Sydney marking the one-hundredth anniversary of women's participation. One may notice the numbers jumped from less than one hundred women in 1920 to almost three hundred in 1928. These gains were enhanced by the efforts of Alice Milliat, who in 1922 staged a "First Women's Olympic Games" in Paris. These games featured fifteen track and field events and were successful both on the track and with spectators. Milliat's plan was to hold these games at the midpoint of each quadrennium. Before the 1928 games, the International Amateur Athletic Federation (the governing body for track and field) prevailed upon Pierre deCoubertin, founder of the modern Olympic Games, to officially open the Olympic Games

**TABLE 1**

WOMEN'S PARTICIPATION IN THE GAMES OF THE OLYMPIAD

| Year | Sports | Events | NOCs* | Partici-pants | % | Year | Sports | Events | NOCs | Partici-pants | % |
|------|--------|--------|-------|---------------|---|------|--------|--------|------|---------------|---|
| 1896 | – | – | – | – | – | 1956 | 6 | 26 | 39 | 384 | 16.1 |
| 1900 | 2 | 3 | 5 | 19 | 1.6 | 1960 | 6 | 29 | 45 | 610 | 11.4 |
| 1904 | 1 | 2 | 1 | 6 | 0.9 | 1964 | 7 | 33 | 53 | 683 | 13.3 |
| 1908 | 2 | 3 | 4 | 36 | 1.8 | 1968 | 7 | 39 | 54 | 781 | 14.2 |
| 1912 | 2 | 6 | 11 | 57 | 2.2 | 1972 | 8 | 43 | 65 | 1058 | 14.8 |
| 1920 | 2 | 6 | 13 | 77 | 2.9 | 1976 | 11 | 49 | 66 | 1247 | 20.7 |
| 1924 | 3 | 11 | 20 | 136 | 4.4 | 1980 | 12 | 50 | 54 | 1125 | 21.5 |
| 1928 | 4 | 14 | 25 | 290 | 9.6 | 1984 | 14 | 62 | 94 | 1567 | 23.0 |
| 1932 | 3 | 14 | 18 | 127 | 9.0 | 1988 | 17 | 86 | 117 | 2186 | 25.8 |
| 1936 | 4 | 15 | 26 | 328 | 8.1 | 1992 | 19 | 98 | 136 | 2708 | 28.8 |
| 1948 | 5 | 19 | 33 | 385 | 9.4 | 1996 | 21 | 108 | 169 | 3626 | 34.2 |
| 1952 | 6 | 25 | 41 | 518 | 10.5 | 2000 | 25 | 121 | | 3947 | 38.0 |

*NOCs: National Olympic Committees
Mixed events included.
We think that women also competed in sailing in 1900.
Source: IOC Department of International Cooperation.

to women.[21] Nearly four thousand women competed in the Sydney Olympic Games.

Table 2 shows comparable statistics for the Olympic Winter Games. Generally, the percentages of women participants has been a little higher in the Winter Games.

Table 3, presenting the percentages of women's events, projects that by the 2002 games in Salt Lake City, 47 percent of events will include women competitors.

Yet another example of assertive advocacy by international women sport leaders involves the use of Olympic Solidarity Funds. The International Olympic Committee regularly lends financial assistance to members of the Olympic movement, particularly from developing countries. On the occasion of the first IOC Conference on Women, a direct question emerged: What were the data on distribution of Solidarity Funds by gender? Participants learned that the information had never been disaggregated by gender. At the second IOC Conference, data were forthcoming along with assurances that "we can always do better." The following illustrates the general low level of the use of these funds for women athletes and an even lower utilization in coaching and leadership training. From the Olympic Solidarity Fund women received the following: 21

**TABLE 2**
WOMEN'S PARTICIPATION IN THE OLYMPIC WINTER GAMES

| Year | Sports | Events | NOCs | Partici-pants | % | Year | Sports | Events | NOCs | Partici-pants | % |
|------|--------|--------|------|---------|------|------|--------|--------|------|---------|------|
| 1924 | 1 | 2 | 7 | 13 | 5.0 | 1968 | 3 | 13 | 29 | 211 | 18.2 |
| 1928 | 1 | 2 | 10 | 26 | 5.6 | 1972 | 3 | 13 | 27 | 206 | 20.5 |
| 1932 | 1 | 2 | 7 | 21 | 8.3 | 1976 | 3 | 14 | 30 | 231 | 20.6 |
| 1936 | 2 | 3 | 15 | 80 | 12.0 | 1980 | 3 | 14 | 31 | 233 | 21.7 |
| 1948 | 2 | 5 | 12 | 77 | 11.5 | 1984 | 3 | 15 | 35 | 274 | 21.5 |
| 1952 | 2 | 6 | 17 | 109 | 15.7 | 1988 | 3 | 18 | 39 | 313 | 22.0 |
| 1956 | 2 | 7 | 18 | 132 | 17.0 | 1992 | 4 | 25 | 44 | 488 | 27.1 |
| 1960 | 2 | 11 | 22 | 143 | 21.5 | 1994 | 4 | 27 | 44 | 523 | 30.0 |
| 1964 | 3 | 13 | 28 | 200 | 18.3 | 1998 | 6 | 31 | 54 | 788 | 36.2 |
|      |   |    |    |     |     | 2002 | 7 | 37 |    |     |      |

Mixed events included.

Source: IOC Department of International Cooperation.

percent of scholarships allowing qualifying athletes with no support from country to attend Atlanta, and 34 percent for Nagano (1998). Only 8 percent of scholarships for coaches to attend training went to women. And only 13 percent of participants in sport leadership training seminars were women.[22]

If one attempts to calculate the importance of the Olympic sport "icon status" in sheer dollars and cents, the figures undoubtedly would be staggering. A 1996 U.S. Olympic Committee Board of Directors report showed the budgets for the last quarter of the century.

| | |
|---|---|
| 1973–76 | $13 million |
| 1977–80 | $56 million |
| 1981–84 | $97 million |
| 1985–88 | $182 million |
| 1989–92 | $308 million |
| 1993–96 | $426 million |

In making a case that the eye-catching, heart-stopping, icon status of sport should assure its inclusion in an examination of gender, leadership, and power, I should close the argument with what Michael Kimmel called the "nation's recent love affair with the magnificent performance of the U.S. women's soccer team as it won the World Cup."[23] He comments on how the athleticism of their on-field performance was counterpointed by their "femininity-assuring" heterosexuality with television late night host David Letterman. Sport icon

**TABLE 3**

WOMEN'S PARTICIPATION IN THE OLYMPIC GAMES: PERCENTAGE OF EVENTS

| | Games of the Olympiad | | | Olympic Winter Games | | |
|---|---|---|---|---|---|---|
| Year | Total Events | Women's Events | % | Total Events | Women's Events** | % |
| 1900 | 86 | 3 | 3.49 | – | – | – |
| 1904 | 89 | 3 | 3.37 | – | – | – |
| 1908 | 107 | 3 | 2.80 | – | – | – |
| 1912 | 102 | 6 | 5.88 | – | – | – |
| 1920 | 152 | 6 | 3.95 | – | – | – |
| 1924 | 126 | 11 | 8.73 | 16 | 2 | 12.50 |
| 1928 | 109 | 14 | 12.84 | 14 | 2 | 14.28 |
| 1932 | 117 | 14 | 11.96 | 14 | 2 | 14.28 |
| 1936 | 129 | 15 | 11.62 | 17 | 3 | 17.64 |
| 1948 | 136 | 19 | 13.97 | 22 | 5 | 22.72 |
| 1952 | 149 | 25 | 16.77 | 22 | 6 | 27.27 |
| 1956 | 151 | 26 | 17.21 | 24 | 7 | 29.16 |
| 1960 | 150 | 29 | 19.33 | 27 | 11 | 40.74 |
| 1964 | 163 | 33 | 20.24 | 34 | 13 | 38.23 |
| 1968 | 172 | 39 | 22.67 | 35 | 13 | 37.14 |
| 1972 | 195 | 43 | 22.05 | 35 | 13 | 37.14 |
| 1976 | 198 | 49 | 24.74 | 37 | 14 | 37.83 |
| 1980 | 203 | 50 | 24.63 | 38 | 14 | 36.84 |
| 1984 | 221 | 62 | 28.05 | 39 | 15 | 38.46 |
| 1988 | 237 | 86* | 36.28 | 46 | 18 | 39.13 |
| 1992 | 257 | 98* | 28.13 | 57 | 25 | 43.86 |
| 1994 | | | | 61 | 27 | 44.26 |
| 1996 | 271 | 108* | 39.85 | | | |
| 1998 | | | | 68 | 31 | 45.58 |
| 2000 | 300 | 132* | 44.00 | | | |
| 2002 | | | | 78 | 37 | 47.44 |

*Including mixed events.
**Including mixed events from 1924 to 2002.
Source: IOC Department of International Cooperation.

status offers an opportunity for the transformation of old myths, but too often it is an opportunity not taken. We need to find out why.

# Women's Personal Development through Sport and Activity

I suspect that the readers of this book are quite aware of the detailed litera-ture available cataloging the health benefits of an active lifestyle for women.

In preparing this essay, I recalled an experience with a faculty colleague that clearly illustrates this point.

Fifteen years ago, as chair of the Faculty Senate Committee on the Status of Women, I joined a faculty union representative in attending the final Board of Trustees meeting of the year to "fight for" the tenure of a young feminist poet and literary critic who was in danger of losing a tenure decision. A model of the intellectual feminist iconoclast, she was a "rising star" of women's studies faculty dispersed in various departments of the university, but she had garnered a mixed bag of narrow wins and losses moving up from her home department to School and Council of Deans. Many factors, especially her merit, won the day, and she remains at my university, an honored full professor. It is a large, urban, commuter institution, and I have rarely spoken to her over the years. Imagine my surprise recently to see her hurrying out of the gym at 8 A.M., cheeks rosy and hair damp from a shower. Perplexed, I glanced from her clothing bag to her face, to her bag and face again. "Oh, yes," she smiled as a reaction to my puzzlement, "you gym people had it right all along," and she hurried off to the interior of the campus.

We may not love the "gym people" designation, but it is good to know that the message about activity and health has broken through the old mind/body dichotomy. The 1996 U.S. Surgeon General's Report has pointed out the following:

- People who are usually inactive can improve their health and well-being by becoming even moderately active on a regular basis.
- Physical activity need not be strenuous to achieve health benefits.
- Greater health benefits can be achieved by increasing the amount (duration, frequency, intensity) of physical activity.[24]

Unfortunately, while the gender gap in sport and physical activity can be observed in all societies and microcultures within societies, the gap is much more pronounced in societies where custom combines with poverty and low levels of economic development to restrict girls and women from participation.[25] Even in the United States, a recent study revealed that both personal and structural/environmental factors abound in association with physical inactivity among diverse racial and ethnic groups of middle-aged and older women.[26]

Thus, the case to be made for the importance of the inclusion of sport and physical activity issues in any discourse that addresses the health and quality of life of women is fairly simple and straightforward. I close this section, however, with a plea that feminist scholars begin to exercise, in their praxis, the political will to advocate for opportunities at sport as their due and natural human right.

Margaret Schuler traces this line of thought in general terms as a major conceptual advance by feminist advocates.[27] Paragraph 18 of the 1993 Vienna Declaration and Program of Action captures the essence of the argument: "The human rights of women and the girl-child are an inalienable, integral, and indivisible part of universal human rights. The full and equal participation of women in political, civil, economic, social and cultural life at national, regional and international levels and the eradication of all forms of discrimination on grounds of sex are priority objectives of the international community."[28]

As made clear in the Flor statement already cited, sport and physical activity involvement (as distinct from sheer manual labor) is explicitly covered as an aspect of "social, economic and cultural life."[29] In institutionalized and community sport, in the United States, and in many international bodies, "nondiscrimination language" has been added, but reality lags far behind the words.

The interdependence of the progress of women's sport with the general development of women is made even clearer in a book from the British development agency Oxfam. From a long background of development experiences, Oxfam has evolved two definitions that are important in this context: (1) *empowerment* is "gaining the strength, confidence and vision to work for positive changes in one's life, individually and with others"; and (2) *capacity building* consists of "activities on a spectrum from helping people to help themselves (personal/local level) to strengthening civil society organizations in order to foster democratization and the building of strong, effective and accountable institutions."[30] The author concluded that skills and leadership training for women "should be backed up with confidence and self-awareness building." Sport and physical activity can be seen as natural means of supplying such back-up programs for strength, confidence, and self-awareness building.[31]

Briefly, what are these demonstrated health and capacity-building benefits of an active lifestyle? For adolescents, they include:

- Higher levels of muscular strength and improved muscular and cardio-vascular endurance
- Lower risk of obesity and chronic inactivity
- Association with higher self-esteem, body image, confidence, and peer relationships

- Association with lower risk of unwanted pregnancy, later coital initiation, and lower participation in risky sexual practices
- Building of peak bone mass, reducing the adult risk of osteoporosis[32]

For women, an active lifestyle reduces the risk of:
- Dying prematurely
- Dying from heart disease
- Developing diabetes
- Developing high blood pressure
- Developing colon and selected other types of cancer

Additionally, an active lifestyle:
- Reduces blood pressure in those suffering from high blood pressure
- Helps build and maintain healthy bones and teeth
- Reduces feelings of anxiety and depression
- Increases mobility and decreases falls in older people[33]

The foregoing are all well-documented findings within the medical community. Additionally, anecdotal evidence supports three other possible benefits and uses of sport and physical activity for the empowerment and capacity building of women. Women and Sport South Africa has been funded for an "anticrime" project for women. The organization has been charged governmentally to develop an accredited self-defense course. The course will have the purpose to "train trainers to empower our women throughout the country to protect themselves and their families against crime."[34] Here in the United States, a similar chord was struck by sport sociologists noting that women use sport, on both a symbolic and a real level, to reclaim and repossess themselves from restrictive patriarchal practices. The physical empowerment of sport is seen as a metaphor for personal empowerment.[35]

At the second International Conference in Namibia and the second IOC Conference on Women, periods of time were given after presentations for interventions from delegates in order to share their experiences. Individuals from areas of the world of great conflict (Rwanda, Bosnia, Northern Ireland) recounted how the tragedies of life in refugee camps were made a little more bearable when aid workers were able to organize games and play periods for their children. This was a pleasant distraction and seemed to engender hope that the present circumstance was only temporary. Life would begin for them again. Additionally, U.N. representatives described instances where games and sport were one vehicle by which reconciliation was temporarily reached among former combatants after conflict was controlled.

It has been documented that sport has a significant potential role in the process of globalization.[36] Women and women's sport must be purposefully included in the positive aspects of globalization. It is a basic human right of women to be offered opportunities to foster their empowerment and capacity building, including institutionalized facilitations to full and equal participation in social, economic, and cultural forms. These are the necessities to enable women to lead and to assert influence in their own lives and in their communities. Sport science and medical literature indicates the vital role that sport, exercise, and physical activity can play in the achievement of these basic rights. How do we assure that women have opportunities to develop through sport and exercise? At the very least, I suggest that we make it happen best if we integrate sport and physical activity matters consistently in feminist scholarship and advocacy.

## Why the "Sport Question" Is Problematic

By this time, a reader of this text may well be asking, If all the preceding is accurate, why isn't sport at the forefront of mainstream feminist scholarship and praxis? Good question! Simply asking the question represents a positive step in the present state of affairs. After all, the absence of sport analysis discourse in mainstream women's studies has not yet occasioned much notice.

Elizabeth Darlison addresses these matters quite directly. She suggests that the relationship of sport and physical activity to the important social objective of sustainable development, particularly as regards gender, has not been understood and is thus much undervalued. Why the lack of understanding and recognition of sport's benefit to social and economic policies across portfolios? Her attributions run to two areas: (1) the inability of those individuals and organizations most closely involved with sport and physical activity both to fully understand the breadth and significance of sport's potential contribution and to "market" the contribution effectively; and (2) the lack of capacity and commitment (in government and academic and other circles) to create supportive environments where the development potential of sport and physical activity could be realized.[37]

Certainly the claims of undervaluing are bolstered by study of documents produced by governmental and nongovernmental organizations during the Beijing Plus 5 assessment. A U.N. Division for the Advancement of Women

Expert Group Meeting report from Tunisia focused on women and health concerns. An important section of the report dealt with intersectoral partnerships. It stated, "While the Ministry of Health is usually in charge of the health sector within government, other Ministries can also impact health prevention and care, Finance, Education, Labor, Environment, Youth, Planning, Women's Affairs, Social Welfare."[38] The omission of any reference to a sport and recreation sector seems telling.

In the United States, the President's Interagency Council on Women convened a national satellite conference in 1996 to begin the assessment of actions taken and needed in regard to the Platform for Action. A book was compiled of all recommendations forwarded by tens of thousands of NGO representatives attending. The recommendations were organized around twelve themes in seventy pages of text. Two hundred and seventy-five organizations were listed as participants, but none was a sport-oriented organization. Two small references, contained in seven lines of text, were even remotely related to sport and physical activity concerns. In the education section, in order to promote leadership and esteem, it was suggested to use currently successful women role models from several fields including "sports and the arts."[39] In the health section, in improving nutrition and health, and to prevent disease, it was suggested to launch a national public health initiative for girls and adolescents to promote healthy behavior, good nutrition, and sport and physical education, and to provide education on sex and reproductive health, prevention of substance abuse, and STD including HIV/AIDS. These sport interventions seem extremely limited in scope and clearly reflect general public information and perceptions rather than insights from professional and scholarly sources, as was the case with other themes.

Of course, identification of problematic aspects of sport inclusion in feminist scholarship and praxis must acknowledge the "masculinist" baggage replete in the territory. Even after almost thirty years of Title IX activism, twenty years of feminist criticism of sport, and a decade of profeminist male scholars' critique, texts originating in the new millennium still sound the old themes. Kimmel states, "Sport has become both metaphor and reality of American masculinity—its language dominates other discourses as metaphor, while sports have become increasingly important among young boys as the arena of demonstration and proof."[40]

Pronger levels his criticism at the academic aspect of sport study. He labels it "exercise techno-science," a discipline with a strong male bias and complicit in the production of traditional gender power relations. With care and restraint, he traces the qualities in exercise techno-science, including detachment and objectivity in positing the body itself as a "useful, dominable, resource." Particularly these concepts are called into play in the current emphasis on knowledge and techniques to "create the high performance sport body." He also, however, describes the commodification of the body in the mass physical fitness industry. Pronger proposes a feminist exercise techno-science, but it remains much more science "fiction" than his earlier descriptions.[41]

Yet another explanation for the indifference of feminist mainstream scholars to the analysis of sport is the continued dominance of males in control of sport. Though the numerical dominance is being challenged, the only world region in which equity is approached is within the quota systems maintained in the Scandinavian countries.[42] There has been some literature proposing that high-level sports women prefer male coaches. This was explained by K. Fasting et al. in a recent study.[43] These European researchers reported that women in the sample who had never had a woman coach were initially negative toward having one. After playing for a woman coach, the attitude was changed. Athletes then stated that women coaches were better psychologists; they asserted a belief that women athletes were different psychologically from men and that men coaches did not seem able to take the difference into account. These findings notwithstanding, across decades of monitoring, R. V. Acosta and L. J. Carpenter note that the percentage of women coaching keeps declining.[44]

Additional to these research-based explanations for the relative paucity of interconnectedness between mainstream feminist social science analyses and sport science, I conclude with a few experiential-based possibilities. The traditional sport realm may be perceived to symbolize many influences that a feminist scholar may disdain. It may suggest, for example, wealth and leisure and the irrelevant "pastimes" of an elitist minority. Athletics may symbolize an economic and social status that is undeserved and that is closed to women except in the passive role of spectator. Another possibility is that the sport realm is perceived to be inhabited by conservative men and women who disavow feminism and with whom little scholarly or cultural linkage seems likely.

There surely may be grains or trainloads of truth to each of these possible reasons for the relative absence of consistent collaborative effort among sport scholars and mainstream feminists. I suggest here that there is too much at stake to leave things as they historically have been. It is my hope that this book may take our joint efforts to a deeper and richer level.

## Conclusion

This essay argues at many levels. One level is a call for inclusion and diversity. Cornerstone principles of feminist approaches, *inclusion* and *diversity* in this instance refer to those feminist scholars coming from the exercise and sport-based disciplines and advocates who specialize in the matters of the universal right of girls and women to empowerment through sport and physical activity. These are feminists not visible in the "icon view" of sport, whose names are not familiar in association with sport. These are individuals whose work is devoted to opening the benefits and potentials of sport and physical activity as a universal right—to women across the life span, to the poor, to the racially and ethnically diverse, to those of diverse sexualities, and to the differently able.

Because their philosophical and scholarly orientations are so divergent from mainstream views of both sport and traditional sport science, these individuals have contended with marginalization within the very professional and scholarly realm they inhabit. Let them no longer be rendered invisible among the mainstream emancipatory movements within which feminists are the most active. Inclusion would certainly benefit feminist sport scholars. It can also serve an important purpose within mainstream feminism.

Almost fifty years ago, the renowned psychologist George Kelly pointed out an important constructivist dynamic that can be usefully invoked to identify a potential contribution of the inclusion of sport feminism in consideration of women, leadership, and power.[45] Kelly suggested that an individual's efforts toward profound psychological change were inherently perceived as destabilizing (thus mildly to deeply dangerous) to one's global self-concept and worldview. Thus, he argued, openness to such change is enhanced by the availability of "laboratories" in which to safely and temporarily "experiment with" new identities, skills, and roles.

We know that one plane of meaning of sport is the "icon status" aspect. Here sport exists as an enterprise of global import. National pride and revenue totals rise and fall with contest outcome. On other levels of meaning, however, sport and physical activity can be seen as "merely" play. Indeed, core characteristics of play, game, and sport definitions are qualities of being unproductive and separate from "real life."[46] Our courts, gymnasia, and fields around the world could be used (and in some instances noted herein, are being used already) as laboratories to safely "try on" new sexual identities and new methods of decision making and consensus building. In contexts ranging from single-sex women's outdoor questing to activity programs associated with therapeutic approaches to healing post-traumatic stress disorder, new meanings of self-embodiment are emerging.[47] New research on leader-follower dyads, teams, and groups (with varying gender ratios and behavioral expectations) could be created, modified, and reconstituted with near-complete flexibility. Collaborative research concerning decision making, risk taking, centrality and marginality, competency building, perceived attribution, and more could be completed. Cross-racial, cross-gendered task group efficacy could be explored in the "benign" context of play and sport groups.

The sport and physical activity phenomenon shares the complexity, paradox, and contradiction of other social and behavioral sciences. Traditions of the past, organizational frameworks of academic life and physical architectural realities of departmental housing and placement, have tended to isolate and marginalize feminist sport scholars from mainstream feminist praxis. There is much to be gained by the forging of new bonds and bridges.

# Notes

1. C. Krammerae and D. Spender, *The Knowledge Explosion: Generations of Feminist Scholarship* (New York: Teachers College Press, Columbia University, 1992).

2. S. Birrell and C. Cole, *Women, Sport, and Culture* (Champaign, Ill.: Human Kinetics Press, 1994); K. Fasting, "Ensuring Equal Opportunities in Sport: Government's Role," paper presented at the Women and Social Issues Symposium, International Federation of Sports Medicine, Orlando, Florida, 30 May–2 June 1998; J. McKay, M. Messner, and D. Sabo, *Masculinities, Gender Relations, and Sport* (Thousand Oaks, Calif.: Sage, 2000); C. Oglesby and K. Hill, "Gender and Sport," in *Handbook of Research in Sport Psychology*, ed. R. Singer, M. Murphey, and L. Tennant (New York: Macmillan, 1993).

3. M. Messner and D. Sabo, *Sex, Violence, and Power in Sport: Rethinking Masculinity* (Freedom, Calif.: Crossing, 1994); S. Walk, "Moms, Sisters, and Ladies: Women Student Athletic Trainers in Men's Intercollegiate Sport," in *Masculinities, Gender Relations, and Sport*, ed. J. McKay, M. Messner, and D. Sabo (Thousand Oaks, Calif.: Sage, 1994).

4. C. Oglesby, *The Encyclopedia of Women and Sport in America* (Phoenix: Oryx Press, 1998); D. Kluka, *Women, Sport, and Physical Activity: Sharing Good Practice* (Berlin, Germany: International Council of Sport Science and Physical Education, 2000).

5. M. Schuler, *From Basic Needs to Basic Rights: Women's Claim to Human*

*Rights* (Washington, D.C.: Women, Law, and Development, 1995); Patricia Flor, "U.N. Commission on the Status of Women Perspective," paper presented at Second International Conference on Women in Sport, Windhoek, Namibia, 19–22 May 1998.

6. J. Sandoz and J. Winans, *Whatever It Takes: Women on Women's Sport* (New York: Farrar, Straus, and Giroux, 1999), 3–4.

7. B. Pronger, "Feminist Exercise Science," *Studies in Physical Culture and Tourism* 4 (1996): 21–40; McKay, Messner, and Sabo, *Masculinities, Gender Relations, and Sport*; Messner and Sabo, *Sex, Violence, and Power in Sport*; S. Birrell and N. Theberge, "Ideological Control of Women in Sport," in *Women and Sport: International Perspectives*, ed. M. Costa and S. Guthrie (Champaign, Ill.: Human Kinetics Press, 1994).

8. Carole Oglesby, *Women and Sport: From Myth to Reality* (Philadelphia: Lea and Febiger, 1978); E. Gerber, J. Felshin, P. Berlin, and W. Spirduso, *The American Woman in Sport* (Reading, Mass.: Addison-Wesley, 1974); Carole Oglesby, "Epilogue," in *Sport, Men, and the Gender Order*, ed. M. Messner and D. Sabo (Champaign, Ill.: Human Kinetics Press, 1990).

9. McKay, Messner, and Sabo, *Masculinities, Gender Relations, and Sport*, 6.

10. Arlene Blum, *Annapurna: A Woman's Place*, 20th anniversary edition (San Francisco: Sierra Club, 1988), xi.

11. Oglesby, *Encyclopedia of Women and Sport in America*, 1, 8, 38, 69, 80, 123, 154, 225.

12. Ibid., 2.

13. Ann O'Hagan, in Sandoz and Winans, *Whatever It Takes*, 160–62.

14. Darlene Kluka, *Women, Sport, and Physical Activity: Sharing Good Practice* (Berlin, Germany: International Council of Sport Science and Physical Education, 2000), 33.

15. Flor, "U.N. Commission on the Status of Women Perspective," 2.

16. J. Vibar-Bauzon, "The Role of Sport and Physical Activity in the Global Development of Women," paper presented at the Second International Conference on Women and Sport, Windhoek, Namibia, 19–22 May 1998; Kluka, *Women, Sport, and Physical Activity*; L. Xingwana, "The Role of Sport and Physical Activity in the Global Development of Women," paper presented at the Second International Conference on Women and Sport, Windhoek, Namibia, 19–22 May 1998; C. Pelak, "Women and Sport in an International Context: A Case Study of Post-Apartheid South Africa," paper presented at the Women and Sport Symposium, Bowling Green University, Bowling Green, Ohio, 7–8 May 1999.

17. Women and Sport South Africa, *Women and Girls: Get Active*, White Paper on Sport and Recreation in South Africa (Capetown: Western Cape Department of Sport and Recreation, 1997), 1.

18. Oglesby, *Women and Sport*, 195–204.

19. United Nations, 23d Special Session, *Further Actions and Initiatives to Implement the Beijing Declaration and Platform for Action* (New York: UN-DAW, 2000).

20. E. Darlison, *Gender, Sport, Physical Activity, and Social Development*, technical report prepared for UNESCO (Paris: UNESCO, 1999).

21. B. Spears and R. Swanson, *History of Sport and Physical Activity in the United States* (Dubuque, Iowa: Brown, 1983).

22. International Olympic Committee, "The Promotion of Women in the Olympic Movement," paper prepared by the Department of International Cooperation, Lausanne, Switzerland, February 2000.

23. M. Kimmel, "Series Editor Foreword," in *Masculinities, Gender Relations, and Sport* ed. M. McKay, M. Messner, and D. Sabo (Thousand Oaks, Calif.: Sage, 2000), xii.

24. U.S. Surgeon General, *Physical Activity and Health: A Report of the Surgeon General* (Washington, D.C.: GPO, 1996), 1.

25. Darlison, *Gender, Sport, Physical Activity, and Social Development.*

26. A. King, C. Castro, S. Wilcox, A. Eyler, J. Sallis, and R. Bronson, "Personal and Environmental Factors Associated with Physical Inactivity among Differing Racial-Ethnic Groups of U.S. Middle-Aged and Older Women," *Health Psychology* 19, no. 4 (2000): 354–65.

27. Schuler, *From Basic Needs to Basic Rights.*

28. Ibid., 1.

29. Flor, "U.N. Commission on the Status of Women Perspective," 30.

30. D. Eade, *Capacity-Building: An Approach to People-Centered Development* (Osbord, U.K.: Oxfam, 1997), 15–16.

31. D. Scoretz, "Beijing + 5: Physical Activity as a Human Right," *ICSSPE Bulletin* 29 (2000): 4–46.

32. President's Council on Physical Fitness and Sport, *Physical Activity and Sport in the Lives of Girls* (Minneapolis: Center for Research on Girls and Women in Sport, University of Minnesota, 1996); L. Jaffe and R. Manzer, "Girls' Perspectives: Physical Activity and Self-Esteem," *Melpomene* 11, no. 3 (1992): 14–28.

33. U.S. Surgeon General, *Physical Activity and Health*; L. Gauvin, J. Rejeski, and B. Reboussin, "Contributions of Acute Bouts of Vigorous Physical Activity to Diurnal Variations in Feeling States in Active, Middle-Aged Women," *Health Psychology* 19, no. 4 (2000): 365–76; B. Drinkwater, "Women and Exercise: A Physiological Review," in *Exercise and Sport Science Reviews*, ed. R. L. Terjung (Lexington, Mass.: Collamore Press, 1984).

34. Xingwana, "The Role of Sport and Physical Activity," 6.

35. Birrell and Theberge, "Ideological Control of Women in Sport."

36. J. Maguire, "Globalization, Sport Development, and the Media/Sport Production Complex," *Sport Science Review* 2 (1993): 29–47; J. Maguire, "Globalization, Sport, and National Identities," *Society and Leisure* 16 (1994): 293–323.

37. Darlison, *Gender, Sport, Physical Activity, and Social Development*; see also U.N. Division for the Advancement of Women, Expert Group Meeting Report, Tunis, Tunisia, 1999, and Eade, *Capacity-Building.*

38. U.N. Division of Women, Expert Group Meeting Report, Tunis, Tunisia, Department of Economic and Social Affairs, New York, 28 September–2 October 1998, 13.

39. American Association of University Women, Church Women United, National Associations of Commissions for Women, Women's Environment and Development Association (AAUW), *Building on Beijing: U.S. NGOs Shape a Women's National Action Agenda* (Muscatine, Iowa: The Stanley Foundation, 1999).

40. Kimmel, *Masculinities*, xiii.

41. B. Pronger, "Feminist Exercise Science," *Studies in Physical Culture and Tourism* 4 (1996): 21–40, quotes on p. 28.

42. Fasting, "Ensuring Equal Opportunities in Sport."

43. K. Fasting, S. Scraton, G. Pfister, and A. Burruel, *The Experience and Meaning of Sport and Exercise in the Lives of Women in Selected European Countries*, technical report prepared for the International Olympic Committee, Lausanne, Switzerland, 1999.

44. R. V. Acosta and L. J. Carpenter, "Women in Intercollegiate Sport: A Longitudinal Study: Twenty-Year Update," unpublished manuscript, Brooklyn College, Brooklyn, N.Y., 1998.

45. G. Kelly, *Psychology of Personal Constructs* (New York: Norton, 1955).

46. J. Huizinga, *Homo Ludens: A Study of the Play Element in Culture* (Boston: Beacon Press, 1939).

47. P. Martella, "Wholeness, Healing, and Risk Taking in Women Outdoor Leaders," Ph.D. diss. (Philadelphia: Temple University, 2000); President's Council on Physical Fitness and Sport, *Physical Activity and Sport in the Lives of Girls* (Minneapolis: Center for Research on Girls and Women in Sport, University of Minnesota, 1996).

## Want to Learn More?

### International Olympic Committee (IOC): Women in the Olympic Movement

This site gives the history of women in the Olympic movement all the way up to the present day. There is current information about the IOCs, including the resolutions of the second IOC World Conference on Women and Sport and the activities of the IOC's women's and sport working group.

International Olympic Committee
Section for Women's Advancement
Department of International Cooperation
Mrs. Katia Mascagni Stivachtis
Château de Vidy
1007 Lausanne, Switzerland
Telephone +41-21-621-6419
Fax +41-21-621-6354
E-mail katia.mascagni@olympic.org
www.olympic.org/ioc/e/org/women/women_intro_e.html

### MEDSCAPE's Women's Health MedPulse

This site provides clinicians and other health care professionals with a timely source of clinical information relevant to their patients and practice. It helps to make available to a broad medical audience clinical information with the depth, breadth, and validity needed to improve the practice of medicine.

www.medscape.com/Home/Topics/WomensHealth/womenshealth.html

### The United Nations Division for the Advancement of Women (UN-DAW)

This site features information about UN-DAW, whose mission is to advocate the improvement of the status of the women of the world and the achievement of their equality with men. It aims to ensure the participation of women as equal partners with men in all aspects of human endeavor. It promotes women as equal participants and beneficiaries of sustainable development, peace and security, governance, and human rights. It strives to stimulate the mainstreaming of a gender perspective both within and outside the United Nations system.

United Nations Division for the Advancement of Women
2 UN Plaza, DC2-12th Floor
New York, NY 10017
USA
Fax (212) 963-3463
www.un.org/womenwatch/daw

### Women Action: Beijing + 5 Review

Women Action is a global information, communication, and media network that enables NGOs to engage in the Beijing Plus 5 review process. Its long-term goal is women's empowerment, with a special emphasis on women and the media. Another goal is to develop a communications network and information-sharing strategy that allows women in every world region to participate in the five-year review of the implementation of the 1995 Beijing Platform for Action.

www.womenaction.org

**Women's Sports Foundation (WSF) United States**

The mission of WSF is to promote the lifelong participation of all girls and women in sports and fitness, and to create an educated public that encourages females' participation and supports gender equality. Women's Sports Foundation events bring together individuals committed to the cause of women's sports and fitness. These gatherings provide information, celebrate achievements, and offer networking and advertising opportunities.

Women's Sports Foundation, Information Referral Service
Eisenhower Park
East Meadow, NY 11554
Telephone (800) 227-3988
E-mail wosport@aol.com
www.womenssportsfoundation.org/templates/index.html

**Women Sport International (WSI)**

WSI was formed to meet the challenge of ensuring that sport and physical activity receive the attention and priority they deserve in the lives of girls and women and to meet the need for an international umbrella organization that can bring about positive change for girls and women in these important areas of their lives.

WSI is both an issues- and action-based organization. Its members represent over thirty countries and a broad range of expertise and interest in the following areas: sports science medicine, health and fitness, nutrition, coaching, administration, and education, as well as athletes and girls and women who want the opportunity to make sport and physical activity an ongoing part of their lives. The aim of WSI is to bring about increased opportunities and positive change for women and girls at all levels of involvement in sport and physical education.

Women Sport International
P.O. Box 743
Vashon, WA 98070
USA
www.de.psu.edu/wsi/index.htm

# Notes on Contributors

SUSAN C. BOURQUE received her B.A. and Ph.D. at Cornell University. She was a founding member and a former director of the Project on Women and Social Change at Smith College. She is the author of four books, including *Women of the Andes: Patriarchy and Social Change in Two Peruvian Towns*, which was awarded the Hamilton Prize. She is Esther Booth Wiley Professor of Government at Smith College.

BARBARA A. BREHM received her Ed.D. in applied physiology from Teachers College, Columbia University. She is the author of *Essays on Wellness and Stress Management: Increasing Your Stress Resistance* and co-author of *Our Health, Our Futures: A Project by and for Adolescent Girls*. She is Associate Professor of Exercise and Sport Studies at Smith College.

JILL KER CONWAY received her B.A. and M.A. at the University of Sydney and her Ph.D. at Harvard University. She is the author of numerous books, including the award-winning autobiography *The Road from Coorain*. She is a visiting scholar in the Program in Science, Technology, and Society at the Massachusetts Institute of Technology and President Emerita of Smith College, 1975–85.

SUE J. M. FREEMAN received her B.A. at Rutgers University and her M.S. and Ph.D. at the University of Wisconsin, Madison. A founding member and former director of the Project on Women and Social Change at Smith College, she is the author of *Managing Lives: Corporate Women and Social Change*. She is a practicing psychologist and Professor of Education and Child Study at Smith College.

VELMA GARCÍA-GORENA received her B.A. from Smith College and Ph.D. from Yale University. She is the author of *Mothers and the Mexican Antinu-*

*clear Power Movement.* She is Associate Professor of Government at Smith College.

MYRON PERETZ GLAZER received his B.A. from City College of New York and an M.A. and Ph.D. from Princeton University. He is the author of seven books, including *The Whistleblowers: Exposing Corruption in Government and Industry* (with Penina Migdal Glazer). He is co-director with Christine M. Shelton of the Project on Women and Social Change and Barbara Richmond Professor of Sociology at Smith College.

PENINA MIGDAL GLAZER received her B.A. at Douglass College and her M.A. and Ph.D. at Rutgers University. She is the author of five books, including *The Environmental Crusaders: Confronting Disaster and Organizing Community* (with Myron Peretz Glazer). She is Marilyn Levin Professor of History at Hampshire College.

MARY JO KANE received her M.A. and Ph.D. from the University of Illinois, Champaign-Urbana. She is an internationally recognized scholar on the relationship between sport and gender and has published numerous research articles on this and related topics. She is the Director of the Tucker Center for Research on Girls & Women in Sport in the College of Education and Human Development at the University of Minnesota. She also holds the Dorothy McNeill Distinguished Chair for Women in Sport and Exercise Science.

MAUREEN A. MAHONEY received her B.A. from the University of California at Santa Cruz and her Ph.D. from Cornell University. She is Dean of the College at Smith College, where she is also an adjunct professor of psychology. Prior to that, she was Professor of Psychology and Dean of the School of Social Science at Hampshire College.

CAROLE A. OGLESBY received her B.S. and M.S. from the University of California at Los Angeles, a Ph.D. in physical education from Purdue University, and a Ph.D. in counseling from Temple University. She has been a professor at Temple University since 1980. She has recently edited an *Encyclopedia of Women and Sport in America* and is President of Women Sport International.

CHRISTINE M. SHELTON is a co-director with Myron Peretz Glazer of the Project on Women and Social Change, and Associate Professor and Chair of the Department of Exercise and Sport Studies at Smith College. She received her B.S. and M.S. from James Madison University. She is the former Executive Director and a Past President of the National Association for Girls and Women in Sport (NAGWS) and current Vice-President of the International Association of Physical Education and Sport for Girls and Women (IAPESGW). Her research and theoretical work considers gender, race, and cross-cultural issues in sport.

MIRIAM SLATER received her B.A. at Douglass College and her M.A. and Ph.D. at Princeton University. She is the author of *Family Life in the Seventeenth Century: The Verneys of Claydon House* and co-author with Penina Migdal Glazer of *Unequal Colleagues: The Entrance of Women into the Professions, 1890–1940*. She is the Harold F. Johnson Professor Emerita of History at Hampshire College and a research associate with the Project on Women and Social Change at Smith College.

# Index